MR BENETT OF WILTSHIRE

*In Loving Memory of Georgia*

# Mr BENETT
# of
# Wiltshire

*the life of a county
Member of Parliament
1773 – 1852*

## ROBERT MOODY

First published in the United Kingdom in 2005
by The Hobnob Press, PO Box 1838, East Knoyle, Salisbury SP3 6FA

British Library Cataloguing in Publication Data
A catalogue record for this book is available from the British Library.




ISBN 0-946418-40-3


Typeset in 11/12.5 pt Scala
Typesetting and origination by John Chandler
Printed in Great Britain by Salisbury Printing Company Ltd, Salisbury

# Contents

Illustrations are between pages 152 and 153

# *Acknowledgements*

M y thanks are firstly due to the History of Parliament Trust, London, for permitting me to see the unpublished article on John Benett for the 1820-32 section by Stephen Farrell. I am grateful to the History of Parliament Trust for allowing me to read this article in draft and to Dr Farrell in particular for his assistance.

A considerable number of letters written either by or to Benett and letters and journals in which he is mentioned are to be found in a variety of record offices and libraries, and I would like to thank the following for permission to reproduce all or part of such of them as are in their custody: the Wiltshire and Swindon Record Office; the Berkshire Record Office; the Hampshire Record Office; the Staffordshire County Record Office; the Somerset Archive and Record Service and the Wyndham Family Trustees; the Fox Talbot Museum, Lacock and the William Henry Fox Talbot Trust; The Alexander Turnbull Library, Wellington, New Zealand; The Woodson Research Center, Fondren Library, Rice University, Houston, U.S.A.; Boston Public Library, Rare Books Department, Boston, U.S.A., by courtesy of the Trustees. My thanks are also due to the Trustees of the Bowood Collections, Bath Record Office, Coutts & Co's Archivist's Department, the Dewey Museum, Warminster, The Athenaeum and Brooks's Clubs, and James and Polly à Court.

The Library of the Wiltshire Archaeological & Natural History Society in Devizes contains much information about Benett and I am grateful to Dr Lorna Haycock, its Sandell Librarian and Archivist, for first suggesting that I should attempt an account of his life.

Finally, I would particularly like to thank Sir Henry Rumbold, Bart., Benett's great-great-great-grandson, for his kindness in allowing me to reproduce the portraits of his ancestors and also the picture of the 18th-century Pythouse.

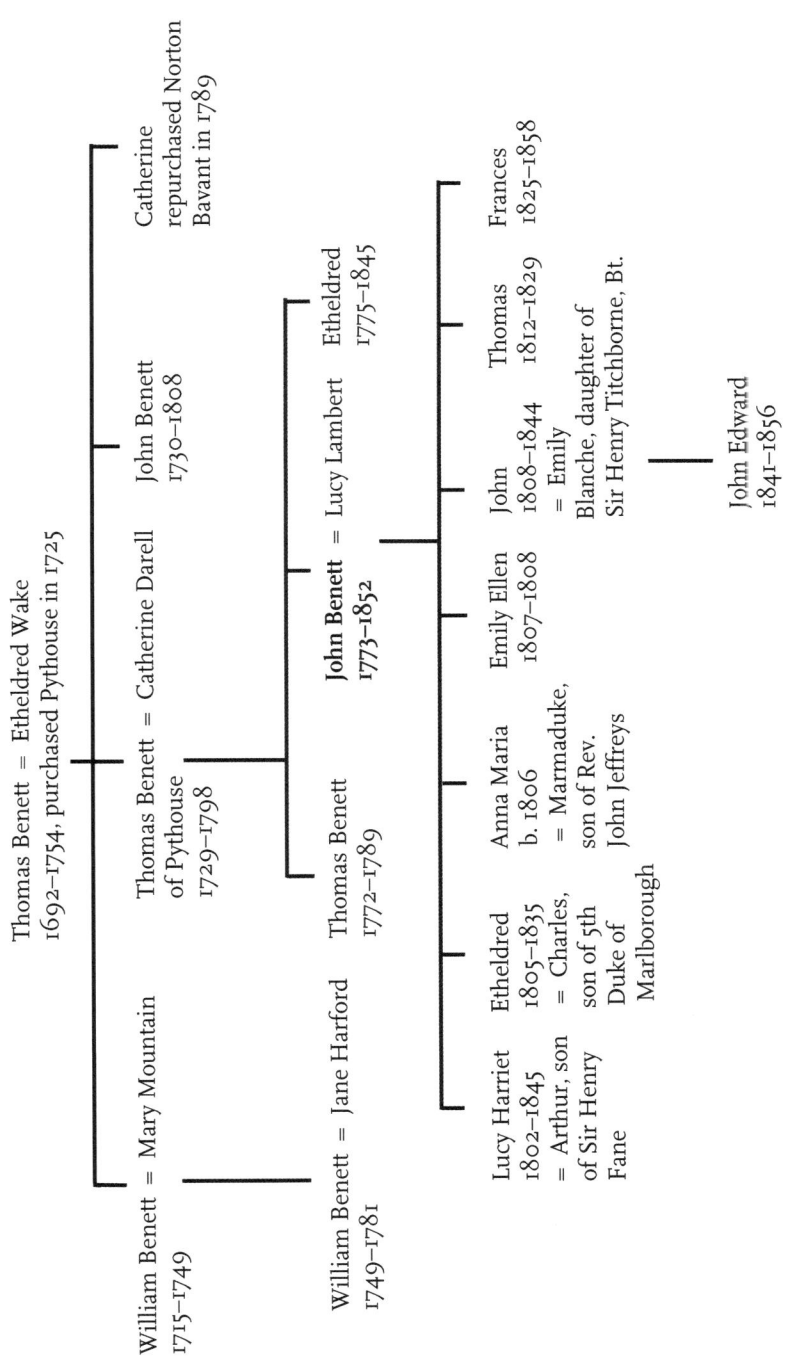

Thomas Benett = Etheldred Wake
1692–1754, purchased Pythouse in 1725

William Benett = Mary Mountain
1715–1749

Thomas Benett = Catherine Darell
of Pythouse
1729–1798

John Benett
1730–1808

Catherine
repurchased Norton
Bavant in 1789

William Benett = Jane Harford
1749–1781

Thomas Benett
1772–1789

**John Benett** = Lucy Lambert
1773–1852

Etheldred
1775–1845

Lucy Harriet
1802–1845
= Arthur, son
of Sir Henry
Fane

Etheldred
1805–1835
= Charles,
son of 5th
Duke of
Marlborough

Anna Maria
b. 1806
= Marmaduke,
son of Rev.
John Jeffreys

Emily Ellen
1807–1808

John
1808–1844
= Emily
Blanche, daughter of
Sir Henry Titchborne, Bt.

Thomas
1812–1829

Frances
1825–1858

John Edward
1841–1856

*John Benett's Family*

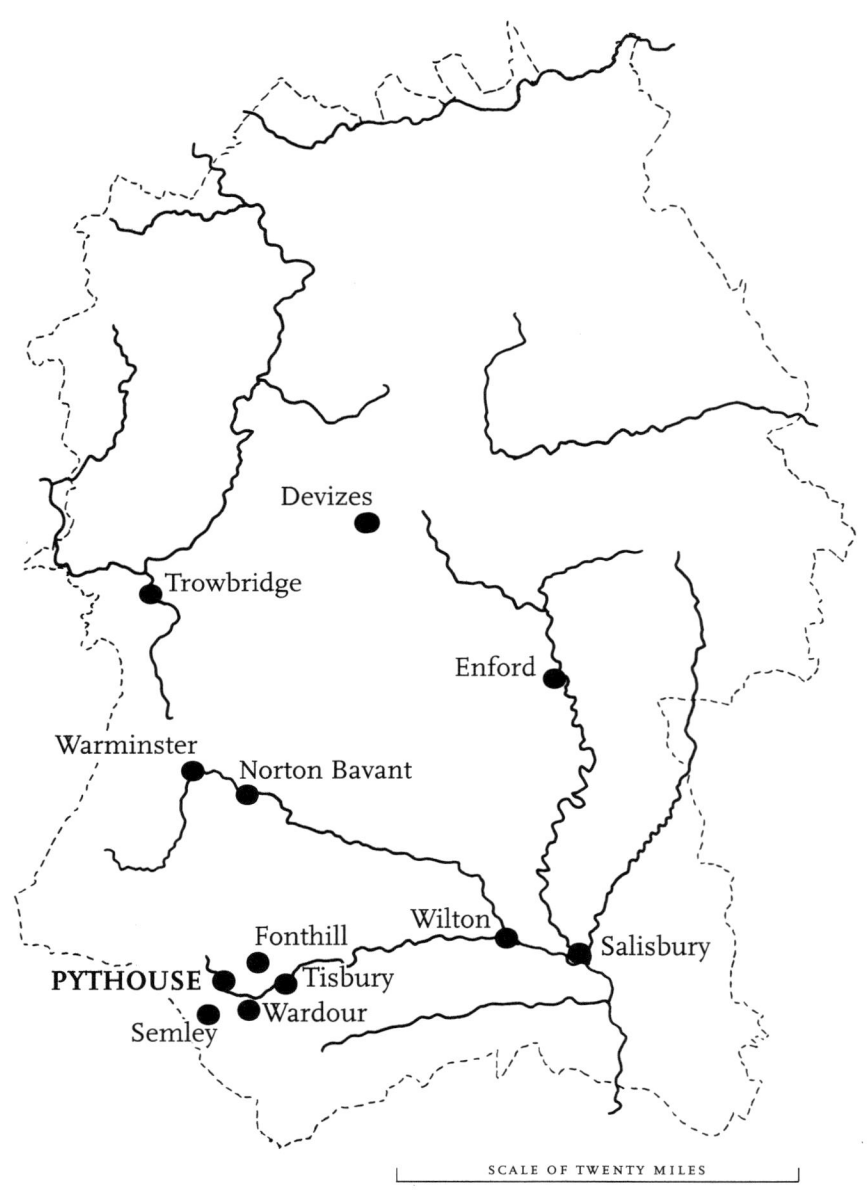

Devizes

Trowbridge

Enford

Warminster

Norton Bavant

Wilton

Fonthill

Salisbury

**PYTHOUSE**

Tisbury

Wardour

Semley

SCALE OF TWENTY MILES

*Location Map of Wiltshire*

# *Introduction*

In 1845, John Benett stood at the grave side as the body of John, his only surviving son, was laid to rest. Not at Norton Bavant, some ten miles away, beneath the floor of that part of the church there called the Benett aisle where his ancestors lay and where the inquisitive traveller would find a brass commemorating the life of an earlier John Benett, a clothier, who had died some 400 years before. John was to lie, not amongst his ancestors, but in the cemetery not far from Wardour Castle, the magnificent seat of the Arundells in the south-western corner of Wiltshire, and recently consecrated as a final resting place for the many Roman Catholics who lived in that part of the county.

Young John's widow, the sister of Lord Arundell's late wife, had asked that her husband's body might be laid to rest beneath the floor of the splendid chapel hidden within the great house, but her request had been declined. So, the burial ground it was to be and Arthur Fane, the rector of Warminster and husband of John's eldest sister, Lucy, was kindly permitted to assist in conducting his brother-in-law's funeral service. Perhaps the tall, elderly father would have preferred his son to lie where *he* would soon lie, but he was tolerant of those who chose not to adhere to the faith of his fathers and so the fact that his son had married the daughter of a Roman Catholic baronet did not perhaps concern him unduly. At least his son's wife had produced an heir, another John, who surely would one day be a credit to his grandfather and even live to see the dawn of the 20th century in the great house on the hill that he had built not far away, and which stood on land that had belonged from a very early date until soon after the Civil War to his great-grandmother's family, the Bennetts of Pythouse.

Perhaps Benett reflected upon what he had achieved throughout his long and eventful life. Of course, he had the advantage of inheriting *his* father's estates as a young man in his early twenties, whereas young John had always been the heir in waiting. Neither the university nor the army held any great attraction for his boy, who had incurred a great many debts and married and produced a son and travelled, but otherwise appears not to have made much of his life. When *he* was young, he had never expected to inherit, and it was only when his elder brother, Thomas, had died shortly before his 17th birthday that he would have realised that his destiny, as owner of his father's estates, would be that of a country gentleman. But that comfortable and unexciting existence was not for him. After his father had died, in no time at all he had had his writings published and had designed and built an impressive new mansion. Later he had engaged in two of the most violent and contentious parliamentary elections that Wiltshire had ever known, and was injured when the mob threatened to destroy his farm machinery and his splendid new house. But that was all in the past. By now he had sat in Parliament for over a quarter of a century and was a figure respected by most, if not all, the people of Wiltshire. Indeed, it was reported not many years later that 'the name of "Mr Benett of Wiltshire" has been a parliamentary "household word" over all England.'[1] How different it had been when his effigy had been burned and all sorts of libels against him had been published, and he had to endure the barbed tongues and sharp pens of such men as Henry Hunt and William Cobbett.

A seat in Parliament was what he had always wanted and, having achieved it at enormous cost, he was determined to retain it until he was not fit enough to travel and make the journey to London from Pythouse, the splendid mansion house that he had built so many years before. Although, so far as is known, none of his Benett ancestors had enjoyed a seat in Parliament, several members of the old Bennett family of Pythouse, from whom he was descended through his great-grandmother, had done so, and a portrait of Thomas Bennett who had been Prince Rupert's Private Secretary and one of Samuel Pepys's tormentors in Parliament, had pride of place on the walls of his house as well as a portrait by Sir Peter Lely of Prince Rupert himself. Any hope that he might have had that one of his sons might one day sit in Parliament was now therefore dashed as the body of his son was laid to rest.

# 1

## *His Family and Early Years 1773-1797*

John Benett had been born on 20 May 1773 to Catherine, the wife of Thomas Benett, a country gentleman living in a house called Pythouse near Tisbury in the south-western corner of Wiltshire He was his parents' second son and was baptised on the following 6 July by the curate of the parish of Tisbury in the church at Norton Bavant, a tiny village some ten miles from Pythouse. Catherine was Thomas's second wife, his first wife having died childless quite shortly after her marriage. She and Thomas were married in 1771 and had already produced a first son, named Thomas after his father; and so the arrival of young John must have been welcomed by his parents, and by his father in particular, as another potential heir to his estate.

Thomas, a second son, had been left the Pythouse estate by his father, Thomas Benett of Norton Bavant. The Benetts had been settled at Norton Bavant since the 14th century at least, and in 1390 one John Benett claimed to hold land there, probably as lessee of the Dominican nuns of Dartford in Kent.[2] The family flourished as clothiers and farmers and one notable member was Thomas Benett who died in 1558, having been a close associate of Cardinal Wolsey and Precentor of Salisbury Cathedral, where his monument can still be seen. In 1565 the family's arms, consisting of 'Gules, three demi-lions rampant Argent, a mullet for difference' were confirmed by William Harvey, Clarenceux King of Arms, when he made his visitation to Wiltshire. In 1611 the lessees of the manor of Norton Bavant joined together to buy the freehold of their respective holdings, with William Benett, being the lessee of most of the land, becoming holder of the manorial rights. Successive members of the family were thereafter recognised as Lords of the Manor.

Thomas's father died in 1754 having bought the Pythouse estate in 1725. He undoubtedly made this purchase because his mother, Patience, was the granddaughter of Thomas Bennett, who had owned the estate until his death in 1663, and whose family (originally called Pyt alias Bennett) had been in possession of it, as freeholders, from a very early date. Thomas Bennett's son and grandson sold it in 1669 after the family had been heavily fined during the Commonwealth as supporters of the Crown. Patience's father, John Bennett, had been steward to Henry, 3rd Lord Arundell of Wardour and Member of Parliament for Shaftesbury. Her brother, Thomas, as well as being Private Secretary to Prince Rupert, had, in 1677, succeeded to his father's seat in Parliament. Until the marriage of Patience to William Benett of Norton Bavant in 1686, there had been no known connection between the two families.

Thomas, the purchaser of the Pythouse estate in 1725, demolished the old mansion of the Bennetts and built a new house, on a different site and in an elevated position to take advantage of shelter from the hill to the north and extensive views to the south. The house in which John was born less than fifty years after it was built was by no means large, having two principal floors built over a basement and beneath an attic storey. There were three bays on each front and so the house probably had only four rooms on each floor. In addition there were the usual servants' quarters with stables and a pigeon house, and the front was enclosed with 'courts and gardens in the confined and formal style of that period'.³ The house was, therefore, of modest size and was in fact intended as a dower house for occupation by Thomas's widow, Etheldred, one of the six daughters and co-heiresses of William Wake, Archbishop of Canterbury.⁴ However, although she was granted by her husband's will the right to live in the new Pythouse for the rest of her life, having lived all her married life in her husband's ancestral home at Norton Bavant, she preferred to remain there during her widowhood.

Not a great deal is known of the activities of young Benett's father. However, many years before, he had attempted to secure election as a fellow of All Souls College Oxford as founder's kin, and also as Member of Parliament for Heytesbury, a 'rotten' borough close to his ancestral home at Norton Bavant. In the one he was successful and in the other spectacularly unsuccessful and the story of these adventures would undoubtedly have been related to his sons, one of whom, John, must surely have known about his father's unsuccessful attempt to enter Parliament when he succeeded where his father had failed.

Thomas's mother, Etheldred, was the granddaughter of the wife of Sir Richard Hovell, who was born a Chichele. She was thus a direct descendant of William Chichele, one of the brothers of Henry Chichele, Archbishop of Canterbury who died in 1443 having founded, jointly with Henry VI, All Souls College Oxford in 1437. By the statutes of the college, all kin of the founder were to be entitled to become fellows and once elected, whether resident or not, were entitled to share in the surplus revenue of the college known as 'augmentation of commons'.

Needless to say, the election of more fellows would reduce the benefits available to the existing fellows, and as the centuries passed since the death of the founders, the college attempted to keep the numbers down by raising personal objections to potential candidates.

Thomas duly lodged his pedigree under the seal of the College of Arms but to no avail. The fellows refused to elect him and so he appealed to the Archbishop of Canterbury who decided in his favour following which *The Gentleman's Magazine* reported:

> We heard at Doctor's Common, by the Archbishop of Canterbury and his assistants, Dr Paul, Dr Bettejworth & Baron Clarke, an appeal brought by Mr Bennet, a kinsman of Archbishop Chicheley, founder of All Souls College Oxford but rejected at the last election in November, it was determin'd, in favour of the applicant, to annul the last election, and to issue monition to the college from the Archbishop, the visitor, to admit him into a fellowship as his right by consanguinity, and to pay full costs.[5]

Notwithstanding this, the fellows ignored the archbishop's decision, and so Thomas and his parents had no alternative but to commence more formal proceedings against the college, in an effort to compel compliance with the archbishop's order. They knew that the fellows of All Souls would do everything in their power to thwart them and so decided to seek the aid of one of Etheldred's nephews Martin Folkes.[6] He was the son of her sister Dorothy and an eminent antiquary, who had been President of the Royal Society since 1741 and who, in 1750, was elected President of the Society of Antiquaries. He was, of course, well acquainted with the details of his cousin's descent from the brother of one of the founders, and so made and signed a very lengthy statement demonstrating that Thomas was indeed one of the founder's kin. No doubt it was considered that the fellows of All Souls would be impressed and indeed persuaded by the evidence of such an exalted witness.

In September 1750, Thomas was ordered by the fellows to show proof of his pedigree, and in November the sub-warden and fellows of Wadham College provided a certificate that:

> Thomas Bennet Gentleman Commoner and Student in Civil Law in the said College hath for the three years past been personally known to us and have [sic] behaved himself piously, soberly and honestly. And we do to the best of our knowledge believe and certify that the said Thomas Bennet hath neither held, taught, wrote or believed anything contrary to the Doctrines or Discipline of the Church of England.

During 1751, William Blackstone,[7] who had been a fellow of All Souls since 1744 and whose *Commentaries on the Laws of England* is widely considered to be the best general history of English law, lodged a statement to the effect that the fellows were correct in their decision, as in his opinion Thomas had failed to disclose proof of his pedigree before the election. Further, the fellows themselves provided a lengthy statement giving their reasons why they chose not to elect him. They were singularly unimpressed by the pedigree produced by the College of Arms, declaring in their Answer to Thomas's claim:

> from the Gross Errors and Notorious Falsehoods which have appeared to the College of All Souls in pedigrees attested by the same Authority And from the known Contempt with which all Courts of Justice have Treated that Authority no Faith or Credit in law is to be given thereto!

The archbishop was invited to ignore the evidence provided by Dr Folkes on the grounds that 'he was not a legal or competent witness as being interested in the point in question', meaning, one presumes, that as his mother was a member of the Hovell family he too might be entitled to seek election as Founder's kin.

If the fellows were unimpressed by the evidence of the College of Arms and the eminent President of the Royal Society, they were even less impressed by Thomas's academic performance! They stated that:

> The appellant (i.e. Thomas) did appear in order to perform all the exercises usually performed or required to be performed by such persons as stand candidates for Fellowships in the said College and these respondents (i.e. the Fellows of All Souls) say that the Appellant was in no Degree equal for the scholastic merit to the Gentlemen Elected by the College and particularly his Compositions were mean, his Translations Notoriously faulty and erroneous and he appeared in the Publick Disputations to be so entirely ignorant of the first Rudiments of Logic & Natural Philosophy That he could not at all enter into the parts of either opponent or respondent but after a pause of above a quarter of an hour was obliged to be dismissed from his seat without propounding or answering a single argument or performing any branch of that Exercise and therefore these respondents do not believe him to be duly qualified according to the Statutes of the said College to be elected a Fellow of the same and these respondents further answer to the said article do hereunto annexe the Theme (i.e. essay) of the said Appellant marked with the letter A and other his Translations of one of Sully's Epistles and a paragraph from the Spectator marked with the letters B and C which they pray may be taken as part and parcell of this their answer which said

Theme and Translations are of the proper handwriting of the said Appellant and signed with his own name.

A hearing of the appeal did not take place until 21 February 1752, and a further two years were to pass before the archbishop ordered in March 1754 that Thomas should be admitted as a fellow of All Souls and on 14 April the college confirmed to the archbishop that he had been duly admitted.

Costs of only £50 were awarded against the college and as Thomas's proctor's bill amounted to no less than £191 11s 2d [8] initially he was seriously out of pocket. In 1765 there was published *Stemmata Chicheleana: or a genealogical Account of some of the families derived from Thomas Chichele, of Higham-Ferrers in the County of Northampton,* included in which are pedigrees of a large number of the descendants of Archbishop Wake, in one of which Thomas is highlighted as having become a fellow of All Souls fifteen years before. Thomas was exceedingly fortunate that he succeeded in his claim as in 1750 William Blackstone had published his *Collateral Consanguinity* to show the absurdity of claims such as Thomas's. Supported by his arguments the college admitted only one more kinsman until 1762 when, fortified by an archiepiscopal verdict, more kinsmen flooded in.[9]

No sooner had he been elected a fellow of All Souls and shortly after his father's death, Thomas embarked on another adventure. Having inherited the Pythouse estate, Thomas probably thought of himself as a man of sufficient standing to enable him to seek a seat in Parliament. In April of 1754 a General Election was called, whereupon he mounted a challenge to the Ashe family of Heytesbury, a village only a mile from Norton Bavant. Heytesbury was a classic 'rotten' borough where 26 voters returned two Members to Parliament. These voters were the tenants of a small number of burgage tenements. The majority of these were owned by the Ashe family who, in accordance with the usual practice, expected their tenants to vote as they directed. The two family candidates were Pierce à Court Ashe and his brother William à Court, who one would have expected to have been friends as well as neighbours of the Benetts of Norton Bavant.

One wonders why Thomas chose to stand as he must have known that he had not the slightest chance of success. In the event, he attracted only 2 votes whereas 19 were cast in favour of Pierce and 17 in favour of his brother. The two who were bold enough to vote for Thomas were Richard Dann and Thomas Yates, who both cast their other vote in favour of Pierce.[10] He knew that traditionally it was only the tenants of the burgage tenements who were entitled to vote and so, following the election, Thomas asked his friend and lawyer John Howard of the Inner Temple to attempt to discover whether a charter had ever been granted to Heytesbury, no doubt with a view to seeing whether the very limited suffrage could be questioned and thus the result of the election challenged. Howard reported :

> I have searched carefully amongst the Records of the most Antient date down through every reign to the present time for any charter granted to Haytesbury . . . But I do not find any such one granted. If you would have further search made let me know directly and it is pretty chargeable for they charge at the rolls for liberty to search a shill[ing] for every year searched.[11]

Although the Ashe family's control appeared to be unassailable, Thomas's activities were a cause of anxiety to them, and on the 5 June 1754 Pierce reported to his brother William:

> Our neighbour endeavours still to ingratiate himself with the mob. Jack Bennet was over here Monday at our club feast and yesterday some part of ours was at Norton to compliment Squire Thomas. They expected 30 guineas towards their subscription but came away entertained only with some Norton Ale so they lost my two guineas and got nothing. That was as much noise and disturbance as the day of the election produced. I am afraid our intelligence was groundless they certainly at least think of continuing at Norton by the stock of fuel laid in.[12]

Pierce and William would have known that Thomas's elder brother William had inherited the Norton Bavant estate on the death of their father earlier in the year, and that Thomas had inherited the Pythouse estate. So his description as 'Squire Thomas' was surely a somewhat flippant allusion to Thomas's transformation from the status of a younger son to that of a landowner in his own right. It appears from this letter that the Ashe brothers may have heard rumours that, during the minority of Thomas's nephew William, the Norton estate would be disposed of, but this was not in fact the case. Jack Bennet was undoubtedly Thomas's younger brother, the 24 year old John, who had just come down from Oxford before entering the church. Thomas did stand again in 1761 but withdrew before the poll commenced.

The Pythouse estate that young John's father had inherited was of modest size and extended to only about 300 acres. So shortly before he was married for the second time, he increased his land holdings by buying from Sir Henry Paulet St. John the manor of Enford[13] in the north-east corner of Salisbury Plain, an estate that extended to about

1500 acres. It seems a little curious that he should have purchased an estate some twenty-five miles from Pythouse. The reason may be that it was at one time thought that the Benetts of Norton Bavant were descended from one John Benet who according to a pedigree published in the 19th century lived at Enford in about 1339.[14]

Thomas's second wife and John's mother Catherine was the daughter of John Darell, a banker of York Street, St James's Square in London. She was co-heir to her brother who left her a fortune of £18,000, and her sister Hariett was married to Richard Croftes, Member of Parliament for Cambridge University. By a strange coincidence, she was descended from Florence, the sister of Archbishop Chichele, who married the archbishop's steward Sir John Darell of Calehill.[15]

The management of the household was Catherine's responsibility and the keeping of meticulous accounts was an important part of this duty. The account books[16] were kept by her personally and not by a housekeeper and they provide us with a most detailed picture of every penny spent at Pythouse, both in and about the house and farm shortly before Benett's birth and during his early childhood. During the first year of her marriage the total spent amounted to £1573 16s 9½d and, as she received from her husband £1437 5s 10¾d, the deficit was carried forward to the following year.

The expenditure was divided into 12 sections as follows:

| | | |
|---|---|---|
| 1. | For repairs & taxes on Pythouse and farm | 203 0 5 ½ |
| 2. | Turnpikes, carriage of goods & other matters belonging to no account | 10 4 9 |
| 3. | Irregular bills | 7 4 6 |
| 4. | Mr Benett's cloathes and particular expenses | 60 12 6 |
| 5. | My own cloathes and particular expenses | 36 5 9 ½ |
| 6. | Jaunts and other pleasurable expenses | 16 4 2 ½ |
| 7. | Servants' wages and liveries | 102 2 5 ½ |
| 8. | Stable and dogs | 75 5 10 |
| 9. | Cellars | 98 5 6 |
| 10. | Garden | 28 18 11 |
| 11. | Housekeeping | 286 5 4 ¼ |
| 12. | Farm account debtors this year | 397 8 5 |

£1573 16 9 ½

Included in the expenditure under section 1 were 2s 6d per quarter for the *Salisbury Journal* and 3d for the carriage of some oranges and lemons from Salisbury. Included in section 2 were 'Palmer's travelling expenses to Sarum & Shaftesbury' and stationery purchased from Easton's in Salisbury. On Boxing Day, Pythouse was visited by carol singers from nearby Tisbury and Ansty. They received 10s 6d and 2s 6d respectively (presumably because more singers came from Tisbury than from its smaller neighbour) and on the same day one shilling was paid to 'Tom Spencer who came as a Christmas fiddler'. On the following day the singers from Donhead arrived as well as a party from Semley (both villages close to Pythouse) who received 2s 6d respectively. Catherine even recorded other very small sums paid to 'Boys who came fiddling'.

In section 3, five shillings were given to 'Chosley for finding three guineas dropt out of Mr Benett's pocket' and, on 22 February 1772, there was included in Catherine's very modest expenditure on 'my own cloathes and particular expenses' one guinea to the Semley bell ringers for ringing the church bells when 'little Thomas was born' and £1 11s 6d to the Tisbury ringers; also the surprisingly large sum of ten guineas to the midwives who attended her on the birth of Thomas.

On 'jaunts and other pleasurable expenses', £5 19s was spent in April 1772 on a visit to Sarum, Longford and Wilton (presumably to see Longford Castle and Wilton House) and in August the very large sum of £8 5s on a trip to Blandford Races. Included in the servants' wages and liveries were five guineas to Henry Bailey 'who acts occasionally as Butler'. The gardeners' wages accounted for almost the whole of the sum spent in the gardens. From the housekeeping account a very clear picture of the household's diet can be seen. A great deal of fish in particular was consumed with, for instance, 2s 10½d being spent in April on a crab, a lobster, 2 flounders and an eel and in October 1s 6d for 2 plaice and 100 oysters. In March 1772, plate tax for 500 ounces of plate at 5s per 100 ounces was paid.

Catherine's account books for 1776 and 1777 have also survived with 3s being paid to a 'ratcatcher for his Secret of Poisoning Rats' and 1s to a gardener 'for finding a Hare which Mr Benett shot'. A half year's land tax and window tax amounting to over £15 was paid in 1777 as well as 2 guineas 'given towards the relief of the Parish of Aldbourne in Wiltshire where there has been a great fire'. In May of this year a fee of 2s 6d was paid at Fonthill House for showing the house to the Miss Bennetts of Hartgrove[17] and in the same year the sum of £17 was paid to 'Mitchell coachmaker at Salisbury for a new Phaeton with Harness for a pair of horses and a large Trunk'. By this time, clothes had to be purchased for Catherine and Thomas's young children, Thomas born in 1772 and John born in the following year as well as for their daughters Etheldred and Anna Maria.

In May 1776, Catherine paid 13s 5d for almost six yards of cloth to make shirts for 'my son John', and in June the surprisingly large sum of 4s for a pocket handkerchief bought from 'Harry Bishop, Mr Foulkes's footman'. In October, two pairs of leather gloves were purchased for him at a cost of 2s and early in the following year, 2s 4d were paid for two white worsted stockings bought in Shaftesbury.

Between April 1777 and February 1778, a total of £4 3s 2d was spent on ' My son John's clothes and expenses'. During that time, on no less than seven occasions, 2s was paid for the purchase of shoes for the fast growing four-year-old John, £1 10s 6d for 'two suits of cloathes and a pair of breeches', 7s 6d for a brown beaver hat, 10d for a pair of gloves, and early in 1778, £1 9s 6d for '2 suits of Fustian cloathes'.

In 1780, when Benett was a child of seven, his mother died in childbirth and so for the second time Thomas was left a widower. It seems that following her death, Thomas became increasingly eccentric and we can glean a delightful picture of his character and of the household within which young Benett was brought up from the contents of a letter written by the Rev.Charles Egerton, curate of Blandford, in 1785:

> We stopt a night at Mr Bennett's who lives near Shaftesbury. This man may well be called a perfect character. He is a man of large fortune, has the most excentric ideas of everything especially of womankind who he considers as universally fools: imagines he knows everything better than any man else, and will endeavour to prove that a Physician, Lawyer, Statesman, Goldfinder, etc. etc. are fools compared with himself. Notwithstanding all this he is really a very good-natured man and exceedingly pleasant companion. We arrived there about three and found him and his maiden sister, the veriest old maid in nature, going to dine with his brother Doctor B, rector of a neighbouring parish. He insisted on our going with him and away we went, Miss Bennett and Mr Bragge enjoying a tête à tête on the way. The doctor and his lady were agreeable people, but nothing extraordinary. I shall therefore only say that we spent a very comfortable afternoon and returned to Pythouse to supper.
>
> Mr Bennett, having lost a cause the day before at Salisbury in which he endeavoured to invalidate a will which left £2000 a year away from him, was not so entertaining, says Bragge, as usual. However he made me laugh most heartily tho' I did not thank him for keeping me up from half past twelve when everyone else went to bed, till half past one, giving me an account of the trial, which he said had cost £1500. He is reckoned a very close man, though I am sure he's very hospitable in his own house. He told me that £2000 per annum was nothing to him as he

had £4000 and never spent it, but he thought it his duty towards his children. He has one little boy who was born with his head rather out of shape, and as he as usual knew better than the midwife, undertook to put it into shape which he has done with a vengeance.

His servants are all in due proportion strange. If you ask him where he got his butler he says from the gibbet, but I believe the gibbet never presented such a scarecrow. His coachman, a tall meagre fellow with long straight grey hair, and his footmen stiff and awkward like those whom you see introduced into a pantomime, render the group quite complete and truly worthy of Mr Bunbury's cognisance.[18]

The cause that Thomas had lost and that was referred to in this letter related to the family's ancestral estate at Norton Bavant. On his father's death in 1754, this estate was held in trust for the infant son of Thomas's elder brother William. William had made a most unsuitable marriage. According to a statement made probably in connection with the cause referred to in Charles Egerton's letter:

being an Eldest Son was a great favourite with his Parents although by the foregoing Settlement rendered totally independent of them the latter of which proved his ruin As he very early in life grew refractory And being Heir Apparent to so good Estate He did not want for abettors of his Folly. Drinking and other intemperance soon destroyed an original and good constitution Which was entirely broke up And he died of Dropsy About 26 April 1749. Sometime previous to his Death he Married one Mary Mountain an Inkeepers Daughter at Stockbridge in Hampshire Where he used to spend Much of his Time in the lowest Company and left her at his death with Child of William Bennet the present supposed Testator who was born About the 10th of June 1749 but of a tender constitution and subject to fits and considering His Father's Health at the time he was begot And His Mother a Drinking Woman It was almost a miracle that he lived to be a man.

William 'the supposed Testator', appears to have been no more respectable that his father, for when he married an apothecary's widow in Bath it was said that he was drunk during the ceremony, fainted during the performance of it and that the bride was given away by his under footman. Philip Dart, one of the witnesses to the new will that was inevitably signed after the wedding had taken place, was the disreputable clergyman who performed the ceremony and was said to be planning to marry the widow himself once William had died. He would have done so had not the milliner to whom he was already engaged refused to release him!

Needless to say, William did indeed die soon after whereupon his widow inherited the whole of his estate, subject to the payment of a number of legacies, and now, as a rich widow, promptly remarried. Efforts were made to prove that William did not have testamentary capacity when he made his will and it is no wonder that the Reverend Charles Egerton was kept out of his bed until well after midnight while Benett's father related the whole story to him. The Norton Bavant estate was eventually ordered by the Chancery Court to be sold and was purchased by Thomas's spinster sister Catherine in 1789.

As he got older, Thomas spent some of his time at his house in Bath and, while he was there, his young children wrote to him commenting on his health and giving him news of the happenings at Pythouse. For instance his 13-year-old son wrote to him in 1786:

> Dear Papa
> I am glad to hear your Headache has left you I hope your soreness will soon be well. Mr Stephens sends his Compliments to you, and is glad to hear your Lumbago has left you. Trooper has taken Physic twice. The Horses are well. Carlo went out a Hunting a little while ago and came home with a wire about his neck, and Pedro was lost a whole night, and the next Day came Home with a wire. Cosmo has a bad Eye – Captain Yeo has sent to Mr Dick Whatly who is Horse and Dog mad to get him some Greyhounds out of Norfolk Suffolk and Cambridge. Captain Yeo does not like Cosmo. The Miller has found a Hare Siting and I wish you was here to Shoot her. Mr S says Jack is turned out a Capital Horse, and that he has some thoughts of entering him for Sweepstakes. All the House sends Compliments to you. I am Sir your dutiful son
>
> John Benett[19]

and again in 1788:

> Dear Papa
> I am glad to hear your Leg is so much better and hope you feet will soon be sound. I am glad to find you are in your old lodgings. I hope Mr Smith and Family are well. Aunt has been free from Cholick ever since you left us. Herod was shod Saturday his Warts have been done with Aqua fortis but is not strong enough to do much Good. James has a Pot of Mercurial Ointment to rub his Heels which are very sound. The Dogs are not pleased that they are chained up and are getting angry. We have not heard of any more mad Dogs. I believe the Stable Rat is dead but Mr [?] watches Day and Night. We have cut another Cucumber and Asparagus twice and Brocole in great abundance. Mr Kneller can walk with the help of Miss Charlot and a stick. Mr South has been here every Saturday to see Mr Hill who has

been cheated out of a Horse by a Shaftesbury rogue. Compliments from all the House. I am obliged to finish my letter to let James go to Bed.
I am your most dutiful Son

John Benett[20]

Nothing is known of the young Benett's education, although in 1819 he was described as man 'of moderate private education' and it is likely, therefore, that he was educated either at home or at a private academy.[21] In 1789, his future prospects changed dramatically when his elder brother, Thomas, died just over a month before his 17th birthday. A note on the back of the portrait painted when he was five years old reads, 'This is the boy who was accidentally shot near the old Chapel at Pythouse and to whom his father said "Tom you are dying, die like a man"'!

Thomas continued to increase the size of his estates by purchasing land at Semley in 1792[22] and 1796[23] and an estate in Chicklade in 1797[24] – both very close to Pythouse. By the time of his death that occurred shortly after he bought the Chicklade estate he also owned land in Sutton Veny and Warminster, as well as the manor of Kington at West Stour and the advowson of Askerswell in Dorset,[25] the manor and farm at South Litchfield and a mansion and park called Freemantle Park at Kingsclere both in Hampshire.[26]

Having completed his education and following his elder brother's premature and unexpected death, Benett went neither to university nor into the army, but appears to have remained at home to assist his father in managing his estates and farming such of the farms as were not let. His younger brother William, who would have to make his own way in the world, did proceed to Wadham College, Oxford and then to Lincoln's Inn and to a career at the bar. In 1790 Nathaniel Palmer, for 36 years his father's 'Friend Companion and Assistant in his Private Affairs' (as he was described in the brass set up in his memory in Tisbury church), had died, and so during the last few years of his father's life, Benett undoubtedly took Nathaniel Palmer's place as his father's assistant and so was well equipped to assume on his father's death the responsibilities expected of a country landowner.

In April 1795, Benett (by now a young man of 21) was asked by his father's younger brother, Dr John Benet, the rector of nearby Donhead St Andrew, who had so hospitably and unexpectedly entertained the curate of Blandford, to act as godfather to his fifth son. He wrote:

Dear Jack
I intend making a complete Christian of my youngest boy George on Easter Tuesday and if you will come to Lower Donhead by half past two

o'clock to answer for the young man's future good behaviour I shall be obliged to you. You will meet the Grove family[27] & the Penruddockes.[28] We are engaged on this occasion (as Mrs Grove brings two boys for the same purpose) to dine at Ferne[29] and we shall be happy to have your company with us in the chaise. . .

> Believe me your sincere and aff. Uncle
>
> John Benet [sic][30]

However, Benett decided to decline his uncle's invitation by writing:

Dear Uncle
I thank you for the honor you offer me of being Godfather to my cousin George but I am too little acquainted with the duties of that office to venture upon the business. . . I should not be able to perform with Propriety and hope you will not esteem my declining this matter any Disrespect or disregard to yourself or to my cousins as I shall be happy to do anything for you within the compass of my knowledge and abilities.[31]

Having in April baptised his two-year-old son and made him a 'complete Christian', in June the rector of Donhead St Andrew had to suffer the loss of the infant's mother and by her death, according to the announcement in the *Salisbury and Winchester Journal*, 'her husband and children have lost an affectionate wife and mother and those of her acquaintance, who knew her amiable qualities, will severely feel the loss of her friendship'.[32]

Benett's father died in 1797 and on the 24 May was buried with his ancestors at Norton Bavant, leaving his two surviving sons, John and William and his two daughters Etheldred and Anna Maria. Benett now therefore, as a very young man, found himself master of his father's considerable property and with the prospect of life as an obscure country gentleman spread out before him.

## 2

## *His marriage, the building of a new Pythouse and his encounters with Henry Hunt and Archdeacon Coxe 1797-1817*

On his father's death, Benett came into possession of all his father's estates, including the house in which he had spent his childhood and early years. Pythouse was a typical early Georgian house with two principal floors built over a basement and beneath an attic storey. The square building had three bays on each front and so probably had only four principal rooms on each floor. By the terms of his father's will, all his plate, family pictures and busts, and the 13 pictures left to him by his London lawyer and friend John Howard ( including a picture of the Rape of Helen by Luca Giordano some 10 feet long) were to pass as heirlooms to the possessor for the time being of the house, and so the quite modestly sized house must have been overflowing with pictures. Marble busts of his grandparents and mother would have added a further touch of distinction to the interior of the house of which the young Benett was now master.

Whether he retained all his father's domestic servants cannot be said, but what is known is that, in August 1797, he paid Hair Powder Tax of one guinea for his housekeeper. It may be that he had dispensed with the services of the footmen so graphically described by the curate of Blandford, as he paid no tax for any other servants in the house[1] notwithstanding the fact that in his will his father directed that 'for 92 days after my death Housekeeping shall continue at my mansion House called Pythouse in the same manner in which it was carried on there in my lifetime'.[2]

The year following his father's death was a momentous one for Benett when his father's 83-year-old spinster sister, Catherine, died at Pythouse, leaving him the estate at Norton Bavant that had been in the possession of his ancestors for at least 400 years. Benett probably knew that he was his aunt's heir but it must have given him great satisfaction that so soon after inheriting his father's estates, he also became the owner of the Norton Bavant property, that consisted of the manor house close to the church, a newly erected corn mill and ten freehold farms consisting of about 750 acres of arable meadow, pasture and down land. The acquisition of this estate, when added to the lands he had inherited from his father, transformed Benett into a landowner of some consequence.

It is likely that as soon as his father had died, Benett would have become a magistrate for the county, and he was certainly named as one of those sworn to act in this capacity early in 1802.[3] In November of 1797 his name was one of the three nominated to be placed before the King, who would then 'prick' one of them to be High Sheriff of the county for the coming year.[4] Benett was duly chosen to assume this office that had been held by his father before him in 1758. Benett would have found himself as a young man in his mid-twenties incurring considerable expense in attending the judges at the assizes, and being responsible with the magistrates for maintaining law and order throughout the county (not an easy task in the absence of a regular police force). He would be liable to receive instructions from the judges and magistrates and, although by this time the standing of those who were likely to be chosen had risen, earlier in the century there had been 'a sort of tacit conspiracy to let the office fall either on the minor gentry or on a young man who had succeeded early to his father's estate'[5] – a perfect description of Benett's situation. Serving as High Sheriff, however, would have brought him into contact with most of the men of influence throughout the county, connections that would prove invaluable and indeed essential when later he sought to be elected as one of the county's representatives in Parliament. It is also probable that, his name having been 'pricked' to serve as High Sheriff, it was at this time that the Lord Lieutenant of the county, the Earl of Pembroke and Montgomery,[6] appointed him one of his deputies. One further public office also came his way in 1799 when, following the announcement of the appointment of three Commissioners of Appeal in Income Tax cases for the southern division of the county, Benett, together with Sir John Methuen Poore[7] and Michael Hicks Beach,[8] was named to act in case of vacancies.[9]

In 1798, Benett found himself becoming involved in a matter that was to occupy a great deal of his time in the years to come. The liability of landowners to the church for tithes, that is for a tenth part of the produce of the land, had for many years been a cause of friction and dispute between the laity and the clergy. Instead of physically handing over animals or harvested produce, the custom had grown up in some parishes for moduses, that is money payments in lieu of tithes, to be paid, and for many years this had been the practice in Benett's home parish of Tisbury. However, Thomas Prevost, the vicar of Tisbury since 1791, refused to accept payment in this way and commenced proceedings in the Bishop of Salisbury's Episcopal Court against John and Samuel Bracher, occupiers of land in the parish. A number of landowners, led by Benett as the principal owner, were determined to resist the vicar's claim, and agreed to do whatever they could to assist the Brachers. On 15 June, they entered into an agreement with a Warminster attorney named John Thring by which they instructed Thring to defend the actions that had already been commenced and any future suits that Prevost might institute. They agreed to pay all of Thring's costs, charges and expenses in the proportions to which the rent or the annual value of each of their respective estates bore to each other.[10] This action by Benett, so soon after inheriting the Pythouse estate, was certainly not calculated to endear him to the ecclesiastical authorities, and the decision of Prevost to take action against two of his parishioners was doubtless the event that kindled his interest in tithes and his determination to see their reform. As well as commencing these proeedings, in 1801 Prevost also filed a bill in the Court of Exchequer against Benett and others to account for tithes in kind.[11]

Amongst the property Benett inherited from his father and settled by his will was land at Enford, Norton Bavant, Tisbury, Semley, Longbridge Deverill and Chicklade, all being subject to the payment of land tax. In 1799, therefore, he decided to redeem this tax 'with his own proper money' consisting of £6057 1s 11d 3% Reduced Bank Annuities[12] also, doubtless, inherited from his father.

Since 1793 England had been at war with France and it is almost certain that, having attained his majority in the following year, he enlisted as a private[13] in the yeomanry cavalry of Wiltshire. This was formed in 1794 after an appeal in the *Salisbury and Winchester Journal* for 'hunters coursers and bold riders'[14] to volunteer their services. Benett joined the Hindon troop, all the officers of which would have been personally known to him. It was necessary for Benett to find his own horse of at least fourteen hands, saddle, and leather breeches, and all pay received from the Government for the troop was equally divided between officers and men without distinction, all of whom would be gentleman or yeomen or 'other persons' approved by the Lord Lieutenant. If he failed to attend when called out to suppress riots or tumults, he would forfeit the sum of twenty pounds, and if he was absent from training a fine of two guineas would be imposed. [15]

In 1800 he was advanced to the rank of cornet, and would doubtless have looked splendid in his uniform as he set off for a day's exercise with the Hindon Troop, made up mainly of farmers and farmers' sons. The daughter of a member of one such troop recalled the scene as her father prepared for a day with his regiment, 'What polishing of sword and epaulette! What brushing of bearskin and broadcloth! With what admiration we used to walk round my father when he was fully equipped, and he affecting all the time to take it as a mere matter of course'.[16] Not many years after Benett joined the troop, a cornet's uniform consisted of a blue cut-away coat with tails turned back with white cloth, a red standing collar enriched with gold braid, with matching cuffs and with intricate gold braiding to the elbow. The front was laced with gold braid, with three rows of gilt ball buttons. With this was worn a white cloth waistcoat and breeches, both fastened with gilt ball buttons. On the left shoulder was a gold bullion epaulette, denoting the wearers rank[17] and so, as a tall young man of 26, Benett would surely have cut a dashing figure as he rode out of the park of Pythouse to join his troop.

The Treaty of Amiens of 1802 heralded what, it was thought at the time, would be a period of peace but this illusion was soon shattered by the resumption of hostilities between England and France in the following year. The threat of invasion was extremely serious, and so it was necessary to bring all the yeomanry cavalry troops up to strength. On 14 July 1803 a General Meeting of the Lieutenancy was held in the Town Hall in Devizes, attended by the Lord Lieutenant and 30 deputy lieutenants including Benett.[18] At this meeting a number of resolutions were passed in order to carry into execution the Act that had been recently passed to provide for the defence and security of the realm. A meeting of deputy lieutenants and officers was held at Salisbury on 26 July and Benett was one of those who signed a number of resolutions including one:

> That the several captains should receive into their troops any yeomen or gentlemen, not exceeding one hundred in each troop, on their engaging to find such necessaries and arms and appointments as the allowance from the Government shall be found inadequate to procure[19]

And another:

> That the sum of one shilling weekly be allowed the wife and each child of militia men under 10 years of age from this week to the next Michaelmas Quarter Sessions to be holden in this county when a new Order will be made.[20]

Benett's friend Thomas Grove,[21] as captain of the Hindon troop, acted very speedily by arranging for a notice to be inserted in the *Salisbury and Winchester Journal* on 1 August to the effect that 'all those gentlemen and yeomen who wish to enter the Hindon Troup of Wilts Yeomanry are desired to attend at Hindon on Wednesday the 3rd day of August at 11 o'clock in the forenoon in order to be enrolled'.[22]

On 8 August the *Salisbury and Winchester Journal* announced:

> The Officers of the Wiltshire Yeomanry Cavalry have resolved to augment their troops to 100 men and it is not doubted but the whole 10 troops will speedily be filled. This resolution was made on 26 inst. But the order for advertising it in our last was by some accident mislaid.[23]

As a consequence, the Wiltshire regiment very quickly recruited over 700 men. Having been advanced to the rank of lieutenant in 1804, Benett doubtless attended with the Hindon troop when the whole of the Wiltshire regiment assembled at Devizes for 14 days permanent duty, with the Hindon troop being quartered at Marlborough. At the end of the duty the regiment was congratulated on 'the rapid improvement it has made in discipline and exercise, and upon the regular, steady, and soldier-like behaviour of every individual.'[24]

It seems that the last winter of the 18th century was a hard one, and so Benett, as a young batchelor with an ample fortune, could not fail to be touched by the plight of his needy neighbours, and in particular those living in and around Semley, a village of some 500 souls almost within sight of Pythouse. In January of 1800, the *Salisbury and Winchester Journal* reported:

> Among the charitable attention of the opulent to their poor neighbours during the inclement season, those of John Benett Esq of Pyt-house, have been eminently serviceable, and have procured for him the fervant thanks and blessings of the poor of Semly [sic] etc.[25]

Also as the new century dawned, as patron of the benefice of Askerswell, a small village near Bridport in Dorset, Benett was called upon to choose a new rector. The advowson of Askerswell had been acquired by his great-grandfather, William Benett of Norton Bavant, in 1699 and in 1789 Benett's father had presented the Reverend John Colmer to the benefice.[26] For some reason, that appointment appears to have lapsed as, in 1801, Benett re-presented Colmer to the living.[27] As will be seen, this 'act of kindness', as Colmer was later to describe it, was greatly appreciated by him, notwithstanding that in the same year he became rector of Crickett Malherbe in Somerset and, in 1807, rector of

Littleton Drew in Wiltshire, whilst remaining rector of Askerswell until his death in 1842![28]

As a tall twenty-eight year old bachelor with an extensive estate and income, and probably presenting a dashing image in his cornet's uniform, Benett would make a most desirable husband for one of the daughters of the neighbouring gentry. In 1801 he was married in the church at Boyton, a village not far from Norton Bavant. His bride was Lucy, only surviving daughter of Edmund Lambert of Boyton, who was half brother of the eminent botanist Aylmer Bourke Lambert.[29] He was one of the original fellows of the Linnaean Society and, since 1796, its Vice-President, a post he was to hold for no less than 46 years. She was Benett's second cousin once removed, being also descended from William Wake, Archbishop of Canterbury – Lucy from his daughter Amy[30] and Benett from his daughter Etheldred. The Lamberts had been settled at Boyton since 1573, and so both Lucy and her bridegroom were descended from families of minor gentry long resident in the south-western corner of Wiltshire. The match would no doubt have been regarded by all their friends and relations as being entirely suitable.

No portrait of Benett as a young man survives, but his nickname of 'Long John' and a portrait painted later in his life, enable us to be sure that he was an extremely tall man and probably well over six feet in height. A portrait of Lucy, wearing a high waisted dress of the period, and almost certainly painted shortly before her marriage, hung during the whole of the 20th century at Pythouse.[31] This portrait has been attributed (probably wrongly) to Sir Thomas Lawrence[32] and almost certainly because amongst the family letters is one from Lawrence written in 1807 (endorsed 'insolent letter'!) and reading:

> Sir
> You must be well convinced that I should not have bestowed the time I have upon the picture if I had not intended to finish it. That time is of rather more use to me.
>
> If you will care to give directions where it may be sent the picture will be completed by the end of next month.[33]

Lucy doubtless brought with her a substantial dowry and it is said that this injection of wealth (together with that inherited from his father) persuaded Benett to embark on what must be considered his most lasting, and certainly his most visible, memorial. The Pythouse that he inherited from his father had been built by his grandfather, initially as a dower house for his widow, but in the event it was left to and occupied by

Benett's father as a second son; it was therefore a house of modest proportions. It is likely in consequence that as soon as he had decided to marry he resolved to transform the house in which he had been brought up into a mansion in the latest neo-Grecian style, that would be a grand house within which to bring up his family, to be a statement of his increasing wealth and an impressive focal point of an estate that was to grow very considerably over the next few years.

Benett did not demolish his grandfather's house (parts of which were retained and can still be seen, including a staircase leading to the second floor and a room panelled in typical 18th century style) but he encased it with new ranges. The main entrance was approached by a wide flight of steps that ended beneath four massive unfluted Ionic columns supporting a pediment, on which the Benett arms impaled with the arms of Lucy's family were proudly displayed. On each of the side elevations there are further Ionic porticoes with recessed loggias, inside which can be seen the walls and windows of the earlier house. The cast-iron rainwater heads are dated 1805 – the likely year in which the work was completed.

What is remarkable is that the house was built to Benett's own design.[34] In producing a neo-Grecian façade, Benett demonstrated that he was familiar with the very latest and fashionable architectural ideas, and it may be that he had seen George Dance's reconstructed Stratton Park in Hampshire or James Wyatt's Dodington Park in south Gloucestershire, both completed at much the same time as the new Pythouse. It has been said that, after 1810, the Greek Revival was ' the very criterion of architectural distinction'[35] and so having built his new house well before that date, Benett must have been justly proud of his thoroughly modern creation. It is perhaps a measure of Benett's achievement that one writer should number Pythouse amongst England's thousand best houses, although it is doubtful whether he would have thought of himself, as the writer suggests, 'a true radical' when he designed his house as 'a temple in the Greek style adopted as 'democratic' by the American and French revolutions'.[36]

Owner-architects were not entirely unknown at the time but were certainly a rarity. While the house was being rebuilt, Benett and Lucy lived in the house on his nearby Chicklade estate[37] that had been purchased by his father shortly before his death; and he is said to have 'supervised the execution of them (i.e. his own designs) . . . rising at 5 o'clock every morning for that purpose'.[38] The front elevation is very similar to that of Dinton House (subsequently called Philipps House) designed some eight years later by Jeffry Wyatt[39] (later Sir Jeffry

Wyattville) and about five miles from Pythouse. Had Philipps House been built *before* Pythouse one would have been forgiven for believing that Benett had been inspired by Wyatt's work. However, it is likely that William Wyndham,[40] for whom Dinton House was built and who was one of Benett's closest friends, asked Wyatt to design a house for him taking *his* inspiration from Pythouse! Were Benett to return to his house today he would be surprised not only to see it very considerably enlarged but also to see that the glazing bars to the windows of the upper two floors of the entrance front have been removed and replaced with plate glass. A pencil drawing of the entrance front thought to date from *c*. 1815[41] presents a very vivid picture of the house as designed by him.

Benett retained the orangery on the bank to the west of the house and also the gatepiers, with bands of rocky rustication, that had belonged to and were probably built at the same time as the earlier Pythouse.

The most unusual feature of the interior of the house was, and of course still is, the dramatic main staircase of 20 steps that rises in one arm and returns in two, being supported by cast iron shafts decorated with iron circles and arches of various shapes and sizes. The long library retains the character of a room in the earlier house and here Benett inserted segmental arched recesses. The plaster cornices in the spacious entrance hall display the crest of the Benetts of Norton Bavant described as 'out of a mural coronet, or, a lion's head, ar'. On the whole, the remainder of the interior is remarkably restrained, although Benett must have been pleased to have been able to acquire the magnificent chimney pieces that he placed in the two state rooms on each side of the marble floored entrance hall[42]. They are believed to have originated in northern Italy and one of them is said to have been dated 1553 and referred to the Martinengo family.[43] The Pythouse estate adjoins the estate of Fonthill, and in 1801 William Beckford,[44] who had begun the process of demolishing the magnificent Fonthill Splendens, instructed Mr Phillips to offer for sale by auction, 'valuable building materials of the two wings and offices of Fonthill Mansion . . . and magnificent Statuary Chimney-pieces enriched with Statuary figures (four and five feet high) supporting the Mantles of exquisite sculpture and classically designed'.[45] It is possible that Benett purchased the chimney pieces at this sale or, if not, perhaps at the further sale that took place in 1807 when several more marble chimney pieces were sold. Fonthill Splendens was soon to be replaced by Beckford's prodigious Fonthill Abbey. This, as will be seen, was purchased by Benett following the collapse of its tower, and so it is possible, and perhaps even probable, that Benett rescued the chimneypieces from the ruins and thus introduced two exotic features to the two principal reception rooms.

Having built his new house, it is certain that Benett would have taken the opportunity of filling it with new and fashionable furniture, such as the pair of Thomas Hope 'Empire Type' card tables and the dining table almost 16 feet long when fully extended, with a set of 12 dining chairs and fine new chandeliers. These were all amongst the contents of the mansion that the executors of the widow of John Fane-Benett-Stanford, the last of Benett's descendants to live there, offered for sale by auction in 1957. However the sale catalogue also mentions a Dutch walnut armoire, a Dutch walnut bureau and other early 18th century furniture. These are more than likely to have originally been part of the furnishings of the Pythouse partly incorporated by Benett in his new house, as well as a Ch'ien Lung armorial dinner tea and breakfast service bearing the Benett coat of arms, that had been purchased by Benett's father in 1789. Also to be seen in the new house would have been the portraits of Benett's ancestors, the Benetts of Norton Bavant, as well as a few portraits of members of the original Bennett family of Pythouse (including a fine portrait of Thomas Bennett who had been private secretary to Prince Rupert), and the Italian paintings ( including an enormous painting of the Rape of Helen by Luca Giordano) left to his father by his London lawyer in 1766.[46] Probably in the hall would have been the marble bust of Benett's grandfather, Thomas Benett, that had formerly been in the earlier house, on the base of which is the inscription 'T:B:Arm:Sol:Emp:et Dom Aedif.An 1727'. A translation of the expanded wording – Thomas Benett Armiger Solum Emptor et Domum Aedificator Annus 1727 – would be 'Thomas Benett Esq. purchaser of the land and builder of the house'. Marble busts of Thomas's widow, Etheldred, sculpted after her death by the celebrated sculptor Joseph Wilton[47] and of Benett's mother Catherine, would also have adorned the new house.

It seems that the designing and building of the new Pythouse was not the first time that Benett had applied his mind to architectural matters. It is said that he also designed the stables at another Wiltshire house, Stockton House, built soon after 1800. [48] These handsome stables are 'in the same chequerwork as the chapel wing from which the motif of the paired arched windows is taken'.[49] As an amateur architect, Benett appears in Colvin's *Dictionary of British Architects 1600-1840*[50] – a somewhat surprising place in which to find the name of a Wiltshire country gentleman.

In 1802 Lucy's father, Edmund Lambert, died and one of the first provisions of his will was a gift of £500 to Benett:

> upon trust that he will lay out the same in erecting and completely finishing within a distance of 200 yards of his mansion house at Pythouse aforesaid a chappel [sic] large enough to contain 30 or 40 persons for the purpose of having Divine Service performed and a Sermon preached therein once every Sunday and Christmas Day agreeably to the Established Church of England and do and shall finish the same with proper and convenient seats and a decent reading desk and pulpit and Communion Table and other necessary articles of furniture in such manner as that chapel may be ready for consecration and the performance of Divine Service within 2 years after my death.

He further provided an additional sum of £600 the income from which was to be paid to such clergymen as should from time to time perform Divine Service in the chapel.[51] Tradition has it that the chapel was built for Lucy in particular, and therefore it is likely that the gift in her father's will was made to provide a place of worship for her Benett proceeded to erect the chapel,[52] perhaps to his own design, in the gothic style with a burial vault below. However, it has been said that the Bishop of Salisbury refused to consecrate it as it was thought to be intended for private use only. When Benett signed a will in 1817, he expressed a wish to be buried in 'the Chapel lately built by me', and so it is possible that by that time the chapel had been completed.[53]

However, it is more likely that the building of the chapel, situated in a woodland setting behind the present mansion, was never finished, although the roof with its lierne vault remains miraculously almost intact. Some of the external masonry has been incorporated in another building on the estate and a number of the stone finials lie in groups on the grass surrounding the building. Norton Bavant having always been the burial place of his Benett ancestors, now that Pythouse was firmly established as the principal residence of the family, there can be no doubt that he intended the vault beneath his new chapel to be used in future; the straight pathway leading through laurel bushes and evergreens provides a suitably funereal approach.

His experience and expertise acquired when rebuilding Pythouse would have been well known to his friends. In 1811 the immensely wealthy Bristol merchant and banker Philip Miles[54] purchased the manor of Abbots Leigh, a few miles to the north-west of the city and, following the death of his wife and remarriage, he decided to commission the architect Thomas Hopper[55] to design a new mansion for him on the estate. In

1814, Benett was a witness when an agreement was entered into between Miles and Hopper. The agreement says nothing about the style of the house but merely provides for its dimensions. It further provides that should Hopper die, then Benett was to act as arbitrator in deciding what should be paid to his estate. The house that was built is in almost every respect identical to Pythouse – so much so that one can imagine Miles saying to Hopper, 'There is no need to incorporate in our agreement further details of the house. Build me one like Mr Benett's Pythouse!'[56] The resulting mansion, Leigh Court, clearly inspired by Pythouse, has been described as 'the best house of its date in Somerset'.[57]

In 1804, Benett was elected a member of the Bear Club, originally a group of men who met at the *Bear Inn* in Devizes for social purposes with the fines for non-attendance, annual subscriptions and donations being applied to the schooling and clothing of poor boys in the neighbourhood of Devizes. In time, the club attracted as subscribers many of the nobility and gentry, not only from Wiltshire but also from adjoining counties. Benett was joined by some twenty other new members including the Hon. Henry Addington,[58] the Member of Parliament for Devizes who was created Viscount Sidmouth in the following year. Benett's friend Thomas Grove of Ferne had been a member since 1802 and quite probably persuaded him that he should join, and become well acquainted with, a group of well to do and influential men from all parts of the county, most of whom attended the annual dinner held each August in Devizes.[59]

Having completed the building of his new house, Benett turned his attention to the acquisition of as much land in the neighbourhood as became available for purchase, with the intention, one may be sure, of providing it with an estate large enough to complement its size and grandeur. In 1802 and 1803 Lord Arundell of Wardour[60] had transferred all his estates to trustees with a view to sufficient of them being sold or mortgaged in order to pay some of his debts. These amounted to the enormous sum of £327,623[61] (some £9 million in 2005 terms), and so Benett had the opportunity in 1806 of purchasing from the trustees 335 acres in Semley and 29 acres in Tisbury.[62] In December of the same year the chance of purchasing a much larger property presented itself when he agreed to buy the manors, lordships and advowsons of Berwick St Leonard and Pertwood (villages very close to the Pythouse estate), amounting to some 1700 acres, for £34,000.[63] Half of the purchase price was to be paid on the next Lady Day, with the other half being due at the following Michaelmas, whereupon the purchase was to be completed.

From his father Benett had inherited a considerable estate in Hampshire. This property of over 1000 acres consisted of a manor and farm at South Litchfield and the nearby manor, mansion and park called Freemantle Park at Kingsclere. His father's will contained a provision that this estate should be sold and the proceeds used to purchase land in Wiltshire, Dorset or Somerset. In order to comply with this provision, therefore, and also to provide sufficient money to complete his new purchase, Benett arranged for the Hampshire property to be sold[64] and, as part of the land was comprised in his marriage settlement he instructed his London solicitors to make arrangements for it to be released from the settlement. In the same letter he supplied them with a draft of an advertisement with full particulars that he suggested should immediately be inserted in the Salisbury, Bath and London newspapers.[65] At the same time, his property at West Stour in Dorset and the 162 acre Wincombe Park farm at Donhead St Mary were offered for sale.[66] The land at Donhead St. Mary was eventually sold in 1807.[67]

Benett duly paid the first instalment of the purchase price of the estate at Berwick St.Leonard and Pertwood. However, he refused to complete the purchase and sought a reduction in price on the grounds that certain persons claimed to have rights to turn cattle on to some of the woods that he had agreed to buy and he also said that there was a discrepancy in the measurements of some of the boundaries. It is not unlikely that Benett raised these objections with a view to delaying completion of the purchase because he did not have the necessary funds available. In due course, the vendors commenced proceedings against Benett but by February 1808 he was writing to his solicitors :

> Dear Sirs,
> I have been prevented attending to the subject of your last letter sooner by the illness of my youngest child which has at last terminated with her life – her complaint (viz water on the brain) was to be fatal and therefore I think her happily relieved and I wish to have the Berwick business finished without further litigation and I think by your letter that they will agree to our terms...[68]

The dispute must have eventually been settled as all the property was conveyed to Benett in November 1809 and in the following year he sold 293 acres at Pertwood and the advowson for £12,068 – a very profitable resale of a small part of what he had purchased. In 1808 he bought a further 206 acres in Semley[69] and also Lower Linley and Upper Linley Farms, being very close to Pythouse and consisting of about 250 acres of land.[70] When, in 1807-8, Lord Arundell sold 800 acres of Tisbury manor, Benett purchased 22 acres to add to the Pythouse estate.[71] At the same time he acquired a small estate of several houses and cottages with some 75 acres of land in East Codford,[72] and consolidated his Enford estate by purchasing the tithes from the Enford and Fifield tithings.[73] In 1809 as a result of inclosure awards, as lord of the manor of Enford and Fifield, he was allotted 770 acres there[74] and, as lord of the manor of Norton Bavant, 1275 acres (including 39 acres for rectorial glebe) to add to his estate there.[75] Occasionally he sold small areas of land. For instance, in 1809 he sold for £860 land in Sutton Veny ( a village not far from Norton Bavant) called Pound Furlong that had been purchased many years before by his grandfather, Thomas Benett of Norton Bavant.[76] When the time came to execute the deed of that property, the Warminster surgeon John Seagram must have been visiting Pythouse, for he acted as one of the witnesses to Benett's signature, as did Thomas Hartnall described as 'Butler to Mr Benett'.

As well as purchasing land in the immediate vicinity of Pythouse, Benett also acquired considerable property at Boyton from Lucy's half brother Aylmer Bourke Lambert, the lord of the manor. It was common practice for leases to be granted for the life of one or more people, and so Benett chose the life of his daughter Anna Maria then aged four to be the 'life' in the seven leases of various houses and parcels of land in Boyton that were granted to him on 6 August 1811. On the same day, he was granted by copy of the court roll, five further parcels of land in Boyton, once again for the life Anna Maria, and also a lease of a meadow called Broad Leaze in Codford St Peter for a term of 99 years if Anna Maria should live so long.[77]

Having given birth to three daughters, Lucy Harriet in 1802, Etheldred Catherine in 1805 and Anna Maria in 1806, Lucy gave birth to yet another daughter, Emily Ellen in 1808; but she, as her father mentioned in his letter to his solicitor, died in her infancy. There must have been great rejoicing, therefore, when, in August of the following year, Lucy presented her husband with a son, subsequently named John. The importance of the arrival of a son did not escape the notice of Charlotte Grove, who noted in her diary, 'Heard the good news that Mrs Benett of Pitt [House] has a *son and heir*'[78] nor of the readers of the *Salisbury and Winchester Journal,* who would have read as the first of the announcements of births, 'On Sunday the 13th instant at Pyt-house in this county, the Lady of John Benett, Esq, a son and heir'.[79] A second son, named Thomas Edmund after his two grandfathers, followed three years later, thus giving Benett every reason to believe that he now had a son who would one day succeed him to the family estates.

Charlotte's diary provides a brief glimpse of the social life of the family at Pythouse at this time. Benett and his wife Lucy were intimate friends of Charlotte's parents, Thomas and Charlotte Grove of Ferne, as well as of Lord and Lady Arundell of Wardour Castle, the Knellers at Donhead Hall, the Helyars of Sedgehill House and the Gordons at Wincombe Park, Donhead St. Mary – all houses within easy travelling distance of Pythouse. It seems that Benett and his wife Lucy were in the habit of giving a ball at Pythouse after Christmas during this period, to which all the leading families of the district would have been invited. When Charlotte went to a fancy dress ball given in January 1811 she met 'a large party' there, and Benett's cousin George, the son of his uncle John, the rector of Donhead St.Andrew, 'dressed up as Miss Easton & deceived us completely'. The Grove family remained at Pythouse for the next two days and played chess and other games and eventually 'with regret left the dear Benetts'.[80]

Benett's activities as a magistate were rarely reported in the press and, when they were, it is probable that, in the case of a theft, it was the fame of the victim of the crime that was noteworthy. For instance, in the summer of 1805, Benett committed a man named William Topp to Fisherton Gaol for trial at the following Assizes, charged with having stolen 'a quantity of old copper the property of William Beckford of Fonthill'[81].

In 1808, Benett had an encounter with the radical agitator Henry Hunt,[82] who was convinced that the landowners of the county were conspiring to do all that they could to get rid of him. Both John Astley[83] and Michael Hicks Beach, two east Wiltshire landowners, brought actions against him for trespass and Benett brought an assault charge arising out of a fracas between Hunt and one of his gamekeepers.[84] In his memoirs Hunt relates:

> I was riding out one morning, shooting with a friend, and as we were passing along a lane, a public high road, I suddenly felt a smart blow on the side, and at the same moment some one seized me by the flap of my shooting jacket, and nearly pulled me off my horse. When I recovered myself, and turned round, my friend, the late Mr. John Oakes, of Bath, who had seen the attack made upon me, was demanding of a ruffian the reason for such outrageous conduct. This ruffian was a fellow of the name of Stone, a game-keeper to Mr John Benett, of Pyt-House, of Corn-Bill notoriety, one of the present members for the county of Wilts. Stone stood grinning defiance, with the double-barrelled gun, cocked, in his hand. Indignant at the atrocity of the assault which, without the slightest provocation, had been committed upon me, I sprung from my horse, and

laid down my own gun on the bank, and walking deliberately up to the scoundrel, I first seized his gun with one hand, and with the other I struck him three or four blows; upon which he let go the gun and fell. This fellow was a notorious fighter, and, as he has since confessed, was hired to commit this assault upon me, with the expectation that I should resent it, which would afford him an opportunity to give me a severe drubbing. His goodly scheme was, however, frustrated; for my first blow, after I came in contact with him, was planted so effectually, and followed up so rapidly, that the hireling bruiser was defeated, before he could make any successful attempt to retaliate.

Having discharged his gun, I returned it to him, and the gentleman walked off, or rather sneaked away, not only having himself received a sound hiding, such as he intended and undertaken to give to me, but apparently ashamed and sensible of his folly. It appears, however, that after he had gone home, about a quarter of a mile, and washed himself and taken dinner, he, on the same afternoon, walked to Pyt-House, a distance of thirty miles, to inform his master of the awkward and unexpected result of the experiment which he had been making. After due deliberation, he was advised to return, and to present at the sessions a bill of indictment against me for assault. If he could procure any witness to confirm his story, so much the better; but, as no other person was present but myself and my friend, this was no easy matter to be accomplished. The bill was, however, found at the quarter sessions, and the indictment was removed by certiorari into the Court of King's Bench, to be tried at the assizes.[85]

In due course, Hunt tells us that he was committed to the custody of the Marshall of the King's Bench for three months.[86] Hunt continues to relate in his memoirs:

The truth is, that Stone confessed that he was hired and well paid to assault me, for the purpose of procuring an indictment against me; and by that means I was to be got out of the way, that this dirty job might be executed in a court of justice in my absence. Stone being discharged from his situation, offered to hire himself as my game-keeper, and to divulge the whole plot, and appear as a witness against his former employers. I, however, rather chose to put up with the loss which I had already sustained, than to employ such a treacherous villain, and to encounter fresh law expenses, which I now began to feel were most ruinous, notwithstanding I conducted my own business in the courts. I had, besides, ascertained that the stock-purse gang were always delighted when they found they had entrapped me into a law suit, although my late successes had caused a heavy drain upon the subscribers, some of whom began to grumble at the expense, and to declare off.[87]

The true sequence of events is to be found, not in Hunt's account, which formed part of his highly egotistical memoirs written in 1820 while serving two years sentence of imprisonment in Ilchester gaol; but in a report that appeared in the *Times* when describing the court hearing – at the conclusion of which he was punished for his assault on Benett's gamekeeper William Stone.[88] This report reveals that Benett, as Lord of the Manor of Enford, where Hunt had a farm, directed his gamekeeper to give Hunt notice that he was not to be permitted to shoot on the land forming part of the manor. For some time, Stone had attempted to serve this notice but eventually, seeing Hunt on a shooting party, he followed him and managed to put the notice in Hunt's pocket but at the same time inevitably he touched him. Hunt dismounted from his horse and attacked Stone in a most violent fashion. According to the newspaper report, Hunt acknowledged the justice of the guilty verdict – no mention of this, of course, in his memoirs – whereupon he embarked on a lengthy speech. He implied that he was being persecuted as a result of a conspiracy amongst his neighbours, arising out of his political principles, with which he then proceeded to regale the court until silenced and sentenced to three calendar months in prison. He was also ordered to find security to keep the peace in the sum of £200 with two sureties in the sum of £100 each.

In common with most country landowners, Benett employed keepers on his estates in an effort to protect his game from the activities of poachers, not all of whom were motivated by the need to feed their hungry families. Some five years before, a number of landowners had inserted in the *Salisbury and Winchester Journal* notices warning against unlawful poaching and threatening the prosecution of offenders. However, Benett's notice was couched in unusually courteous terms. Instead of adopting a belligerent tone, it declared that, 'Mr Benett particularly requests that all persons will refrain from sporting on the Manors of Norton Bavant and Endford, both in the County of Wilts.' This notice was, of course, ignored by Hunt and, as will be seen, Benett was later to tell a parliamentary committee that the incidence of fighting on his estate had persuaded him to give up the preservation of game almost entirely.[89]

Since 1807, the county of Wilts had been represented in Parliament by Henry Penruddock Wyndham and Richard Long.[90] Wyndham was the head of the Salisbury branch of the Wyndham family, and various members of the Long family had represented six different boroughs in the north of the county for over a century. Since 1722 there had been only one contested election of county Members, the candidates generally being chosen by the Deptford and Beckhampton Clubs – meetings of gentry who between them amicably decided who should be presented to the freeholders for election by them. The clubs were named after Deptford in the south of the county and Beckhampton in the north where the meetings were traditionally held. In 1812 Wyndham decided to retire and not seek re-election at the forthcoming General Election, and so the clubs would have met to decide who should succeed him. Although 'A Freeholder' writing to the editor of the *Devizes and Wiltshire Gazette* in 1825 stated that Benett was a member of both of the clubs,[91] it is likely that Benett was one of the gentry from the south of the county who met together and agreed with some from the north that Paul Methuen[92] of Corsham should be nominated. Although the Methuen family had been settled in Wiltshire since the 17th century, the decision to invite him to stand was an indication that the more independent minded of the country gentry – and Benett would certainly be counted amongst their number – had decided that the time had come to select a man who was not a member of one of the families who had traditionally represented the county in Parliament.

Early in October, Sir William à Court,[93] the High Sheriff of the county, gave notice 'that a meeting of the Gentlemen, Clergy and Freeholders of the county' would be held at Devizes 'for the purpose of nominating proper persons to represent the county in the ensuing Parliament'.[94] At the nomination, Long and Methuen were unanimously approved as 'proper persons' to be placed before the Special County Court to be held at Wilton on the 14th, and Methuen asked Benett to nominate him. This he duly did following which, in the absence of any other nominations, Long and Methuen were duly elected. In the evening, the new members with about thirty other gentlemen, amongst whom Benett would surely have been numbered, dined at the Assembly Rooms in Salisbury. The fact that so few decided to dine is confirmation that the uncontested election was of little interest to the freeholders – or perhaps the requirement that each of those attending was expected to pay for his own entertainment resulted in only a handful thinking it worthwhile to do so. Certainly more were expected, as it was reported that the dinner gave 'general satisfaction. It had only one fault – it was too abundant, having been provided in the expectation of a more numerous company'![95] How very different the next county election was to be.

Benett continued to combine his activities as a country gentleman with those of a practical farmer, and no doubt enjoyed seeing his men taking part in the competitions organised from time to time by the Bath and West of England Society for the Encouragement of Agriculture, Arts, Manufacture and Commerce. In the summer of 1811, a 'Trial of Ploughs' took place at Deptford Farm near Wylye, the farm being leased by Robert Gourlay[96] from the Duke of Somerset.[97] Benett must have been exceedingly disappointed that his ploughman with a Scotch plough drawn by 2 oxen took 2 hours and 51 minutes to plough half an acre of land. He was the slowest of the eight competitors whose times were reported, whereas Gourlay's similar plough drawn by 2 horses completed the task in only 1 hour and 51 minutes.[98] However Gourlay's pleasure in his success was soon to be eclipsed when, soon after, his goods were seized by his landlord, the Duke, during a long period of acrimonious litigation between them.

Benett was now, therefore, a very active and substantial 'improving' landowner whose rental income depended on a prosperous tenantry, and whose only other income was derived from his own farming activities. Thus he had a very real interest in attempting to improve agrarian techniques and to increase agricultural production. Indeed, in 1799 and very soon after inheriting his father's estates and commencing to farm on his own account, he became a member of the Bath and West of England Agricultural Society,[99] at whose meetings he would meet many members of the aristocracy and gentry, as well as substantial farmers. In 1813, Thomas Davis published his *General View of the Agriculture of Wiltshire,* in which he observed that there was no society instituted in the county for the improvement of agriculture, and suggested that the farmers of the county would benefit from the publication of papers on agriculture as practised by the Bath and West of England Agricultural Society.[100] In order to remedy this, Benett was largely instrumental in organising the formation of 'The Wiltshire Society for the Encouragement of Agriculture and the Rewarding of Faithful and Industrious Servants'.[101] On 16 February 1813, a meeting of landowners and farmers was held at Devizes at which Benett was unanimously elected President and was ' thanked for his conduct of the Chair and for framing the Rules approved of and adopted by the Society'.[102] The Marquis of Bath[103] agreed to become Patron of the Society and the numerous Vice Presidents in due course included the Marquis of Ailesbury,[104] the Marquis of Lansdowne,[105] Lord Arundell,[106] Sir Richard Colt Hoare[107] and virtually every other prominent landowner in the county (other than the Earls of Pembroke and Radnor). Benett threw himself into the activities of the new society with characteristic enthusiasm and, at a meeting held in June 1813 at the

*Deptford Inn,* he achieved considerably more success than he had at Deptford Farm two years before. In the class for ploughing with 2 oxen without a driver (in which there were only 3 entries) his servant at Berwick Farm took the first prize and his servant at Pythouse the third! He himself exhibited a turnip drill that was no doubt much admired.[108]

Earlier, in March, a dramatic event had taken place on the downs not far from Warminster, when two convicted murderers named George Ruddock and George Carpenter paid the supreme penalty for their crime. The procession to the place of execution included two detachments of the yeomanry cavalry as well as the under sheriff, the magistrates of the division and about one hundred gentlemen on horseback. It was reported that it was thought that no less than 40,000 people were present 'all of whom seemed properly impressed with the solemnity of the occasion'[109] and it is more than likely that Benett was numbered amongst them to witness the enforcement of the law.

The meetings of the Bath and West of England Agricultural Society provided an ideal venue for Benett to demonstate his expertise in practical farming and, at its meeting held in April 1814, his letter describing the system on which he farmed his arable land was read and referred to the Superintending Committee.[110] In the following month Benett would surely have been present at the farm of a Mr Pocock near Warminster, when the drivers of eight ploughs of different construction contended for premiums awarded by the Society and when his swing plough drawn by two oxen was awarded the first premium.[111]

At the same time the Society decided to invite the submission of essays on the vexed question of the commutation of tithes. Tithes, whether collected in kind or by way of so much per acre, had for many years been a cause of disputes between farmers and tithe owners, and progressive agriculturalists invariably saw the whole system as an obstacle to improvement. Further, by the beginning of the 19th century, the Church of England was coming under increasing pressure to reform itself, thus adding to the general feeling, outside the Church at least, that something needed to be done. Six essays were submitted to the Society, the identity of the authors not being known to the judges. Benett decided to incorporate his thoughts on the subject in an essay that was submitted and in due course was deemed the winner and, as a consequence, at the meeting of the Society held on 13 December, he was awarded the Bedfordian Gold Medal. (At the same meeting he was awarded the 1st premium of 5 guineas for his man's performance in the 1814 ploughing match, a prize of 10 guineas for raising a crop of turnips for Spring feeding and a prize of 8 guineas for the best fat heifer.).[112] The

*Salisbury and Winchester Journal* reported that 'the show of cattle and sheep was highly gratifying to the numerous assemblage of agriculturalists present' and had 'the pleasure to notice that Mr. Bennet, of Pythouse, obtained no less than five premiums'.[113]

In his essay, two editions of which were published,[114] and which was 'the result of long reflection on that subject, though it has been very hastily written down,' as he put it, Benett contended that as agriculture was on the decline, it was time to 'remove one of the greatest checks to agricultural industry and improvement, which probably ever did exist in this or any other country'. He argued firstly that as the tithe owner takes one tenth of the gross product without paying any part of the expense of cultivation, the farmers had been unfairly penalised. His second contention was that 'the tithe system casts a bone of contention between the minister and his parishioners' and that, as one great cause of disagreement in the valuation of tithes arose from the nature of the system, 'more dissenters from the Established Church have been produced by this cause than by any other'.

The remedy he proposed was that, in the case of tithes in the possession of lay impropriators, they should be compelled by Act of Parliament to sell or exchange them for land of equal value. With respect to livings held by colleges, he suggested that each college should sell the tithes of all its livings and purchase estates to the value of the whole, such estates to be let and the income paid over to the different incumbents according to the proportions that may be their due.

In Benett's view there were a number of 'great and good effects, which I imagine would arise from a commutation of tithe for land', the last of which was 'not the least in his estimation' and was that ' it would remove that interference in property, which has caused more law suits, more ill-will amongst men, and more defection from the Church to which it is attached, than any other human institution could possibly have effected'.

This essay brought a very speedy response from William Coxe,[115] Archdeacon of Wilts and the holder of the livings of both Bemerton and Fovant in Wiltshire. Coxe, who had been educated at Eton and King's College Cambridge, was Benett's senior by some 25 years and a man who would undoubtedly have thought of himself as intellectually Benett's superior. He had travelled widely and was one of the two tutors who accompanied Lord Herbert, later 11th Earl of Pembroke on his Grand Tour between 1775 and 1780; and had published a number of travel notes as well as memoirs of the House of Austria. Despite Benett's assertion that he did not 'by any means wish to invade the property of the church', Coxe perceived the essay as a serious and dangerous attack on the ancient institution of tithes. Furthermore, it came from a man whose general character in the county was that of ' an able agriculturalist and a sensible man' from whom he hoped he would receive 'satisfaction on a subject of so much delicacy and importance to England, and to the well being of our Established Church'.[116]

In his essay, Benett had suggested that the long expected peace had brought with it 'the expected good, except to the agriculturalist – *to him it had brought evil*' and that agriculture was now 'on the decline'. Coxe pointed out that the recent decline in the price of corn had only occurred because during the recent war the price had increased to such an extent that 'it is allowed by respectable farmers, that their profits within a few years would have purchased the fee simple of their farms'. The core of Coxe's contention was that tithe was a perpetual annuity on all landed property, 'derived from a high and sacred source, of which no believer in Revelation can speak without respect', and when attempting to demolish Benett's observations on improvements and the effect of tithe on the cultivation of waste land he was almost tempted to doubt that he was perusing the work of a practical agriculturalist!

On the suggestion that the existence of the system of tithes was the cause of dissent from the established church, Coxe was particularly dismissive:

> That you should impute so great a portion of dissent from the church to the operation of the tithe system, is proof that you wrote too hastily to give due consideration to your assertions, or it is one of those mistaken judgements, which the most sensible men will sometimes form, when they are biassed by partiality to a darling opinion. Many other causes, much more probable, might have been easily assigned for this evil. I do not deny that a few, and very few, may be found, whose heads or hearts are so perverted, that they imagine they can avenge themselves of their pastor, by refusing to receive the words of truth from his lips. But did it never occur to you, that many have been unfortunately compelled to frequent conventicles, for want of room for their accommodation in the established churches, and many more by the restless desire for novelty.

Coxe continued to remind Benett that the reformers in France had begun by abolishing the prescriptive rights of the church before robbing the great landowners of the inheritance derived from their ancestors, and implied that a similar fate might befall Benett and his fellow landholders. He concluded by arguing that the right of the Church of England to its property was not derived from 'the concessions of parliaments or the favour of princes' but from 'a principle at least as sacred, as any other right enjoyed or exercised in this country' and declared:

> From the wild schemes and flimsy declamations of obscure individuals we have nothing to fear. But our vigilance ought to be awakened, when we observe every symptom of a systematic encroachment on the property of the church among a great body of landholders; when they find a gentleman, so truly respectable as he is, whom I now have the honour to address, suggesting schemes highly adverse to our interests and *already anticipating the sanction of the Legislature for an* INTENDED *Act of Parliament;* when we see his suggestions formally approved by a Society no less respectable; nay, when we find projects of such nature coupled with THREATS, which evince a strong presumption of our weakness, or a design to terrify us into submission. I will quote the very words of the Essayist for they well deserve to be treasured up in memory. "I speak of tithe as a property (not considering in whose possession it is) which, in its nature, is so injurious to the interest of the whole State, that it OUGHT to be, and eventually, I believe, MUST be, commuted for some of equal value to the owners, but will not produce the same evil consequences to the public". (p.4) And again: "Of the truth of this assertion I am convinced – that it will be the *best policy* of tithe owners to take a full and fair equivalent for the ENORMOUS PROPERTY which they now possess; and particularly at this time, *when the country at large* is PROBABLY *willing to give that equivalent.*". (p.8)

Although tithe rentcharges were not finally abolished until the 20th century, Benett's belief that tithe would eventually be commuted was, of course, well founded and it was doubtless with great satisfaction that he lived to see the Tithe Commutation Act passed in 1836.

Benett was not a man to be silenced by the arguments of the erudite archdeacon. Within five months, having obtained the Bath and West of England Society's consent to his essay being incorporated in it,[117] his reply appeared in print prefaced by a statement that the 'reply would have appeared sooner had the Author's other pursuits and engagements permitted him to pay earlier attention to Mr.Coxe's attack on him'. What is surprising is that Benett managed to research and write his reply within such a short time. Benett had many talents but he was by no means a man of letters, and the conclusion must be drawn that he had a considerable amount of assistance in his work. Indeed Coxe initially came to the same conclusion when in one of his letters in reply he states:

> In another part you favour your readers with so much law, that I could not at first avoid suspecting that you had recurred to some country attorney, who is practically versed in tithe cases, and who lent you the aid of his experience and library.

However, Coxe then states that having considered Benett's production 'more leisurely', he was convinced that it contained nothing which he might not fairly call his own compilation as all the authorities quoted, apart from Selden's *History of Tithes*, were mere manuals, compiled for the information of solicitors, or those who had not time for extensive research.

The authorities quoted by Benett in his reply, that ran to no less than 58 pages of print, are so extensive that it seems very unlikely that he would have had the time or expertise to consult them all unaided. For instance, on one page alone, 13 verses from 5 different chapters of the Old Testament are referred to and on another, *Jura Ecclesiastica*, Watson's *Clergyman's Law*, Tertullian's *Apology*, Urban, Bishop of Rome's *Epistle*, Cyprian, Bishop of Carthage's *Epistle* and an edict of the Council of Antioch!

The main thrust of his argument was that the 'right of the Protestant clergy to take tithes, in England, in remuneration for the performance of the duties of the church, proceeds from the *statute law* of the land' and that therefore 'parliament had a perfect right to alter, amend or even abrogate all the laws relating to tithes, as well as other objects'.[118]

In September, Coxe produced no less than three further letters refuting Benett's arguments – all of which were, of course, published and no doubt widely read.[119] He could not resist a little sarcasm when referring to Benett's contention that all tithes were not originally considered as due to the clergy only, but as alms to the poor, by writing:

> Here I cannot refrain from saying that it is grateful to observe your solicitude for the welfare of the poor: I conclude that those who have the happiness of living under your protection must find in you the noblest of characters, the poor man's friend; that the superfluities of your ample fortune are employed in ameliorating their condition. And your influence exerted in protecting them from petty oppressions and parochial vexations.

In 1816, his replies to Coxe's three letters were published and so popular were they that a second edition was produced.[120] Benett's prize essay itself reached an even wider audience when, in 1815, it was reprinted in volume 6 of *The Pamphleteer: respectfully dedicated to both Houses of Parliament* – a periodical printed and edited by Abraham John Valpy and containing papers with an economic and political flavour and probably read by many members of Parliament.[121]

Coxe was by no means the only writer opposed to Benett's plan for the commutation of tithes. On 25 September 1815, there was advertised in the *Salisbury and Winchester Journal* and priced at one shilling *A Letter to John Benett of Pythouse in the county of Wilts Esq showing the Impracticability of Commuting Tithes in the manner proposed in his Essay published by the Bath Agricultural Society...* by An Experienced Land Agent.[122] At the end of 1821, the *Devizes and Wiltshire Gazette* carried the first part of a lengthy communication from 'A.A.', in whose view:

> The subject of tithes has been most amply discussed yet no result has taken place. Mr Benett was for giving land, for this he had a medal...the large quantities of land that are already tied up from all beneficial advantage of change, and barter, and competition, in the hands of the Clergy, and of corporate bodies, and in entailed properties, is an argument unanswerable against Mr Benett.[123]

Following the award of the Bedfordian Gold Medal, Benett sent to the Bath and West of England Society a form of petition to be presented to Parliament. This was duly approved, with the secretary being instructed to write to Benett informing him of this and requesting his assistance in drawing a bill for Parliament, the wording to follow the principles recommended by him in his prize essay.[124]

In September 1815, Coxe had published a fourth letter to Benett, this time on the conduct of the Bath and West of England Society and on its petition to Parliament. In this letter, marking the conclusion of the correspondence, Coxe declares 'I here take leave of this unpleasant controversy, because I do not expect to make a convert of you...'[125] As a consequence of this correspondence, Benett was widely and for very many years thought to be an enemy of the established church and, according to Waylen,[126] the Devizes historian, 'it required the friendly pen of Rev. Charles Lucas[127] of Devizes to convince the world of the orthodoxy of one who so perversely denied the divine right of tythes'.[128]

Since inheriting his father's estate, Benett had been in dispute with the vicar of Tisbury over the payment of vicarial tithes. In 1812 there had been a hearing in the Court of Exchequer in an action brought by Thomas Prevost against Benett and Joseph Trim and Joseph Day, when Tisbury's late-16th century glebe terrier and two 18th-century terriers were produced to Edward Davies, a witness in the case.[129] In the summer of 1816, the dispute came to a head when the case of John Benett esq and others –v– Rev.Thomas Prevost was heard at the assizes in Salisbury. In view of his expertise and lengthy research into the history of tithes, it is likely that Benett was the moving spirit in the case, and may even have paid for the services of the Shaftesbury solicitors and Mr Serjeant Pell, and no less than three other barristers instructed by them. Prevost had, of course, always insisted upon receiving his tithes in kind whereas the plaintiffs claimed that there were in existence moduses consisting of 3d for a cow, 6d for a calf, three ha'pence for a heifer, 1d for eggs and 1d for gardens. The evidence showed that the moduses never varied and had been in existence since time immemorial, except that during the incumbency of the previous vicar there were a few instances where 3s had been paid for a cow, and this sum had been paid by two or three small occupants to Prevost. He contended that moduses could only be established in cases where the payments had been unvaried, and also relied on the circumstances of the augmentation made to the vicarage by the Abbess and Convent of Shaftesbury in 1360, and of two terriers deposited in the Bishop's Registry. After a long investigation, verdicts were returned in favour of the plaintiffs.[130] This successful action against the vicar doubtless contributed to the long-held view that Benett was lukewarm in his professed support for the established church.

The appearance of Benett's essay and letters in print may have encouraged him to think about embarking on another publishing venture. In a trunk at Pythouse was a very large quantity of deeds and other documents relating to his ancestors and their numerous properties – those of the original Bennett family of Pythouse including letters written by members of the family and others during the Civil War. John Britton,[131] writing in 1814, relates that these letters were found in a chest discovered in digging the foundations of the new Pythouse and that, 'these are considered very curious documents, as calculated to elucidate many events in the history of the civil wars in the seventeenth century. It is hoped the possessor will lay them before the public'.[132] William Lisle Bowles,[133] for 45 years vicar of Bremhill in Wiltshire, knew about the collection and wrote to his publisher, John Murray:[134]

> A friend of mine (a gentleman of very large fortune in this county), Mr Benett of Pyt-House, has in his possession a whole trunk full of original letters, written at the beginning of the civil wars by those who were great actors on the king's side. There are not less than 63 letters in Charles's own hand writing, to Rupert, from the year 1642 to '45 . . . As Mr Benett

talks of publishing them, the collection may be worth your notice, but I only throw out this hint.[135]

Murray responded very quickly to Bowles's letter and wrote:

> I feel very much interested in your account of the curious collection of letters which have been discovered at your friend Mr Benett's and I should feel myself most particularly obliged if you used your influence to procure for me the publication of a work of such high interest and respectability. If you require the additional influence of the Marquis of Lansdowne, who has called upon me more than once in company with Mr Benett, I could perhaps get a letter from Dugald Stewart [136] (who is a relation of Mrs Murray) to him, but I think even in this quarter the exertion of your kindness would prove satisfactory.[137]

In the event, Benett did not put his thinking into practice and many years were to pass before he eventually sold most of the letters. It seems that this may not have been the first time that Benett was considering publishing these letters, as in 1807 he had received a letter from one Anne Vavasour in which she writes, 'the collection of letters you are soon to publish will be very interesting to the Public, particularly to me from the circumstance of there being some letters written by one of my own family Sir Wm Vavasour'.[138]

Between 1813 and January 1815, the price of corn had fallen from £5 9s. a quarter to £2 5s.[139] With farmers facing heavier taxes, there was considerable agricultural distress and great pressure on Parliament to do something to alleviate a desperate situation. The Corn Laws attempted to regulate the import of foreign corn and to stabilise prices, but those who opposed them considered that they merely kept the price of bread and also farm rents at an artificially high level.

Parliament was inundated with petitions seeking reform of the Corn Laws; one from Bristol bore as many as 40,000 signatures, and so in 1814 the petitions were referred to a parliamentary select committee. Benett was one of those who gave evidence, at the commencement of which he confirmed that he was a considerable landholder in Wiltshire and that for more than 20 years he had occupied and farmed about 2000 acres of this land, and that he had 'generally turned his attention to the agriculture of the kingdom'. He then proceeded to answer many questions about the rent of agricultural land, the expenses of farming and the cost of labour, and expressed the opinion that the diminution in the demand for labour was entirely due to the low price of corn. In answer to the question, 'What quantity of Corn per week do you think that a labourer in husbandry ought to earn?' he replied 'A bushel' and in reply to the following question asking whether a bushel would suffice for the maintenance of a man, his wife, and two children he replied, 'Yes, certainly; it is what we calculate; we calculate that every person in a labourer's family should have per week the price of a gallon loaf, and three-pence over for feeding and clothing, exclusive of house rent, sickness and casual expenses'. This reply was to receive a great deal of publicity in the coming years, with Cobbett labelling him 'the gallon loaf man' – an epithet still used by some historians. As a result Benett was widely thought of as a man who believed that an agricultural labourer and his family should be able to subsist on what was in effect a starvation diet.[140] Throughout his career, he was a constant supporter of the protection afforded by the Corn Laws and the evidence he gave was seen by many as proof that he was the supporter of a law causing hardship to the labouring man and his family.

Notwithstanding the report of the select committee, a Bill was passed in 1815 excluding the importation of corn until the price of corn grown at home reached 80s a quarter, and Benett continued to be an ardent supporter of the Corn Laws for many years to come.

According to a letter published several years later, Benett 'made himself the most unpopular country gentleman in the County in which he resides – so much so as to be burnt in effigy in several principal towns where his name was posted with epithets of odium and execration'.[141]

He was thus widely perceived as a man who was no friend of the poor, and this view was confirmed in the minds of many when in 1817 he stated before a Poor Law Committee that he would pull down all the labourers' cottages on his estate if Parliament amended the law of settlement so as to allow settlement to be claimed by length of residence.[142] In reply to the perfectly reasonable suggestion from some members of the Committee that if there were no cottages there would be no labourers, Benett replied that it did not matter how far a labourer had to walk to his work saying, 'I have many labourers coming three miles to my farm every morning during the winter' (the working hours were 6am to 6pm) 'and they are the most punctual persons we have'. The uncharacteristically rash suggestion that he would pull down all the labourers' cottages on his estate has led some writers to suggest that this is what he actually did, although there is no evidence to support this view. However, Benett's statement certainly contributed to his unpopularity that lasted for many years.

On 2 January 1815, the *Salisbury and Winchester Journal* published a notice signed by Benett, his friend and neighbour Thomas Grove of

Ferne and 44 other landowners and farmers, that 'conceiving it to be impossible that the British farmers should ever contend on fair or equal terms with foreign powers . . .' they intended to meet at Warminster on 6 January to consider the propriety of preparing petitions to the two Houses of Parliament.[143] Benett's old adversary Henry Hunt, a well known and vociferous opponent of the Corn Laws, being incensed at the short notice that had been given, hurried to Warminster and watched from an upstairs window as Benett and some of his fellow requisitionists:

> as pretty a little snug cabal as ever was mustered on any occasion...went smirking along, little dreaming that they should meet with the slightest interruption or opposition to their measures, which were all ready cut and dry, and safely deposited in the pocket of the celebrated attorney, Mr Charles Bowles of Shaftesbury.[144]

Benett addressed the meeting after some 'wriggling and twisting' according to Hunt, and Keene's *Bath Journal* reports that he declared that:

> unless some measure were devised to enable the farmer to pay his present rent and taxes, the landlords would be completely ruined; and he solemnly declared, that, unless this desired object were carried into immediate execution, he for one would be under the absolute necessity, before that day twelvemonth, of *leaving the country* with his family, to reside where provisions and all the necessaries of life were to be obtained within the reach of his fortune.

Hunt could not resist adding a footnote 'Quere. – If this solemn asserveration of Mr Benett's be correct, (who, bye the bye, is a Landowner to the amount of 10,000*l.* a year) what will be the fate of those who are left behind, without the means of flying from evil?'[145]

Hunt, who was of course a Wiltshire landowner and so perfectly entitled to address the meeting, then spoke at length, making various personal attacks on Benett's conduct as a landlord in Enford,[146] and protested that the proposed petitions were purporting to propose measures for the protection of tradesman and mechanics, whereas it had only for its object 'the benefit and agrandizement of a few rapacious landholders'.[147] According to the newspaper report reproduced in Hunt's *Memoirs,* after a good deal of confusion, the meeting broke up, whereupon ' the Chairman, with Mr Benett and a few of his friends, retired to a private room at the inn, but whether to sign this petition in secret, which they could not carry in public, or to abandon it altogether, we do not know'. According to Hunt, 'the publication of this report in *all* the London newspapers, and in almost every country newspaper in the three kingdoms, first roused a general feeling against the proposed Corn Bill'.

On the day before the meeting, Charlotte Grove noted in her diary that 'My father went to Pyt House. I hope his and Mr Benett's plan answer for the sake of old England' and on the day following the meeting that 'My father returned. They had a good meeting at Warminster though the *officious* Mr Hunt tried to make it as *disagreeable* as he could'![148]

An account of the meeting and of Benett's speech (as interpreted and supplied by Hunt) appeared in the *Salisbury and Winchester Journal* and in the London newspapers, including *The Times*;[149] and as usual Hunt rushed into print with a report of Benett's evidence.[150] Lengthy letters written by Benett and John Bleek were printed in the *Salisbury and Winchester Journal*, in one of which Benett said that the object of the meeting was not to petition in favour of the Corn Laws – was not for the purpose of keeping up the present rent of land – and was not for the oppression of the poor, as had been falsely represented; but was for the relief of farmers with small capitals and for the protection of the agricultural interest of the country. In the same letter he wrote that he had no intention of leaving the country and that 'though I have not £10,000 p.a., as they are pleased to say, I hope I shall not be compelled so to do, and that they will find me at my post in the county of Wilts for many years to come'.[151] Prophetic words indeed! In another letter, he felt that he had no alternative but to go so far as to publish an abstract of the accounts of Enford Farm going back many years in order to refute the allegations that had been made against him.[152] According to William Cobbett's *Political Register*:

> 'the speech, as published, drew down on him the *execrations* of those
> same papers, and, indeed, of the public in general. He said that he never
> uttered such words; that he had been grossly misrepresented. He wrote
> to some of the same papers a *contradiction* of the statement; a *defence of
> himself*. But, in order to get in a short paragraph, he was called upon to
> pay one paper *nineteen guineas*! and, though he had a fortune of, probably,
> 10,000 *l.* a year, he declared that his fortune would have been insufficient
> to obtain the means of defending himself through the same channels
> which had attacked him'.[153]

Benett's letter to the editor of *The Courier* was, in fact, published and in the course of it he wrote:

With respect to myself and to what I have been reported to have said about leaving the country and which has given matter for observation to the Editors of various papers, I can say that I have been more sinned against than sinning and I assure those Editors, who have taken anonymous information as their authority, and those persons who have expressed so much alarm and displeasure, that I have no such intention . . .[54]

An anonymous correspondent signing himself 'Bene=Volus' writing to the *Salisbury and Winchester Journal*, while not agreeing with Benett's views, declared:

. . . By report, however, I know him to be a most active, useful, and responsible country gentleman; and if every casual expression uttered by such men is to be distorted to a meaning calculated to excite popular prejudice against them, they may be induced to withdraw themselves from the service of the public in disgust, and bury their talents in an obscurity which though it may be inglorious to themselves, will be highly injurious to the community at large.[55]

Following the meeting at Warminster, the wording of the petition, that was probably drafted by Benett and that was duly adopted by the meeting, was printed in the *Salisbury and Winchester Journal*.[156] However, it was not signed by as many people as had been hoped, as appears from the following letter written by Benett to the Earl of Hardwicke[157] on 15 February:

I am directed by a Committee which has the management of some Petitions in Wiltshire, in favour of the Landed interest to write to your Lordship and to request in the name of the Committee of which I am one, that your Lordship will do us the favour, to present our Petition to the House of Peers – The Petitions are four in number, for the convenience of placing them at the four sessions towns of the County for signature but they are worded exactly similar to each other – I am sorry that the names do not exactly amount to 500 but they are the names of the most respectable men.

Benett then felt that he had to mention to Lord Hardwicke a matter that had clearly been worrying him and that he feared might prejudice the passage of the Petitions. He continues:

Your Lordship will probably recollect that I was examined before your Committee on the Corn Laws last Spring and that I was then ordered to send you an account of a supposed Wiltshire farm with the expense of its cultivation, with a note of the price of wheat, under different circumstances. I sent such an account as soon as possible, directed to your Lordship in St James's Square; but as it was not printed, and as I heard no more of it, I have been led to fear that your Lordhip never received it – it has since been slightly altered and presented with my evidence before the Commons Committee – I have troubled your Lordship with the mention of this, as I may have appeared guilty of neglect of your Lordship's order.[158]

Lord Hardwicke responded quite quickly to this letter as, on 26 February, Benett wrote to him again:

I have sent the petitions from this neighbourhood to Mr Long MP for this County with a desire that he will have them handed to your Lordship by one of the Door keepers of the House of Lords as you have directed; and I beg to express the obligation the Committee and myself are under to your Lordship for your readiness to accede to our request.

A great opposition has been made to the Petition by a very few persons, with Mr Hunt, who lately stood for Bristol at their head – they endeavoured by false representations of our proceedings and objects at our meeting (by newspapers and handbills) to excite public clamour thereby to intimidate and deter several persons from signing them. They succeeded to a certain extent, because this is a manufacturing county, but their objects are too well known to mislead any but the working manufacturers as I prepared and proposed these petitions. I hope your Lordship will excuse my intruding on your time by stating my objects in so doing to have been to protect the farmer with *small capital*, the farm labourers and ultimately thereby to produce *lower* and *steadier* price of corn on an average year than can I believe ever be obtained by importation. . .[159]

Benett then contined at some length to elaborate on his theories as to how these objects could be achieved.

In 1814, Napoleon abdicated and so it seemed that peace would now return to Europe. However, at the beginning of 1815,the whole of Europe was convulsed by the news that Napoleon had escaped, and on 10 March he arrived in Lyons announcing that he would rescue France from its degradation. As a consequence, the continent's armies began to mobilise once again and the country prepared to put itself on a war footing. The news must have travelled exceedingly speedily as, on 13 March, the Marquis of Bath, who in 1811 had been appointed Colonel of the Wiltshire regiment of yeomanry cavalry, wrote to Benett from his house in Grosvenor Square in London:

Dear Sir

In compliance with the directions I have received from The Lord Lieutenant of the County I must request you to adopt such measures as may enable you to assemble your troop of Yeomanry Cavalry with the least possible delay if called upon to support the Civil Power in procuring the Peace of the County.

Your obedient humble servant<br>Bath[160]

In the event, of course, Benett and the Hindon troop were not called upon to defend the county from Napoleon's army nor, for the time being, to assist in keeping the peace.

For many years Benett had acted as a magistrate, dispensing justice in the south-western corner of Wiltshire and, in particular, committing offenders to the gaol at Fisherton Anger on the outskirts of Salisbury, and to the Bridewells in Devizes and Marlborough for later trial. From the calendars of prisoners[161] a picture can be gained of the criminal activities of those who were brought before him at this time. In 1816, for instance, he committed the 18-year-old Alexander Barrett as 'a rogue and vagabond, having been found in an enclosed field in the night time with two guns for the purpose and with the intent to kill and destroy game at Donhead St Mary'. His companion, William Jenkins, was also committed for the same offence. As a result of disturbances in Mere later in the year, he committed Thomas Norris for breaking windows and appearing naked in the public street and assaulting a constable and also two others at the same time for behaving in a riotous manner. In December, he committed Henry Maidment and Stephen Long for breaking into the shop of Francis Webb at Mere and stealing 80 lbs of fat. In the event Maidment was acquitted and the case against Long was not pursued.

On the night of 10 January 1816, a gang of about 15 men armed with guns and sticks attacked some of Benett's keepers and others employed by him, having during the day been engaged in shooting pheasants in the enclosed plantations at Pythouse. Poaching was, of course, a very serious criminal offence, not to mention the night time assault, and so Benett was very anxious to apprehend those who had not already been taken. He therefore arranged to insert a notice in the *Salisbury and Winchester Journal* offering a reward of 10 guineas for the apprehension of the poachers. Even more serious was the fact that one of the poachers 'flashed' a gun with intent to fire it but, being wet, it failed to discharge. If it could be proved that the gun was intentionally pointed at one of Benett's employees, then a reward of the very large sum of 50 guineas (more than twice the amount that a labourer would earn in a year) was offered to any person who could cause the apprehension and conviction of the man who flashed the gun.[162]

It was well known, though never publicly accepted by Benett, that there were exceptionally large numbers of poverty-stricken people living in the neighbourhood of Tisbury and Pythouse; and their problems, particularly in winter, did not escape his notice. Since his father's death he alone, and after his marriage, he and Lucy together made an effort to alleviate their distress, and this was acknowledged when, in February 1816, the *Salisbury and Winchester Journal* reported:

> In addition to the benefactions we have recently noticed, we feel pleasure in announcing the annual and liberal benefaction of Mrs Benett, of Pythouse, in this county; this humane and good lady stands conspicuously eminent for her benevolent attention to the numerous poor in her neighbourhood; and has within the last few days distributed amongst them a considerable number of linsey[163] articles of apparel, chemises, and shirts, which were received with inexpressible gratitude. We have also the pleasure to notice the liberality of Mr Benett, who has lately given to the poor of his neighbourhood a remarkably fine fat ox. We need scarcely add that these deeds of charity are particuarly worthy of imitation at this inclement season of the year.[164]

Following Hunt's attack on Benett at the meeting in Warminster at the beginning of 1815, Benett doubtless gave instructions that Hunt's activities in Enford, where Benett not only owned a large estate and was lord of the manor but where Hunt was also a landowner, should be closely watched. Were it not for his radical opinions, Hunt would have been thought of as a typical Wiltshire gentleman, and fond of country pursuits including fishing. When he was discovered fishing in the lord of the manor's water, therefore, Benett did not hesitate to take legal proceedings against him and claimed the somewhat ludicrously inflated sum of £1000 by way of damages. In March an enquiry was held in the Sheriff's court and after some deliberation the jury found for Benett but awarded him derisory damages of one farthing![165] Hunt no doubt considered that he was the victor and continued to think nothing but ill of Benett.

Benett continued to interest himself in the affairs of the agricultural community and in March 1816, as president of the Wiltshire Society for the Encouragement of Agriculture, he chaired a meeting of the Society held at the *Bear Inn* in Devizes when it was resolved that 'the distress of the agricultural interest has arrived at such an alarming height, that it is become the imperious duty of all owners and occupiers of land . . . to address themselves to the Legislature . . .'. A large number of resolutions were passed, to be incorporated in petitions to be presented to both Houses of Parliament, and to be sent to the proprietors and occupiers of land in the county for their signatures. They were also to be inserted in the *Salisbury Journal* and the *Farmers Journal*, and 1000 copies to be printed in the form of a letter and sent to each Member of the House of Commons. It is not unlikely that Benett himself drafted the resolutions, although perhaps not the one that stated that the thanks of the meeting be given to 'John Benett Esq. the President for his able conduct of the Chair this day, and for his zealous attention he has given to the affairs of the Society in general'.

No time was wasted. The resolutions that had been passed were immediately printed, and so hastily was this done that Benett's name as chairman was incorrectly spelt 'Bennett'. Once the printing had been completed, in order to save time and while still in Devizes, Benett wrote a note on a number of them and sent them to the Society's vice-presidents requesting them to support the proposed petition. His note to Michael Hicks Beach, a Member of Parliament as well as one of the vice-presidents of the Society, ended with the words '& in gt haste'[166] and only three days after the meeting the Marquis of Lansdowne, writing from London, acknowledged Benett's note and confirmed that he would be happy to give his support to the petition.[167] In October, Benett doubtless attended the Society's Autumnal Ploughing Match, when his worker at Berwick Farm managed to plough half an acre of land with two horses without a driver in 2 hours and 32 minutes, 6 minutes slower than the Marquis of Bath's man and so taking second place. When the time came for the competition to plough the same area with two oxen, Benett's servant, David Ball, was the only candidate. However, he was allowed to start and although the land was extremely heavy, he completed his task in 3 hours and 7 minutes, and so was awarded the first premium in the class.[168]

As one would expect, Benett also continued to take an active interest in the affairs of Bath and West of England Agricultural Society and when, in December 1816, he attended the anniversary meeting of the Society held in Bath, he had by that time become well enough known to be singled out and named in the newspapers as one of the distinguished persons present.[169] He was to attend the annual meetings of the Society regularly, and at the meeting held at the end of the following year, it was reported that, 'on the motion of Mr Benett it was determined after some opposition on the grounds of the inadequacy of the funds of the Society for that purpose, and after a desultory conversation on the supposed causes of such depression, to increase the Premiums for the shew of live stock. . .'[170]

Throughout 1817 Benett continued to sit as a magistrate. Amongst those who were brought before him in February were three men who were all sentenced to three months hard labour having disobeyed an order of bastardy at Tisbury. In May the cases included James Turner for receiving a pair of breeches and a waistcoat knowing them to have been stolen, James Lampard for milking a cow at Semley and stealing the milk, and James Draper for leaving his wife and family chargeable to the parish of Kingston Deverill.

Early in 1817 an assassination attempt was made on the life of the Prince Regent as he drove down the Mall on his return from Parliament. Deeply distasteful as the Prince's life-style was to the vast majority of the people, the attack was seen as an assault not only on the person of a highly unpopular man, but also on the monarchy and constitution itself. Since the end of the Napoleonic war the fear of revolution remained in the forefront of the minds of the propertied classes.

A number of leading Wiltshire landowners decided that their loyalty to the *status quo* should be publicly demonstrated by the presentation of an address to the Prince Regent congratulating him on his happy escape, and so Benett and twenty-nine other freeholders requested the High Sheriff, John Penruddocke, to call a county meeting to pass the necessary resolution to enable an appropriate address to be drawn up.[171] On 17 March a notice was inserted in the *Salisbury and Winchester Journal* advising its readers that a meeting would be held in Devizes at noon on the following Wednesday.[172] During the two days prior to the meeting, Henry Hunt and his friends had circulated handbills announcing Hunt's intention to attend, and so trouble was expected. In the previous November, in Spa Fields in London, Hunt, supported by the tricolour and cap of liberty on a pike, had made an inflammatory speech to an enormous crowd of people and so at the meeting in Devizes it was confidently expected that he would attempt to inflame 'the passions of the uneducated, by instilling into their minds principles injurious both to themselves and to society', as the *Salisbury and Winchester Journal* expressed it in its subsequent report of the meeting. [173]

The meeting was opened in the Town Hall and was attended by the Lord Lieutenant, the Earl of Pembroke and, according to the newspaper report by ' many other personages of high rank, an unusual number of country gentlemen, yeomen and tradesmen'. The crowd wishing to attend was so great that the meeting was soon adjourned to the Market Place. Speeches were made proposing and seconding the motion and then Benett addressed the meeting. After making a number of remarks supporting the proposal, Benett launched into an attack on Hunt and his supporters by declaring that:

> . . . the greater criminals were the audacious men who had been labouring, year after year, by falsehood and calumny, to deceive the community, not only as to their duties, but as to their dearest interests; who had endeavoured to set the poor man in opposition to the rich, and to inspire him with an hatred of all that reason and religion would teach him to venerate and to love; who represented our existing Government as a cruel and oppressive tyranny, and accused all those to whom the exercise of its powers belongs, as destitute of all goodness, as being the worst enemies of the country, and persons whom it would be lawful to resist and expedient to punish. He was speaking of those travelling orators who had of late years raised a clamour in this and the neighbouring counties, who wandered from town to town, and from village and village; to disseminate their doctrines amongst the lower classes of the people; who spared no exertion or expense to corrupt the public mind; who had obtruded themselves upon the public meetings to the exclusion of those who might be able to detect their falsehood, and counteract their designs. . . If any of those men were present, he would tell them that the guilt of that atrocious act which occasioned the present meeting, was imputable to them; that the disorders of the Luddites, and the blood which flowed in suppressing those disorders, were imputable to them; that the guilt of Cashman[174] and his wicked associates was principally their guilt, and that they must answer to impartial justice for the death of that unhappy criminal. . .

Hunt then attempted to address the meeting. According to the newspaper report of the proceedings, he made many attempts to be heard but from every side he was:

> assailed by groans, hisses, and reproaches; and the cries of 'No Hunt,' 'Off, Off,' 'No white feathers here,' 'We'll send Mr Morley to you,' 'We don't want a coward for a leader,' 'Where is the ghost of Cashman?' were particularly audible. In the general confusion, we could distinguish many voices exclaiming that he was not now at Spa Fields.[175]

According to Hunt, Lord Pembroke had ordered his tenants to attend the meeting to oppose him and Benett (whom in his Memoirs he calls

Black Jack, alias the Devil's Knitting Needle – a delightful allusion to Benett's tall and thin stature!) gave the orders to a gang of desperadoes:

> when to be silent and when to bellow, hoot, hallow, and make all sorts of discordant vulgar noises, such as would have degraded and lowered the character of a horde of drunken prostitutes, in the most abandoned brothel in the universe![176]

In the event, the High Sheriff ordered the reading of the Riot Act and that Hunt should be taken into custody. However, according to Hunt, he was rescued by the crowd and carried away in triumph although the newspaper reported that only some few people remained in another part of the market place to hear him speak.

# 3
# The Contested County Election of 1818

B y now, well known throughout the county and personally acquainted with most of the leading landowners, Benett could with some confidence seek a seat in Parliament as one of the two Members returned by the freeholders of Wiltshire.

In 1818 a General Election was pending. The two sitting Members were Paul Methuen, and Richard Long who had decided that he would not seek re-election. In his place William Pole-Tylney-Long-Wellesley[1] was chosen by the Long and other county families to succeed him. The contest was, therefore, between Methuen, Pole-Tylney-Long-Wellesley (commonly called Long-Wellesley or just Wellesley) and Benett. Methuen had inherited Corsham Court and its estate from his father in 1816 and had been one of the two county Members since 1812. Had Benett decided not to stand, Methuen and Wellesley would have been returned unopposed in the traditional fashion (there had been only one contested county election since 1722) and at no, or very little, expense and trouble to themselves. So Methuen must have been extremely angry that Benett, who had proposed his candidature at the 1812 election, should now be opposing him. Nevertheless, he was considered to be certain of re-election, and so the contest was in reality one between Benett and Wellesley, whose personal characteristics and immediate backgrounds could scarcely have been more different.

Benett was the Wiltshireman born and bred, who had always resided in the county, served as High Sheriff and magistrate and, although a landowner, was also a practical farmer and an expert in agricultural matters. Wellesley, on the other hand, was a son of the 3rd Earl of Mornington, a nephew of the great Duke of Wellington, and who, it was said, 'employs his time at his toilet, in the lounge of Bond Street, or in the ring of Hyde Park in the morning: and in Fop's Alley, at the Opera-House, or in voting away the people's money in the House of Commons in the evening'.[2] In 1816, he had married Catherine Tylney-Long, the heiress of the old north Wiltshire landowning family of Long, and a bride who would be able to supply him with the financial means, for a while at least, to maintain his prodigiously expensive lifestyle. It was reported that at the wedding ceremony, Catherine wore a dress costing 700 guineas and a necklace costing 25,000 guineas![3] After his marriage, he lived in the grandest and most extravagant way at Wanstead House in Essex, his wife's property over which he had control under the terms of his marriage settlement, and in stark contrast to Benett's modest establishment at Pythouse. It appears that Wanstead was to surpass Charlton House in splendour, with the interior being a 'uniform blaze of burnished gold' and the parties given there 'had no precedent in expense, variety and extent' since the days of Cardinal Wolsey'.

On 23 February, Benett announced that he intended to stand by publishing the following letter addressed to the Nobility, Gentry, Clergy, and Freeholders of the County of Wilts:

> Gentlemen
>
> Mr LONG having publicly declared his intention to decline the future representation of this county, I take this early opportunity of offering myself to your notice, and of requesting the favour of your support at the ensuing Election.
>
> Should you confer on me the distinguished honour to which I aspire, of representing this truly independent county in Parliament, the strongest expression of my gratitude will be found in the conscientious, diligent, and independent discharge of the duties of that important trust.
>
> Whenever a dissolution of the present Parliament takes place, I will embrace the earliest opportunity of personally renewing my request.[4]

Benett well knew that the cost of a contested election would be immense. Indeed a meeting of freeholders held in the Guildhall at Calne on 6 March went so far as to pass a resolution declaring that 'the enormous expense attending Election Contests deter honest and independent men, of modest fortunes, from offering their services to the country in the Commons House of Parliament, where their talents might be the most effectually exerted for the public good', and another, 'that the best service which every freeholder can render to his country, who is not ashamed to be treated and carried to the poll at the expense of the Candidate, is to stay at home'![5]

Even before making public his intention to stand, it is clear that Benett had commenced the mammoth task of writing to an enormous number of freeholders soliciting their votes, and to others telling them of his plans. On 22 February, he wrote to Lord Folkestone,[6] one of the

Members of Parliament for Salisbury and the Earl of Radnor's heir, seeking his support. He wrote:

> My dear Lord
>
> Mr Long having declared his intention to decline the future representation of this county in Parliament, I am induced by the advice of many of my friends to offer myself as a candidate for that distinguished position.
>
> If your Lordship should think me a fit person for that situation, and will favour me with your interest and support, I should ever feel the highest sense of the obligation.

Folkestone endorsed Benett's letter, 'Answered that I can at present enter into no further engagement than that I will bear his wishes in mind'.[7] As will be seen, Folkestone was a firm supporter and confidant of Methuen, who certainly did not think that Benett was a fit person to represent the county. Neither Benett nor John Tinney,[8] the Salisbury solicitor who was to be his chief election agent and secretary to his election committee, can have realised that Folkestone would be supporting Methuen and was very unlikely to look favourably on Benett's pretensions as, early in March, Tinney wrote another letter to him. Tinney and Folkestone were undoubtedly well acquainted with each other as his letter commences with the quite familiar form of address of 'My dear Lord' and concludes with the even more familiar 'believe me to be, my dear Lord, faithfully and sincerely yours' and it maybe that this relationship persuaded Benett and Tinney that a further approach might be fruitful. In his letter, he says, 'I think that all your best friends at Salisbury are zealous in the support of my friend Mr Benett who has declared himself a candidate and is very generally supported. It would give me great pleasure to learn that your Lordship's name was among the number of his friends with that powerful Interest which you command.'[9]

The wording of the letter to Lord Folkestone was almost identical to many others that he wrote at this time. For instance, on 26 February he wrote to Peter Lovell[10] of Cole Park, Malmesbury:

> Sir
>
> Mr Long having declared his intention to decline the future representation of this County, I am induced to offer myself as a candidate for that honour.
>
> If you will therefore favour me with your vote and interest, I shall ever feel a high sense of obligation.[11]

He could expect almost unanimous support from the voters in the vicinity of Pythouse and so would not have been surprised when as early as 8 February a freeholder named Ord from nearby Semley told him 'of course you are welcome to my vote'.[12] He had earlier written to Lucy's half-brother, Aylmer Bourke Lambert, who replied on 23 February:

> I sincerely rejoice at the contents of your letter; it is what I have long wished for if you recollect I mentioned it to you when last in Town. I shall look *incessantly* for you and write to the Duke of Marlborough by this days post. Can I do anything for you with Mr Chas Long who I dine with tomorrow at the Pay Office. Mrs Lambert joins in all manner of kind wishes...[13]

Lambert was as good as his word as, on the following day, the Duke put pen to paper by writing from Blenheim, presumably to his agent in Wiltshire: 'I beg you to make what interest you can amongst my tenantry & others in Wiltshire in favour of Mr Benett of Pythouse in Wilts who intends to stand for theCounty next general Election.[14] Some weeks later, Lambert engaged in a little mutual canvassing when he found himself dining in London. He wrote:

> Dear Benett
> I have only just time to inform you I yesterday had the pleasure of dining with the Duchess of Marlborough. Lord Blandford[15] was there, to do the honors of his Mother's table & as soon as the Ladies had left the Room, he began canvassing me for Cricklade!!! Agst Gordon, supposing as a Wiltshire man I might have some interest there. I immediately said that I was just going to canvass his Lordship on the same so we soon *settled the Business.*

On 16 March, Wellesley wrote to the *Salisbury and Winchester Journal* with a letter signed 'Timothy Trueman' that had appeared in another newspaper containing an attack on his character. Both this letter and Wellesley's reply, refuting 'Timothy Trueman's' allegations and calling upon him to state his name and to offer an apology, were duly published[16] and this was the first of numerous letters written under fictitious names that were to appear in the press over the next three months. In the following number of the newspaper, the printers stated that they would not insert any anonymous letters or notices with fictitious signatures which in their judgement may, in the slightest degree, reflect on private characters; nor unless the names of the authors had been communicated to them.[17]

The treating and carrying of voters was, of course, a vital weapon in the armoury of the candidates and Benett's friends and neighbours in the south-western corner of the county were quick to let the freeholders know that:

> It has been agreed by Thomas King and Henry Foot, Esqs. And many of the respectable inhabitants of the Chalk Hundred, that they will convey to the poll such of the freeholders in their vicinity (who may require the same) as are in the interest of Mr.Benett, whenever their services may be required, free of every expense to that gentleman; and that they will, in the mean time, collectively and individually, use every exertion to secure his return.[18]

In the same number of the *Salisbury and Winchester Journal* in which this notice appeared, John Bailey, writing from Downton, gave notice that 'several Gentlemen of Downton, with due regard for the independence of the county, have agreed to convey the voters in this District, in the interest of Mr Benett, to the Poll at Wilton free from any expense to that Gentleman'; and J. Roles, writing from Maddington, gave notice that several gentlemen in the hundred of Branch and Dole were willing to do likewise.

In March, Fulwar Craven[19] of Chilton House, who had declined the invitation of a number of freeholders to stand himself, made it clear where his sympathies lay when he requested the publishers of the *Salisbury and Winchester Journal* to announce that 'it was the intention of many respectable freeholders in this neighbourhood to take charge of bringing the friends of Mr Methuen and Mr Benett to the poll at Wilton without expense to him.'[20] In the event, only 46 of those who voted cast both of their votes in favour of Methuen and Benett jointly.

Benett, whose election committee was chaired by his friend William Wyndham of Dinton, and included such well known Wiltshiremen as Thomas Calley,[21] W.B. Brodie,[22] Wadham Wyndham[23] and the Reverend Edward Duke,[24] immediately started canvassing the most important people in the county in the hope that they would persuade the freeholders within their sphere of influence to vote for him.

In a letter to Benett written on 28 February,[25] the Marquis of Lansdowne made it clear that he was not willing to commit himself to support any of the candidates at that time, and so Benett must have been encouraged by the tone of a letter from the Duke of Somerset who wrote on 2 March:

> The event, which you announce to me, was quite unexpected, and may be very important in its consequences to the County of Wilts, the members of which ought certainly to be men of consideration and property within it, and previously known in some public situation. In the above respects, I am not aware that there is any other candidate who has a better claim

than you have to the votes of the Freeholders of Wiltshire, or to the good wishes of those inhabitants who, from various circumstances, must not take an active part in any election. Amongst the latter of course, I reckon myself and feel flattered by the application you have made to me.[26]

Benett's approach to the Earl of Radnor[27] was met with a distinctly frosty response:

> 16 March  Longford Castle
> Sir
> I am sorry to have been prevented giving you a certain answer to your Application – From long Friendship and personal Connexion with the Families of both of your opponents it is impossible for me to assist you in your present pursuit.
> Radnor

Benett must have hoped that he would gain the endorsement of the Earl of Pembroke, the Lord Lieutenant and the greatest landowner in the south of the county. His initial approach did not meet with any success and so at the end of March, Lucy made a further attempt. She wrote:

> My Lord
> The degree of intimacy with which I remember your Lordship's Father to have honoured mine induces me to venture on taking the liberty Mr Benett refrained from, that of again soliciting your interest in his favour so far as to enable him to declare with confidence he has your interest and that your Lordship's tenants should be convinced of the same. Mr Benett is from home continuing his canvass which has engaged him three months already and the necessity of again troubling you will I hope plead my excuse as from the inactivity of Mr Methuen every exertion on Mr Benett's part has become necessary to ensure his success in what will now end in a serious contest, an event he did not foresee when he embarqued in the cause, it having arisen from the long harboured enmity of the Long family which being *concealed* it made it impossible for him to be aware of, till the *effects* appeared. As your Lordship expresses yourself in ignorance of the wishes and intentions of the County, in general, I take the liberty of explaining these particulars and have also the pleasure that the Duke of Somerset, Marquess of Bath, Ld. Arundell[28], Sir Richard Colt Hoare and all the Gentlemen of consequence and old family in South Wilts have espoused Mr Benett's cause, Ld. Radnor excepted. Again offering an apology for the liberty I have taken
> I remain, My Lord, your very obedient servant
> Lucy Benett[29]

Lord Pembroke's reply was brief but courteous:

Madam

I very much regret the impossibility of my complying with a request of yours but having in answer to several applications I received from each of the parties, declared my intention of withholding from all interference whatever I can take no step to direct contradiction to this intention.[30]

Richard Colt Hoare of Stourhead decided to write a note to Lucy rather than to her husband:

I take the liberty of addressing myself to you as being more likely to be at home than Mr Bennet (sic) who is probably still actively employed . . . I beg leave to assure him of my good wishes and vote.

I hope your plants prosper and I wish we were nearer neighbours that you might occasionally take a peek at my collection which is now in the highest beauty – but will be sheared next week.

Truly yours

R.C.Hoare

Some influential landowners had not entirely made up their minds who they would support. William Hicks Beach wrote:

I am sorry there is likely to be a contest for the county of Wilts. I shall certainly support Mr Methuen but I shall not at this time promise my other vote. I intend being at Netheravon on the 15 of April for a few days & should business take you into this part of the county I shall be happy to see you.[31]

It is certain that Benett would have called upon such an important freeholder in the north of the county. However, Lord Churchill[32] had no doubts about where his sympathies lay. On 9 April, he wrote:

Spurning the unconstitutional idea of the County of Wilts being an appendage to the House of Draycott or any other house, and relying on the report of your independence and diligence in public business, I do not want to be solicited for my vote at the ensuing Election, but write to offer it. My interest is very inconsiderable but as it is, it is at your service.[33]

By no means all of the numerous letters received would have been as pleasing to read as this one. Some made it clear that the writer would not be voting for Benett, one suggested that he should 'come forward and advertise your debts' and one in particular contained an unpleasant threat. A man named Coward writing from Wilton on 10 June lays down a challenge:

It having been represented to several of my Acquaintances who are Freeholders of the County of Wilts that you were one of the magistrates that convicted a Poor man named Lovelace late of Compton Hut and committed him to the *Cells* in Fisherton Gaol where he was *loaded with irons* for only picking up a rabbit which his dog accidentally killed while he was loading his wagon with Furze and the same freeholders having further heard that you together with Mr Penruddock ordered James Lampard and Chas Jeffrey, both married men and each of them having seven or eight children *publickly and severely* to be flogged throughout the parish of Compton Chamberlain for the small offence of taking home two Bundles of Broom after having been out all night in the depth of winter watching for poachers on the lands of Mr Penruddock. You will oblige me much by informing me whether or not either of these reports are true and would thank you for an answer at your earliest possible convenience in order that I may contradict those reports if incorrect and which will influence the freeholders in giving their votes at the ensuing election. If you do not think it worth your while to answer this they are determined to call you publickly through the Salisbury Newspaper to do it, which I hope you will prevent.[34]

Benett presented himself as the 'independent' candidate belonging to an old family long established in the county who spent his time promoting the interests of trade and agriculture as opposed to Wellesley – a man who spent his time 'lounging in London society'. By describing himself as independent, Benett intended to convey that he was entirely independent of the great families and groups of gentry who had formerly nominated candidates to be presented to the freeholders of the county for election. The words 'Benett and Independence' can still be seen carved into the stone front of *The Boot Inn* in Tisbury.

The election campaign ran for over three months and, as Lucy indicates in her letter to Lord Pembroke, Benett spent the whole of that time travelling the county canvassing the freeholders – 3736 of whom eventually voted. In his letter to them published on 9 March, he said that he was anxious to introduce himself to every individual 'whose public interests it may hereafter be my duty vigilantly to protect, I shall persevere till I have had the honour of paying my personal respects to every freeholder'.[35] A formidable task, indeed! On 19 March, *Simpson's Salisbury Gazette* carried a letter from him in which he stated, 'I shall not relax my exertions till I have waited on every Freeholder whose name I may be made acquainted with; and I hope that if in any instance I may not have had that honour, it will not be attributed to wilful neglect.[36]

Some potential voters inevitably escaped his attention, for on 28 March he addressed another letter to them saying, 'If I have omitted to wait on any freeholder residing in the places which I have already visited, I beg to assure them that the omission has not been intentional, and that I will return to those places as soon as my engagements will permit, for the purpose of paying my personal respects to every individual'.[37] This announcement may have been prompted by an undated letter that he had received reading:

> As I hear that you are so near as Cricklade I beg to inform you Mr Line called on me and was surprised that you had not called on Mr Wain, Mr Roberts, and Mr Chapman freeholders at Latton & perhaps there are more if you enquire.[38]

A not insignificant number of freeholders did not, in fact, live within the boundaries of Wiltshire – London, Suffolk and the Isle of Wight were the places of residence of some of them. Over a period of three months, more than 300 letters were received[39] addressed mostly to Benett himself, but some to his Shaftesbury agent and attorney Philip Chitty. One particularly touching letter was written on 9 June by a very distant freeholder in response to one seeking his vote:

> I received your letter requesting my Vote at the ensuing Election for the County of Wilts & I am very much disposed to comply with it but deferred returning an answer, till I should ascertain whether it would be in my Power considering ye length of ye journey I must take for that purpose (140 miles this my abode being 70 from Wilton) & being persuaded by my Neighbours and acquaintances and almost compelled by ye entreaties to relinquish all thought of undertaking so fatiguing a task, & being also conscious of my ability to perform it (being nearly 83 years of age) either by riding on Horseback or in a carriage & subject to Rheumatic Pains on getting cold, I am sure you will have ye goodness to excuse my not attendance at ye Poll Wishing you Success.[40]

A parson, Robert Tabor, writing in a seemingly extremely ill-educated hand from Stourton and addressing his letter to 'Mr John Benett esq pit house Wilts', would also have difficulty in attending the Poll:

> I Robert Tabor Clerke of Stourton received a letter from your agent from Shaston to be a vote for your honour if my name will do you are welcome to it for I ham [sic] so lame that I cannot go so far.[41]

Another did not expect to give his vote for nothing. On 28 March, G. Penruddocke wrote from Winsley near Bradford that:

W Dike a respectable freeholder of Limpley Stoke has desired me to inform you that his votes are at your service he expects and would be greatly obliged to you for your influence in getting his son a place as bailiff; he is honest and able and well qualified for an estate of five or six hundred acres.

May I add that I have leisure if you think I would promote your wishes I should be happy to serve my county by executing any commission you may be pleased to entrust me with. I have no vote interest.[42]

And another expected an unusual favour in exchange for passing on to Benett the name and address of an uncanvassed freeholder. He wrote:

I write upon the possibility of a Friend of mine in London being overlook'd & remaining not canvass'd who I believe to have a vote for this county – Address
Nicholas Elliott esq
27 Edgeware Road London
It will not be necessary to pay your respects to him in person so tip him a line.

I have a friend in Sarum – a great Collector of Eggs and if you will secure for me one of the . . . [illegible] tribe you will oblige me.[43]

From March until June, the electors were continually confronted by letters and handbills written by the candidates and their supporters, many of them hiding behind pseudonyms and published in the newspapers circulating in the county. One of the most verbose was 'Titus Trueman' who, in the early stage of the campaign, favoured his readers with his opinion of Benett:

This gentleman is well known to you all, and your interests are perfectly known by him. His life has been laudably spent in improving the system of agriculture, in fertilising the soil which gave us birth. He is a man of superior talents, of learning and science, steadily attached to the government and constitution of his country, of an independent fortune, and of a mind more independent. . . Were England the only country on the face of the earth, had the work of creation been limited to its shore, then a thorough knowledge of its soil, of the nature of its produce, and a competent acquaintance with local circumstances, would have been amply sufficient to qualify a man for a seat in the council of the nation. As England forms, however, only a small, though important and powerful part of the world, a thorough knowledge of her relations with other states is essentially necessary in one who aims at a seat among the legislators of his country. Mr Benett's pursuits have been of a different kind; he pretends not to this; his business has been at home; but gentlemen, your representation will even in this respect, feel no deficiency, if with him you elect.[44]

In a reply to this letter, 'A Wiltshire Freeholder' in comparing the merits of Wellesley and Benett suggests that if Wellesley is to be returned:

The country at large is to benefit from the travelled experience, the diplomatic dignity, the more matured and finished faculties of the head of the house of Draycott . . . while the county of Wilts is to look to her own immediate advantages in the more circumscribed, modest, and unassuming intelligence of Mr Benett; his coolness of intellect, clearness of conception, and facility of delivery; his intimate and practical acquaintance with the soil, the produce, the poor-rates, the tythes, the paupers, and the gossip of his own immediate neighbourhood. [45]

When William Wyndham agreed to act as chairman of Benett's election committee, it is unlikely that he realised what an exceedingly time-consuming and arduous task lay ahead of him. On 3 May, he wrote to Benett:

I hope you are convinced of my sincere desire to serve you in your Election as well as on every other occasion, but I cannot bring myself to think that I shall be doing so by attending such meetings as that intended to be held at Devizes on the 12 and I am sorry to say the more respectable the less likely it is to be beneficial to your interest; you cannot be ignorant of the idea of magisterial influence that is gone further, or the pains that are daily taken to separate the interest of the county gentlemen from that of the small freeholder. I must fear this meeting will tend to increase that feeling, we likewise must recollect that it is not respectability but the number of votes that will decide the Election and for this reason I declined taking the chair at the dinner before receiving your letter.

And as a post script, he adds that 'Mrs Wyndham desires me to add that she hopes you have a better opinion of her than to suppose she would prefer a pair of fine eyes to a good heart'![46]

Early in May, 'A True Friend of Independence' asked the electors to consider 'wherein consists the superiority of Mr Benett over Mr Wellesley. . . Has he fortune in or out of the county, that a county member ought to have, to support the increased expenses, if elected, it will bring upon him? . . . and, lastly, is he so very independent?'[47] The question of whether Benett could be truly independent when he had to look to a number of subscribers to assist him in defraying some of his election expenses was one that was raised by supporters of his opponents on several occasions during the coming months. This suggestion was rebutted in a piece of election literature published by one of his supporters calling himself 'Hamlet, *Secundus*', and in which the reader is invited to contrast the qualities of Benett as opposed to those possessed by Wellesley. Benett:

> Is reproached by his adversaries for his poverty, and his inability to pay the expenses of an election. He feels this most illiberal insinuation as reflecting disgrace only on those who made it; and (whether or not as able to pay his debts as his opponent) that the examples of a Hampden and a Marvell prove that great wealth is not always necessary to independence.[48]

At a time when the qualities and personal characteristics of the candidates appear to have received considerably more attention than the likely policies to be supported or adopted by them if elected, it is no surprise to find the past conduct of the parties being drawn into the public domain in the most startling detail. A particularly striking example of this is the dispute between Benett and one John Fisher, who in 1811 had taken a 10-year lease of one of Benett's farms in Enford. On 28 April, Benett wrote to the printers of the *Salisbury and Winchester Journal* giving his version of the facts as he saw them,[49] to be followed by a lengthy rebuttal from Fisher on 5 May,[50] and on 9 May[51] by a letter from Philip Chitty, Benett's Shaftesbury lawyer. This ended with a detailed financial account showing the receipts and payments in respect of the tenancy from 1812 to 1817 – an extraordinary public disclosure of financial transactions that would normally be of no concern or interest to anyone other than the parties concerned. According to Benett 'This man, thinking to injure me in the estimation of my friends, the freeholders of Wiltshire, most *malignantly* and *falsely* charges me with having broken my word with him', and one can only conclude that he did indeed intend to cause as much damage as he could to Benett's reputation as a landlord. Having already been treated with the sight of one set of accounts, the readers of the *Salisbury and Winchester Journal* had the doubtful pleasure of perusing another version of the accounts supplied by Fisher.[52] In the meantime 'Titus Trueman' waded in with his comments on the dispute headed by a quotation from the 2nd verse of the Book of Judges, 'And the dirt came out'![53] Others gave their views. 'Britannicus' wrote to the editor of the *Salisbury Gazette*[54] at such length that surely the readers of that paper must have become quite weary of hearing of the dispute.

On 1 June, the *Salisbury and Winchester Journal* published a letter from 'John Barley-Corn' who wrote in jest to 'Dear Cousin Moonraker':

You must be out of your wits to kick up a dust about Long Benett. Why should he be a knight of the shire before any body else? What if he has lived like a gentleman at Pythouse these twenty years, and killed his own beef, and brewed his own beer, and made it very good, and been generous enough with it to every body that came, just like his father and grandfather before him – he won't be the better Parliament-man for that. And then he has got all his neighbours to vote for him, and the country gentlemen are all up in his favour, and all the farmers say he is their best friend; and, as a justice, he makes no difference between rich and poor; and he quarrelled with his brother justices about a new jail, because he thought that the expense could be saved to the county by repairing the old jail; and he has thrown away two or three thousand pounds in building a new chapel, that his poor neighbours might not walk three miles to church on a wet Sunday. All this, cousin, is a mere trick, that he has been playing these twenty years, to cheat us out of the county at last: and then he will speak his own mind whether we like it or not. . . This cousin is the truth; but it won't take me in while I can judge for myself and vote for whom I like best.[55]

At the beginning of June, 'A Conscientious Freeholder', having been absent from the country for some time, looked at the 'advertisements', as he called them that had been circulating over the last two months and addressed his fellow freeholders by declaring:

One of them tells me that till within these six years Mr. Long Wellesley was entirely unconnected with the county, that even since that time, the period of his adoption as he calls it, he has never lived a week within its precincts . . . His next assertion is that he comes forward as a country gentleman (not as a Wiltshire country gentleman surely, for he has not a drop of Wiltshire blood in his veins), and I am at a loss to conceive how a residence at a villa in the immediate environs of London in a style of luxury and dissipation wholly incompatible with any thing like the habits of business, can give him the right to the style and title which he here assumes. . .

Of Mr Benett I hear – that he has always lived in the county, an active magistrate and an independent country gentleman; unattached to any party, yet consistent in his principles; a proud boast if it is true: that he assisted Mr Methuen to destroy the preponderating influence of certain oligarchial clubs that had been established among you; that he is the man who by a happy combination of talent and daring, at a county meeting at Devizes, exiled that turbulent fellow Hunt from your confines; this is the story of his friends.[56]

On 12 June, the High Sheriff of the county, Alexander Powell,[57] gave notice that he had received the King's writ for the election of two knights to serve the county in Parliament on 4 August, and that a special county court would be held at Wilton on 24 June when the election would be commenced.

The views of Benett's supporters and opponents during the election campaign provide a picture, although inevitably somewhat prejudiced, of how he was regarded by his contemporaries. From one side he was 'a man of superior talents, of learning and science, steadily attached to the government and constitution of this country; of an independent fortune and of a mind more independent',[58] and 'an extensive practical farmer . . . the improvements in agriculture exhibited on his estates are adopted by all who see them',[59] and in the controversy on the subject of tithes, 'he acquitted himself in a manner highly creditable to his own literary talents and has displayed a fund of knowledge on subjects of political economy in general, that is rarely acquired by one man'.[60] On the other hand, he was a man 'whose principles and conduct have made him obnoxious to every man attached to the religion of his country',[61] and, when it became known that Benett would be standing for Parliament, Lord Malmesbury[62] wrote to his son 'he is in every light a very unfit [person] for the situation – a democrat, a surppressor of tithes, and a supporter of the Catholic question. . .'[63]

'An Observer', writing to the *Salisbury Gazette* from Trowbridge on 11 May, declared:

> Then we have Mr.*Benett*. This gentleman has no recommendations, but the being a resident, country gentleman, of an old family; an active magistrate; an officer in the Yeomanry; president of the County Agricultural Society: as he has officiously attended to the local business of Wiltshire, and has no connection, or interest in, any other county; as he has the misfortune to have avowed the opposition of that distinguished character, Mr Henry Hunt, the chairman of the Spitfields meetings; and as he is even *suspected* of having, at the last election, instigated Mr Methuen to the daring step of canvassing the freeholders at large, without having the sanction of any clubs or committee; let us not become dupes to his shallow pretensions; no, Sir.[64]

'A Busy Body', writing from Zeals on 17 May, told the readers of the *Salisbury Gazette* what kind of speech might be expected from Benett when he addressed a dinner at Marlborough given by 'the friends of independence':

> how much riding, and driving, and chacing, and pacing, he had

undergone; to attend agricultural meetings, sessions, and assizes; his prize cups at Devizes; his patent ploughs, Scotch carts; his letters to Coxe, flax dressing, and his Wiltshire lady. Of course we shall be told how *her* father brought up five hundred votes, and turned the fortune of the day in favour of the Old Moon-Raker's hero of 1772, causing his opponent to strike his flag. . . [65]

One of the merits attributed to Benett during the campaign was his Wiltshire birth and ancestry, as opposed to Wellesley's background. This argument failed to impress 'Veritas, *junior*' who addressed the Old Moon-Raker:

> If the representation of Wiltshire ought not (as you say) to be the appendage of any house or of any family, I would ask, Why should the representation of this county be the birthright of a native of Wiltshire only? And why in particular the birth right of Mr Benett? Why should connection of *blood (which is a mere accident of nature)* give a better title to the representation of a county than connection by *marriage*, which is the most honourable connection upon earth, and which rests upon the *choice* and *preference* of the individual himself.
>
> But even here, taking yourself upon your own fallacious argument, allow me to ask, What is there in the *blood* of *Mr. Benett* that entitles him to 'adulation', such as that to which you bestow on him? And what will be the *degradation* into which the freeholders of Wiltshire will (as you declare) inevitably fall by preferring the *blood* of the Hero of Waterloo to that of the *family of Pythouse?* [66]

On 8 June a notice appeared in the *Salisbury and Winchester Journal* informing the public that the freeholders in 'the interest of Mr Benett' intended dining at Devizes on the 12th. Dinner would be taken at 4 o'clock and gentlemen were requested to take tickets at 10s. 6d. each. As the New Room at the *Bear Inn* was not ready, the Mayor and Corporation of Devizes, 'at the earnest request of several freeholders', had granted the use of the Town Hall for the dinner.[67] In the event, the Town Hall could not accommodate all those who wished to attend and so, according to the newspaper account, 'many were obliged to dine in other apartments'. In his speech, Benett alluded to the charges made against him in the 'manufacturing districts of Wilts' that he proposed a duty of 4s. in the pound on imported foreign wool. He said that the charges were false and absurd. Many speeches followed and the evening was enlivened by 'several appropriate glees' from singers from Salisbury and from Bath, and 'a more highly respectable company from all parts of the county never assembled at Devizes'.[68]

A large number of substantial freeholders had been circulated and invited to join Benett's Election Committee, and on 22 June John Tinney, the Salisbury solicitor and secretary to the committee, arranged for a list of the names of almost 200 freeholders from all parts of the county to be inserted in the *Salisbury and Winchester Journal*, all of whom had signified their willingness to form the committee in Benett's interest.[69] Not all those who were approached, however, were willing to accept the invitation. One correspondent writing on 7 June from Horningsham, and so probably employed from time to time by the Marquis of Bath, wrote:

> In answer to your application to be of your committee I beg leave to state that although I am a freeholder of the County, and as a professional man acting in much public business, I think it probable my appearance in so public capacity for you might be construed as acting in the Character of a Representative of a Great Man who must not be seen to interfere in the County Election.[70]

Tinney busied himself in contacting Benett's supporters throughout the county and responding to their offers of assistance. For instance, on 23 June he wrote to the Highworth solicitors, Crowdy & Son:

> We should have been most happy to avail ourselves of your legal assistance in the taking the poll – and are sorry that your unavoidable absence will render it necessary to complete the arrangements of the Booths for polling without reference to you. Nevertheless I trust you will give us all the assistance in your power, according to your better discretion – not forgetting that for Mr Benett and myself, the nearer you are to us the more agreeable – yet we know that usefulness is at this juncture what is most regarded.[71]

Benett's well known antipathy towards tithes led many to believe that he was no friend of the church and may even have been an atheist. On 13 June, the Rev. Charles Lucas wrote to the *Salisbury and Winchester Journal* setting out part of Benett's response to an enquiry about his religious beliefs and principles:

> I believe in God and in his revealed Will, and endeavour to make that will the rule of my faith and practice. As a Protestant Christian in a Protestant Country I will ever uphold the Rights of Conscience and religious Liberty to all.[72]

A 'Mild Enquirer', writing from Devizes on the following day, reminded the readers of the newspaper that:

Mr Benett has, it seems, endowed a chapel, and we may charitably draw the inference – that if he is not himself a constant attendant at public worship, he encourages it in others; and had he the most remote objection to it, would he have transmitted such a building to his posterity? Would he not rather have built a theatre, a temple to the Olympii, a menagerie, &c. &c for their recreation and amusement?[73]

Methuen, who appears not to have engaged in any very active canvassing himself, kept Lord Folkestone informed of progress, and in an undated letter from Corsham wrote:

I write to tell you how I have got on since my arrival in the County, and I am happy to say nothing can be more satisfactory or more decided than my superiority in numbers over the others.

Benett's friends however think to serve him by leaving me in the lurch, at least by not promising me. I have therefore communicated this to my friends that they may pay him the same compliment. He has likewise endeavoured to get votes from me, that were promised by saying he knew I had no objection to part with them, as I had more than I wanted. Depend upon it whichever wins will not be *in a canter*. I find all the attorneys think the House of Draycott the strongest.

If you mean to attend the Nomination (but do not put yourself out of your way on my account if not perfectly convenient) let me have the pleasure of your company. Ld. Andover and a large Party will be here and a fine row there will be. The *mob* and the *women* are outrageous against Benett. Tinney says he expects to have all his windows smashed, as Benett is to be at his house. I assure you feelings run very high against him, though I hope no greater mischief may happen than what Tinney apprehends,

I think Benett must be hard pushed when his friends resort to such an expedient to serve him at my expense, as to make the Farmers believe that your humble servant was the person who presented Salisbury Jail. . . I am happy to congratulate you on your perfect safety either from trouble or danger. Tinney tells me you are safe as of course you know, beyond all chance.

Pray give my best to Ldy Folkestone and believe me dear Folkestone with many thanks for your kindness on this occasion of campaigning.[74]

The nomination for the election took place in Devizes on 18 June. Each of the candidates would wish to see as many of their supporters in the market place and so their friends made every effort to achieve this.

As an example, small cards were printed and no doubt widely circulated reading:

> Mr Calley, Mr Harding, Mr Craven and other Gentlemen in the interest of Mr Benett, propose meeting at Beckhampton Inn, on Thursday next, at Nine o'clock precisely, where they hope you will join them to attend the Nomination on that day.[75]

The local magistrates knew that there might be trouble, and so they had arranged to have printed and circulated handbills in which they made it clear that they expected 'all classes of persons to conduct themselves peaceably and quietly on the day of Nomination and during the Election', and masters were requested to 'be watchful over their Servants and Workmen, and Parents over their children, so as to prevent their being led into excesses which cannot serve any purpose but to bring disgrace and punishment on themselves'.[76]

Benett arrived in the town on the previous evening and Methuen and Wellesley on the day itself. The market place was overflowing with an immense crowd of people when the High Sheriff proceeded to the monument at the centre of the market place in order to open the proceedings. Each of the candidates was duly proposed and seconded, Benett by his old friends William Wyndham and Thomas Grove, he a distant kinsman and both old friends and neighbours. Methuen was the first to address the crowd at great length and, although he was not treated so unceremoniously as the other two candidates, the uproar was such that he could barely be heard. Benett was next called upon to speak. The High Sheriff did his best to procure him a hearing but cries of 'No Benett, – off – off' from one side and 'Benett for ever' from the other meant that his speech that lasted for nearly half an hour was inaudible except by those standing closest to him. Wellesley had an even more riotous reception than Benett and for almost an hour all efforts to produce silence proved ineffectual. After he had retired, the High Sheriff called for a show of hands and, as this appeared to indicate almost equal support for all of the candidates, thus making it impossible to determine which two of the candidates had the most support, the meeting (or rather the county court, as it should be more properly described) was adjourned to the following Wednesday at Wilton where the election would commence.

While Benett appears to have been treated with undisguised contempt by Wellesley (which was doubtless reciprocated), Benett and Methuen had, of course, been well acquainted with each other for many years. Although Methuen must surely have strongly deprecated Benett's intervention in the election, there appears at this stage to have been no personal animosity between the two, as is demonstrated by this warm but undated letter probably written in the early days of the campaign:

> My dear Benett
> I lose no time in assuring you how happy I should be to supply you with the list[77] you wish for, if I had it. . . I have not heard of any opposition to you and I see no intention of hostility as far as I can judge. I never can forget how much indebted to you I am for the support you gave me, and if it is not repaid as warmly on my part by the same personal exertions, I am sure you will attribute my conduct to the right motive, that of not injuring you as well as myself, as a coalition – or at least the appearance of one would injure us most materially.
>
> > With best compliments to Mrs Benett
> > Believe me my Dear Benett
> > Truly yours
> > > Paul Methuen[78]

Both Benett and Wellesley knew that it would be in their interests if some sort of coalition could be arranged with Methuen, and it maybe that this letter was in response to one from Benett suggesting some sort of arrangement that might be to their mutual benefit. Several handbills were printed and circulated suggesting that such a coalition did exist, and as a consequence Methuen arranged for a handbill to be issued in the name of Anthony Guy stating that, 'Mr.Methuen has not coalesced, and will not coalesce with either Mr.Benett or Mr.Long Wellesley. I think it necessary to declare this because an unfounded report of a Coalition has been circulated.'[79]

Doubtless Methuen was infuriated when Benett's supporters issued a handbill in response declaring that 'Mr Guy may deny as often and publicly as he pleases, the existence of any coalition between Mr Methuen and Mr Benett, or Mr Wellesley. No one suspects him of coalescing with Mr Benett. This gratuitous declaration appears, therefore, as a quibble and an evasion. I challenge Mr Guy, as a Gentleman, to assert that no understanding exists between any of the respective agents of Mr Methuen and Mr Wellesley . . . *there is* a system now going on (call it coalition or what you please) the purpose of which is to injure Mr.Benett and promote the interests of Mr.Wellesley'.[80] It is more than likely that this exchange contributed towards the marked change in Methuen's feelings towards Benett – cordial at the commencement of the election campaign and virulently hostile by the end, as will be seen.

Benett's election committee of almost two hundred freeholders had its headquarters in Salisbury at the *White Hart Inn*, and as many of them as possible dined there during the election campaign.[81] At the meeting held on 20 June under the chairmanship of William Wyndham, a number of resolutions were passed, one of which:

> *Resolved*, That we perceive, with the strongest motions of regret, that attempts have been made to prejudice the minds of the lower classes of society, by the publicity given to false and obnoxious writings, and the circulation of inflammatory hand-bills, which have already produced acts of violence, and can only lead to the commission of injury to the persons and property of all parties, and tend to demoralise the minds of the hitherto industrious poor, even after this contest shall have been determined.[82]

Needless to say, this resolution did nothing to prevent the acts of violence that were to come. On the same day, a meeting of Benett's supporters was held at the *Angel Inn* in Marlborough, following which there was circulated a report of the proceedings. This stated that the committee viewed 'with great regret and dissatisfaction the late tumultuous and riotous Disturbance at the Day of Nomination at Devizes that from the statements they had heard, corroborated by strong facts, those disorders are to be attributed to the adherents and partizans of Mr Wellesley; that persons were forwarded, not having Freehold Property, to Devizes, and liberally paid for their trouble by the same injudicious partizans'.[83] Within two days, handbills were circulating in which Wellesley stated that no persons were forwarded to Devizes at his expense and none were paid for their trouble in disturbing the peace.[84]

One of the more bizarre handbills was addressed to the:

LOWER ORDER

THE MOBILITY

The Friends of      W

Dear Rabble

Stick to your Man! The present

War is only a war of opinion! Be not discouraged! the

Gentlemen of DEVIZES are too much gentlemen to notice

Anything but breaking the Peace; which God forbid! – let

Mr BENETT'S Colours pass freely, and you as freely sport

your OWN! Let it be known that the PEOPLE keep KINGS

on their THRONES!!![85]

As the election campaign proceeded, any support that Benett might have had in the manufacturing towns in the north of the county soon evaporated. In March, Elizabeth Bush writing to Bowles and Chitty from Trowbridge informed them that:

> The canvass of Mr Benett in this place I fear may not be attended with much success unless some Gentlemen known here takes him by the hand and I should not recommend his making his appearance here unless some of the neighbouring Gentlemen come in the Town accompanying him. He is very unpopular amongst the people here.[86]

In May, Benett's agent in Bradford reported that:

> Mr Wellesley's friends have so far succeeded in alarming the minds of the manufacturing men here with the idea of a Tax on Wool to the consequent Ruin of the trade and your name has been so interminably attached with a 30£ per cent Tax that I have found almost all here forsaking your interest in consequence at least those who have concerned themselves affected by the Question. . .[87]

He urges Benett to either advertise or write him a letter refuting any suggestion that he was in favour of such a tax.

On the evening of the nomination in Devizes, there were disturbances in Trowbridge. Thomas Hele Phipps[88] wrote to Benett:

> I am sorry to say there was a riot at Trowbridge last evening brought on I am informed by W [illegible]. . . Long's friends giving the populace beer. The windows of the Wool Pack Inn are entirely demolished. My neighbour, Ludlow and myself have written to the Secretary of State to have the barracks here occupied by troops and if that is not consented to by his Lordship & the same done immediately it will be impossible for us to bring up one voter at the approaching Election – indeed at present they are in great alarm – we intend to bring them up on Thursday next but that must now depend on the arrival of the troops. . .[89]

'Another Stranger', writing from near Salisbury on 25 June, was particularly concerned about the measure of violent behaviour of those opposed to Benett or certainly of the mob, few of whom can have been freeholders and entitled to vote, and while perhaps exaggerating somewhat the friendly feelings of some of Benett's neighbours towards him, was surprised at the attacks now being made upon him. He wrote:

> My friends . . . assure me that he is a gentleman of a very ancient family in the county, of unblemished character, and competent fortune, – that he (as well as his ancestors before him,) has constantly resided *in your own part of the county*, and expended his income among you – that he is beloved by all ranks of people to whom he is really known – an active,

intelligent, and upright magistrate – a good husband, an affectionate father, a kind master, a firm friend. To these testimonies allow me to add another, for which I can vouch on my own observation – I happened some years since to be in the vicinity of this gentleman's residence, at a period when he was suffering under a dangerous illness. The dejected countenances, the anxious enquiries, the heart-breathed prayers of his humbler neighbours, offered up and heard by heaven on his behalf, convinced me he must be the poor man's friend – With this impression on my mind, can I do other than marvel at what I now behold?

Because, in one solitary instance, Mr B., when called on by the British legislature, delivered a certain opinion on the Corn Laws upon oath, I presume, or which , to a man of his principles would be the same, on his honour, I hear him hissed and hooted as if he were the enemy of God and man; – nay, not only so, but threatened, and even so violently assaulted, that his numerous friends deem it necessary to range themselves constantly around him for his personal protection.[90]

As their captain, it is no surprise to find that Benett was supported by the men of the Hindon troop of yeomanry cavalry and Wellesley took great exception to this. On 22 June he issued handbills, one stating that 'Mr Benett's Troop did go into Devizes in military order – they received the word of command from Captain Calley, who formed them into two lines, leading from the *Bear Inn*, to the Market Place, between which issued from the Bear, according to order, the infantry who attended Mr Benett. . .' and another that 'A Troop of Horse, I understand, entered into the Town of Trowbridge late last night, and as I am informed, Mr Mortimer, a magistrate, and a partisan of Mr Benett's has availed himself of this force to intimidate the voters. . . ,[91] and another in which he protested 'most solemnly against the unconstitutional proceedings of permitting the assemblage, in military order, of troops of yeomanry cavalry (though not in uniform), armed with heavy sticks'.[92]

These were serious allegations that immediately brought forth a response from Thomas Calley, who pointed out that Wellesley being a stranger could not be personally acquainted with 'the very respectable freeholders' in whose company he was, that the yeomanry cavalry of Wiltshire would never assemble in or out of uniform without proper constitutional authority, and that out of the great numbers of freeholders with him, not more than 10 or 12 belonged to the troop. John Peniston[93] of Salisbury, a member of the corps, wrote to the *Salisbury and Winchester Journal* that he was not prepared to 'suffer such a libel to pass uncontradicted'. He made it clear that in the market place in

Devizes none of the men were armed with heavy sticks, but that on leaving the town some of them were compelled to arm themselves with sticks to guard themselves from the attacks of 'a desperate mob (unauthorised no doubt) wearing the colours of Mr Wellesley'.[94] As a Roman Catholic, Peniston's support of Benett added credence to the belief that Benett was unacceptably tolerant towards Catholics, and at the commencement of the poll a particularly virulent attack was made upon him when the question was asked:

> What makes this papist, *who has no vote,* stand forward so boldly for the honour of John Benett's insulted troop? I'll tell you . A. – He receives from that troop, in the shape of *pay* and *perquisites* Two hundred pounds per annum! . . . What attaches him to the interest of J.Benet? A. – Because Mr.Benett informed a certain Catholic lord,[95] that if he would give him his interest, he would, if returned, vote for the Catholic Bill ! – NO ATHEISM ! NO POPERY!'[96]

Even at this late stage, letters were being received by Benett from potential voters or from people writing on their behalf. He must have despaired when he received a letter dated 17 June from a particularly touchy freeholder who was certainly known to him. Benett was informed that:

> Mr Jervoise[97] called on me this morning and after talking of the Sarum Election, we mentioned yours. He told me he should go on Wednesday to vote, that he should give his first vote to Mr Methuen & did not know to whom he should give the second. He felt in some degree hurt at what he considered a want of attention on your part whether from inadvertence or any other cause, he says, having seen you at my house some years ago he afterwards going near Pyt House left his card, & which although you have been so often at Salisbury you never returned.[98]

In the event, Jervoise relented and cast his second vote for Benett. At much the same time, he received a somewhat obsequious letter from the Reverend John Colmer who was only too willing to cast his vote for Benett. He wrote:

> When you in so handsome a manner re-presented me to my Rectory at Askerswell I was enabled by that act of your kindness to take a small living in the County of Wilts, of course entitled me to vote in that county. . . I assure you that my vote is *wholly* at your service.[99]

Benett's supporters must have been under the impression that the election to be held on the following Wednesday might once again take the form of a show of hands, as on the 22 June a notice appeared in the *Salisbury and Winchester Journal* reading:

> The Friends of Mr Benett, who so nobly supported him at the nomination at Devizes on Monday last, together with all others in the Independent interest, are most earnestly requested to assemble on Wednesday morning, on Mr Benett's Ground, near the Hustings, about three miles from Salisbury on the Devizes Road, again to aid and support the glorious cause, as a show of hands is again to be proposed.[100]

In the event, no such thing occurred, as the High Sheriff who was responsible for conducting the election must have known that a ballot would be required, and would therefore have arranged for the necessary polling booths to be erected in readiness. He would also have designated separate parts of the election ground to each of the candidates and their supporters, upon which tents would be erected for their shelter and entertainment. Each of the candidates employed a number of attorneys to assist in their canvassing, and Samuel Foot, a solicitor of Salisbury, inserted a notice in the *Salisbury and Winchester Journal* on 22 June:

> All persons desirous of having the privilege of erecting BOOTHS for the accommodation of Freeholders and others, on the ground fixed for the reception of Persons in the interest of John Benett esq are desired immediately to apply to Mr Foot, solicitor, Endless St.[101]

During the course of the election campaign, the supporters of both Benett and Wellesley amused themselves by writing and distributing the words of a number of songs to be sung at their respective meetings. 'A New Song' consisting of ten stanzas of doggerel verse commenced with the words:

> Hark! What tumult rends the sky,
> What clouds of dust arise!
> A Stranger bold, of lineage high,
> Claims Wiltshire as his prize.

The next four verses refer in quite surprisingly polite terms to Wellesley, with the next proclaiming of Benett that:

> His Fathers held the Lands he holds,
> A Native's name he bears;
> A brother true he e're beholds
> When a Wiltshire-man appears.

And concludes by declaring:

But Benett's name, our native Friend,
The Friend of Freedom's Cause,
Prevailing still, the skies shall rend
Beneath no Tyrant's laws.[102]

Wellesley's supporters would have enjoyed reading the following slanderous description of Benett entitled A Caricature:

A-canvassing round the County, we see
A long, lanthorn-jaw'd, wretched creature.
A-straddle across a poor beast – (who but he?)
Of a gentleman – blest with no feature.

His coat it is blue, and was formerly new;
His hat is a gift of his scout, Sir:
His breeches are brown, and well known to each town,
Which this ill Weed has canvass'd about, Sir.

He's tall and he's thin, and his legs are a-twin;
His visage, the picture of grief, Sir;
He seems like a thing that's committed a sin,
And less like a Gent, than a ————, Sir!

O! what shall we say? – when the time comes we may,
And this Candidate view, one and all, Sir:
Why, we'll, with one voice, make Well'sley our choice,
William Tylney Long Wellesley, — and Paul, Sir.[103]

To the tune of *Down Derry* Wellesley's supporters would have sung of:

A tall Man there is and he lives at Pyt-House,
Who longs for a seat in the Parliament House
But, before we all meet in our great county town.
He's a few little foibles, which I will write down.
Derry down, down, down Benett down.

And first there's his fam'd Agricult'ral pursuit,
– The good of a tree is known by its fruit: –
But what good is Mutton? Which surely you'll own
Is too dear to buy, and too fat to get down.
Derry down,&c.

That's harmless: but than he's a RARE friend to trade,
Will sell you a PLOUGH, or a COAT, or a SPADE*,
Fix the price of a building, within half-a crown+;-

And all this he does, just to keep the trade down;
Derry down, &c.

To the Poor too he's generous, and makes out a table,
To see on HOW LITTLE to live they are able –
Says that WHITE BREAD'S TOO GOOD, and THEY OUGHT to eat
BROWN,
Thus you see my good friends how he'll tread the POOR down,
Derry down,&c.

But look at Long Wellesley!! – aye, he is the man,
He's liberal and noble – deny it who can – !!
Despises a Pension, and fears no man's frown:-
Then UP with LONG WELLESLEY, and DOWN BENETT DOWN,
Derry down, down, down, Benett, down.

* The Gentleman boasts a Warehouse for Vending these Articles.
+ And keeps a Builder's Price Book, for the advancement of the
profits of Architecture.[104]

Not to be outdone, Benett's supporters published 'A New version
of Chevy Chase for the Year 1818'.[105] After describing how the 'Young
IRISH WELL****Y, proud and vain' had decided to canvas the
freeholders, the verses continued with:

For soon the News, to Pythouse, brought,
Had reach'd brave BENETT'S Ear,
Who swift dash'd forth in WILTSHIRE'S Cause,
Unknowing Guilt or fear.

For many gallant 'Squires of Note'
Stood ready to defend,
With all their Tenants to their Backs,
This steady WILTSHIRE'S Friend.

And so on for another fourteen verses in which it is implied, amongst
other things, that Wellesley's father, as Master of the Mint, would be able
to hand him the key when his 'purse sinks low'! 'The Pedigree' to be
sung to the tune of 'The Tight Little Island', mocks the changes in the
surname of Wellesley the Dandy's family from Colley to Wesley to
Wellesley and eventually to Pole-Tylney-Long-Wellesley.

Perhaps the most original of the many squibs that were
distributed was clearly produced by Wellesley's supporters:

WILTSHIRE RACES
On Wednesday, June 24th 1818.—-
The FREEHOLDER'S PLATE
Will be run by any "Thorough Breds," who can
Prove their necessary Qualifications—The best of Heats.
To be seen and entered at the Steward's post on the Morn-
ing of that day. If any disputes arise, to be determined
by the high Sheriff, or whom he shall appoint.

The Thorough Breds already expected to start, — are

|  | Rider | Colour |
|---|---|---|
| Mr. Corsham's Turncoat, by Changeable............ | D.Ollapod. | Uncertain |
| Mr. Illweed's Corn Bill, by self Interest............ | A.Shark | Pythouse Mixture. |
| Duke Wellington's Nephew, by Independence........... | W.Waterloo. | Wellington Blue. [06] |

In accordance with tradition, the election was opened at Wilton on 24 June. Anticipating a repeat of the riotous scenes at the nomination in Devizes, the High Sheriff arranged for railing to be erected around the cross in the market place to prevent men on horseback from disrupting the proceedings. Benett took the precaution of arriving early, preceded by a cavalcade of freeholders on horseback and in carriages, and they so filled the area in front of the town-hall that when Methuen arrived he could not reach the cross without getting out of his carriage. Wellesley was much too grand to contemplate walking to the cross and insisted on a way being cleared so that he could arrive at the cross in his carriage. Once all three candidates were in place at the cross, the King's Writ and the Bribery Act were read and the High Sheriff sworn.

Methuen was first proposed and seconded and then Benett, by William Wyndham and John Gale Everett[107] of Heytesbury, and thirdly Wellesley. Each of the candidates addressed the freeholders and during his address Benett referred to the fact that some considered that he was not a man of sufficient wealth to represent the county by declaring:

Gentlemen, I am not new in this county, but I am in new circumstances – I am a new candidate for a seat in the House of Commons  I have omitted on all occasions to speak of my family; but I owe it to my ancestry to say, that they have been known in this county for five hundred years. Some of them have been military men, and some of them statesmen, but none of them sinecurists.[108] Had they been sinecurists, it would not then have been said of me, that I was too *poor* to represent the county of Wilts.

When Benett had finished speaking he retired amidst the cheers of his friends and the hisses and groans of his opponents. There appears to have been particular personal animosity between Benett and Wellesley who paid a handsome compliment to Methuen and cordially shook the hands of both the proposers of Benett and Methuen on finishing his speech but no such acknowledgement was afforded to Benett. The High Sheriff then adjourned the proceedings to the hustings. He knew that there would be a considerable amount of disorder and so arranged for 205 special constables, all drawn from Salisbury and the immediately surrounding villages, to be sworn in. Each was paid 20 shillings for their services.[109]

Having arrived at the place of the election, a field called Old Camp Ground some three miles from Salisbury and adjoining the road leading to Devizes, all three candidates addressed the assembled company, although Benett's speech was inaudible above the clamour of his opponents. In his letter to the freeholders, written and published on the first day of the poll, he told them that they should not be 'intimidated by the obstruction which have hitherto prevented your access to the poll in my favour. The prevalence of violence and disorder cannot be of long duration'. At the end of the first day Methuen had polled 185 votes, Wellesley 162 and Benett 85.

During that evening, the house of John Tinney, the highly respected Salisbury solicitor who gave his services to Benett gratuitously throughout the election, came under attack from the mob supporting Wellesley. Seeing that his house was threatened, he confronted the mob and ordered them to disperse, but was struck on the head with a bludgeon by a man called Macklin. Philip Chitty, Benett's Shaftesbury solicitor, was in the house at the time and gave evidence at the subsequent trial that Tinney 'fell to his knees with blood copiously flowing'.[110] Although Tinney escaped further injury, as he had earlier predicted, the windows of his house were smashed by missiles thrown by the mob.

The poll was opened at nine o'clock on the second day, whereupon Methuen arrived to address the crowd. Wellesley appeared at half past ten and immediately deplored the outrageous attack, as he described it, on John Tinney. Benett attempted to be heard but he was interrupted to such an extent and greeted with the usual hisses and groans that this speech appears to have been incapable of being reported. Wellesley then spoke, followed by the announcement by the High Sheriff of the state of the poll; Methuen 736 votes, Wellesley, 509 and Benett, 410. As usual, the candidates once again addressed the crowds. Methuen was heard and Benett proceeded to obtain a partial hearing thanks to 'the exertions of Mr Long Wellesley', but was once again unable to fight against the constant uproar of the opposition. When Wellesley left the hustings, he was reported to have been cheered 'by the greatest assemblage we ever witnessed out of the metropolis'. It is clear from this that the election, and more particularly the sight and presence of a close relation of the hero of Waterloo, attracted an immense number of people to what in normal times was a quiet field in the Wiltshire countryside.

Some of those who had offered to convey freeholders to the poll encountered some quite unexpected difficulties. It will be recalled that it was anticipated that the mob might attempt to prevent voters known to support Benett from leaving Trowbridge. Just as serious was the problem of securing suitable transport. One correspondent informed Benett:

> I was surprised that Mr Wellesley has retained all the horses in Cirencester. I shall try Fairford. . . my neighbour John Howse told me last night he might harness his team of Oxen and put them to the car rather than you should be disappointed in your votes at Poulton.[III]

On the third day, Methuen was the first to address the multitude and the main thrust of his speech was directed at refuting the claim that he had entered into some sort of coalition with Wellesley. He sought to obtain the High Sheriff's consent to swear on the Bible that he had brought with him that he had formed no coalition, but Benett's brother William came forward and insisted that no gentleman could doubt Methuen's word. Wellesley's arrival, with his band and cavalcade and banners with his armorial bearings, was marked, as on all other days, by the playing of the national anthem. He was heard without difficulty, unlike Benett, whose arrival on the hustings was greeted by hisses and groans and his departure 'by the delectable sounds of goose music'!

To obtain a fair hearing was always a problem for Benett (not to mention for the newspaper reporters who attempted to record what he had said) and some 25 years later it was remarked that:

> During the memorable contest between Mr Benett and Mr Long Wellesley, Mr Benett greatly annoyed at the frequent interruptions he had met with on the hustings near Wilton, designated a large number of the lower classes who interrupted him, as a *mob* – and this he repeated several times, which rather tended to increase the hubbub than allay it. Lord Radnor was standing near at the time, and exclaimed 'how to the –

can ye expect to be heard by addressing them in that style – call them *gentlemen!*' said his Lordship.[112]

At the end of the third day, Benett had polled only eleven votes fewer than Wellesley. Benett must have thought that he had victory in view and so Wellesley was prompted to inform the freeholders that:

> The little ground I have lost this day, has arisen purely from accidental circumstances. At the moment that the poll was closed, the booths were crowded with my friends giving their votes, one hundred and forty of whom were then on the ground, and could not be polled from not being up in time. Had they arrived half an hour earlier, I should have more than maintained my majority. Every exertion was made, every nerve strained by Mr. Benett to place himself above me today. With all those exertions he was unable to attain his object; and I speak with the most perfect confidence when I state to you that tomorrow night an end will be put to the exultations of Mr. Benett and his friends, by your seeing me with a majority so commanding, that there will no longer be a doubt of my success.[113]

And so it was to be as by the end of the fourth day, Wellesley had indeed increased his lead. As a result, Benett immediately addressed the freeholders by claiming:

> My opponent, Mr. Wellesley, has obtained a transient superiority on the Poll, from unforeseen circumstances. Many of my friends have been prevented from presenting themselves by the system of terror acted upon before and since the election, wholly incompatible with the rights of the electors and the principles of the constitution. But the triumph which is gained by such extraordinary means cannot be of long duration.
>
> All obstructions at the place of election are removed, and my friends may come to the hustings without danger or insult. Be not intimidated, Brother Freeholders, the day of our triumph is near.[114]

In his speech at the close of the fourth day of the poll, Wellesley said that he was Benett's best friend when he had told him not to 'spend his own money, nor make me spend mine'. The cost of the election was enormous and Wellesley's financial position exceedingly precarious. His return to Parliament was vital to protect him from his creditors.

The reports that appeared in the *Salisbury and Winchester Journal* at this time appear to show Wellesley in an exceedingly favourable light, and so it is no surprise to find Benett informing the freeholders on Monday 29 June that he had the authority of the printers to say that one of the reports was sent to them by Wellesley's agent and will be charged for as a common advertisement!

No voting took place, of course, on Sunday, although it appears that the candidates and many of their supporters appeared at the hustings. Benett's friend and supporter Thomas Calley had just been defeated at the parliamentary election that had taken place at Cricklade, in the north of the county, and Benett was hoping that many who had supported Calley would arrive to support him on the following day. No long speeches were made and according to one account 'throughout this day the utmost decorum was observed'!

On the Monday, battle was recommenced. Benett arrived escorted by a large number of freeholders decorated with his favours and Methuen in his barouche with purple banners. Wellesley made his usual dramatic and showy entry. The ingenuity of the candidates must have been sorely strained to find something original to say and 'having heard the first you are prepared for the second, while this refreshes your memory with regard to both', as the *Salisbury and Winchester Journal* so succinctly put it. On this and the following days, Wellesley's lead over Benett continued to increase and by Wednesday evening, the seventh day of the poll, Methuen had a commanding lead with Wellesley ahead of Benett by 380 votes. Benett must by now have realised that his chances of securing election were receding and when, by the end of the following day, Wellesley's lead had increased by a further 57 votes, he decided to concede defeat. On Thursday evening, he informed the High Sheriff that it was not his intention to poll any more votes and then addressed his supporters:

> Gentlemen, it is with deep regret that I have to inform you that my resources have failed me in the northern and other parts of this county; and I beg to inform you that I consider it fruitless any longer to continue this contest, which I am sure you will regret as much or more than myself. Gentlemen, I beg to return you my most heartfelt thanks and gratitude for your attendance on me, which has been necessary for the safety of my person; and I have only to add, that I hope you, or some of you, will see me safely escorted to my home.

It was then reported that 'He departed immediately for Pythouse, accompanied by all his horsemen.'

On 2 July, Charlotte, the daughter of Thomas Grove, Methuen's proposer and Benett's old friend, recorded in her diary, 'Today Mr Benett gave up his election finding the conduct of his opponent & mob there is no chance of his succeeding'.[115]

According to the *Salisbury and Winchester Journal*:

> There being an ardent curiosity to know how the numerous freeholders of this county exercised their elective franchise in the recent arduous

contest, we doubt not but the poll-book, which is advertised for publication on Tuesday next, will be read with great assidity in all parts of the county.[116]

The poll book, priced at 7s. 6d., was duly published thus enabling everyone to know how each of the freeholders had voted. The number of plumpers, that is, those who voted for only one candidate rather than two, was thought to be of interest, and so the *Salisbury and Winchester Journal* carried a paragraph that read:

PLUMPERS – The following statement of the poll, at the conclusion of the late contested election for this county, affords a proof that the number of *plumpers* is no testimony of superior strength. Such votes arise frequently out of adventitious circumstances and, as in the present instance, often proceed in an inverse ratio to the total majority

|  | *Methuen* | *Wellesley* | *Benett* |
|---|---|---|---|
| Plumpers | 185 | 412 | 445 |
| General votes | 2637 | 1597 | 1127 |
|  | 2822 | 2 009 | 1572[117] |

In the hundred of Dunworth, in which Pythouse was situated and which included most of the surrounding villages, Benett's support was at its greatest. Of the 81 votes only 2 were cast in favour of Wellesley, 16 in favour of Methuen and 63 in Benett's favour. Indeed, in Semley all 9 freeholders voted for Benett alone and in Tisbury all 19 freeholders also voted for him although 5 of them cast their other vote in Methuen's favour. In Westbury, only one freeholder who lived not in Wiltshire but in Somerset, voted for Wellesley. It was in the manufacturing towns in the north of the county that Benett failed to collect any material number of votes. For instance, in Trowbridge, where 318 votes were recorded, only 19 were in his favour, and in Malmesbury only two freeholders voted for him.

The cost to the candidates of fighting the election was enormous. Some years later Wellesley, in writing to Lord Chancellor Eldon,[118] estimated his expenses at 'not less than between £30,000 and £40,000'[119] – and this was probably an underestimate.

The *Salisbury and Winchester Journal*, reporting early in August, declared:

By information, which we have received from different parts of the county, we are led to believe that the expenses of the late election, so far as they relate to Mr Benett, will be borne entirely by the gentlemen, yeomanry, and tradesmen, who are represented as being determined that no charge whatsoever shall be made on the person whom they consider to be the champion of their independence.[120]

In the event, comparatively small sums were subscribed and so Benett was left with a burden of debt that remained with him for the rest of his life.

Benett's sister Etheldred, writing to Gideon Mantell[121] in September, paints a vivid, although naturally somewhat partisan, picture of what had occurred:

A contested election sets even Geology at defiance, and a Brother's life at stake, you may well suppose rendered the scene much too interesting for me to think with effect on any other subject. Our opponent finding honorable means were of no avail against the Man, who was really the choice of the County, stuck at nothing, however dishonorable, to attain his end. He has carried his Election, but by means which have made him detested by all the respectable part of the County. By bribery and corruption of every kind he raised a Mob against us, and the mischief he has done by the demoralization of the lower classes is most deplorable and will be dreadfully felt for years.

My Brother's life was preserved through the Election by means most honorable to him, most gratifying to all his family. – The Yeomen of the County (not the yeomen Cavalry as Mr. L.W. has falsely reported) seeing the urgency of the case, from the highest to the lowest gave up all their own concerns for the whole time of the Election lasted and at the risk of much personal danger, expense and inconvenience, kept up a spontaneous Guard of from four hundred to six hundred daily, and without whom my Brother could not have moved but at the risk of his life, so dreadfully had Mr.Wellesley poisoned the minds of the lower classes against the Man whose conduct they had all been eye witnesses for more than 20 years. A most striking proof how far Beer and falsehood will go with ignorant People. – Ours however is the Triumph, and I trust that a time will come when Mr Wellesley will find the County of Wilts. is not to be carried a second time by bribery, falsehood and intimidation, nor would it now if we had been aware that such dishonourable means would have been used against us, but Mr Wellesley was deep in electioneering, it was my Brother's first attempt, and as there has not been a contest in Wiltshire for 46 years, no one suspected such conduct therefore [and] could not guard against it.[122]

The 'spontaneous guard of from four hundred to six hundred', later called 'the Wiltshire Cossacks' referred to by Etheldred was seen by many to be not so much a bodyguard but a force that, whether intentionally or not, served to intimidate the supporters of Benett's opponents. It is more than likely that the truth lies somewhere between the contrasting views.

Although defeated, Benett could not resist one final letter to the freeholders. On 10 July, writing from Pythouse, he suggests that having elected Wellesley, the representation of the county was intended to be the appendage of one family, that of the Longs into which he married and as a result of this connection and their influence he achieved success. Benett wrote:

> I offered myself as a Candidate for your representation, with the legitimate pretensions of being a private gentleman, of a family as ancient, as honourable, and independent as any in this county; having resided my whole life amongst you, and endeavoured to perform all the duties attached to my station. I had no Treasury influence, no high alliances, no immoderate fortune to boast of. The whole of my interest in the county of Wilts proceeded from the affections of those who have long known me as their friend, whose attachment cannot be bought; it is my estimation above all price; and I trust that my conduct will always be such as to ensure me a continuance of it.

He attributed his failure to secure sufficient votes to achieve victory to:

> The scandalous falsehoods which circulated under anonymous signatures, by hand-bills, and other papers, the opening of houses of public resort, and the inflammatory speeches which were daily and hourly addressed to the populace in the streets and ale-houses of the manufacturing and other large towns, exceed in infamy anything which has been known in the most corrupt borough elections. These proceedings occasioned the numerous assaults which were committed on my friends and myself, and established that system of intimidation which prevented a number of my voters (though in many instances not till after they had been beaten and the carriages in which they would have been conveyed broken to pieces), from coming to the poll in my favour. Others in the same circumstances, were induced to vote against me: thus has the freedom of election been grossly violated, and the unbiassed suffrages of the freeholders have not been obtained against me.[123]

Many years later, the *Devizes and Wiltshire Gazette* described Wellesley as 'one of the best electioneers in the Kingdom and who, by his dexterity, a few years since, obtained the representation of Wilts (when scarcely known to half a dozen persons in the county) in opposition to a gentleman who had resided in it all his life'.[124]

Later in July, both Wellesley , writing from Wanstead House, and 'One of the Family' (presumably a member of the Long Family or somebody writing on its behalf) responded to Benett's letter and refuted his allegations.[125] He appears to have had the last word in the election that produced an unprecedented volume of advertisements, letters and speeches, most of which were very shortly afterwards reproduced in *Kaleidoscopiana Wiltoniensia or, a Literary, Political, and Moral View of the County of Wilts during the Contested Election for its Representation, in June 1818* . . . by An Observer, and extending to over 400 pages.[126]

As if this was not enough, at least two other publications appeared in quick succession. The first, printed in Devizes, was *An Impartial Account of the Most Material Circumstances, which led to the result of the Late Election of members, for The County of Wilts: with the origin of Clubs and Quorums in the County.*[127] This account was far from impartial and was probably written by the Rev. Charles Lucas, one of Benett's supporters. Lucas writes:

> A spirit of opposition the most violent, was excited against a respectable Gentleman, long known, and of ancient family in the county, – and a triumph secured in favour of an entire stranger, of whom little was known, – who, without fortune himself, gained by marriage the most ample means of dispensing, general, useful and active benevolence , but who was distinguished more by a general character of selfish extravagance, than by the knowledge of his having, with all his wealth ever made ONE POOR MAN HAPPY; – yet on THIS MAN, the BLESSINGS of the poor were showered, – and on his rival, (who had employed HIS wealth as it ought to be employed,) CURSES loud and deep from almost every cottage and manufactory in the County!

The writer continues by reminding his readers that Benett 'was the first to point out to MR METHUEN, the propriety and necessity of standing on truly independent grounds . . .' and ends with:

> One word more, on the cry of BARLEY BREAD and POTATOES. Because Mr Benett said a man could not support his family on seven shillings a week, *although* many lived on Barley Bread and Potatoes, which although evidently implied, that he considered such a fare a hardship, that he *recommended* such provision for the lower classes of the community.

> > 'The whole of the misery of my Parish
> > and I believe of my Country, is OCCASI-
> > ONED BY THE LOWNESS OF WAGES',

Mr. Benett says THIS! And it need not be added, that it is become the DUTY of every freeholder to READ HIS EVIDENCE, that he may be convinced by his own eyes, of the badness of that cause, which required the assistance of such gross and palpable falsehoods to support it.

The Reverend Mr Lucas, if he was indeed the author of this pamphlet, would have done well to have re-read Benett's evidence before the parliamentary committee himself, as his interpretation of it is far from accurate.

The publication of this pamphlet was closely followed by an extraordinary diatribe aimed at Benett's conduct, pronouncements and principles entitled *Letters to the Gentlemen, Clergy, Freeholders, Manufacturers, Tradesmen, and Inhabitants, of the County of Wilts in reference to the Events of the Late Election.*[128] In three letters, extending to 67 pages in all, the author, writing under the pseudonym of 'Sydney', combined invective with sarcasm. When recollecting Benett's speech made on his withdrawal from the contest he wrote:

Oh! What a soul touching scene must have presented itself!! Oh! What a tale to tell the county!!! Was there ever humiliation in all the world before like this? Was ever humiliation rendered more complete? As a man composed of flesh and blood, I feel for him from the very bottom of my soul; and I am quite certain, that had I been similarly situated, and at that moment placed in Mr Benett's grisly situation; I should in the agony of my mind have beaten my breast; and in the heart rending language of Job, loudly exclaimed, 'cursed be the day in which I was born, and the night in which such a wretch as I was conceived!' What! Mr Benett, a Gentleman of wealth, consequence, and respectability, residing the whole of his life on his own estate, in the midst of his friends and tenantry; a candidate for the representation of his native county; President of the Wilts Agricultural Society; a Magistrate; an Officer; faith, I believe, in a troop of Wiltshire Yeomanry; ay, and to sum up the whole *'the poor Man's Friend!'* sounding such a retreat as this!! Is this the Mr Benett, who for these last twelve months we have heard so much talk about, and who has been here, there, and everywhere soliciting the suffrages of the freeholders, making cocksure of being elected and whose poor head for months past has been running on nothing else upon earth, but the honours that awaited him? Vain calculation! Is this the man so defeated, so disappointed, so crest fallen?

And later continued:

Gentlemen, Mr Benett in order to prop up his rotten and expiring cause, is pleased to descant on the hereditary patriotic virtue of his family; he has recently discovered that the late Mr Goddard,[129] of Swindon House, owed the success of his memorable election, *not* to the patriotic spirit of the county of Wilts; but to one *Mr Lambert*, Mr Benett's wife's father: in the name of fortune who is his *prompter*, when he stands up to talk so absurd, so ridiculously nonsensical? Let us hear no more such insufferable cant as the *hereditary* virtue of families: at least on such an occasion as this: it is nothing more than vain, idle, empty talk; like *'sounding brass, or a tinkling cymbal'*.

During the course of the election campaign, it is likely that the organisers of the forthcoming triennial meeting of the 'Salisbury School for the gratuitous Education of the Infant Poor, on the Plan of Rev. Dr. Bell,[130] and in the faith of the Church of England' were in a dilemma as to which of the candidates were likely to be elected and so should be invited to act as stewards. In the event, they invited all three and so when a notice of the meeting to be held on 23 July was published, Methuen and Wellesley were duly described as Members of Parliament, with plain 'John Benett Esq' joining not only the successful candidates but also his old rival Archdeacon Coxe as one of the stewards.[131]

On 22 July, Benett's election committee met at Salisbury under the chairmanship of William Wyndham and passed twelve resolutions, including ones declaring that the committee would be permanent and that the meeting be adjourned to the Wednesday in the week of the Summer Assizes, 1819, at the *White Hart Inn* in Salisbury.[132] Little did they know that they would indeed be meeting in the following year in order to attempt once again to secure Benett's election to Parliament. Another of the resolutions declared that:

> We are of the opinion that the final result of the Poll was not the expression of the free and unbiased sentiments of the Freeholders at large: that a system of intimidation was established in many districts, and other means inconsistent with the freedom and purity of election were pursued, by which many independent Freeholders were restrained from presenting themselves at the Poll; or were otherwise prevented from giving their votes according to their unbiased judgement, in favour of Mr Benett.

Methuen's undated letter to Lord Folkestone, probably written at this time to thank him for his support during the election, reveals his true feelings about Benett as a person and about the resolutions passed at this meeting:

I cannot enough thank you for your very kind attention to my Interest, and the trouble you have taken in my name. I see the thing with the same eye that you do, and I assume you have done so from the first moment I heard what was going on.

Respecting L. Wellesley you may be assured he is frightened out of his wits (such as they are) and not without reason as you shall learn. He has taken up 32000 [pounds] of Brooks and Williams the annuity gentlemen at 16 per cent, by which, his Election has cost him in fact (supposing that sum will clear *all*) 100,000 till it is paid, as it is I believe 5000 a year which he has to pay, being the legal interest of the sum I mention. Before the Election I believe no man in England was more entirely done . . .

Respecting Benett there is nothing he may not say or do, I am convinced. Mr Grove told me the other day, that he and his friends met him going into Wilton and endeavoured to prevent his proposing me at the Election declaring there was a Coalition. After what . . . at the Hustings, when you were so kind as to act as my friend and make an explanation from Benett declaring his disbelief in a Coalition, can any man ever look upon Benett in the light of a man of veracity or honesty? I only wish I had insisted on the transaction on that occasion being published, as it ought to be known to the whole County. . .

My retiring is a *stale story*, attempted last time, and I have no doubt depended upon by Benett. I will never be bullied out by him and I hope if I ever do retire from any reason such as health or wishing to be quiet when I get old, I may not see my place occupied by a man devoid of common truth and common honesty, I have no doubt Astley will oppose Benett whenever he comes forward.

A postscript to this letter written at its head declared:

I cannot help thinking Benett's friends should have been made [to] say whether their Resolutions were intended against me or not as I am sure they were worded intentionally in an ambiguous manner in order to give a greater éclat to their Champion's pretensions.[133]

At the end of July, the prosecution instituted by the Corporation of Salisbury against James Macklin and others for a breach of the peace in assaulting John Tinney and for riotous conduct was heard at the Assizes sitting in Salisbury.[134] Benett's pyrrhic victory over Hunt three years before must have encouraged him to take further action to protect what he perceived to be his exclusive fishing rights in the river Avon where it passed through the manor of Enford; for, at the same sitting, a special jury heard his long-running action against one Jesse Coster for trespass arising out of his fishing in the river there. Benett's counsel traced by an extract from the Domesday Book, his title to the manor of Enford supported by grants from the Crown in the reigns of Edward I, Henry VIII, James and Elizabeth, all conveying the rights of fishing to his predecessors. However, the defendant's counsel produced the evidence of 'many old and respectable inhabitants' to prove that for the last 70 years they had fished in the river without interruption or objection. Benett must have been dismayed that the jury returned a verdict in favour of the defendant which established to the owners of land in the parish a right of common fishery for ever.[135]

Following the election, dinners were organised in various parts of the county for the entertainment of the supporters of each of the candidates, presumably at the candidates' expense. At a dinner given in Salisbury in August attended by nearly a hundred of Methuen's friends, in a rare display of magnanimity, after the health of Methuen and Long Wellesley had been drunk, it was reported that, 'the health of Mr Benett of Pythouse was also given three times three'.[136]

Although Benett had been defeated, he was expected to show his gratitude to his supporters by entertaining them at very considerable expense and on a most lavish scale. In August, some 700 of them dined in a marquee erected in the grounds of Pythouse, and one of the principal guests was his neighbour Lord Arundell. The ladies were, of course, excluded although when the health of Benett's wife, Lucy, was toasted she appeared at the window of the library with some other ladies and made it known that she would like the company to accept a toast – The Glorious Minority of 1818 – from her. A large number of people from the neighbourhood surrounded the house 'greeting the company and showing their perfect sympathy in the sentiments of the day' and were duly rewarded by being entertained three days later.[137]

Later in the month, the inhabitants of Warminster, ' who took no part in the disgraceful proceedings which occurred during the election', were rewarded with a large loaf of bread and a plentiful supply of strong beer paid for by some of Benett's friends in the town.[138] And on the 31st a 'splendid dinner' was given in the Assembly Rooms in Salisbury for a company consisting mostly of country gentlemen and farmers. In his speech he alluded, not for the first time, to the part played by Lucy's father in the last contested county election by declaring:

> No one could possess more love for the county of Wilts, or more zeal for
> its independence, than Mrs Benett, and the feelings she appeared to have
> inherited from her father, the late Mr. Lambert, who, it was in the
> recollection of some persons, attended the contested election of 1772 with

five hundred of his friends; their votes turned the scale in favour of Mr. Goddard, and the independence of the county was for that time secured.

One of the numerous toasts was to 'The Wiltshire Cossack' and John Peniston, who, with Benett's friend Henry King[139] of Chilmark, had lead the horseman who attended Benett throughout the election, responded. He proposed: 'The Freedom of election, uninfluenced by force, unawed by popular clamour'.[140]

In the months after the election, Benett's solicitors and other agents would have been kept busy in settling – and in some cases disputing – the numerous claims for the payment of expenses incurred on his behalf. The part played by John Tinney is graphically described in a memoir of his life, included in a 'Biography' of notable Salisbury people published some years later:

> In Mr Benett's contested election for the county in 1818, the partialities of friendship, and the odious manner in which the feelings of the mob had been wrought upon by Mr Long Wellesley, induced him to offer Mr Benett his services gratuitously. The populace assailed his windows with stones, and when some of the voters tendered for the latter were considered to be doubtful; by calling through our streets for a *screwtinney*, as they purposely pronounced it they pretty significantly expressed the value of his support. We still remember the good-humoured smile with which he met at the assizes a question from Serjeant Pell, at that time supreme with the common juries and the galleries on the Western Circuit. It was an action against Mr Benett for some electioneering expenses, we believe, and Mr Tinney was a witness for the defendant. The learned Serjeant, as of counsel for the plaintiff, thought he had a fine opportunity to gratify vulgar prejudices by having an attorney in the witness box. 'I suppose, Mr Tinney,' said the Serjeant, 'You made a good thing of this election?' 'Not one farthing. My services to Mr Benett were gratuitous.' The Serjeant sat down – it was enough.[141]

Practically nothing is known about the character of Lucy. However, an entry in the journal kept by the Irish poet Tom Moore[142] (who, in 1817, had moved with his wife Bessy to Sloperton Cottage not far from Bowood, the seat of his patron the Marquis of Lansdowne) paints an extremely unflattering picture of her. On 11 November 1818 he recorded:

> Mrs Phipps & Bennet (sic) (the would-be Wiltshire Member) called & asked me to dinner – wished to stay at home with Bessy, but the dear girl insisted on my going, as I had refused them so often . . . the dinner, dull

enough – Bennet a very haranguing minded gentleman – and his wife odious – full of airs, with a hard, grinding *Tartar* voice, and presuming beyond everything – produced and read some verses she had written on Sheridan's death – The verses, better than one would expect from her, but the voice & confidence intolerable – how much more delightful to have a woman's mind a perfect *blank* than to see it scribbled over with all this wretched impertinence –[143]

This was not the first time that Moore had met Lucy as they were both at a ball held in Devizes in the previous month. Afterwards Charles Lewis Phipps,[144] a close neighbour and friend of Moore and also a friend of the Benetts, 'took charge of Mrs Benett (our would-be member's wife) in her carriage and I came home with Mrs Phipps in hers – Oh the days of my youth'.[145]

Lucy must have appeared to Moore as typical of the sort of women that Bessy, originally an actress, would have dreaded to meet. One of Moore's reasons for moving out of London, and away from the brilliant world of high society in which he moved so easily, was 'to exempt his wife from the mortification of vicinity to a society which would not have received her'.[146] We may be certain that Lucy would have been reluctant at this time to 'receive' her – an attitude that contrasts starkly with the kindly behaviour shown to her by the Marquis of Lansdowne and his wife. Further, one can perhaps deduce from Moore's remarks that Lucy had literary aspirations and that she was anxious to show her work to the man who is remembered as the national lyricist of Ireland, and who, it has been said, 'alone among modern poets, united the arts of poetry and music'.[147] He may even have refused a number of earlier invitations to dine with the intention of avoiding having to meet her. Certainly he would not have wished to place 'my sweet Bessy', as he calls her in his journal, in the position of being snubbed by her. On the other hand, Benett, who inevitably met people of every sort and condition in the course of his agricultural and parliamentary pursuits, would surely have greeted her with lofty courtesy.

After the excitement of the election, Benett's life would have returned to something like normality, sitting as a magistrate and, having been captain of the Hindon troop of yeomanry cavalry since 1811, organising the regular training of the troop. Members of the troop received notice, often very short, of call out through the medium of the *Salisbury and Winchester Journal*, and on 15 March 1819 members of the troop would have read that:

The Hindon troop will parade in field-day order on Lady Down, on Wednesday the 17th March inst, and the two following days at eleven o'clock in the morning.

Pythouse                                        John Benett, Captain[148]

On the same day, the newspaper carried an advertisement for C. Greenwood's new maps of Wilts, Dorset, Somerset, Cornwall and Devon, the survey for which was shortly to commence, with a list of those who had already subscribed for them. As virtually every nobleman and country gentleman living in Wiltshire is included in the list, it is no surprise to find that Benett had committed himself to taking the maps for Wiltshire, Dorset and Somerset.

Benett also busied himself with the affairs of agriculture, and in December, at the meeting of the Bath and West of England Agricultural Society held in Bath, he was one of those appointed to the committee to arrange ploughing matches.[149] The last of the numerous dinners he attended throughout the year was held at Warminster during December, having been postponed in consequence of the Queen's death. In his speech that followed the pattern of all the others he had made, he was able to provide a little variation by recording his pleasure at being in Warminster and in the vicinity of 'Norton Bavant, a spot where his family had resided upwards of 500 years'. He also paid tribute once again to Lucy by declaring that 'no person could be more devoted to the cause in which they were embarked than Mrs Benett, that she had imbibed the principles of independence from her ancestors, that she would anxiously instil the same principles into the minds of her children; and he trusted that these children would on a future day appear as champions of Wiltshire and Independence'.[150]

In July of the following year, while in Norfolk attending Thomas Coke's[151] famous sheep-shearing gathering and agricultural meeting at Holkham,[152] he was given some startling news. Paul Methuen had applied for the Chiltern Hundreds and so would be retiring from Parliament.

# 4
# Two More County Elections 1819-1820

As soon as the news of Methuen's retirement had reached Benett, he returned post haste to Wiltshire. One of his supporters later wrote, 'Our champion was pledged to offer himself on the first vacancy, and we know how he travelled, or rather flew from Norfolk, to redeem this pledge'.[1] One can imagine his astonishment at learning that his rival for the seat was none other than John Dugdale Astley,[2] a long-standing friend who last year had actively assisted him and was a member of his election committee. During the course of the 1818 election campaign, Astley's father had died and from him he inherited considerable wealth. This included very large estates in Staffordshire, Warwickshire and Shropshire as well as at Everleigh in the east of Wiltshire. He now therefore had the financial means to bear the enormous cost of a contested election and perhaps had anticipated that Benett, who had to rely on subscribers to defray some of his expenses, would not be willing to embark on another ruinously expensive undertaking. On various occasions after his defeat, however, Benett had said that he would hold himself in readiness to fight another election and the fact that his election committee remained in being is, perhaps, some indication that it was thought that Methuen would soon seek to retire.

Rumours that Methuen might retire were circulating in the county and on 2 July Charlotte Grove noted in her diary: 'There is a report that Mr Methuen is going to resign being Member of the county'.[3] Further, before leaving for Norfolk, Benett had taken the precaution of drafting his Address to the Freeholders, and this he left with Lucy who, before publishing it, had called on Astley presumably to inform him that she was about to do so. As Methuen was at Astley's house when she called, the meeting must have been fraught with difficulties.

On 7 July, it was announced that the election would be held only twelve days later. The candidates and the county had had to endure a campaign lasting over three months in the previous year and perhaps it was thought that, with the nomination taking place on 16 July, the preparations for the election would be conducted peaceably, with the election itself passing without incident. How different it was to be!

Not only Benett himself, but all his family and friends were amazed that Astley should have decided to stand against him. On 11 July, Benett's sister Etheldred wrote to her fellow geologist, Gideon Mantell:

> You will be surprised to hear that we are again employed in all the horrors of a contested election. Mr Methuen has thought it proper to accept the Chiltern hundreds and by all the circumstances attending it, it is generally supposed that he has sold the County. Mr. Astley who is now come forward was a warm supporter of my Brother at the last election, and his name stands second on the list of those gentlemen who passed a unanimous vote of thanks to him for his conduct on that occasion and publicly pledged themselves to support him the first opportunity that offered, my Brother, of course, feels bound to redeem his pledge to the County and his friends are unanimous in their support of him on the present occasion . . . I venture, therefore again to request you to use your influence with your Wiltshire companions in our favor. I am sure you will excuse this hurried and blotted scrawl at the present moment and with my best compliments to Mrs Mantell
> > Believe me dear Sir
> > Your very humble Servant
> > Etheldred Benett [4]

On Wednesday the 7th at 10.30am, Benett arrived at the Assembly Rooms in Salisbury where he explained to some 300 of his supporters the peculiar position in which he found himself, and expressed his astonishment that Astley, 'a man with whom I have been on terms of intimacy for many years, and who has always professed friendship for me', as he put it, was to be his opponent. He pointed out that Astley was a rich man, and he himself was comparatively poor; but his character was well known to the county of Wilts. He also said that he had lately been several times in the gallery at the House of Commons when subjects of the greatest national importance were discussed and decided. They were occasions which should claim the attendance of the Members for Wiltshire, but he had not seen both of them in their places on these occasions. Some friends had advised him not to enter the threatened contest: to those he replied, 'I am bound to do it, and to redeem the pledge I have given; it will hurt my purse, but, thank God, not my character'. He concluded his speech by saying that he would be going directly to his friend Mr Phipps, of Westbury, and then to seek for Astley, perhaps to attempt to persuade him to withdraw from the contest. A *Sketch of a speech delivered by Mr Benett of Pythouse at the Assembly Rooms, Salisbury* was published by Brodie and Dowding and copies together with copies of the Election Address were distributed to Benett's supporters. These included George Purefoy Jervoise who, it may be recalled, had considered himself neglected by Benett at the time of the 1818 election.[5]

Astley felt compelled to counter the charge that he had acted improperly in standing against Benett by issuing a handbill addressed to the freeholders and saying that it was well known that he had thought of standing himself in the 1818 election, but had only decided not to do so because his position then was 'not so clearly and absolutely independent as a County Member's ought to be'.[6] Having now inherited his father's very considerable property, he had the means, unlike Benett, to bear the enormous cost of a contested election.

On Friday Lucy arrived in Salisbury, having been cheered as she passed through Wilton. On her arrival in the city the populace took the horses from her carriage and drew her to her inn.[7] On the following day, Benett was in Warminster where the chairman of his election committee, William Wyndham, presided at a meeting at the *Bath Arms Inn* at which over £3000 was raised within a few minutes to support the campaign. In the *Salisbury and Winchester Journal* published on 12 July, a notice appeared informing the freeholders that, 'to wait upon many of the freeholders is impossible and to make the usual preparations for a Contested election by preparing sufficient conveyances for my friends may be equally out of my power'. Another notice reported that Benett's election committee had resolved that a subscription be opened at both the banks in Salisbury for the purpose of defraying his election expenses.[8]

Rumours had been circulating that Methuen had given Astley advance notice of his intention to resign, and had even employed a spy to report when Benett was out of the county. Astley insisted that he and Methuen should sign and publish a declaration to the effect that there had been no pre-concerted arrangement between them as to the time and mode of Methuen's resignation, and that the first intimation of his decision to resign that he had given to anyone, other than his family, was to John Fuller[9] of Neston Park on 27 June. This declaration was duly printed as a handbill and published in the *Salisbury and Winchester Journal* on 19 July.[10]

Methuen was incensed that he had been obliged to sign the declaration, and even more by the suggestion that he had arranged for Benett's movements to be watched. He therefore wrote to Lord Folkestone for his advice:

You will be annoyed, I know, that Astley told me he could not get on unless I would sign the enclosed declaration. I could not refuse him though I feel a touch indignant at such a measure being necessary.

I must tell you *in strict confidence* that Mr Bleek[11] of Warminster, a most active agent for Astley, came yesterday to me, enjoining secrecy but telling me that Benett has asserted in Devizes Market Place publically he had found out that I kept a man near Pythouse for a month to watch him out of the county. I told Bleek I should notice nothing that was not reported to me on the authority of the person who heard it and he went away saying he would get the Rev. Mr.Thring to swear the fact before a magistrate and he would then bring me the Paper.

If I do receive such a document I shall send it off on express to you to know what I ought to do. My own opinion and Mr Joy (who is my confidential friend) is that I should call together a few of my most intimate friends (two or three, you and Goddard perhaps with him) and consult as to what measure I ought to take. Calling him out, I consider out of the Question, as my object of course is first to disprove a lie and expose him. He may then take his own course with me. This is Mr Joy's decided opinion on the subject.[12]

As nothing more was heard of the matter, it is likely that the Rev. Mr. Thring decided that he did not wish to become involved, and that, in any event, if Benett did say anything in the Market Place in Devizes, he probably merely repeated the rumours that were abroad without asserting that they were true.

On 19 July, it was also reported that on Tuesday last both candidates arrived in Salisbury and:

a very perceptible interest, in Mr Benett's favour, has within the last few days manifested itself, not only in this city but throughout the county at large: the freeholders recollect that he bore his disappointment last year with much manliness and good humour and the unexpected opposition raised against him by an old friend who supported him at the last election has gained him many friends. In short, there is now a most striking contrast between the popular feeling now and at the last election. At the moment, Mr Benett is considered by numerous classes, not only here but throughout our county, as the champion of independence[13]

On Friday, the nomination took place in Devizes in accordance with tradition. As expected, a huge crowd of people assembled in the Market Place (including the poet Tom Moore who walked to Devizes to witness the proceedings)[14] and after the candidates had been proposed and seconded they each attempted to address the multitude. However, the uproar was such that the addresses of neither of them could be heard by any other than those standing closest to them. No one was probably very surprised to find that Henry Hunt was present, nor that he then proceeded to regale the assembled company with his views and, as he was a well known opponent of Benett's, appeared to be supporting Astley! Amongst other things he said, 'that a great deal has been said about what Mr Benett has done for the county, but he has not, to my knowledge, served the county on any material instance. I was bred up, I may say, between both the candidates, one of whom I can say nothing in favour of', and concluded by proposing three cheers for Astley. The High Sheriff was about to proclaim the time of the election when a Mr Eyre intervened and said that Hunt's public principles were 'the most mischievous, subversive of property, and everything most to be preserved and held in esteem', and that Astley should disclaim any connection with such a person. This Astley proceeded to do, whereupon the High Sheriff announced that the election would commence on the following Monday. The forthcoming election, preceded by the nomination, was widely perceived as being a matter of interest not only to the people of Wiltshire but also to a much wider audience, and so on 20 July the readers of the *Morning Chronicle* in London and elsewhere would have been able to enjoy an account of the nomination in Devizes.[15]

Astley was no doubt horrified that Hunt had made an appearance at the nomination and that the impression had been given that he had Hunt's support. Benett's friends lost no time in taking advantage of this and promptly arranged for handbills to be printed and circulated and reading:

Orator HUNT !!

*JUST ARRIVED IN THIS COUNTY*
*The Celebrated Spa-Fields Orator,*
**HENRY HUNT,**
*He was first discovered at the Market-Cross, Devizes,*
On the Day of **NOMINATION,** Speaking in favor of
MR. ASTLEY *! !*

**FREEHOLDERS of Wiltshire, REFLECT ON THIS.**[16]

By now, Tom Moore was sufficient a friend of Benett's to do what he could to give him his support and on 24 July recorded in his journal:

Had written to Lord Holland about some votes for Benett – received a long answer from him, begging me to state particularly to Benett or his friends that it was *because* he believed him a friend to religious liberty & an enemy to all disqualifying Tests that he gave him his good wishes in the contest.[17]

The first stage of the election took place at Wilton as usual. After the candidates had been proposed, they each addressed the huge crowd. The High Sheriff then proposed a show of hands but as some people held up two hands, he suggested the holding up of hats and declared a majority in favour of Benett. Not surprisingly Astley demanded a poll, and so, as everyone knew was inevitable, the proceedings were adjourned to the hustings where the polling booths had been erected.

The vast crowd moved to the familiar field outside Salisbury, and an onlooker would have been astonished, but not perhaps surprised, to see that:

> a great contest had ensued between the friends of the respective candidates for possession of the ground immediately in front of the hustings: in this strife (which was maintained with great obstinacy, principally by farmers' servants and by numbers of other persons of a low description in society) the party in Mr Benett's favour proved predominant.[18]

As a result of this conflict, Astley's friends would, of course, have found it difficult, if not impossible, to reach the polling booths and so, when the poll was closed at 4 o'clock, 302 freeholders had voted for Benett and 199 in favour of Astley. Later, one voter said:

> When I went up to the poll, I was obstructed; a bludgeon man wearing the colours of Mr Benett refused to let me pass. I insisted on going up to the booth and the fellow said, 'I'll not allow you to go, for you have got the wrong colour'. He repeated that, 'I should not go, for he was hired at 3s. 6d. per day to prevent Mr Astley's voters going to vote; he was paid for doing it and he would do that for which he was hired'. I took him to the poll clerk, and on his expressing contrition for what he had done, I suffered him to go.[19]

The High Sheriff knew that even more disorder would be expected on the Tuesday, the second day of the poll. In anticipation of this, he had arranged for 200 special constables to be sworn in and his own javelin men were also in attendance. As soon as the polling booths had opened, battle commenced between the partisans of the candidates to establish supremacy in front of the hustings. It was reported that more than 200 men from Bradford and Trowbridge armed with bludgeons were present with instructions to clear the ground for Astley.

One of them later declared before the High Sheriff that Thomas Timbrell, one of Astley's agents, had gone to the *George Inn* in Trowbridge on the day before, announcing that he wanted 300 men to go to the election and that those who had served in the militia under Astley must certainly go. Timbrell later denied this report and said that he would take action against the printers of the *Salisbury and Winchester Journal*.

The special constables were hopelessly outnumbered and powerless to restore order. Stones were thrown at 'many respectable people who were on the hustings (many of whom were ladies) and also at the persons in the polling booths', and ' hundreds of heads were broken and numberless contusions received'.[20] A man from Shaftesbury was stabbed in the side and 12 others were sent to the Infirmary in Salisbury suffering from severe injuries. The battle continued for three hours, at the end of which Benett's party won the day and drove their opponents from the field. As a consequence, just after midday, the High Sheriff ordered the polling to cease and adjourned the election to the next day. Benett had polled 190 votes and Astley 151.

The breakdown of law and order was so serious that word was sent to General Lord Howard, commanding officer of the district, who replied that he had ordered two troops of the 16th Lancers to a destination within eight miles of the city to await orders from the magistrates.

As Astley's supporters had been dispersed, he found himself in the position of having to return to Salisbury without his usual entourage, and decided to take the road through the villages of Durnford and Stratford-sub-Castle rather than taking the highway leading from Salisbury to Devizes. Having reached Stratford, his open carriage overturned, not as a result of the removal of the linch-pin of his carriage as was later rumoured, but as a consequence of the inebriated condition of his drivers! He thus had to suffer the indignity of being forced to walk into Salisbury – even having to place himself under the protection of Benett's friends, if the contemporary newspaper report is to be believed.

A letter from 'A Candid Dissenter' published on 26 July is a rare example of one of Benett's opponents mixing criticism with praise, observing:

> He is a man of good plain understanding, a good husband, a good father, a good neighbour, and a pleasant hospitable companion; a man of very moderate private education and from his publications evidently without any pretension to literary attainments. His religious principles have long been questionable and his indifference to the cause of the established

Church, and to every other tolerant sect, is sufficiently evidenced by his strong attachment to the cause of Popery which brought him the presence and support of the Roman Catholics in his cause at the last election – his troop of horsemen headed by one of that intolerant persuasion . . . Mr Benett is a man of a handsome private fortune. But avowedly dependent on his several subscription friends for the payment of his election bills with the list of his subscribers constantly staring his independence in the face. He is an active magistrate and esteemed by many of his opulent neighbours but long before he became a candidate for the County he unfortunately made himself the most unpopular country gentleman in the County in which he resides – so much so as to be burnt in effigy in several principal towns where his name was posted with epithets of odium and execration.[21]

During the 1818 election campaign little was said about the religious beliefs of the candidates. However, in 1819 much play was made of Astley's High Church principles and alleged intolerance towards dissenters, as opposed to Benett's well known tolerance towards the religious practices of both Roman Catholics and Protestant Dissenters. In 1816 rioters had disrupted the meetings of Independents held at Ansty, a village not far from Pythouse, and Benett was said to have been the only magistrate who declared that the rioters should be brought to justice and punished. As a consequence, Benett appears to have had the support of dissenters throughout the county and a notice was now published declaring:

> Lest any person should doubt the truth of a statement which has just appeared of Mr. Benett's generous and friendly conduct when our rights, as Protestant Dissenters, were invaded last year: We, the undersigned, resident Dissenters, do voluntarily assert that we had the most prompt and efficacious assistance from Mr. Benett, and from Mr. Benett *only*, on that trying occasion.
>
> Had he not advocated our cause at this memorable period, the consequence might have been disastrous to the '*rights of conscience*', instead of terminating as it did, in triumph of '*religious liberty*'.
>
> We call upon our dissenting friends throughout the County, to rally round the standard of *religious freedom*, and to give their Votes to a Man, who has *proved* himself our Champion in '*the hour of Danger*'.[22]

Further, John Bleek[23] writing to the *Salisbury and Winchester Journal* after the election stated:

> that a certain individual had, by himself and his family, addressed letters

to various dissenting ministers in the county accusing Mr Astley in the harshest terms of biggotry and intolerance: that one of these letters was addressed to the Rev.Mr.Seymour of Bradford, and had been read by him to his congregation from the pulpit and that another letter of similar import and from the same quarter had been addressed to the Rev. Mr. Kent of Trowbridge. . .[24]

Bleek later corrected this statement by saying that the letter was not actually read but that the minister recommended his hearers not to support Astley and that at another chapel in Bradford a similar letter *was* read by the minister to his congregation immediately after partaking of the Sacrament.[25]

It is clear that the family referred to in Bleek's letter was the Everett family of Heytesbury. John Gale Everett, a prosperous cloth manufacturer, was an old friend of Benett's, a member of his election committee and one of those who 'resolved to convey the voters of the Hundreds of Warminster and Heytesbury, in the interest of Mr Benett,to the hustings at Wilton, free of expense to that gentleman'.[26] Later in the year, a letter written by Charlotte Everett was reproduced and declared:

> . . . can we give our votes and support to a man who is such a notorious Bigot that he will never employ a poor person if he goes to meeting – and who has been known to discharge such for the sin of worshipping God according to his conscience? On the other hand, Mr Everett has intimately known Mr Benett the last twenty years and, though he has been grossly misrepresented for electioneering purposes, has always found him a steady friend of the poor, and a staunch friend of religious Liberty. . .[27]

As Astley was well known as a High Churchman, it was not difficult for his opponents to portray him as a man who was intolerant to dissenters. On 19 July the *Salisbury and Winchester Journal* printed a notice to the effect that:

> JOHN BRICKER of the Parish of Laycock in the county of Wilts, on his Oath said that on Good Friday April 9th 1819, Mr Astley threatened to withhold from him Parish Relief, in case he should apply for it, IF HE CONTINUED TO GO TO THAT HOUSE, namely the DISSENTING CHAPEL, sworn before Thos Calley and also before Wm Wyndham of Dinton.[28]

In response, 31 members of the Wiltshire Militia, of which Astley was major, signed a notice certifying that Astley was:

> a humane, charitable man and allowed us full and free liberty of

Religious Worship, either public or private, and preaching and private Prayer meetings were often held (with his permission) in a tent within one hundred yards of his own Tent; that he never disturbed us, but, on the contrary, allowed several men who preached belonging to the regiment, absence for that purpose.

This was followed by a similar notice signed by 56 other members of the militia! One would be forgiven if one doubted this display of religious fervour on the part of the Wiltshire militia and wondered whether a very slight amount of pressure might have been exerted on them to support their commanding officer!

On 26 July the *Salisbury and Winchester Journal* published a letter from 'Fidles' who wrote (after reminding his readers of Benett's conduct after the Ansty disturbances):

Has Mr Astley been able to disprove the charges which have been made against him of intolerance and intimidation? Never! All the lame attempts which have been made to do so, have only tended to fasten upon my mind the conviction that the charges are true, and I am constrained to believe, that on the election of Mr Astley religious liberty would find him a decided foe.[29]

This letter was followed by a notice headed:

Endowed Chapels
The Crisis is Important; every energy should be exerted, and not a moment to be lost. It should be universally known – That the TRUSTEES of PROPERTY, left to ALL PLACES OF WORSHIP, may VOTE at the ELECTION and that the Property, so left, will qualify as many Voters as will ensure 40s per annum to each Trustee

It is probable that this notice was inserted by Benett's supporters who considered that many, if not most, of the trustees of dissenting meeting houses and land belonging to them would be likely to support him. The not inconsiderable number of dissenters were under considerable pressure, therefore, to cast their votes in Benett's favour.

The election was the talking point of every one in the county, and when on 26 July Tom Moore, the poet, recorded in his diary that he, Mrs Phipps, the wife of his great friend Charles Phipps, and Bessy, his wife, 'as Benettites' beat their opponents as 'Astleyites'[30] their victory was a foretaste of what was to come.

Having closed the poll, the High Sheriff then had to decide where the election should be continued on the following day. Very heavy rain during the Tuesday afternoon doubtless turned the hustings field into a muddy quagmire and so it was decided to continue the election in a large malthouse near St Martin's church in Salisbury, where any disorder could probably be more easily contained.

The Wednesday morning was no doubt required to erect the polling booths in the malthouse and so the poll was opened again at 3 o'clock. It remained open until closed at 8 o'clock in the evening, by which time Benett had polled a further 386 votes with Astley gaining a further 260.

In the Earl of Radnor, Benett found a powerful opponent. One account of the election relates:

> Lord Radnor's steward, wearing Astley's colours, attended the sheriff's assessor during the poll, 'to support the disputed voters in Mr Astley's interest'. On being asked by Benett's counsel whether he had attended at Lord Radnor's direction, he was hastily warned by Astley's counsel and replied that he did not choose to answer. The handbill which related these facts quoted the vote of the House of Commons that it was an infringement of the privileges of the House for a peer to concern himself with elections.[31]

Trowbridge in the north of the county was a manufacturing town in which Benett was particularly unpopular. Indeed, in the 1818 election, out of 170 electors only 18 voted for him. The son of George Crabbe, the poet and rector of Trowbridge and a friend and supporter of Benett, recounted his father's experiences:

> During the violence of that contested election, while the few friends of Mr Benett were almost in despair of their lives, he (i.e. George Crabbe) was twice assailed by a mob of parishioners, with hisses and the most virulent abuse. He replied to their formidable menaces by 'rating them roundly'; and though he was induced to retire by the advice of some friends, who hastened to his succour, yet this made no change to his vote, habits or conduct. He continued to support Mr Benett; he walked in the streets always alone, and just as frequently as before; and spoke as fearlessly. Mr. Canon Bowles, who was near him on this occasion, says, in a letter to the present writer, – 'A riotous tumultuous and most appalling mob, at the time of election, besieged his house, when a chaise was at the door, to prevent his going to the poll, and giving his vote in favour of my most worthy friend, John Benett of Pyt House, the present member for the county. The mob threatened to destroy the chaise, and tear him to pieces, if he attempted to set out. In the face of the furious assemblage, he came out and calmly, told them they might kill him if they chose, but, whilst alive, nothing would prevent his giving a vote at the election, according to his promise and principles, and set off, undisturbed and unhurt, to vote

for Mr. Benett.[32]

The contest was an excuse for all sorts of lawlessness. On 22 July it was reported that:

> Mr Ashley of Melksham, a friend of Mr Benett, had a stone thrown at him on Tuesday morning as he was walking down the street of that town, by a boy wearing the colours of Mr Astley, which broke his head in a dangerous manner. A neighbouring magistrate immediately issued his warrant for the apprehension of the boy, who was twice rescued from the custody of the constables. . . A lady with her servant in a gig was nearly killed at Trowbridge on Thursday last by the partisans of Mr Benett.[33]

On 2 August it was reported that:

> Lady Tuite passing through Trowbridge having red trimmings to some part of her equipage or livery the populace thought this indicative of a favourable opinion to Mr Benett and instantly set up a cry against her and with the most brutal violence followed her to the turnpike and but for the speed of her horses she must have been seriously injured by the vollie of stones thrown at her carriage.[34]

The polling continued reasonably peacefully for the remainder of the week and on the Friday, the fifth day of the election, Astley polled 3 more votes than Benett – the first time that he had overtaken his opponent. Throughout the following week no acts of violence were reported and, as before, at the end of each day the number of votes cast for each candidate to date was published and widely circulated. On Monday 2 August, it was announced that the poll would remain open until 3 o'clock on Wednesday – the last moment allowed by law. By now tension was mounting as it could be seen that, by the close of the poll at the end of the previous week, 4,303 votes had been cast, with Benett's majority over Astley amounting to only 143.

On the day before the close of the poll, there were several fracas at the malthouse, one rather ludicrously caused 'by a friend of Mr Benett parading the room with the sleeves of his coat turned inside out; this was resented by Mr Astley's partisans who hissed and pushed and hustled him from one end of the room to the other'. When Benett appeared with Lucy and William Wyndham's wife 'their husbands could not have been more grossly accosted by abuse of every kind than these ladies were'.[35] The poll closed at 7.30 in the evening and although Astley had polled 16 more votes than Benett on that day, Benett and his supporters must have known that victory was assured.

Wednesday was the day of triumph for Benett. As the poll closed, he was walking up and down the lane near the malthouse when his supporters rushed out with a view to chairing him to the *White Hart Inn*. He told them, of course, that this would not be appropriate until the High Sheriff had declared him the victor. He was shortly summoned indoors where the High Sheriff and the assessors were waiting to declare him the victor and to invest him with the sword and spurs of the new Knight of the Shire.

While Benett had been with the High Sheriff, his supporters had hoisted up a pole stating his majority of 166 and the words 'See the Conquering Hero Comes'. The band struck up the appropriate tune whereupon the procession, supposed to consist of no less than 5000 people, proceeded to the Market Place. Here Benett delivered another of his interminable speeches – this time, of course, to the cheers of the crowds, and in conclusion he:

> exhorted the vast multitude which was assembled before him to preserve peace, order and tranquillity; to show no insults to the adversaries whom they had defeated, but to take them by the hand, and conciliate their friendship. This was the part which he intended to act towards Major Astley; he had gone out of town that morning, or he (Mr Benett) would have gone, now that the contest was closed, and shaken him by the hand. He (Major Astley) was an honest man, but had erred in judgement: he should, therefore, the next time that he saw him offer him his hand as he would to a child who had unintentionally done him mischief. He concluded by exhorting his friends not to be found in the streets of Salisbury at a later hour than 10 o'clock.[36]

On 7 August, the *Morning Chronicle* carried a copy of a letter addressed by Benett to the freeholders of the county in the course of which he wrote:

> The glorious victory, which I owe to your virtuous exertions in the sacred cause of independence, is at length achieved, and I am placed in that elevated station to which I aspired upon no other principles than those which, I am sure you would finally approve, and dignify by your general sanction to obtain your favour has ever been the main ambition of my life.[37]

On the 12th, the *Devizes and Wiltshire Gazette* carried an article that was surely submitted by one of Benett's supporters living in the south of the county. It reads:

> After an unexampled contest for fifteen days, Mr Benett comes in M.P. for the county by a majority of 166. There is a wonderful similarity in this

contest to that of 1772. Pride, Purse and Prejudice, have been humbled by the Independent spirit of the County. And it is to be hoped that the freedom of the county now recovered will bring in an aera [*sic*] for another half a century. Our northern neighbours, who live at a great distance from the scene of the action, were roused the moment they heard of the unconstitutional proceedings on the day of Nomination, and at the commencement of the poll: and were resolved that the democratical mobs of Trowbridge, Bradford, Calne etc urged on by the ultra-aristocrats, who endeavoured to make them the tools of their ambition, should not carry the day. At the Close of the Poll, there were seven coaches of the Northern reserve.

May the Northern lights ever reflect the Freedom of Wiltshire. Let the freeholders remember this contest – that truth will at length beat down falsehood, – that it is more honourable to send their own member to Parliament at their own expense, than be sent up to the Poll to vote for a stranger at his.[38]

On the same day as this notice appeared, there was published *A Word at Parting being Algernon's Address to the Freeholders of the County of Wilts stating some of the occurrences at the late contest for the county, the characters of the contest considered, with opinion concerning the course of the event*.[39] No copy of this work, that was offered for sale at the price of 2s 6d, appears to have survived.

Following his victory, numerous dinners and other celebrations were held throughout the county. On 30 August, the annual Venison Dinner was held at Devizes at which Wellesley presided with Benett sitting as vice-president. Wellesley must have suffered some embarrassment as it was reported that 'unfortunately owing to some mistake of the former gentleman's game keeper, there was no venison provided'.[40] Doubtless Benett took secret delight in his rival's discomfiture! The Venison Dinners were provided at the expense of the county Members in order to give the freeholders an opportunity of meeting with their representatives in Parliament. Some indication of the animosity felt towards Benett in Trowbridge is afforded by his reference to the fact that he had been invited to and would liked to have attended the Venison Dinner in Trowbridge, but he had been informed that ' his presence would endanger the peace of the town and the safety of his friends'.

Knowing that Benett would not be present at the dinner in Trowbridge, his opponents took the opportunity in their speeches to launch a series of attacks on him and his supporters. Methuen revealed his true feelings when he said:

I will not say that I came here to meet Mr Benett: it would afford me no pleasure to meet that Gentleman. I cannot be a hypocrite; or to meet that man as a friend, who has either been a principal in the act, or has sanctioned by his agents the foulest calumnies against my character . . . could he have attained the temporary elevation he now enjoys had nothing but legal and constitutional means been resorted to? Are horses hoofs, bullies and bludgeons the instruments of purity of elections?

On the same occasion, Mr James Long said:

We opposed Mr Benett because we knew but little of him and what we did know of him was *bad*. He was an admirer of the horrors of the French revolution, and probably that induced him to try the experiment with the bludgeon men at the place of Poll. . . With regard to Mr Benett's religion . . . a statement . . . had already appeared in the public prints which shews the gross ignorance of Mr Benett with regard to the worship of the Established Church . . . When that beautiful and important portion of the morning service the *Te Deum* was about to be performed, *he did not know where to look for it.*[41]

On the same day that the Venison Dinner was held in Devizes, a public dinner was held in Salisbury for 300 of Benett's supporters, all no doubt at his considerable expense. The words of three glees with choruses and a song to be sung to the tune of 'Rule Britannia' were printed and distributed to the assembled company who, after a considerable amount of alcoholic refreshment, no doubt enjoyed celebrating Benett's victory with some hearty singing. The author or authors of the glees indulged in considerable flights of fancy by writing:

See! The Conquering Hero come!
Praise him in triumphal songs:
He hath matchless glory gained:
And hath Wiltshire's fame maintain'd.

Chorus

BENETT'S name to Wiltshire dear,
Conquering hero! Welcome here!

Groves of laurel round him rise,
Garlands stretch towards the skies.
The noble Patriot loudly greet,
BENETT'S name with joy repeat.

Chorus

BENETT'S name to Wiltshire dear,
Conquering hero! Welcome here![42]

And so on!

On the following day, 400 poor men, women and children were 'regaled at the malthouse with a profusion of viands left untouched at the preceding day's entertainment'. Benett and his wife Lucy were both present and 'ingratiated themselves much with their humble friends by paying them attention during their repast . . . and they seemed all fully convinced of the *falsehood* of that widely spread rumour that Mr Benett was not a friend of the poor'.[43] On this occasion in response to the toast to his wife's health, Benett said that she 'inherited her constitutional energy of character from her father Mr Lambert of Boyton; and then went on to relate how towards the close of the aforesaid election of 1772, Mr Lambert came to the rescue at the head of 500 freeholders, who at once placed Mr Goddard at the head of the poll, and secured the county's independence'.[44] No doubt Benett learned from his father-in-law's experience the utility of an organised *quasi* army of supporters in achieving victory in a contested election.

One particular song was published at this time, doubtless by Benett's supporters, and this quite amusingly describes how Methuen, Astley and Benett were thought of at the close of the election. *Victory or The Wiltshire Election* was printed by Harrisons of Devizes and intended to be sung to the tune of *Derry Down*:

The great Wiltshire Contest is ended at last,
And all the noise, nonsense, and hubbub is past;
So I'll sit in quiet and briefly recount,
The Events that were manifest near Sarum's Mount.
Tol de rol, lol, tol, tol de rol, lol,
tol de rol, lol de rol, lol de rol, lol.

Mr. Methuen retir'd, and trimm'd his cravat,
Yet looking askaunt for applause and éclat;
And raising his person in elegant style,
He deck'd his sweet face with a flowery smile.
Tol de rol, lol &c.

And first Major Astley was drawn o'er the course,
With blue and gold streamers to strengthen his force;
And crown'd with Nobility mountainous high,
While tag-rag and bob-tail resound to the sky.
Tol de rol, lol &c.

Of good Major Astley we'll say not a word,
His pledges of Honor, his glory of sword; -
Desertion in Friendship however array'd,
E'en in gossamer met it reflecteth a shade.
　　Tol de rol, lol &c.

And second, John Benett rode over the Plain,
Twelve hundred stout Horsemen appear'd in his train;
And boldly proclaim'd both by colours and shout,
They were not to be frighten'd by rabble or rout.
　　Tol de rol, lol &c.

Words, wagers, and warfare, like proud seas arose,
And those who were friends became deadliest foes;
The Head and the Bob-tail for Astley were strong,
But the strength of the body, has prov'd the head wrong.
　　Tol de rol, lol &c.

The hearts of true Wiltshire Men carried the day,
And Benett our chosen was then borne away;
With firmness, with honor, with Victory crown'd,
Our shouts my brave boys, shall old Stonehenge rebound.
　　Tol de rol, lol &c.

So now Major Astley pray make your best bow,
And take all those with you who kick'd up the row;
And when you shall venture on Salisbury Plain,
The staunch friends of Benett will meet you again.
　　Tol de rol, lol &c.[45]

Although the election was over, Benett was extremely irritated that many handbills containing what he considered to be libellous allegations were widely circulating and the newspapers were full of very extensive reports of the speeches made at a number of dinners and of letters from anonymous correspondents making all sorts of allegations against him. One handbill in particular caused him concern, which read:

CORN BILL
BE IT KNOWN
AND
LET IT NOT BE FORGOTTEN
THAT THE
C O R N B I L L

WOULD NEVER HAVE BEEN THOUGHT OF
BUT FOR
Mr. JOHN BENETT
BY WHOSE HARD
S W E A R I N G
PARLIAMENT was deceived into the
MEASURE[46]

Benett made it clear in the press that as the evidence he had given to the parliamentary select committee occurred, of course, when he had no vote in Parliament, the provisions of the corn laws should certainly not be laid at his door.

On 2 September, the *Devizes and Wiltshire Gazette* published a letter from an anonymous correspondent calling himself 'Q in the Corner' that articulated very clearly the animosity towards Benett felt by many people in the county. He wrote:

> . . . Now the people of this town of any note, are many of them great friends of Mr Benett; but yet Mr Astley was not afraid of a broken head, when he came to Devizes; and therefore there must be something, which makes the poor of the land unfriendly to the presence of Mr Benett. It is true that he says he lamented the low rates of wages and that 'the *poor man could not maintain his wife and two children on the present low wages!*' but this has nothing to do with it, unless he can prove that *he* always gave *high* wages . . . Did Mr Benett ever raise the wages of his mechanics or the labourers in his employ? Has he not rather reduced them all he can? . . . It seems therefore to me, Mr Editor, something very like hypocrisy for a man to talk in this way about the poor; as for saying that he was well respected in his neighbourhood, – I was in Tisbury the other day and * * * * !
>
> As to wishing that the poor in other districts might be as *well acquainted* with him as the poor in *his own* neighbourhood; I do think that they would rather *remain as they are* and request him to suspend his good intentions till he can *act* as well as *speak* like a Member of Parliament; and that will *never* be.[47]

So numerous and serious were the attacks on him and reported at great length in the newspapers, that he could not let them pass without some sort of response, and so, on 9 September, a letter from him was published in the *Devizes and Wiltshire Gazette*:

> I beg to call your attention to the Devizes Gazette of this and last week which is crowded in every column with the ravings of that combination of

persons, who, baffled in their attempts to render this County no better than a close Borough, have not the strength of mind to bear their disappointment with becoming fortitude, and therefore give vent to their feelings by pouring forth on my head every species of abuse, however low or improbable.

He explained that he did not attend the Venison Dinner in Trowbridge because:

> I would not again expose the lives of my friends to the violence of a drunken mob under the command of Mr Astley's agents, and I could not foresee the advantage which was taken of my absence; as I never by act or word, injured any of these Gentlemen who were present at that dinner, and there made such outrageous attacks on my character; and, in my speeches at the election dinners, I have always made a point to abstain as far as possible from mentioning my opponents, considering it as inconsistent with the character of a Gentleman to calumniate those who are precluded by absence from making any defence. [48]

He decided not to enumerate each of the individual allegations made against him save for two, one of which was perhaps quite serious and the other laughably trivial. The first charge, that he had rejoiced at the horrors of the French Revolution, he quite easily refuted. The other, that he had 'looked for the *Te Deum* in the wrong part of the Prayer Book', as he put it, he dealt with by condemning the person who would have spent his time observing such a thing during the course of Divine service. This letter did not prevent Methuen from continuing to condemn Benett's supporters. In a speech he delivered at a Venison Dinner held later in the month in Bradford he said:

> He [Benett] is the last man in the world that I would select for observation; he supported me at my first coming forward for the county. I expressed my gratitude for it; but does that expression of gratitude give Mr Benett's partizans a right to knock me down – to trample me under their feet – to pursue me with rancour and violence? From Mr Benett I could take much; I have no antipathy against him, but as for his clan (I beg to be understood here as only alluding to a part, and a small part, of his supporters) I shall always speak of them as I think of them.

Despite Methuen's assertion that he had no antipathy towards Benett, we know from his private letter to Lord Folkestone that this was not true, and these feelings undoubtedly stemmed from Benett's decision in the previous year to seek to enter Parliament in opposition to him and Wellesley.

On one occasion in September, the poor of Broadchalke were 'plentifully supplied with cheese, strong beer and cyder' followed by music and dancing[49] and in October, Benett attended a dinner at Devizes, in his speech making it clear that he was a friend of religious liberty and reform. At this dinner it was suggested that there were nine prisoners incarcerated in the Bridewell, one of whose debt was apparently incurred because he voted for Benett. A subscription was promptly raised to enable them all to be freed, with Benett making up the deficiency. On the Thursday following he visited Sherston. Two miles away he was met by a large body of freeholders bearing flags, and he entered the town with the bells ringing, and 200 freeholders then dined in the three inns.[50]

Benett made sure that his supporters were rewarded, and in particular Henry King of Chilmark, to whom he presented a silver claret jug engraved with the following inscription:

> This is to record the gallant and preserving conduct of Henry King, Esq., of Chilmark, who, in the years 1818 and 1819 rode for 25 days at the head of more than one thousand brave and independent horsemen, to support at the hustings the freedom of election, by defending the candidate of his and their choice from the personal violence of a misguided party. Their efforts secured the election of John Benett, Esq., on the 4th August, 1819, and the names of 'King and the Wiltshire Cossacks' will live in the hearts of all who value the independence of the County of Wilts, and be more imperishable than the metal on which this is inscribed – John Benett Esq., M.P., to his much esteemed friend, Henry King Esq., A.D.1819 [51]

Benett's sister Etheldred must have been relieved to be able to put the election behind her and once again address her mind to her geological interests. On 20 September, she wrote to Gideon Mantell:

> I have waited for a frank[52] from our new member to thank you for your two last obliging letters, and for the kind support which my Brother received from your Friends all of whom I believe were on our side. Mr. Robt. Strange of Devizes was one of my Brother's agents. You will have seen by the Papers what a protracted business it was, but it is not possible for you to form an idea of the anxiety and fatigue of it, the Election last year was nothing to it; Mr. Astley's Agents followed Wellesley's plan of attempting by violence what they could not carry by honest means, nor could we for a moment consider the Election safe untill [sic] it was actually declared; Mr. Astley is now doing all the mischief in his power by endeavouring to keep the County in so great a ferment as possible, and the consequence has already been a radical reform meeting of the Towns

of Bradford and Trowbridge, but fortunately having no leaders the People separated without mischief and though another meeting was talked of no day was fixed and it seems to die away. You will believe that amidst all this bustle Geology has been quite out of the question . . . I did hope to have set to work immediately after the Election but Wiltshire Elections do not now terminate with the close of the Poll, and the Paper war is still carried on with the utmost virulence by our opponents. . .[53]

Following the election, the Salisbury solicitor G.Butt, transcribed from the original poll book details of how the freeholders voted and the result, having been corrected by the Check Books of the candidates, was printed by Brodie and Dowding of Salisbury. From this it can be seen that, as one might have expected, Benett was widely, and in some areas almost unanimously, supported by the voters in the south-western corner of the county. In Tisbury, all 23 freeholders whose votes were accepted voted for him. They included, perhaps rather surprisingly, the Rev. Dr. Thomas Prevost, the vicar with whom Benett had crossed swords so recently over the question of tithes. However, when Joseph Green of Ansty attempted to vote for him he was rejected on the grounds that he was a Roman Catholic. In Semley, all 16 freeholders voted for him, except for two men named Bigg who lived in Bristol and voted for Astley. In Mere all 84 electors voted for him and in the hundred of Dunworth as a whole all but two did likewise.

While the votes of the clergy of the established church were almost evenly divided between Benett and Astley (with Archdeacon Coxe and the Dean of Salisbury not surprisingly voting for Astley), of the 36 dissenting ministers recorded, only 6 attempted to vote for Astley, and of these one withdrew his vote and another was rejected. It is not unlikely, therefore, that Benett received a large number of votes from dissenting freeholders that may have been decisive in securing his victory. One of Benett's more unusual supporters was a draper named Thomas Ellen who, as clerk to an Independent Meeting in Shaftesbury, was paid 40s a year out of land in Semley and whose vote was duly accepted.

The fact that the whole world could see how any man had voted led to some quite unexpected results. William Stagg, writing to the *Devizes and Wiltshire Gazette* in October, related that, having accepted an invitation to sit on Benett's election committee, he naturally then felt obliged to vote for him. For many years, he had been permitted by Astley's father to course at Everleigh and did not think that casting his vote against Astley would affect that arrangement. However, on 30 September he took his dogs on Collingbourne Down and 'started a hare when I was immediately served with a forbiddance, though not myself on Mr Astley's property'. This was signed by Astley himself. The writer of the letter concluded, 'I shall leave you and the Freeholders of Wilts to judge the motive for the forbiddance'.[54]

Public interest in the result of the election was such that James Gilmour, the Salisbury printer, produced for sale an elaborately designed record of each day's result with the final majority in Benett's favour printed in gold on a deep red background. Further, a meticulously worked sampler, showing the votes daily received by each of the candidates, has also survived.[55]

One writer must have enjoyed likening the contest to a day at the races and went to the trouble and expense of having his satirical composition printed and circulated. Doubtless many readers joined in the fun by reading about:

### The Wiltshire Races

Between Mr Benett: black horse, Farmer; rode by Mr Goodwill, Rider's Colour, Scarlet and Blue. Major Astley's brown horse, Lag; rode by Mr Everley, Colour of the Rider, Purple.

This wonderful Race was for the important Prize of a seat upon an old Bench, which had been in use for centuries, and is supposed to be lined with Gold and fringed with Place and Pension, and was to be decided in one Fifteen Mile Heat. Lag the favourite at starting, seven to four on Lag.

This astonishing Race took place on Monday the 19th July 1819, on the Plain of Wilton, but was removed for conveniency of running to Malt Downs near Salisbury; the Wood of the former Place having obstructed the fair Course of the Horses.

Farmer took the lead at starting, and kept it gaily for five Miles, till coming into Pound Note Valley, where Lag pushed hard to shoot ahead, and had at one Time positively got his Nose as far as Farmer's Flank; but Goodwill kept his horse close and steady, being confident in his great length and strength, he having rode him a breathing gallop on the same course against Welleslyan and Methuen Horses.

In coming up the steep Hill of Examination, Farmer shewed his Blood and Bottom to admiration, by beating Lag in prime stile in an easy Gallop, a whole Yard and a Distance[56]

The expense of the two elections was enormous and left Benett and Astley financially embarrassed. Lady Holland,[57] who, with her husband, supported Benett, said:

the expense of the contest will ruin both parties as they are merely country gentlemen of very moderate fortunes, and the whole of Benett's income is not sufficient to pay the interest of the debt he incurred in the last election.

She subsequently amended this to 'Astley has £100,000 in ready money and a good landed estate, Benett is a pauper'.[58] Methuen reckoned that Benett had spent £18,000 in 1818 and £35,000 in 1819, with only £8000 being subscribed for him.[59] In reality, Benett's expenditure far exceeded these amounts.

It is just as well that Astley had a 'good landed estate' as he was forced to sell nearly all his property in Staffordshire, Warwickshire and Shropshire to meet his expenses. These were said to amount to £100,000 with as much as £5000 being spent on ribbons for his supporters. However, he was able to retain his estates in Wiltshire and was rewarded with a baronetcy in 1821. Benett's persistent independence as well as relative poverty prevented any such honour being bestowed on him.

In an effort to reimburse Benett for some part of the huge sum of money he had spent, or had yet to spend, contributions were sought from his well-wishers. On 16 August it was reported :

> We are informed that the subscriptions towards defraying Mr Benett's expenses in that contest for the representation of Wilts are going on very successfully in every part of the county. One subscription is of so peculiar a nature, that it is worth recording. On the 9th instant, the sum of £200 was paid to Messrs Stephensons, Remington & Co by Messrs Sykes & Co by 'A Friend to Independence on account of Benett's committee'.[60]

This contribution, although substantial and equivalent to perhaps £6000 in 21st century terms, would have had to have been repeated very many times to make any material contribution to Benett's expenses.

John Tinney, who acted as Benett's chief election agent, was undoubtedly involved in negotiating the payment of large sums of money on his behalf and attempted to reduce the amount to be paid where possible. A Bath attorney named Boord was employed to canvass any voters who might have been in Bath, and he claimed £197. His claim was heard at the Assizes held in Salisbury in July 1822 and, according to one report, 'so zealous was Mr Boord for Mr Benett that one of his clerks perished from exertion'![61] His counsel declared that:

> the day of success and triumph was indeed a glorious one to Mr Benett but the day of payment had now arrived, which is indeed a dark and

dismal one, considering the vast and enormous expense the defendant had been put to.

Benett adopted a lofty position and said that he relied on his professional advisers as to what should be paid. After a few minutes consideration, the jury awarded Boord damages of £140.[62]

Boord's claim was not the last to be made against him arising out of the election. At the end of 1823, Benett's friend and stalwart supporter, John Peniston of Salisbury, was writing to Newman and Sons, presumably a firm of solicitors:

> I was surprised at the receipt of your letter never having heard of your client's claim nor aware of any committee of Mr Benett's being in existence since the close of his election in 1819. I immediately waited on that Gentleman with your letter who stated that he would give immediate directions to his agents, Messrs Bowles and Chitty of Shaftesbury to have the claim examined [and] paid.[63]

Now aged 46, Benett duly took his seat in Parliament and immediately voted against the Address. On 30 November, he voted for Lord Althorp's[64] motion for a committee on the state of the nation and on that day made his maiden speech. That he should be on his feet so soon after entering the House demonstrates the level of his confidence, and willingness and ability to make his mark in Parliament. Before the House were measures proposed by the Government to control the widespread disorder and unrest occurring throughout the country. Benett said that he rose with considerable diffidence to address the House but considered it his duty to express his sentiments. He agreed that there were many proofs of sedition in the north of the country but doubted that there was sufficient call for such strong measures as would affect the liberties of the whole kingdom. Benett's view was that although the delay in granting Parliamentary reform was in part responsible for causing disorder, the main reason was the poverty and distress of the people. When men were in a state of want, and almost of starvation, their complaints ought surely to be heard. Every person knew that the people were all but starving, and that starving people are the readiest to receive the poison of mountback orators. So far as the county that he had the honour to represent was concerned, provisions were low but there was no money to buy them, and no opportunity of procuring any by employment. Instead of passing any coercive measures, the Government ought to devise some means of procuring food for the people.[65] He addressed the House again on 7 December in a debate on the Seditious Meetings Prevention Bill when he said that he hoped that three years would be sufficient for the operation of the measures proposed and trusted that a Select Committee would be appointed to consider the distress of the country and propose some relief. He soon demonstrated his independence by voting against the bill on the grounds that this bill, together with the other six bills introduced by the Government to define the powers of the local executive, was an unwarranted attack on the liberty of the subject.

At last, therefore, Benett had succeeded in securing a Parliamentary seat. However, his performance in the House did not meet with the approval of all of his friends. His neighbours and life long friends, the Grove family of Ferne, appear to have taken exception to his opinions and the way in which he voted, and Charlotte Grove recorded in her diary that 'he [her friend John Still] perfectly coincides with me in regard to Mr Benett's conduct in the House of Commons',[66] and, as would soon be apparent, her father demonstrated his disapproval in a very public way. The political differences between the Pythouse and Ferne families appear to have brought their friendly relations to an end, for a while at least.

However, within less than six months disaster struck. In January 1820 George III died and as a consequence Parliament would be dissolved. Benett was now faced with the daunting task of fighting yet another election. Two contested elections in consecutive years were an unusual occurrence, but three in a row would be almost unprecedented. The enormous cost was certainly more that a man of Benett's means could stand. In the previous elections his friends and supporters had given some financial support, and now they were to be asked to do the same once more.

It was rumoured that Benett would not be seeking re-election, but a letter published on 14 February in the *Salisbury and Winchester Journal*[67] and on the following day, somewhat surprisingly, in the *Morning Chronicle*,[68] published in London, made it clear that he would indeed be standing. Astley had already given notice that he would be a candidate, as had Wellesley, and so another ruinously expensive contest seemed likely. As soon as Benett knew that Parliament would be dissolved following the King's death, he began writing to men of influence throughout the county canvassing their support. Many replies were received and most of them pledged support for him.[69]

Benett's sister Etheldred also did everything she could to help, but the two letters she wrote to him from Norton Bavant in February demonstrate most graphically the concern she felt about the turn of events and the difficulties that yet another contested election would present:

My dear John

I have no doubt of your success if your votes can be got to the Poll but how that is to be accomplished God knows; if you attempt to carry them nothing can save you from utter ruin; no friend of yours can wish you to spend a shilling for they must know the failure of the subscription at both last Elections has already thrown an overwhelming debt upon your property, and one that you will never see cleared as long as you live. We are out every day, people are evidently pleased with our calling but it is evident that they expect it as a matter of course, your interest in this neighbourhood as everywhere else is much improved. Mr Henry Wansey junr[70] is much pleased with your Parliamentary conduct and is in consequence actively canvassing for you, he has much influence with the little voters in Warminster where he told me you had upwards of twenty more than last year . . . Mr H. Wansey told us Mr Rogers of Berkeley is against you on the old story of the Tithe business and as he has much influence round Berkeley it would be adviseable to get somebody to choak him off such a stale subject . . . Wellesley did not get out of his coach at Warminster and the Horses were ordered for Rood Ashton so he has been consulting the Longs, his Delicacy would not permit him to canvass till after the Royal Funeral, we have no doubt of his standing if possible . . . but the Wellesley interest is certainly at a very low ebb in Warminster your friends had heard of only five who had the least idea of voting for him.

And on 22 February, she wrote:

Of course you have seen Wellesley's advertisement which some of your friends here begin to hope was letting himself down easy and that he would retreat from the Poll, but yesterday I met Mr Starr in Warminster who has lately been in various parts of the county and being Astley's tenant was more likely to hear the truth than those openly attached to your cause alone, that he is strongly supported by the Government interest which is silently at work for him in every direction and that they are determined to bring in two Ministerial Members if possible, he therefore desired me when I wrote to tell you this that you must not be thrown off your guard by any thing that might appear in the papers for that it was certainly necessary for your friends to keep on the alert. We dined at Mr John Everett's yesterday, Mr Wyndham called there in the morning on his way home from Mr Heathcote's near Melksham, while at Mr Heathcote's he called on Richard Long who told him that Wellesley had asked him (Richard Long) to nominate him, which he has positively refused to do . . . it is agreed on all hands that the Mobility are more come round to your side but the Masters still remain inflexible.[71]

After the expense of the two earlier elections, Benett was certainly in no position to fight another unaided, and so on 28 February a notice appeared announcing that a meeting would be held at the *Bear Inn* in Devizes to consider and adopt such measures as might be necessary to secure his re-election.[72] At this meeting, chaired by William Wyndham, a subscription was opened for raising the enormous sum of £20,000 or such less sum as might be necessary.[73] He also had the support of Lord Holland[74] who wrote:

> In consequence of your steady and independent opposition in Parliament to the unnecessary and unconstitutional measures of the last short session I beg you to accept my best wishes for your success at the ensuing election in Wiltshire. If this letter or anything else in my power can be of service to you I will thank you to write. . .[75]

Benett continued writing to as many people as he could seeking their support. For instance, on 7 February he wrote to George Purefoy Jervoise who, until recently, had served as one of the Members of Parliament for Salisbury. Although Jervoise had voted for Benett in both the 1818 and 1819 elections and so was likely to do the same again, he was taking nothing for granted when he wrote:

> I expect shortly to be engaged in another contest for the representation of this county. Mr Astley commenced an active canvass by himself and agents a week ago, and Mr Wellesley's friends are doing the same. My Parliamentary duty will not allow me time to make a personal canvass but my friends are in many places performing that duty for me, and with great success. My interest in the manufacturing districts is much improved which with the powerful support which was given me on the last occasion can leave no doubt on my mind of ultimate success. May I request the favour of you again to give me your support which will add much to the great obligation which I feel I now am under to you.[76]

On 13 February, Benett wrote to Lord Holland to thank him for his support and for his approval of his conduct in Parliament on the various repressive measures:

> I agree with your lordship in considering those measures unnecessary and unconstitutional. And, further, I believe the tendency of some of them to be exceedingly dangerous, for by the restraints they impose on the public and constitutional meetings, they point out to the disaffected the only effectual mode of executing their dangerous purposes.[77]

Shortly afterwards, he wrote to James Crowdy, one of his supporters and a solicitor in Highworth in the north of the county:

> I have been so much engaged in writing and other matters regarding the threatened contest that I have not had time to inform you how assurances are in respect to it.
>
> I have not attempted a personal canvass for two reasons, first because my parliamentary duty would not allow the time to compleat it, and secondly I did not consider it quite correct to do so till after the royal funeral.
>
> My agents and friends have however canvassed the whole county most actively and it appears that my interest is being much increased. The manufacturing towns are now almost wholly with myself or Mr Astley as far as I can learn. Mr Astley's canvass has been and continues to be carried on with much activity, but I cannot hear of anything being done for Mr Wellesley, though some of his agents I find have declared his intention of again offering himself .
>
> I certainly shall stand alone, and not interfere in regard to either of the other parties. I shall ever be very cautious how I trust anyone in election matters. There cannot be any doubt as to the result of this election, though it would be much better to have a quiet one.
>
> I shall go to London tomorrow to No. 7 Clevedon Row, St.James. The moment Parliament is dissolved, which I expect will be within a month, I shall return and will then wait on my friends at Highworth who have in two contests already supported me nobly.
>
> I hope you will excuse me till that time, and believe me, my dear sir
> I remain your faithful and obedient servt.
> John Benett
> I beg you will give my best regards to all your family.[78]

When a letter from a 'Loyal Freeholder' appeared in the *Devizes and Wiltshire Gazette* on 2 March inviting the readers 'to see what Mr Benett has done . . . he certainly has voted through thick and thin for the Radicals, and I sincerely trust the loyal freeholders will put it out of his power to do further mischief',[79] they must have thought that this was the first of many letters that would appear in the county newspapers, either extolling or denigrating the qualities of the hopeful rivals for the two county seats seats.

Numerous printed notices would also be expected to appear and one, addressed to the 'Independent Freeholders of the County of Wilts' by 'A real Friend of the Cause of Constitutional Independence', after suggesting that it was well known that both Wellesley and Astley, as soon as they had been elected in 1818, became a members of the Beckhampton club declared that:

> It is also *notorious*, that the members of that Club, who for many years appointed Representatives for this County, have been supporters both of Mr Long Wellesley and Major Astley, in whose persons they are endeavouring to re-establish the system of dictating Members to the County, which was broken through by *Mr Methuen*, and for which if for nothing else, he is entitled to your thanks. Resist, brother Freeholders this attempt, this coalition of Clubites, redouble the exertions you so gloriously and effectually made for Benett and Independence in 1819, and have at least One Representative of your own choosing.[80]

One song that was printed and circulated, possibly at this time, is worthy of note in that it attempts to identify policies that the writer thought Benett supported:

A New Song written by A Shearman
Who has been for a long time out of
Employ owing to Gigs[81] and Frames

JOHN BENETT is a hero bold
of noble enterprise
For if you do but hear him speak
'Twill make your courage rise.

Chorus

And if he do but gain our trade
'Twill fill our hearts with joy
For Gigs and Frames to be put down
Then we shall have employ.

Then our poor wives and children too
We'll leap and sing and say
God bless JOHN BENETT of Pyt House
For him we'll ever pray.

For W – s – y L – g and A – l- y too
They are no friends of we,
For lately in the House L – g said
That no Reform should be.

We have a vote – we have a voice –
And we'll do all we can

That we may keep JOHN BENETT still
An INDEPENDENT MAN.[82]

The author of this song was right in thinking that Benett was a supporter of reform, but mistaken in believing that he would be able, or indeed willing, to do anything to halt the progress of industrial mechanisation.

Benett's relief must have been immense when, early in March, Wellesley informed the freeholders that:

> After a dispassionate examination of the consequences naturally arising from a contest for the Representation of the County, I find that to secure my availing of the great majority of the voters ready to poll in my favour, would be attended by an indefinite expense; I am therefore reluctantly compelled to relinquish the honour of continuing, now, to be your Representative.[83]

Wellesley's financial position was desperate and so he had no alternative but to withdraw. Indeed, two years later, he and his wife and children had to flee to France to avoid his creditors.[84] Some time after, having given an account of a duel that Wellesley had recently fought in Calais, the *Devizes and Wiltshire Gazette* reported that the duel 'completely exonerates the former gentleman (i.e. Wellesley) from a charge made by some of his Wiltshire friends, at a time when there was some misunderstanding between Mr Benett and Mr Wellesley'.[85] Neither the nature of the charge nor of the misunderstanding, is recorded. According to Wellesley's obituary published in the *Morning Chronicle* after his death in 1857, he was 'redeemed by no single virtue and adorned with no single grace'![86]

On 2 March, the High Sheriff, Ambrose Goddard,[87] gave notice that a Special County Court, would be held on 14 March at Wilton in accordance with tradition and where the election would be held. There had been very little time, of course, for canvassing or for a large number of letters to be published in the newspapers circulating in the county as had occurred in 1818. One notable letter, addressed to 'A Freeholder of the County of Wilts', was, however, published in the *Salisbury and Winchester Journal* and widely circulated as an election broadsheet. This was from the celebrated preacher Rowland Hill,[88] who wrote from Surrey Chapel in London when it was thought that there would be a contested election:

> As MR BENETT has so fully proved himself a decided friend to Religious Liberty, and is by no means to be registered among the mock patriots of

the day, as a wanton oppositionist to the Government without any just or weighty cause: indeed, as he votes in Parliament free and independent of any party designs, such are the persons we want to protect our civil and religious rights according to the frame of *our most excellent* constitution, and such are the characters on whom alone we can depend for the national prosperity of our Country.

Under these principles I shall be happy to give *Mr Benett* my warmest support. LIBERTY *without* LICENTIOUSNESS *I believe to be the rational principles which guide his mind.*

I am happy a full refutation of the calumny of his hard heartedness to the Poor has been effected. How is it possible that a Man of his principles can be cruel to the Poor, while especially as a Member of Parliament, he should be looked up to as a legitimate defender of their cause?

It is much to be lamented that any Gentlemen should suffer so sorely for their services in Parliament on our behalf, when Sir William Guise was returned for Gloucestershire, in many districts the voters were sent up without any expense to the Member, while others were mean enough to make Sir Wm pay heavily for their favors; . . . it is to be hoped that Mr Benett will meet with many such liberal and patriotic electors through the County of Wilts'.[89]

On the day of the election, a very large crowd of people accompanied the candidates from Salisbury to Wilton. Benett's election committee knew that enormous numbers of people would be expected and so engaged in a little of what we would now call crowd or traffic management by issuing a notice to:

inform the friends of Mr Benett who intend accompanying him to Wilton that the procession will move from St Anne's St at 9.30 am. To avoid confusion it is requested that Gentlemen who are on horseback will form in Brown St facing towards St Anne's St; those on foot will assemble in St Anne's St. COLOURS will be worn on that day.[90]

The candidates and their supporters arrived at Wilton with Benett's procession consisting of more than a thousand of his friends (probably led by Henry King) and more than twenty carriages. Benett was proposed by Abraham Ludlow[91] and Astley by Benett's old friend and neighbour Thomas Grove. Grove did not approve of Benett's conduct in the last Parliament, and his daughter Charlotte recorded in her diary on 4 March that her father would be voting for Astley rather than Benett.[92] In the event, it was not necessary for him to vote at all because, as expected, no other nomination was forthcoming, and therefore Benett and Astley were duly elected Knights of the Shire. Benett then addressed the multitude and was greeted with 'long and continued applause'. How different from so many of his earlier appearances before the electors of the county. He concluded his lengthy speech, after referring to the contests of the previous years, by declaring, 'If you cannot forget, forgive as I do . . . I entreat all parties to forgive. Let there no longer be 'No Benett, No Astley' but ' Benett and Astley'.

In the Assembly Rooms in Salisbury on the same day, more than 300 people sat down to dinner with Benett sitting on the High Sheriff's right and Astley on his left, and it was reported that the friends of the new members decorated with their respective colours sat intermixed at the tables and the utmost harmony and conviviality prevailed![93]

Following the election Lord Malmesbury wrote to his son ' . . . the election is also over in Wiltshire – but Benett is such a strange man that he will keep up the spirit of animosity as long as he can'.[94] Quite what Malmesbury had in mind is not clear, but what is known is that any personal differences he might have had with his erstwhile friend, Astley, were soon forgotten. At the end of the month it was reported that:

> Mr Benett yesterday paid a visit to his friends in the neighbourhood of Melksham and thanked them for their support during the late contests. His arrival was announced by the ringing of bells etc. Mr Benett has indeed (says our informant) been actively engaged since his re-election in thanking his friends generally throughout the county and has everywhere been received with the most marked respect.[95]

In the following month a meeting of freeholders was held in Devizes, at which a number of resolutions were passed, including:

> That in our opinion the Freeholders who participate in the present Glorious Triumph, ought to participate in the heavy expenses by which it was achieved – expenses which far exceed all previous calculations – over which Mr Benett never presumed to exercise any control, – but without which, his success could not have been ensured
> That a subscription be now opened to answer those expenses. . .[96]

It is unlikely that any material sums of money were received, and some years later an elector, in a letter addressed to Lord Radnor,[97] asserted that 'the *loudest* talkers contributed the least towards Mr Benett's expenses on a former occasion, which he and his family will feel to the end of their days'.[98]

# 5

## His early years in Parliament, Friendship with Thomas Moore, Purchase of Fonthill Abbey and the Death of his Wife, 1820-1829

In the 1820 Parliament, Benett voted for the Whig opposition, while Astley voted for the Government. When the state of agriculture, and the Corn Laws in particular, was being debated Benett was a prominent speaker in the House, and extracts from his speeches were reported *verbatim* in the newspapers of the county so no one need be unaware of his opinions. According to his obituary, 'he was returned to Parliament as a Whig of the old school but all his predilections were of a truly Conservative character. . . and on all occasions resisted in the most determined manner any relaxation of the protective duties on corn'.[1] Although Benett held himself out as independent, all Members of Parliament at this time were in reality independent in that there was no party organisation as we understand it today. However, many Members made a practice of supporting either the Government of the day or the body of Members who opposed it. Benett, however, always voted as he thought would be in the best interests of the country – and of the people of Wiltshire in particular. Nevertheless, as a rule, Benett was considered to be a Whig. The Whigs in general stood for Catholic emancipation and for electoral reform, both matters of principle that had Benett's support; in 1823 the *Devizes and Wiltshire Gazette* referred to his Whig principles and 'zeal for Catholic Emancipation'.[2] It is more than likely that his feelings of tolerance towards Roman Catholics stemmed from the presence of his neighbours the Arundells at nearby Wardour, and the fact that there were more Catholics in Tisbury and the surrounding parishes than in any other part of Wiltshire. Indeed by 1839 more than three-quarters of all the county's Roman Catholics were his near neighbours.[3]

In 1829, the Roman Catholic Relief Act, that had, of course, Benett's wholehearted support, was passed, and in the following year

John Peniston of Salisbury, who was a prominent Roman Catholic, was writing to Benett:

> I am glad to learn Lord Arundell has been with you. The pleasure of such a meeting I am sure must have been mutual, and I sincerely join you in the gratifying feelings his friends must experience on such a man resuming his hereditary rights. I should be laughed at were I to express my feelings in becoming a really free man. It was easy for those who felt no privation to consider ours imaginary.[4]

During the course of both the 1818 and 1819 election campaigns, Benett's Christian beliefs were called into question. It was rumoured that he was an atheist and that he had not been seen in church since he was High Sheriff,[5] although another said that he knew that was false, 'for I saw him myself, *with my own eyes*, within these six months'.[6] Whatever his beliefs may have been, a curious event took place in the church at Norton Bavant on 22 July 1820. For on that day his eldest daughter, the 17-year-old Lucy, and her sisters Etheldred and Anna Maria and her brothers John and Thomas were all baptised together! Surely he cannot have failed to remember that Lucy and the two boys had already been baptised in the usual way as infants at Pythouse and Etheldred and Anna Maria had likewise been baptised as infants, in their case in London at St. George's Hanover Square![7]

Following the 1820 election, as a county Member of Parliament, the pattern of Benett's life was quite dramatically transformed. Before standing for Parliament in 1818, he was not particularly prominent in public life. However, on 24 July 1820 he sat for the first time as a member of the Grand Jury at the assizes held in Salisbury and not only as a member, but as the foreman[8] – a post he was to hold for many years to come. The Grand Jury always consisted of prominent landowners and so it a surprise to find that he had not exercised this judicial function before this time.

As the senior county Member, he took the chair at the annual Venison Dinner held in Devizes in August. The dinner, according to the *Devizes and Wiltshire Gazette*, was 'certainly a public one open to every freeholder who may choose to attend; and if we mistake not, the original intention of it was to give the representatives of the county an opportunity to annually meet their constituents'. It is, perhaps, surprising that only 15 freeholders chose to attend the dinner provided at the expense of the Members. In response to the toast to the independence of the county, Benett observed that there was not a more independent county in the kingdom – nor more independently represented.[9]

To hold a county meeting was an accepted and popular way of drawing the wishes of the people to the attention of the legislature and so, following the death of George III, a county meeting was held at Devizes, at which the Earl of Pembroke proposed and Benett seconded a resolution that a loyal address be sent to the new King. His speech (in which he referred to the 'pathetic and eloquent appeal with which Lord Pembroke had introduced the Address') was followed by speeches from the Marquis of Lansdowne and the Duke of Somerset.[10] A more controversial meeting was held there in the following January. The trial of Queen Caroline had generated an immense amount of sympathy for her and, as a result, another county meeting was held there to 'consider the propriety of declaring their unabated and unalterable attachment to the Constitution and of expressing their regret at the late unconstitutional proceedings against the Queen and of petitioning both Houses of Parliament to take the most effectual measures for the removal of every obstacle to a satisfactory and final arrangement and to prevent a recurrence to measures of a similar tendency, and the revival of discussions equally mischievous to the public morals and dangerous to the peace of the county'. It was reported that 10,000 people were present and that the windows of all the houses in the market place were crowded with 'ladies of respectability, presenting a rare assemblage of elegance and beauty'![11] Doubtless it was necessary for Benett to employ all his skills as a public orator in addressing such a multitude, that was so peaceful and approving of the purpose of the meeting that it was not necessary for a single special constable to be sworn in to keep the peace. Benett said that he was happy to present the petition in support of the Queen because he thought the proceedings against her, 'unjust, impolitic, and inconsistent, and last, not least, because they were directed against a woman'. Shortly after the meeting, the petition, signed by the High Sheriff and 100 freeholders, in which it was prayed that 'the House would use its efforts to put a termination to the odious and uncalled for proceedings against the Queen', was duly presented to the House by Benett.[12]

In April a meeting of freeholders who had supported Benett in his struggle to enter and remain in Parliament was held, and a number of resolutions were passed including one that declared:

> That in our opinion the Freeholders who participate in the present Glorious Triumph, ought to participate in the heavy expenses by which it was achieved – expenses which far exceed all previous calculations over which Mr Benett never presumed to exercise any control, – but without which, his success could not have been ensured.[13]

Another resolution was passed that a subscription be opened to answer those expenses. It is unlikely that any very material sums were raised to relieve Benett from the burden of debt that he now carried.

In May 1820, having sided with the opposition on the civil list, Benett presented a petition signed by 6000 clothiers and clothworkers, as well as eleven magistrates. It complained of the number of manufacturers who, in consequence of the introduction of machinery, and other causes, had been driven out of work and were compelled to have recourse to parochial relief.[14] While Benett surely regretted that men were reduced to having to apply for parish relief, he was doubtless realistic enough to know that there was nothing Parliament could do to prevent the inevitable development and utilisation of new methods of production. Two days later in a debate on the criminal laws, Benett said that although the shocking punishment of embowelling and quartering persons convicted of treason could no longer be imposed, the power of mutilating the bodies of such persons after death still remained in the hands of the executive authority. It seems that such an uncivilised practise had recently occurred and so he urged that steps be taken to prevent it.[15] At the end of the month, he was appointed to a select committee on agricultural distress, in June he voted for a reduction in the standing army, and he was in the House and voted on a number of occasions in July.

Henry Hunt, whilst languishing in Ilchester gaol, published a number of letters '*To The Radical Reformers, Male and Female of England, Ireland, and Scotland*' and in them continued with his vendetta against Benett. In December 1820 he wrote:

Let us now change the scene. What a pretty mess the CORN-BILL Gentry are got into! Ha! Ha! Ha! It is impossible not to laugh at the ridiculous figure they cut. . . Will any kind friend in Wiltshire inform me what is become of Mr. John Benett, of Pyt-house, the great CORN-BILL champion? I cannot help laughing at his dupes, his gulls, the Wiltshire yeomanry: they have sent him to parliament as a member for their county! Oh, how he is laughing in his sleeve at them! I heard one booby said, in Devizes market, that now they had got Hunt in prison, and BENETT, in parliament, the price of corn would soon get up again. We all know what is become of Mr.WEBB HALL. Oh how quiet and snug he is with his large salary as Secretary to the Board of Agriculture! Hunt, the great opponent of the CORN-BILL is in jail; JOHN BENETT and WEBB HALL are the great champions for the measure; the one of these is in parliament, and the other has 500l. a year as Secretary to the Board of Agriculture; each has his SOP, and both are silenced. Ha! ha! ha![16]

The readers of the *Devizes and Wiltshire Gazette* would, perhaps, have been surprised to read in August that at the annual meeting of the Wilts Auxiliary British and Foreign Bible Society, 'Mr Benett and Mr Astley, members for the County, enlivened the meeting by their excellent and appropriate addresses'.[17] While Astley was a well known churchman, Benett was certainly not noted for his support of religious organisations of any kind, although he did attend, with Astley, the annual meeting of the society in 1822 when, 'Mr Benett M P was one of those who gave their able assistance'.[18] It is likely that as Benett knew that Astley would be attending these meetings to support the society, he felt that he should do likewise. His attendances were very nearly the only times he showed any interest in societies with a religious flavour. Apart from the support that he gave to the parish churches of Tisbury and Norton Bavant (in which he had, of course, a particular interest), his name was always conspicuous by its absence from the lists of subscribers to appeals of a religious nature. For instance, when, in 1815, a list was published of the names of virtually every person of substance in the county who subscribed to a fund for the furtherance of the 'Distribution of Bibles, Testaments, Prayer Books, and small Religious Tracts, to the Poor', Benett's name was not to be found amongst them.[19]

In February 1821, Benett was addressing the House once again, after a Member named Palmer had complained that, for the last three years, he had been attempting to have his name put on the commission for Wiltshire (i.e. to act as a magistrate), and had made his application through Benett to the Lord Lieutenant. Benett's response was one that must have been repeated many times before and since – that he had written to the clerk to the Lord Lieutenant with Palmer's request but had received no reply to his letter![20] It is likely that suggestions were being made that the Lord Lieutenant had not acted entirely impartially in this matter, as shortly afterwards a letter was published, signed by no less than 80 Wiltshire magistrates. It stated that 'having heard with regret certain insinuations of political partiality in your official character as Lord Lieutenant have been openly made against your Lordship, they aver their conviction that it was impossible that any decision of yours, in your official capacity, could have been influenced by the slightest bias of political partiality'.[21] It is significant that Benett's name is not amongst the signatories to this letter.

As during February Benett was in London attending the House, he would have been near at hand when his wife Lucy gave birth to a daughter at 36 Berkeley Square, the residence of Lady Glynne.[22] This child, given the name of Frances at her baptism at Tisbury in the following month, but always known as Fanny, was destined to be the only one of Benett's children to outlive him. In years to come she was to be her father's favourite daughter, and his companion at Pythouse during the last years of his life. In the following month it was reported that he was one of those who attended a 'grand dinner' given by the Marquis and Marchioness of Lansdowne at Lansdowne House in Berkeley Square. Here he would have met his fellow Wiltshiremen Lord Folkestone[23] and Lord Arundell as well as Lord Nugent,[24] the Member of Parliament for Aylesbury, and many others.[25]

In March, Benett presented to Parliament a petition on the subject of agricultural distress, and another similar petition from the eastern part of Wiltshire, both of which were ordered to be printed.[26] As a well known expert on agricultural and country matters, he was probably listened to with some attention when in April, on the second reading of the Malt Duties Repealed Bill that had his hearty support, he said that it was time for the landowners to take the cause of agricultural distress into their own hands and to endeavour to accomplish their own relief.[27] Three days later he was speaking again on a motion for a committee to enquire into the state of the game laws. These old laws were so anachronistic that, as Lord Cranborne[28] said in the debate, in some cases a son was qualified to shoot game (presumably because he was the owner of the estate in which the game was to be found) but the father was not. Benett considered that poaching was the parent of every crime and he proposed that, by making game cheap, the result would be that it would not be worthwhile for the poacher to steal it. In April and again in June, Benett was on his feet supporting a motion that there should be a repeal of the tax on horses engaged in agriculture.[29] On 18 April, in a debate on parliamentary reform, he said that he hoped to see the time when the House of Commons would once more represent the people, and when seats should not any more be sold like cattle in the market. He said the sale of seats was arranged upon a scale of such systematic corruption, that they brought different prices according to the freedom of voting.[30]

In April 1821 he was attending a dinner at the Council Chamber in Salisbury, and on the same day a Ball and Supper at Devizes for 160 people to celebrate the King's Birthday.[31] Later in the year he spoke at the annual dinner of the Wiltshire Society at the *Albion Tavern* in Aldersgate Street in London, when the Duke of Somerset presided with Benett on his right and Astley on his left.[32] This society was formed to raise donations and annual subscriptions for the purpose of apprenticing the children of poor persons from Wiltshire living in London, and also for lending them money at the expiration of their apprenticeship to establish them in business, 'if their conduct shall have been meritorious'. In the following year Benett was appointed the sixth president of the society.

The conduct of members of Parliament was constantly under the scrutiny of the public and, when it fell short of what was expected of them, they could expect their perceived shortcomings to be the subject of critical letters to the press. Benett was, therefore, perhaps not surprised to read in the press at the beginning of May a letter boldly headed, 'To JOHN BENETT, Esq. M.P.' The correspondent, signing himself 'with infinite respect and deference, YOUR SINCERE FRIEND' opened his letter by saying that he had 'narrowly watched' Benett's conduct since he had been in Parliament and was of the opinion that he had frequently given his vote *unthinkingly*. His complaint was that Benett appeared to vote for all manner of matters to be referred to a committee as 'a convenient and easy answer'. A 'sober, a considerate, and an intelligent member of Parliament' before he votes for a committee should be convinced not only of a grievance but also of the practicability of applying a remedy.[33] One wonders whether Benett's sincere friend appreciated that in numerous instances the whole House sat as a committee in order to debate prospective legislation.

In July, Benett was in Norfolk attending the celebrated Holkham Sheep Shearing meeting held at Holkham Hall, seat of Thomas Coke. He, as a member of Parliament for Norfolk, a renowned agriculturalist, and a protectionist who favoured parliamentary reform, had a great deal in common with Benett. The meeting was attended by the Duke of Sussex,[34] 6th son of George III, and at the dinner at the end of the first day, Coke proposed Benett's health 'whom he was glad to see here, as he was deprived of that pleasure two years since, when Mr Benett was suddenly called away, as an election was about to take place in his county, to the freeholders of which he intended to offer himself and he (Mr Coke) was glad to see that gentleman at Holkham as representative for Wiltshire, and as independent a man as ever'.[35] In the course of his speech in response, Benett entered into a defence of the breeding of merino sheep, declaring them to be more profitable than Southdowns. Merino rams had been imported in an attempt to save the Wiltshire horned sheep, but the lambs were born at least a month too early, and Benett's confidence in their merits proved to be ill-founded, as by 1844 there was reported to be no Merino blood left in Wiltshire.[36]

*John Bull* thought the Annual Holkham Sheep Shearing complete 'Humbug'! It noted that Benett was one of the 'celebrated farmers and agriculturalists' present and asked 'how much this anniversary has to do with agriculture and how much with politics and are there people to be found who will believe that the Duke of Sussex would travel to Norfolk to look at fat beasts, or Mr Joseph Hume[37] leave his trade of 'cutting up' Ministers to inspect wethers and ewes'.[38] Whilst Benett doubtless found it useful to meet politicians and other influential people at these meetings, there can be no doubt that his interest in the practice and theory of agriculture was the prime reason for his attendance at them.

In the previous year he had attended the Merino Spring Show in London, and in responding to a toast to his health, he observed that he was a very old member of the society though latterly had seldom been able to attend. At the end of a characteristically long speech he said that there never was so happy a prospect of entire success and important national advantage from this race of sheep (i.e. Merinos); it was especially a great satisfaction to see such beautiful and valuable carcasses.[39] In May 1821, he once again attended the Merino Show at Aldgridge's Repository in St Martin's Lane. At the dinner at the end of the second day attended by the Duke of Norfolk[40] and Thomas Coke amongst others, he demonstrated his interest and expertise by saying 'a few words in defence of exhibiting the sheep lean, which, from their age and folding, must necessarily be so; observing that though the wool might be injured by great poverty, it was not hurt by that degree of leanness consistent with wholesome working conditions'.[41]

In 1813 the *Salisbury and Winchester Journal* had reported that Benett's friend John Gale Everett of Heytesbury 'possesses such a choice stock of Merino sheep, that he has actually refused to take One thousand pounds, which have been offered him for 60 of them by a gentleman of great agricultural repute in this county'.[42] In the light of Benett's enthusiasm for the breed and the fact that by 1813 he had certainly acquired a considerable reputation as an agriculturalist, it is tempting to think that it was he who was 'the gentleman of great agricultural repute' who was prepared to lay out such an enormous sum of money to acquire 60 merino sheep.

Thomas Moore visited Pythouse at the end of October 1821 and in his diary provides us with an insight into Benett's state of mind at this time. He records that on the 31st:

> Breakfasted with Phipps and Benett (member for the County). Mrs Phipps at Benett's near Salisbury – resolved to go there and set off in a chaise for Benett's – changed horses at Warminster, passed Fonthill Abbey and arrived at four – magnificent sunset – dined, sang and slept.

Nov 1st A walk after breakfast with Mrs P. – she in my travelling cap, which became her mightily – after breakfast through the grounds with her, Benett & Phipps – a beautiful place, but its master at his wit's end for money and haunted in this Paradise by duns.[43]

It is more than likely that the party dined off the Chinese armorial service that had been bought by Benett's father in 1789, no less than 246 pieces of which survived to be sold with almost all the other contents of the house in 1957.[44] Moore's principal claim to fame at the time was his publication of *Irish Melodies* with music by Sir John Stevenson,[45] and so the party at Pythouse undoubtedly enjoyed hearing Moore's poetry set to music and sung by him. His singing had an extraordinary effect on his listeners, and one writer, commenting in 1889 on Moore's talent, declared that 'either people were more musically sensitive and sympathetic in those days than in the present, or the singing must have had unparalleled power, for both ladies and gentlemen were frequently obliged to leave the room in floods of tears over the melodies.[46] Next day, he was captivated by the beauty of the park at Pythouse and the splendid view across Benett's estate, but could not resist making reference to his host's parlous financial position.

In the autumn Benett would be seen at the annual meeting of the Bear Club in Devizes,[47] and the dinner held at the *Black Horse Inn* in Salisbury after the Salisbury Infirmary anniversary service in the Cathedral there.[48] Year by year he would have spent an enormous amount of time travelling around the county attending innumerable meetings and banquets. For instance, in 1825 he attended the lavish dinner given in Salisbury by his distant kinsman James Bennett, the newly elected 28-year-old mayor of the city.[49] James Bennett, a silversmith and clockmaker, was a direct descendant of William Bennett[50] of Berwick St John, whose nephew had sold the Pythouse estate in 1669. Benett knew of his relationship to the young mayor and is reported on one occasion to have written in his diary, 'rode into Salisbury today and saw my cousin the watchmaker'.[51]

During the Spring of 1822, Benett was in attendance in the House as usual, and as soon as Parliament had been opened in February, was on his feet expressing the view that the severe distress in his county was caused by excessive taxation.[52] On the 18th he delivered an exceedingly long speech on a motion calling for a Committee on Agricultural Distress.[53] The proposed abolition of the salt tax was debated on a number of occasions at this time and Benett, who was always wishing to see a reduction in taxation, spoke in three of the debates, urging the abolition of what he called 'the most mischievous of imposts'.[54] In April, he delivered a very lengthy speech in which he 'conceived no immediate relief could be afforded to tenants but from the landlord and to enable the landlord to remit their rents the reduction of the rate of interest on mortgage would be most material.'[55] April also saw Benett presenting a petition from certain agriculturalists in Wiltshire complaining of distress, and declaring that he was a 'friend of the principal of free trade but in the present unnatural state of the country it was impossible to have free trade'. In response to his speech introducing the petition, the Marquis of Londonderry[56] (who four months later, his mind deranged by pressure of work, was to take his own life by cutting his throat) expressed astonishment at what Benett had said and implored members to go home to the country with their minds free from the 'gloomy apprehensions, the gloomy pictures and prognostics of Mr Benett'! [57]

At this time, the county of Wilts returned no fewer than 34 members to Parliament. When Lord John Russell[58] tabled a motion that a Reform of the House of Commons was necessary, Benett was one of only seven of these who voted in the minority in its favour.[59] On two consecutive days in May, Benett spoke at great length, and as a well known advocate and supporter of the Corn Laws, 'denied that the Corn Bill had given any monopoly to the land owners and he would not now ask for a higher rent than was given in 1792 because he anticipated a very great reduction of taxation and it was for the landlord to look for relief from that circumstance'.[60] On one of these occasions, he said that he did not intend to trouble the House at much length, and then proceeded to produce a dazzling array of figures and statistics. This certainly demonstrated his command of his subject but at the same time must surely have driven many members from the chamber.[61]

At the end of May he spoke against the repeal of duty on foreign wool[62] and in June he 'denied that the landed interest had any disposition to inflame the public mind and that landowners had submitted to all aggravated injuries which had been heaped upon them with a degree of patience which had become culpable, since it involved the tenantry of the county in their ruin.'[63] During the same month, Benett demonstrated his continued support for Catholic emancipation by voting in favour of Canning's[64] motion for the admission of Catholics into the Upper House. His fellow county member, Astley, voted against it.

In 1821 and 1822 Henry Hunt, who was languishing in Ilchester gaol as a result of the part he played in the Smithfield and St Peter's Field reform meetings, made further attacks on Benett in his letters to *The Radical Reformers*. In January 1821, he refers to Benett's speech made in 1817 in which he had said that the people were neither seditious nor blasphemous, but there would always be some scoundrels who would wish to create disturbances in the state. Hunt then suggested that Benett might have condescended to say who the scoundrels were, and then made a veiled attack on him by suggesting that the true scoundrels were those 'upon the look out for plundering the people, and grinding the face of the poor'; and that Benett might have said:

> avoid the hypocrite as you would a pestilence, and if you know a scoundrel who, in canvassing for election, becomes all things to all men, a Tory with the Tories, a Whig with the Whigs, a moderate Reformer with the moderate Reformers, and a Radical with the Radicals, sanctified with religions, although an atheist by profession and practice – if you should meet a scoundrel of this class, a bankrupt in fortune and character, prowling about with a lank unmeaning form, a cadaverous shark-like visage, the emblem of a black rankling heart within, fly from his touch, for it is as venomous as the tooth of a viper.[65]

Although in the next paragraph Hunt refers to the 'imaginary monster which I have described above', there cannot have been many of his readers who did not conclude that he was describing Benett himself.

Early in the following year, in mocking those farmers who had been opposed to reform, he wrote:

> Only think that those yeomanry cavalry bucks should, after seven years of peace, be holding public meetings all over the country, to petition the Honourable House for redress, for reduction of taxation, and for retrenchment and economy. The Webb Halls, the Ellmans, the John Benetts, the Ilotts, and the Bath Agricultural Asses, are for petitioning the Honourable House for redress, for relief from distress; but these wiseacres are for leaving the way in which this is to be effected, entirely to the discretion of some collective wisdoms that brought them into the scrape.[66]

In the face of these attacks, Benett displayed a considerable degree of forgiveness when in February he supported the petition signed by some 5000 inhabitants of Preston praying for some mitigation in the punishment meted out to Hunt, and which contributed to his release from prison.[67]

In April, Hunt wrote that 'the notorious JOHN BENETT, of Corn Bill celebrity, the Wiltshire member, has discovered that the country is not in so bad a state as some would make it out to be; and he sees great hope of relief for the farmer, and appears to have set his heart upon a *good slice* of the Chancellor of the Exchequer's 3,000,000 *l*. that is to be lent at 3 per cent.'[68] In his July letter to *The Radical Reformers*, having made a number of exceedingly disparaging remarks about Sir Thomas Baring,[69] he wrote, 'The farmers say he is playing the second act of the farce exhibited by John Benett, Esq. at Warminster, a few years back, relative to the Corn Bill, as related in the 36th and 37th Numbers of my Memoirs. Mr.Benett then threatened to leave us, and go and live in France, if the Ministers did not pass an Act to keep up the price of corn and his rents. The people of England said to Mr.Benett, 'who the devil cares where you go to live; go to France or to the devil, and be ——, for what we care'.[70]

It likely that these attacks came to Benett's notice, but he did not deign to respond to them (at least not in public) and continued as usual to attend the assizes held in Salisbury as foreman of the Grand Jury, and to play a very active role as president of the county agricultural society. At the annual meeting held in Devizes in July he was unanimously re-elected as president, having been proposed by Henry Hoare,[71] son of Sir Richard Colt Hoare of Stourhead. He had travelled from London that morning to attend the meeting and said of 'his friend Mr Benett that whether in or out of Parliament he had uniformly and zealously advocated the agricultural interests; and that in so doing he had shown himself truly desirous to promote the welfare of the inhabitants of his native county, and solicitous for the prosperity of the Empire at large'.[72]

By this time, it appears that Benett had become inducted into the mysteries of freemasonry, as in September it was reported that, when the Lodge of Temperance and Morality of Free and Accepted Masons met to celebrate their anniversary at Market Lavington, 'with a number of other brethren John Benett esq M.P. honoured the lodge with his presence as a visiting brother'.[73] Although a number of Masonic lodges had been established in the county for some years, by 1813 only six were in existence with three more established by 1825.[74] This report of his visit to the lodge in Market Lavington seems to be the only record of his activities as a freemason.

Throughout the 1820s Benett continued to do his duty as captain of the Hindon troop of yeomanry cavalry. In 1817, new regulations had been issued by the Government providing for three troops of the regiment to assemble for permanent duty for not more than six days in any year, the time and place to be notified to the Lord Lieutenant, and by him to the King. Benett would have received the same pay and allowances as a regular cavalry officer. The troop, therefore, met for training at regular intervals, and in September 1822 the Salisbury troop joined the Hindon troop for 4 days' duty under the command of Benett, 'whose approbation they obtained for the steadiness of their conduct in the field'. On the last day 100 of the two troops sat down to an 'elegant and sumptuous entertainment' at Wardour Castle provided by Lord Arundell, who was captain of the Salisbury troop and whose health Benett proposed.[75] He would perhaps have done well to propose Arundell's financial health as well, for behind the façade of the sumptuous entertainment held at the magnificent mansion was a scene of near ruin. Arundell had inherited his title on his father's death in 1817 and the Wardour estate from his grandmother, the widow of the 8th Lord Arundell. This estate was far too small to maintain Wardour Castle and the lifestyle expected of a peer, and so in 1825 Arundell's creditors met and agreed to accept 13s. 4d. in the pound in settlement of his debts. Following this he and his wife[76] left the country to live more cheaply in France until 1834.[77] Not to be heavily in debt was the exception rather than the rule amongst early 19th century aristocrats, and Lady Arundell's brother, the first Duke of Buckingham,[78] dragged his estates into the most spectacular bankruptcy of the century. Benett was also indebted to his bankers for most of his life, but the comparatively modest cost of maintaining Pythouse, and the apparent lack of extravagance in his mode of living, enabled him to retain until his death an estate of respectable size, notwithstanding an enforced sale of land after the 1819 election.

Benett's estate and modest mansion were situated within a short distance of two of the most remarkable houses in Wiltshire. Wardour Castle, the largest Georgian house in the county, designed by James Paine[79] and begun in 1769, incorporated a spectacular chapel the size of a large parish church. It contained a magnificent collection of vestments for use by the priests who ministered to the many Roman Catholics living in the extreme south-western corner of the county. Benett was certainly on friendly terms with the Arundells.

It is unlikely that the same would be said of Benett's relations with the master of the other house, or rather abbey, whose estate adjoined his own. The world of William Beckford, who, since 1807 had been living in what has been described by Nikolaus Pevsner as 'the most prodigious romantic folly in England' was far removed from Benett's world of county politics, agricultural meetings and practical farming, yeomanry cavalry training and parliamentary debates. It is well known that Beckford was generally avoided by the neighbouring gentry.

How different from the unostentatious furnishings of Pythouse were the contents of Fonthill Abbey, that Beckford, beset by financial difficulties, proposed to sell by public auction at the Abbey in 1822. The sale catalogue prepared by Christie's whetted the appetite of the rich and famous throughout the land. The proposed ten-day sale caused a sensation, and people flocked in their thousands to this remote corner of Wiltshire to pay to see not only the contents, but also the Abbey itself. The original date of sale was postponed to 1 October and again to 8 October, and on 23 September the *Salisbury and Winchester Journal* had reported that 'there were seldom fewer than 600 admitted daily'.[80] During this time Beckford was secretly negotiating a private sale of the whole of the Abbey and most of its contents, as well as the surrounding estate, to the immensely rich John Farquhar.[81] On the day the auction was to have commenced, the sale was cancelled and contracts exchanged with Farquhar. However, the disappointed viewers of the contents of the Abbey had another opportunity to view and purchase when, in the following year, Farquhar instructed Phillips, Christie's rival auctioneer, to sell Beckford's spectacular treasures. A thirty-seven day sale was planned and John Constable,[82] who visited the Abbey before the sale, paints a wonderful picture of what he saw:

> Imagine the inside of the Cathedral at Salisbury or indeed any beautifull Gothick building magnificently fitted up with crimson & gold, antient pictures, in almost every niche statues, large massive gold boxes for relicks &c &c,. beautifull & rich carpets, curtains, & glasses – some of which spoiled the effect – but all this makes it one whole, strange, ideal, romantic place – quite fairy land.

It is no surprise, therefore, to find that Benett was amongst the crowds who flocked to see this wonderland, although it is likely that he was also casting an experienced eye over the land surrounding the Abbey, sensing that it might not be long before Farquhar would also wish to dispose of it. In September, the *Salisbury and Winchester Journal* reported that 'amongst the distinguished visitors who have been at the Abbey last week we find Mr Benett MP, the Countess of Pembroke, the Marquis of Bath and the Bishop of Winchester & Lady'.[83] Benett's family would surely wish to see the wonders of the Abbey for themselves, and so on 20 October it was reported that 'amongst the company last week' were Lord Pembroke, William Wyndham and his family and Benett and his family.[84] It may not be fanciful to suppose that the Wyndhams and the Benetts decided to join forces in a joint family outing to the Abbey.

By this time it appears that, notwithstanding his first somewhat inauspicious meeting with them five years before, the poet Thomas Moore was a firm friend of the Benett family, as on the 19th October he records in his diary:

Set off at about eleven in my little pony carriage, with the carpenter's pony, and the carpenter himself to drive me. Arrived by dint of hard beating in three hours at Warminster. Took a chaise there, and got to Benett's before six. Company at dinner, Heber,[85] Sir Alexander Mallet,[86] a Miss Partridge and the Phippses.

20 Oct Set off to walk to Fonthill – no sale going on Monday.

21 Oct Drove over to see Wardour. Home in time to attend the ladies to the sale at Fonthill. Stayed there till five. . . Got Mrs Benett to let me have a cup and saucer out of a broken set she bought in order to take home some little memorial of Fonthill to Bessy. Stayed at Pythouse.

Oct 22 Up at seven – set off in a chaise for Warminster taking with me several volumes on tithes, which Benett lent me, besides his Controversy on the same subject with Archdeacon Coxe.[87]

Whilst the rich and famous were moving amongst the luxuries of Fonthill, the weavers working in the manufacturing towns of Warminster and Bradford were meeting to consider what action to take following a reduction in wages. In January 1822, 1200 weavers converged on Warminster and attempted to intimidate the employers into withdrawing the recently imposed scale of wages, at the same time wrecking the houses of the weavers who were continuing to work. Soon after the rioters marched to Heytesbury, where they demolished all the spring looms that they could find. On the following day, 37 members of the Salisbury troop of yeomanry cavalry marched into Warminster and shortly afterwards the Hindon troop arrived, with both troops then forming into a squadron under Benett's command. Several rounds of ball cartridges were delivered to each of the men, who shortly afterwards received orders to march to Westbury where rioting was anticipated. All being quiet, however, the squadron proceeded over the following days to Trowbridge and Bradford and then back to Warminster. Here Benett dismissed the troops after expressing to them 'the thanks of the regiment's Colonel, the Marquis of Bath, and also his own particular thanks for their ready attention to their duties'.[88] There can be no doubt that the presence of the yeomanry cavalry in the manufacturing towns was decisive in preventing any further disturbances, and the *Salisbury and Winchester Journal* considered that thanks were:

eminently due to the Magistrates who adopted decisive and vigorous measures on this occasion, and to the Yeomanry for their prompt attention in the hour of danger: whilst the firmness of those manufacturers, who would not yield to an illegal combination of workmen, and the ready assistance of their well disposed neighbours merit equal praise.[89]

At this time fancy dress balls for the fashionable were extremely popular, and the newspapers would invariably have provided their readers with details of those who attended and the characters that they represented. Benett appears to have had an aversion to such occasions, as his name is rarely found in the accounts in the newspapers, and certainly never with a description of his costume. However, in January of 1823 it was reported that 'Mr Benett. Mrs Benett and family' attended a fancy ball at Old Park, Devizes, the seat of Mr A.H.Hardman. Considerable stamina had to be shown by those who attended, and particularly by those who stayed to the very end. The guests arrived at about 9 o'clock and were ushered into the drawing room where tea and coffee were served. A band then summoned the company to dance and this continued until 1 am when the supper room was thrown open, where 'every delicacy the season could offer' was provided. Dancing then resumed and continued until 5 o'clock when the company departed.[90] Perhaps Benett preferred the company and conversation to be enjoyed at the large dinner parties given by his friends and acquaintances. Thomas Moore records in his journal that on 5 January he was taken by the Phippses to dine at Bowood as a guest of the Marquis of Lansdowne. The Benetts were amongst the large party who listened to Moore sing 'several of the "Irish Melodies" which seemed to produce considerable effect'.[91]

Soon afterwards, Benett was in Devizes again to attend the Quarter Sessions, and at the beginning of February in London for the opening of Parliament. It was not long before he was addressing the House yet again on the question of the Corn Laws. He spoke at considerable length in opposition to the measures being proposed by the Government, and declared that a reduction in the level of taxation would be the only way to afford relief to the landed interest and to benefit all classes. He was looking in particular to see a repeal of taxes on tallow candles and malt and especially on beer.[92] In a debate on the financial state of the country he was pleased to hear that there would be a reduction in the Window Tax, as in his view the tax tended to make country gentlemen desert their ancient and spacious dwellings and drive them to the metropolis.[93] The House was debating the question of excise duties in June when Benett suggested that, if the Chancellor would not spare the revenue produced by the duty on beer, then instead there should be an extra, or special, duty on such malt as might be used by common brewers only.[94]

It was well known that both Benett and Astley were in favour of some measure of reform, and from time to time they were addressed publicly with advice as to its desirable extent and nature. In March, the *Devizes and Wiltshire Gazette* published a letter from 'A Freeman' who prefaced his suggestions in a particularly flattering way:

> I beg leave to premise, Gentlemen, that, however your decisions may have been at variance to one another, upon some questions, it is my humble conviction, that you are both independent men, and act from conscientious principles. I firmly believe too that this county and kingdom at large has not been better served by its Representatives, in the memory of the oldest inhabitant.[95]

In the same month, the House was debating the Army Estimates, during the course of which some members were questioning the financial provision to be made for the corps of yeomanry cavalry throughout the country, and some even calling for their abolition. As one would expect, Benett rose to defend the Wiltshire corps in particular and thoroughly approved of the proposed financial grant. Because he disliked the existence of a regular standing army, he expressed his approval of the yeomanry force, 'which was composed of people of England'.[96] Benett spoke in the House again on a number of occasions during the following months and in May, when the Game Laws were being considered, he declared that in his view most of the offences in the country might be considered as resulting from the severity of the laws. Offenders were gradually trained for poaching to shop lifting and then to house breaking and occasionally murder.[97]

By the 1820s Benett was the proprietor of very extensive landed estates, and so he must have been saddened to have to part with some of them to reduce his borrowings and pay some of his creditors. Benett was a practical man who understood that there was no future in building up enormous debts without the means of servicing them, even though, as a Member of Parliament, his creditors would not be able to pursue him through the courts. He therefore took the sensible course and in 1823 recouped £100,000 by selling a total of 2,378 acres of land in Berwick St Leonard, Chicklade and Boyton in Wiltshire, and Motcombe, Keynton and Stour in Dorset to John Farquhar,[98] who in the same year purchased Fonthill Abbey from William Beckford. The *Devizes and Wiltshire Gazette* considered that 'if the property purchased by Mr Farquhar from Mr Benett (our county member) be added to Fonthill, the domain will then form one of the most splendid estates in this kingdom. Fonthill Abbey is itself a residence for a Prince'.[99] It was part of the agreement entered into on 16 May that a deposit of £20,000 would be paid to Harry Phillips of New Bond Street to be held by him pending completion of the transaction, but that £5000 of this sum would immediately be advanced to Benett, who was doubtless urgently in need of the money. It was also agreed that following completion of the sale, Benett would become Farquhar's tenant at a rent of £3,663 a year, under a lease that could be determined in four or eight or twelve years time, and that Benett would be entitled to grant underleases.

As with other land transactions in which Benett was involved, controversy followed the sale of the land in Berwick St Leonard. Prior to the sale to Farquhar, Benett had owned the advowson and had presented to the living in 1822. In 1823 one John MacIntyre, probably an assignee from Farquhar, had presented and also in 1826, when the Reverend C.H. Grove became the incumbent. However, this was disputed by Benett, presumably on the grounds that he had not included the advowson (nor indeed the lordship of the manor) in the sale. In the edition of *The Clerical Guide and Ecclesiastical Directory* [100] published ten years later, the identity of the patron was stated to be '*in dispute*'. By some unknown means, but probably as a result of litigation, Benett had recovered the advowson by 1840 and later sold it to the Marquis of Westminster.[101]

This was not the first time that the ownership of an advowson had caused Benett some difficulties. The right to choose and appoint the incumbent of a benefice was very often in the ownership of the principal landowner in the parish in which the church was situated. As will be seen, the fact that the Lord Chancellor, and not Benett as Lord of the Manor, had the living of Norton Bavant within his gift was a cause of irritation to Benett and his sister Etheldred. So it is no surprise to find him attempting to acquire the advowson of Tisbury, that had been in the ownership of the Arundell family since the 16th century.

Some three years earlier, Benett was party to a monstrously voluminous deed whereby, in consideration of the sum of £1000, the advowson of Tisbury was apparently transferred to him.[102] To acquire the right to appoint an incumbent who would be sympathetic to his liberal and tolerant religious views was perhaps his motive for entering into this transaction. However, he may not have fully appreciated that what was transferred to him was subject to the residue of an existing nine-year lease of the advowson that had been granted by Lord Arundell – and that allowed, of course, the lessee to make presentations to the living. Further, as the lease appears to have been virtually perpetually renewable without payment of any fine to the lessor, it is difficult to discern why Benett should have thought it worthwhile paying the considerable sum of £1000 for what seems to have been a worthless asset. To add to the confusion it is likely that the transaction was never properly completed as, three years after the deed was entered into, Lord Clifford,[103] who was one of Lord Arundell's trustees and a party to the deed, was writing to Philip Chitty, Benett's Shaftesbury solicitor, that he had received a letter, suggesting that:

> the advowson of Tisbury and Tollard Royal sold to Mr Benett had been paid for by him and the money remitted to me many years back. I am willing to believe this is a complete misunderstanding on his part, but as the assumption seems to have gained some credit, I will trouble you to inform me by return of Post whether, and when and by whom Mr Benett paid this purchase money and what sum it amounted to including principal and interest.[104]

It must be the case that Benett did not in reality acquire the advowson at all, as others continued to present to the living until 1877 when the then Lord Arundell[105] sold the advowson to Benett's grandson, Vere Fane-Benett-Stanford.[106]

Although in 1823 Benett had been compelled to raise the very large sum of £100,000 to reduce his borrowings, he could not let pass the opportunity in the following year of purchasing Middle Linley Farm, situated just to the north of the woodland at the rear of Pythouse itself.[107]

It seems that by this time Thomas Moore did not perhaps find Lucy, Benett's wife, quite so odious as when he first met her in 1818. On the first Sunday in June, he 'went to a dance at Mrs Benett's (our M.P.'s wife) – some pretty people there, amongst whom was Miss Houlton'.[108] Whilst in London, dances such as the one that Lucy had hosted were attended exclusively by fashionable society; in the country Salisbury races were an important event in the social calendar. According to an account written in 1843, 'hither the higher classes came to display their showy attire and splendid equipages, and the multitude to enjoy a cheap and social amusement, enhanced by the exhilarating effects of pure air and a change of scene'.[109] Benett was one of the six notable figures who in 1823 subscribed 10 guineas towards the purchase of a gold cup for next year's meeting. The Race Ball held at the Assembly Rooms in Salisbury and attended by nearly 300 people must have been a glittering affair, with the Earl and Countess of Pembroke, Lord and Lady Arundell and Viscount Folkestone (the Earl of Radnor's heir) honouring it with their presence. Benett and his family were also, of course, amongst the company.[110]

There is no evidence to suggest that Benett took any particular interest in the history of his family or estates, although he did record a brief and not entirely accurate account of the ownership of the Pythouse estate in a book of 'Accounts of Estates and many other useful memoranda beginning 1829'.[111] Further, it was presumably he who told John Britton, the Wiltshire antiquary, some years before about the letters at Pythouse that had once belonged to Prince Rupert. It appears that at this time Britton was attempting to obtain some information about Pythouse, as in September 1823 Benett wrote to Britton apologising for:

> not having given you the information you wish to have concerning this Place sooner. If you can spare the time and will favour me with your company here for a day I will give you every information which it may be in my power to give. . .[112]

It is clear, therefore, that ,although Benett may not have pursued any antiquarian or historical interests himself, he was perfectly happy to assist Britton with his enquiries. Having suggested a number of days upon which Britton might call at Pythouse, he went on to say that, 'should you not be able to favour me with your company, if you will give me your direction, I will give you such account as I can'.

Together with the races, the theatre was the other form of popular entertainment at this time. It is not likely that Benett, as a serious minded Member of Parliament, would have been a patron of the theatre, although in 1828 a comedy and farce were performed at the theatre in Salisbury under the patronage of Lord Arundell and the Salisbury troop of yeomanry cavalry. However, music was an entertainment that found favour with those who would not, perhaps, think it proper to be seen at a theatre. In the 18th century an annual Musical Festival was held in Salisbury and, after a break of some years, it was resumed in 1800, and continued every few years until 1828. In 1824, Benett was reported to have been present at the Festival, the performances of which were generally held in the Cathedral,[113] and four years later he and two of his daughters were present at the last of the festivals.[114]

Despite attending the Salisbury festivals, it seems that Benett had no particular interest in music nor any aptitude for it. There were certainly musical instruments in the house of his father who, in his will, mentions his harpsichord, music and musical instruments, as well as his German flutes and music for wind instruments.[115] However, in September 1824, the *Devizes and Wiltshire Gazette* reported:

> At a meeting of the Bear Club at the Bear Inn in Devizes during the evening Mr Ings and Mr Swayne favoured the company with some excellent songs and Mr Benett having last year said that he would sing a song, provided Mr Pearse would write it for the occasion, our worthy Borough member pledged himself to the company that within two

months of the next anniversary he would get one ready, and give it to Mr Benett, in order that that gentleman might set it to music and put his vocal powers in training.[116]

At the meeting of the Club held in 1825, although 'some delightful songs were sung by Mr Harrington, Mr Ings and Dr Sainsbury', no mention is made in the report of the meeting of Benett treating the company with a display of his vocal powers. One can only assume that the boast made two years previously that he would sing a song was made at the end of a convivial evening, and that the reminder of it a year later was not, perhaps, entirely welcome!

Early in 1824, Benett presented anti-slavery petitions from Wiltshire towns on no fewer than five occasions, although during the year he spoke only three times in the House. Whenever the Game Laws were being considered, he was always at hand to give his fellow Members the benefit of his views. In a debate on the Game Law Amendment Bill in March, it appears to have been suggested that, if passed, the future of fox hunting might be in doubt. Benett said that no man in England was fonder than he of country pursuits, and of fox hunting in particular. If he thought that the Bill would have the effect of abolishing the sport he would most strenuously oppose it. However, he said that the Bill could in no way affect fox hunting. Every fox hunter was a trespasser under the law as it stood, and would have as much right to draw a fox after the passing of the Bill as they had now.[117]

Benett appears to have generally enjoyed good health, but on 1 April the *Devizes and Wiltshire Gazette* reported that 'our county member has for some time been extremely indisposed and is totally unable to attend to his parliamentary duties'.[118] His sister Etheldred rushed to London to be with him, and told her fellow geologist James Sowerby[119] when writing to him at the end of May, that she 'came to London in such haste this year in consequence of the very dangerous illness of my eldest Brother that I could not bring anything with me except a few specimens for the Geological Society which had been previously packed'.[120] However, he appears to have made a good recovery from his illness as, early in May, he was once again on his feet in the House. In July, when he attended the dinner at the annual meeting of the Wiltshire Agricultural Society, after the loyal toast, 'Mr Benett's restoration to health and his presence among them was hailed with 3 times 3 times 3', and one of the speakers declared him to be 'one of the most active, most zealous and best Members the County of Wilts ever produced'.[121]

Having had the satisfaction of seeing his old rival Wellesley withdraw from the 1820 county election, Benett must have hoped that he had seen the last of him as a contender for a county seat. He must have had some misgivings, therefore, when in July it was reported of Wellesley in a London paper that, 'he may shortly be expected to revisit his native country, and under the superintendence of his Noble father, Lord Maryborough,[122] the whole of his debts will be speedily liquidated'. More seriously, at the same time, the *Devizes and Wiltshire Gazette* had 'heard through a reputable quarter, that at the next dissolution of Parliament, Mr Long Wellesley will, positively, again offer himself as a candidate for the representation of the county.'[123] The cost of another contested election was something that Benett's financial situation could not possibly bear.

In 1824 he became a member of two London clubs, where he would have met and become acquainted with many Members of Parliament and other influential men. Firstly, he was elected a member of Brooks's Club[124] in St.James's Street. His proposer was the 2nd Earl of Sefton[125] and his seconder, General Ferguson.[126] In G.M. Trevelyan's view, Brooks's was 'the most famous political club that will ever have existed in England'. Benett remained a member for the rest of his life, and it has been said that in his day 'members were the instigators of reform bills and progressive legislation of all sorts, the club acting as a sort of Whig committee room to both Houses of Parliament'.[127] As a supporter of most of the legislation of this kind, therefore, Benett would have found himself in congenial company at Brooks's.

The other club of which Benett became one of the first 612 members in 1824 was the recently founded Athenaeum. From Wiltshire came his friend Lord Arundell, his half-brother-in-law Aylmer Bourke Lambert and the Marquis of Bath, from the world of politics, George Canning, Sir Robert Peel[128] and the Duke of Wellington as well as the King of the Belgians, the Duke of Sussex, Sir Humphrey Davey and Sir Thomas Lawrence.[129]

It was also in 1824 that Benett's name first appears in Boyle's *Court Guide* as living at 19 Albermarle Street in Mayfair – the house that was to be his home in London while attending Parliament until 1832.

Thomas Moore appears to have been fascinated by Fonthill Abbey and so, in the summer of 1824, he decided to pay it another visit and he records in his diary that:

> To make sure of our admission there drove first to Bennet's. No one at home but Anna, who represented her father's hospitality most worthily; asked me where we meant to sleep, and on saying at Hindon, though she knew neither who nor how many were in the party exclaimed 'That is

impossible: papa and mamma will be home from Salisbury in one hour or two, and you must all come here'.[130]

It was at this time that Benett's assistance was sought in an effort that was being made to place a youth as apprentice to a cutler in Salisbury. Although by 1824 the prosperity of the manufacturers of cutlery in Salisbury was being eclipsed by those in Sheffield, there were still several working cutlers in the city. The most prestigious of these was Henry Shorto[131] who had inherited his father's business in 1797 and, as well as producing high quality cutlery, was also a renowned fossil collector. Benett decided to write to John Peniston to ask him to discover whether any of the Salisbury cutlers would take an apprentice, and told him that his first choice would be Shorto, who had voted for him in both the 1818 and 1819 elections and was probably well known to him. He was certainly known to his sister Etheldred as a fellow fossil collector.

In response to Benett's letter, Peniston wrote:

Immediately on receipt of your letter with its enclosure I waited on Mr Shorto who I am sorry to say though gratified with your preference declines taking an apprentice.

I afterwards called on young Goddard and he also after some consideration called at my house this afternoon to express his determination of not receiving an apprentice.

There are two other cutlers in Town who are literally working men though each keeping a shop no doubt superior to either of the others in practical knowledge but moving in quite a different sphere, the name of one is Nash residing in Catherine Street, the other Botly living in the Market Place. I have not spoken to either of these, doubtful whether such a situation would be eligible.

I hold your Note from Mr Spring Rice[132] until I receive your Answer[133]

It is clear that in response to this letter, Benett asked Peniston to speak to the other two cutlers, despite his reservations as to their suitability. Benett was doubtless disappointed in the reply:

Mr Botly's engagements at Weyhill in one week and mine at Marlborough in the last prevented my seeing him 'til yesterday. I regret to inform you he declines taking an additional apprentice having one who has been with him about 2 years he states that he cannot do justice to both until the one has served half his time this wants a year and a half of being accomplished. I the more regret it both from observation and enquiry finding that a young man well disposed might acquire a good practical knowledge of the cutlery business under such a Master.

There is yet another person of the name of Nash who I believe does not want for knowledge but I doubt if there be much more to recommend him.

Mrs Peniston requests me to return her best acknowledgement for your kind remembrances in the shape of a brace of very fine birds.

Hoping the cold which prevented you attending the Sessions will speedily take its departure.[134]

In September, Benett was present at a dinner held at the *Bear Inn* in Devizes following the installation of the new mayor of the borough. According to a report in the *Devizes and Wiltshire Gazette* the mayor's cards of invitation were on a most liberal and extensive scale; and (to use the words of Mr Benett) 'eminent as Devizes always has stood for its hospitality and conviviality, it shewed itself pre-eminent on the present occasion'. In responding to the toast to the Wiltshire Yeomanry, Benett said that he had been an officer and private thirty years, and although (he good humouredly added) he had not had an opportunity of shewing his prowess in the field of battle, nor of embruing his hands in blood, yet the Yeomanry Cavalry, as a body, were entitled to the support of the country.[135]

Throughout the whole of his adult life, Benett adopted an entirely 'hands-on' approach to farming, keeping, it is thought, almost all his land at Norton Bavant and at Pythouse in hand, and taking an intense interest in its management. An example of his interest in the *minutiae* of agricultural practice is a letter he wrote to the Bath and West of England Agricultural Society and read at the Society's annual meeting in Bath in December 1824 regarding the shoeing of oxen. He wrote that his smith would attend the Cattle yard for the purpose of shoeing oxen in the presence of the members of the Society, 'thus exemplifying the merits of his system'. When the précis of a letter from Dr Wilkinson in Geneva regarding the yoking of oxen was read, Benett said that he had seen pigs as well as cows used in draught-work but it was only where the farmers were very low [presumably meaning very poor]; and that if oxen were so used after they were three years old till they were six, it would be most useful in promoting their growth. He said he would willingly lend oxen for three years to persons who would use them for draught work. Later in the meeting he spoke highly of the merits of Messrs Wingrove's road roller and proposed that they should be awarded the Society's silver medal. He also spoke of the value of salt as manure. He said that he daily conveyed tons of salt to be used as a set-out for wheat, and considered that it would destroy weeds. He had ordered some of the finest salt and was trying experiments, the results of which he hoped to be able to submit to the Society.[136] True to his word, at the December 1825 meeting of the Society, he detailed several experiments that he had made, finding that single salted wheat did better than double salted. He was also persuaded that salt would cure rot in sheep.[137]

As one of the county members of Parliament, Benett must have felt that he should appear at some of the public balls held at Devizes as well as Salisbury, and so in January 1825 he and 'the two Miss Benetts' were seen at the assembly that 'presented a brilliant display of beauty and fashion'. [138] According to another report, the company was 'more numerous, we believe, than on any former occasion; and we doubt whether any country Assembly has surpassed, or ever will surpass, the beauty, elegance, and fashion, which was displayed on that evening'.[139] Later Benett alone, without any other member of his family, was one of the 150 people who attended the last assembly ball of the season at Devizes.[140]

Parliament sat again as usual in February, and in March Benett urged the Government to equalise the duties on the export and import of wool, and that the duty on the export of yarn would be lowered in the same proportion. At each sitting of Parliament a large number of petitions were presented by members, such petitions invariably being signed by enormous numbers of people and covering an extremely wide variety of subjects. However, sometimes the petition would be signed by a very few, as when in 1825 Benett was asked by a member of the Tucker family, who ran 'an academy for young gentlemen' in the remote village of Imber on Salisbury Plain, to present to Parliament a petition for the repeal of the House and Window Tax on Scholastic Establishments. It was reported that almost all of the scholastic profession in Salisbury signed the petition that would then have been delivered to Benett. It was further reported that Mr Tucker 'had received an answer from that gentleman stating that he would feel much pleasure in acceding to his request and would support the prayer in the petition in which he entirely concurred'.[141] In exceptional cases, the petition would be signed by one person only, as when in March 1825, he presented a petition from the notorious litigant, Robert Gourlay,[142] complaining that he had lost his property as a result of delays in the Court of Chancery.[143] One cannot imagine that Benett had much sympathy for Gourlay, who was well known for his longstanding dispute with the Duke of Somerset who had evicted him from his farm at Wylye. In the following month Gourlay was confined in the House of Correction for attempting to horsewhip Henry Brougham.[144]

Benett was in attendance at the Wilts County Sessions held in Salisbury in April, when a great deal of time was spent in listening to the arguments of counsel on the powers of magistrates to legislate with regard to what were at that time called lunatic asylums – and to the asylum at Laverstock near Salisbury in particular. Benett observed that the law was to blame, and said that a new bill relating to asylums had been introduced by Lord Lansdowne, but that it had been taken out of his hands by the Lord Chancellor, where it then rested.[145]

As usual whenever the Corn Laws were debated, as an acknowledged expert on all agricultural matters, Benett was expected to make his views known. So when in May 1825 the Importation of Corn Acts were being debated, he made it clear that he could see no good reason to propose granting what amounted to a bonus of £140,000 to the importers of corn at the expense of the corn growers.[146] In the same month, in a debate on wages of labourers out of Poor Rates, he said that no man in the country was more anxious than he was to see the poor comfortably provided for, but he believed that it was not in the power of Parliament to legislate effectively on the subject.[147] In the following month, the House was discussing the provision of an annuity of £6000 for the child of the Duke of Cumberland,[148] the least popular of the sons of George III, who enjoyed a very unsavoury reputation. In a rare display of humour, Benett congratulated the House on the burst of honest indignation that the grant had excited. When he saw gentlemen of different political sentiments united on a question of this nature it almost made him doubt the necessity of a parliamentary reform![149] The *Devizes and Wiltshire Gazette* reported further that much as Benett was disposed to contend for the necessity of Parliamentary Reform, he confessed his conviction was a little shaken by the proceedings of this night – for whilst he saw gentlemen on the benches opposite so warmly setting themselves against such propositions, he was still disposed to think well of the representatives of the people.[150]

At this time, the long struggle for the emancipation of Catholics was reaching a critical stage. Benett's support for religious toleration was well known, whereas the Earl of Radnor enjoyed great popularity as an advocate of preserving the Protestant constitution in church and state. On 25 March, according to a report in the *Devizes and Wiltshire Gazette,* Salisbury was 'all gaiety' as the various clubs in the city paraded with their banners and bands and:

> the feeling in the city is universal with regard to the subjects of the Church of his holiness the Pope. The Friendly Societies, some of them consisting of 110 members, in the effusion of their loyalty coupled the

*John Benett as a child, at the age of 6*

*Old Pythouse, before its rebuilding by John Benett*

*The new Pythouse, designed by John Benett (engraving from a watercolour by John Buckler)*

*above: caricature of Benett, emphasising his stature*

*above right: Lucy Lambert, painted probably before her marriage to Benett*

*right: Benett in old age*

*Fonthill Abbey, as purchased by Benett*

1819.
## WILTSHIRE COUNTY ELECTION.

SHEW of HANDS on the first Morning, at Wilton, in Favor of Mr. BENETT.

# FINAL
# STATE OF THE POLL.

| | | | |
|---|---|---|---|
| 1st Day - - - - Mr. BENETT | 302—Mr. ASTLEY | 199—Maj. for Mr. BENETT | 103 |
| 2d Day - - - - Mr. BENETT | 190—Mr. ASTLEY | 153—Maj. for Mr. BENETT | 37 |
| 3d Day - - - - Mr. BENETT | 386—Mr. ASTLEY | 260—Maj. for Mr. BENETT | 126 |
| 4th Day - - - - Mr. BENETT | 331—Mr. ASTLEY | 315—Maj. for Mr. BENETT | 16 |
| 5th Day - - - - Mr. BENETT | 277—Mr. ASTLEY | 280—Maj. for Mr. ASTLEY | 3 |
| 6th Day - - - - Mr. BENETT | 204—Mr. ASTLEY | 189—Maj. for Mr. BENETT | 15 |
| 7th Day - - - - Mr. BENETT | 190—Mr. ASTLEY | 251—Maj. for Mr. ASTLEY | 61 |
| 8th Day - - - - Mr. BENETT | 88—Mr. ASTLEY | 123—Maj. for Mr. ASTLEY | 35 |
| 9th Day - - - - Mr. BENETT | 97—Mr. ASTLEY | 95—Maj. for Mr. BENETT | 2 |
| 10th Day - - - Mr. BENETT | 80—Mr. ASTLEY | 100—Maj. for Mr. ASTLEY | 20 |
| 11th Day - - - Mr. BENETT | 44—Mr. ASTLEY | 68—Maj. for Mr. ASTLEY | 24 |
| 12th Day - - - Mr. BENETT | 34—Mr. ASTLEY | 47—Maj. for Mr. ASTLEY | 13 |
| 13th Day - - - Mr. BENETT | 104—Mr. ASTLEY | 83—Maj. for Mr. BENETT | 21 |
| 14th Day - - - Mr. BENETT | 59—Mr. ASTLEY | 75—Maj. for Mr. ASTLEY | 16 |
| 15th Day - - - Mr. BENETT | 50—Mr. ASTLEY | 32—Maj. for Mr. BENETT | 18 |

TOTAL *at the Close*
of 15th Day - } Mr. BENETT 2436—Mr. ASTLEY 2270

## Majority in Favor of Mr. BENETT 166.

SALISBURY, AUGUST 4, 1819.

Brodie and Dowding, Printers, Sarum.

*Election notice, 1819*

Duke of York with the King. Nothing could be more grateful to the feeling of every man attached to the constitution of his country than such a toast. Next followed the Earl of Radnor with appropriate toasts of respect – Lord Folkestone's name was not mentioned, nor Mr Benett's, ncr Mr O'Connell's nor Mr Cobbett's.[151]

The coupling of Benett's name with Daniel O'Connell,[152] who in 1823 had formed the Catholic Association, and the radical William Cobbett,[153] both in their different ways unpopular in many quarters, was a clear indication that he too was opposed by many in the county. This may have given rise to rumours that he would be forced to retire from Parliament, but these were firmly squashed when, at a meeting of the Wiltshire Agricultural Society in July, he observed that he was determined to retain the representation of the county, as long as his conduct met with the approbation of his constituents. The *Devizes and Wiltshire Gazette* followed this report of Benett's speech by adding, 'We trust that this declaration will be sufficient for the non-insertion of the letter of "A Freeholder"'[154] – presumably a letter suggesting that he either would or should be retiring. In his speech, Benett complimented the ministry on the many liberal measures they had carried through Parliament and it was his opinion that England never stood on so high a pinnacle of glory as at the present moment. He spoke highly of the establishment of Mechanics' Institutions and ventured to assert that the higher orders of society were less acquainted with political economy ten years ago than the lower orders were now.[155]

Mutual friends of Benett and Tom Moore were Charles Lewis Phipps and his wife Sophia of Dilton Court. Phipps was the second son of Thomas Hele Phipps of Leighton House and, in common with Benett, a magistrate, a deputy lieutenant of the county, and an officer in the Wiltshire yeomanry cavalry. One can imagine the scandal, therefore, when in March it was reported in the papers that Phipps had fought a duel in the New Forest with a man named Starkey. Phipps's second was Captain Hardman and after the event Phipps asked Hardman to write to Benett to explain what had happened. It appears that Phipps and Starkey had a quarrel over poaching by one of Phipps's labourers, and as neither would apologise, honour could only be satisfied by resorting to a duel, notwithstanding the fact that since 1818 to engage in a duel was a criminal offence. In his letter Hardman told Benett that the first bullet went through Starkey's hat and the second wounded Phipps in his right leg. The seconds then met and agreed that both were satisfied, whereupon the contestants shook hands. Hardman told Benett that a medical man was at hand who prescribed all sorts of medication, but that 'as he was guided hitherto by me in this affair, so he must be in the present instant and in place of the Doctor's stuff I made him drink half a bottle of champagne with me and for which he was all the better and I have no doubt that even Sir Astley Cooper[156] would approve of my physic'.[157]

While the gentry, certainly in the case of Phipps and Starkey, appeared to consider themselves above the law, the common criminal, if caught and convicted, could expect to be exceedingly severely punished. Rural crime in early 19th century England was endemic, and Benett, in common with numerous other landowners and farmers, was from time to time a victim. In December of 1825 a man named Gray and his accomplice were committed to Fisherton gaol on the outskirts of Salisbury for breaking into one of Benett's barns and stealing a considerable quantity of corn. This theft was doubtless reported to Benett and, expecting a further robbery, one of Benett's servants named Trim and his two sons laid in wait. In the early hours of the morning they surprised Gray and his companion, who arrived at the barn with a horse and cart with the intention of stealing more corn. After what was reported to have been 'a most desperate resistance', the two offenders were arrested and carried to gaol. As a reward, Trim and his sons received from the Wylye Association a gratuity of £5 for 'the intrepidity of their conduct and their faithful discharge of their duty to their master'.[158] At this time severe punishments were, of course, meted out to those convicted of what would now be considered quite minor offences. For instance in 1836 James Jacob was committed to the House of Correction for one month for damaging a fir tree at Hindon belonging to Benett.[159]

Ever since the contested elections of 1818 and 1819, Benett had been desperately short of money, but nevertheless continued to buy and sell land – hoping, no doubt, by selling to raise funds to pay some of the interest on his borrowings. In August, he called on Charles Ashe à Court,[160] the brother of Sir William Ashe à Court[161] of Heytesbury. In 1825, Sir William was appointed ambassador to Portugal and so, while he was abroad, his brother looked after his interests at home. The purpose of Benett's visit was to offer to sell a small area of woodland in the parish of Longbridge Deverill and, as Charles put it when writing to his brother, 'he had the modesty to ask 1000 guineas for it' – a sum far in excess of what Charles thought it was worth. In his letter to his brother, he also mentioned that Benett had received a most advantageous offer for his mill at Boyton, that Charles was confident would be accepted. He continues:

In the course of conversation Benett let out to me in confidence his expectation of an entire dislocation of the Fonthill property on old Farquhar's death & his determination in such case to strain every nerve to purchase that portion of which is in Tisbury Parish & which adjoins his property. It would require a very large sum to do this; and would oblige him to dispose first, of his Enford Estates; & possibly (to make up the sum,) of the . . . farm of Norton, lately occupied by Pocock. If he should do so, he will give you the first offer of the property; which certainly if at all at a fair price, would be a most magnificent addition to your estate. It is a farm of about 800£ or 850£ a year and worth I should think some 20,000£. It might be mortgaged for nearly the full amount of the purchase money. However as Benett puts an if in the case, the probability is he will not sell, tho' I believe he is sadly distressed for money; so much so, that he has just purchased an Estate upon which I have a mortgage, not having a single shilling to pay for it; which will of course oblige me to withhold the title deeds. He is an arrant Jew to deal with.[162]

There was clearly 'no love lost' between Benett and his neighbours at Heytesbury, and this feeling perhaps originated from Benett's father's attempt to win a seat in Parliament as a member for Heytesbury in opposition to the à Court family's interests. Charles Ashe à Court's unflattering description of Benett as a notorious 'Jew' must reflect Benett's reputation as a hard and uncompromising man to deal with, certainly as far as property matters were concerned.

While seeking to sell some property, Benett could not resist, at the same time, the temptation to increase the size of his landed estate by purchasing property either adjoining or in the vicinity of his existing estates, and notwithstanding the fact that, by so doing, he would be plunged further into debt. In November 1825, he made a comparatively small purchase when he bought two farmhouses known as Parhams and 86 acres of land in nearby Semley.[163] In the following month, four days before Christmas, the badly constructed tower of Fonthill Abbey , some 225 feet high, collapsed. Following this John Farquhar, who had purchased the Fonthill Abbey estate from William Beckford only two years before and who, according to Charlotte Grove's diary, when the collapse occurred, did 'eat his dinner as contentedly as if nothing had happened',[154] suddenly agreed to sell virtually the whole of the estate to Benett. In view of the speed by which the contracts were signed, Benett may perhaps have already been talking to Farquhar in an effort to purchase some of the property. We know that only a few months before he had confided in Charles Ashe à Court that he was determined to attempt to purchase some of the Fonthill estate on Farquhar's death, and so was undoubtedly caught by surprise when the collapse of the tower at the Abbey enabled his ambition to be fulfilled, if a little earlier than he had expected.

On 22 December and on 27 December, two contracts were entered into.[165] Benett must have spent a good deal of time over Christmas talking to the Shaftesbury solicitors Bowles, Chitty and Chitty who prepared the contracts and, presumably with Farquhar, in order to agree so speedily the terms that were incorporated in them. By the first of the two contracts, Benett agreed to purchase Farquhar's estates in Tisbury and Fonthill Gifford amounting to 2,450 acres.[166] By the other, he bought 504 acres of land within a wall or fence called Abbey Wall for £10,000, all the timber and timberlike trees, the advowson of Fonthill Gifford with its glebe lands, tithes and other rights, the mansion house and lands at Fonthill Gifford in the occupation of John Still, the incumbent (who held the property for his life), and the materials of the abbey that were to be valued by a London surveyor nominated by Farquhar and by Benett's nominee. This was John Peniston, his friend and stalwart supporter in the county elections, who practised as a surveyor and architect in Salisbury. Farquhar agreed to make good title within three months and Benett to pay the sum of £10,000 provided for in the second contract on or before 11 October following. At the same time, Farquhar sold 1400 acres to Benett's old friend Henry King, the leader of the 'Wiltshire Cossacks' at the time of the 1819 election.

Within three months of Benett's agreement to purchase, it was reported:

> This magnificent structure is at length uninhabited; it is stripped of the whole of its costly furniture, and most of the principal windows are taken out. But a few months since, it was little expected that this princely mansion would so soon go to ruin, and become a place of shelter to the feathered tribe.[167]

However, Farquhar's not entirely unexpected death occurred soon after, for he died intestate in 1826 and a dispute between his beneficiaries resulted in the sale and purchase not being completed until 1838![168] In 1827 it was reported that 'in consequence of the writings not being in readiness, the purchase money is not yet paid'.[169] It is likely that Benett welcomed the delay, as he certainly did not have the funds readily available to complete the contracts. In the meantime, he appears to have treated the property as his own, with Peniston proceeding with the task of measuring and valuing the remains of the Abbey. In the autumn of 1827, Peniston wrote to Benett's solicitor, Philip Chitty:

I have been away from home the whole of last week or you would sooner have received the accompanying valuation. I think it necessary, on the part of Mr Benett, to observe that unless he gets prompt possession of the Abbey, judging of the future by the past, he will require an abatement for injury done to the property, much of the glass and some portions of it the most valuable having been destroyed between our first survey and final valuation.[170]

On Christmas Eve, Peniston, whose meticulous schedule and valuation of all materials in the ruined building survives,[171] wrote to Benett:

. . . I am at a loss to say what price should be fixed for the mettallic contents of the fallen tower. It is I take it a species of lottery and I think you had better decline taking any specific sum – but say I am open to receive any tender they may be disposed to offer. But let their proposals be specific as to what they included in their bidding.

I understand there was the remains of the lead cistern, pipes, etc in the Fountain Court. Is it intended this to form a portion of the property to be bid for? The extent of the sum offered will guide my recommendation.[172]

Benett must have received a very high offer as on 27 December Peniston was writing to him:

Though I expected a treasure in the ruins of the tower I was not prepared for its extent, and though no doubt the party willing to give the sum you state must be well acquainted with its value, I think it too eligible an offer to be refused.

I will go over to the abbey on Wednesday next. In the meantime I will thank you to obtain what information you can and tell me with whom I may confer on the subject. I was in Bath last week and being acquainted with Mr G Underwood the architect I have desired him to notify to the builders with whom he is engaged the articles we have to dispose of. In the spring I trust we shall find desirable market.[173]

In the following year, Peniston was negotiating the sale of stone and lead to Edward Blore,[174] almost certainly the noted architect who was undertaking work for the Seymours, probably at nearby East Knoyle. In August he wrote to Benett asking the whereabouts of the statue of the late Alderman Beckford which stood in the entrance hall at the Abbey, and whether Mr Seymour had 'fetched away any stone'.[175]

Between 1826 and 1838, Benett continued to deal with the property as if he were the owner. In 1833 the *Salisbury and Winchester*

*Journal* reported 'part of Fonthill Abbey where the tower once stood still remains a magnificent ruin, but the other part is now fitted up as a mansion under the direction of the present owner John Benett Esq M.P.'[176] This report was, perhaps, a little premature, although as can be seen from the image produced by John Buckler[177] and published in 1829, a substantial part of Beckford's building was unaffected by the collapse of the tower. What is certain is that after a while Benett did indeed begin some work of restoration. J.B.Nichols writes:

> The ruins of Fonthill Abbey remains at present (1835) much as represented in this plate (i.e. Buckler's image) except that its owner John Benett esq M.P. for Wilts is gradually connecting the Brown Parlour and Yellow Rooms into a residence by the addition of offices and other buildings. They proceed, however, very gradually and no part is now inhabited. Mr Beckford himself had the curiosity to visit the place some weeks ago and expressed much approbation of its appearance as a ruin.[178]

Lack of the necessary funds almost certainly prevented Benett from completing the work, and so he continued to sell as much of the remains of the Abbey as possible. Indeed, in as early as 1828, it was advertised that 'materials from this most splendid building are now on sale', including 'the splendid range of plate glass and painted windows in St Michael's Gallery' that 'would to a gentleman fitting up a Picture Gallery or Library be a most valuable acquisition'. The advertisement declared that 'builders of Churches or Chapels may also find windows, stone architraves, mullions and Gothic Ornaments well calculated for such edifices'. Interested parties were requested to apply to Mr Jay[179] at the Abbey itself or John Peniston in the Close of Salisbury.[180] At the same time, the *Devizes and Wiltshire Gazette* reported that 'Fonthill Abbey, that chief of modern architectural gewgaws, is now a heap of ruins'.[181] It is thought that most of the remains of the Abbey were in fact taken down before Benett eventually disposed of the whole of the property.[182]

It is certain that at this time Benett's wife Lucy was suffering from ill health, as she was more often than not absent from the numerous balls that one would have expected her to attend with Benett and their young and eligible daughters. Indeed, it was only the Miss Benetts who attended the first Salisbury Ball of the season at the *White Hart* Rooms in December of 1825.[183] It would have been impossible, of course, for them not to have been chaperoned, and so it is likely that they attended with William Wyndham and his family. However at the Assembly Ball held at Devizes soon afterwards Benett quite properly accompanied his daughters, who found themselves in the company of

'200 fashionables'.[184] Furthermore 'Mr Benett & family' attended the Shaftesbury Second Subscription Ball in the following February, so perhaps Lucy did join the rest of the family on that occasion.

Benett continued to attend the annual meetings of the Bath and West of England Agricultural Society, having been appointed one of the vice-presidents of the Society in 1817. At the meeting held as usual in Bath in December 1825, it was proposed that a petition be presented to Parliament to ask that before any alteration be made to the Corn Laws, there should be an enquiry as to the state of the country, and the prices at which landed interests could bring corn to the market. Benett was quick to say that he regretted that the subject of the Corn Laws had been brought forward, and he had the strongest objection to the petition as coming from the Society. He thought it 'extremely unpleasant to agitate this great question at such a meeting which, without introducing subjects that might divide men's minds, sought to promote the arts and manufactures, as well as improvements in agriculture'. As a consequence the proposal was withdrawn.[185]

His expertise in agricultural matters was widely recognised. For example, in 1828 he sat on a committee of the Society to consider two essays on the best practical means of improving the British fleece, including both carding and combing wool. In the event, the committee decided that neither of the essays merited the proposed award of £10, but in view of the efforts displayed by the writers, they decided that they should each be granted a gratuity of £5.[186] Again, in 1830 the secretary of the Society wrote to him telling him that he had been appointed to a special committee to report on the merits of an essay that had been submitted on the subject of wool, and that it would soon be sent to him 'for his perusal'.

Parliament sat once again in February 1826 and Benett was soon addressing the House on a number of occasions. It was being proposed that a measure should be introduced prohibiting the issue of small currency notes and, in response to a petition against the measure, Benett proposed that the aim of the proposals to establish a sound currency could be effected by compelling those who issued notes under the value of £5 to give security for their payment.[187] On the following day, he spoke in support of a request to bring in a bill for the repeal of the usury laws, on the grounds that money would then be available to country gentlemen at a lower rate of interest than at present.[188] Soon after he was urging that notes should be payable in London as well as in the place where they were issued.[189] When the Corn Laws were again being debated in March and a petition against these laws being considered,

Benett contended that landed proprietors and agriculturalists could not support the present system of taxation, maintain the poor, give tithes to the clergy and pay the church and county rates if the price of their produce was lowered, as would surely be the effect of a repeal of the Corn Laws.[190] Having done his best to defend the reputation of the corps of yeomanry cavalry some three years before, they were under attack again in a debate on the Army Estimates. When a resolution was before the House that £156,271 be granted for defraying the charge of the volunteer corps for 1826, many speakers called for their complete abolition. Benett, of course, would have none of it. He said that there was nothing military about them. They were merely armed constables, and he had seen them on several occasions suppress very dangerous riots without so much as presenting a pistol or drawing a sword. In his opinion they should continue to be called out for three or four days a year.[191] It would not be long before Benett was to be thoroughly thankful that the yeomanry cavalry were still a very necessary force, and a force to be reckoned with.

In March two of Benett's employees, James Lambert and John Gray, stood trial for stealing nine bushels of barley belonging to him. When two of his other men attempted to apprehend the culprits, one of them, an elderly man, was beaten over the head with a stick by one of the criminals who, in turn, was severely beaten by the old man's son. When the injured criminal complained to the trial judge about his treatment at the hands of the old man's son, and said that he was under the care of the doctor for two months, the judge said that the young man's conduct was 'justifiable, faithful and laudable' and, despite their pleas for mercy on account of their families, the judge promptly sentenced them to be transported for seven years.[192]

Back in Parliament in April, in a debate on a motion for leave to bring in a Bill to prevent the cruel and improper treatment of dogs, Benett said he would give his ready support to any bill which would have for its object the prevention of such a brutal exhibition as that of dog fighting.[193] When the Corn Laws were debated yet again at the beginning of May, he spoke at very great length on the 2nd, and again on a number of other days during the first two weeks of the month. Part of his speech delivered on the 2nd was reported by the *Devizes and Wiltshire Gazette*, not in its usual parliamentary column. In its report its readers would have read that Benett thought that the price of labour did not rise in the same proportions with everything else during the last forty years. The price of labour did not increase within that period more than 33%, while the weight of taxation was increased full 300%. The labourer was consequently in a worse situation now than forty years ago.[194] As one of the charges made against Benett from time to time was that his labourers were underpaid, it was surely in his power to increase their wages. Although to do so, and to pay more than was customary in his part of the county, was probably a course of action that he would have found impossible to take.

While the ailing Lucy remained at Pythouse, her husband lived as usual at No 19 Albermarle Street for the current session of Parliament, during which he was particularly active. On 15 April, he called on Thomas Moore at Sloperton Cottage while on his way to the Phipps's. He stayed a while and pressed both Moore and Bessy to go up to town to his house there, that he said he would have to himself due to Lucy's illness.[195] Moore and Benett appear to have become firm friends and for most of May Moore was staying in Albermarle Street. On the 8th Moore breakfasted with Benett, whom he found 'all kindness and hospitality' and when, two days later, they were breakfasting together again 'M. Alexandre, the conjurer paid me a visit and amused us very much with some specimens of his ventriloquism'. On the following day, before Benett spoke in the House on the second reading of the Corn Bill, they decided that they should pay a visit to the phrenologist, Deville, in the Strand, calling in at Brooks's on the way to collect Sir Francis Burdett,[196] at that time Member of Parliament for Westminster and later for North Wilts. Moore records:

> After having explained to us (in his cockney way 'Nature abhors a vacuum etc) the principles of the science, he proceeded to examine our heads, had some suspicion who Burdett was, but did not know me in the least – found no poetry in my head. On Benett's asking him whether he discovered in my head any particular talent, said he had seldom seen a head with so 'Active and general an organization'[197]

Unfortunately, Moore does not record what the phrenologist thought of Benett's head. Despite Deville's apparent lack of success, a week later Moore and Benett paid him another visit, this time taking with them the Houltons,[198] particular friends of Moore; and also William Lisle Bowles, the poet and antiquary and vicar of Bremhill, a village not far from Moore's cottage in Wiltshire. On the 21st Benett left London, 'so that I have his house now all to myself', as Moore records in his diary.[199] Moore seems to have left Albermarle Street by the end of the month, as on the 30th he received a letter from Benett to say 'that he will have everything ready for me at his house in town on Wednesday – has been very anxious that Bessy should come up too, as he has the house all to himself, but the dear girl is wise enough to stay where she is'.[200] Although Moore's wife Bessy seems by now to have been very happy in the company of Benett, to risk having to meet any of her husband's other influential and fashionable friends with whom she was not familiar was something Moore, always touchingly solicitous for her comfort, clearly wished to avoid.

On the first of June, Parliament was dissolved and the election of two Members to represent the county of Wilts was once again, in accordance with ancient custom, held at Wilton. In addressing the freeholders, Benett said that to represent the county was the highest object of his ambition. After he and Astley had been returned unopposed, he made it clear in his speech that he was an advocate for a reform of the representation of the people in Parliament, and that he would take away representation from many of the boroughs. Parliamentary reform was, of course, to be a recurring topic of debate during the next few years, and with Old Sarum, perhaps the most 'rotten' borough in the county if not in the whole country, lying only a few miles from Wilton, the iniquities of the old system of representation were very near at hand for all to see. Benett and Astley continued to represent the county until the passing of the Reform Act, and the acrimony of the 1818 and 1819 elections appears to have been soon forgotten – it was Benett who proposed the health of Astley's son at the celebrations held to celebrate his 21st birthday. Once again, it was only the young Lucy and Etheldred and not their mother who accompanied Benett at the festivities.

In July Thomas Moore, who was staying at Wardour Castle, recorded in his diary on the 19th, 'Set off with Lord Arundell, Mr Jones, Bowles and myself to walk to Benett's – Mrs Benett not well enough to see us – the place looking quite beautiful'.[201]

One of the two annual Venison Dinners, given by the members for the county to such of their constituents as might choose to attend, was held in Devizes at the *Bear Inn* in August. Benett travelled from Pythouse, and he and Astley very nearly found themselves dining in the company of each other alone. The *Devizes and Wiltshire Gazette* reported:

> We have heard with no little concern that five gentlemen only (viz two from the town, two of the immediate neighbourhood and one from a distant part of the county) formed the entire party to sit down with their Members to a sumptuous dinner at which two haunches and one neck of venison were exhibited. . . they both declared that so long as they should be favoured with the company of a single freeholder, they would, from year to year, give their attendance. . . we would submit to the

consideration of the freeholders at large, the propriety of relieving their Members from an attendance, productive only of inconvenience and unnecessary expense.[202]

Parliament met again in November and Benett spoke on the 21st in the debate on Hume's amendment to the Address. Late that night Canning wrote to the King reporting on the proceedings that he described as 'unusually tedious and disagreeable', adding that 'it would be difficult to say who *spoke for* or *against* the amendment' and listing Benett as one of those who voted against the amendment.[203] Later, when it was proposed to postpone a further debate on the Corn Laws, Benett made it clear that he was not only averse to a further delay, but was becoming exasperated by the failure to bring the matter to a conclusion. He said that the suspense in which the country would be left would be a great evil, both as regards trade and all transactions in leases and rents, and he strongly deprecated the appointment of any more committees to examine the operation of the Corn Laws. Such a step was needless after the mass of information that had been collected on the subject.[204]

Having been persuaded that it was necessary during the course of the 1818 election campaign to publish details of the income and expenditure relating to his estate in Enford, Benett must have been exceedingly displeased to find his conduct as landlord of the property being yet again brought into the public domain. At the end of November 1826 a letter appeared in the press, signed by an anonymous correspondent using the name of 'Agricola', stating that a 'charge brought against the Member for Wiltshire would be utterly unworthy of notice, but for the *impression* such a charge, without being explained, is calculated to make on the public mind'. The substance of the charge was that in 1777 the estate was let at £600 p.a. when the price of a labourer was 6 shillings a week, whereas now the estate was let at £1,800 p.a. when the price of a labourer was 7 shillings a week. The writer of the letter declared that, 'As the Member for Wiltshire has been persuaded to take no notice of this charge a second time, I therefore shall take the liberty, knowing the facts, to do it for him, whose high sense of rectitude, and feelings of benevolence, want no defender'. He then proceeded to answer the charge by quoting a number of figures, including the fact that the current rent was £1,260 and not £1,800 p.a., that Benett had purchased the tithes, both great and small, valued at £300 p.a. and, over and above all this, had 'constantly abated his rent from 10 to 20% according to the pressure of the time'.[205]

On 7 February 1827 and the day before the sitting of Parliament resumed, Benett's wife Lucy died in Bath[206] at the age of 42. As a consequence, shortly afterwards and again in March, Benett was granted leave of absence from the House on account of this 'severe domestic affliction'. The cause of her death is unknown, but her absence from most of the balls regularly held during the past few years would suggest that she had been in ill health for some time; and her death in Bath that she had joined the many other ailing gentlefolk who hoped that there they would find a cure. She was buried with her ancestors at Boyton and was survived by her teenage sons, John and Thomas, and her daughters Lucy, Etheldred and Anna Maria, and the infant Fanny.

Benett was back in Parliament again in June, and when Canning brought forward a proposition to advance into the market the corn then bonded in the country, his opinion was that this was not called for in the circumstances; and that, in any event, before the House sanctioned the importation of Canadian corn, he thought that they should be told what quantity was likely to be introduced.[207]

On 21 July, Tom Moore took advantage of Benett's position as a Member of Parliament (and almost certainly not for the first time) to frank one of his letters so that it could be sent free of charge. Writing from Sloperton Cottage, his letter was addressed to Benett at Pythouse but then readdressed to him at 19 Albermarle St:

> My dear Benett
> Pray, frank the inclosed for me – It is in answer to a Member of the Committee of the General Assembly of the Church of Scotland, who has written to me to propose that I shall undertake a translation of the Psalms for them!!
> I was sorry I missed you here and Bessy is affronted.
> Loves to the girls – I beg pardon for being so familiar.
> Yours ever
> T.Moore.[208]

Moore even went so far as to suggest to others that they should take advantage of Benett's privileged position. In the following year he wrote to H.C.Robinson:[209]

> If you find any difficulty in procuring franks you may send the packet through the medium of John Benett Esq MP 19 Albermarle St (or if it should be above Members' privilege) through the hands of Mr Croker[210] Admiralty.[211]

On 29 July Moore recorded in his journal:

> Taken by the two Benetts to Dulwich, where I have some days been meditating a visit to Dr. Glennie, with whom Byron[212] was at school –

Glennie not at home but we were shown into a good garden, where we amused ourselves among the Strawberry beds, and Ethel Benett, having sworn me to secrecy, told me she and Lord Charles were engaged to be married. . . a good deal of laughing on our drive back.[213]

However, Moore found it difficult to keep a secret as, on 3 August, he wrote to Mary,[214] the widow of the poet Percy Bysshe Shelley:

Should your memorabilia extend ( as I hope they will) to many sheets, you can send them for me under cover of our County member John Benett Esq MP Pythouse Salisbury. The marriage, of which I half trusted you with the secret, is now declared and Benett's pretty daughter Ethel is to be in a month or two Lady Charles Churchill. We are going to pass a few days at Pythouse this month.[215]

Etheldred's husband-to-be was Lord Charles Spencer Churchill,[216] second son of the 5th Duke of Marlborough.[217] On the face of it, this was a brilliant match. However, ten years before, Charles, then an officer in the army and well known for his dandyism, had been involved with his brother, the Marquis of Blandford,[218] in some exceedingly disreputable proceedings. Blandford had met the sixteen-year-old daughter of a respectable Dublin provision merchant, then living in London, and persuaded her to marry him. He insisted, for family reasons, that the ceremony be performed in secret, and so she and Blandford went through a ceremony of marriage according to the rite of the Church of England at her parent's house – the ceremony being performed by Charles, posing as a clergyman! Needless to say, the truth was soon revealed. In addition to this, Charles was officially declared insolvent in about 1824, although his mother had from time to time arranged for the family trustees to pay his debts.[219] If this were not enough, Charles's father was a duke whose wife had left him, who had installed his mistress in a house at Blenheim Park with a number of his children by her, had squandered all his money and was living in impoverished circumstances in a corner of the Palace. Despite this, his name was a famous one, and when he accompanied Benett to a banquet given by the new mayor of Salisbury in the following year, the company was told that it was honoured by the presence of a descendant of the great Marlborough![220]

On 16 August, Tom Moore and his wife Bessy set off for their visit to Pythouse. Having changed horses at Warminster, they arrived between 5 and 6 in the afternoon. Moore records, probably to Bessy's relief, 'No company there but the husband elect, Lord Charles and a young Mr Jefferies'. Next day they set off to see Stourhead in Benett's coach and four 'with the lovers on the box'. The following day was a Sunday, and after Moore had taken Bessy to mass at Wardour, they went to see the ruins of Fonthill Abbey, now, of course, ostensibly belonging to Benett. Lord Charles seems to have become a reformed character after his misspent youth, as Moore records:

> Lord Charles (who may possibly end in a Saint) took his pretty Future to church this morning to receive the sacrament, and thought it not decorous to go sightseeing afterwards. Benett drove Bessy round the grounds of Fonthill while I took a solitary walk. Endeavoured to excogitate something during my stay here but could not – Much pressed to prolong our stay till the wedding (next Friday) but cannot spare the time. Bessy a good deal amused with the wedding raiment and trinkets – all splendid (and all on tick).

Having ordered horses, Moore and his wife started for home on the Monday, having 'received while at Benett's two packets of Mrs Shelley's communications relative to Lord Byron – had to pay 8s 6d for their *over* weight'.[221]

The wedding of Etheldred with Lord Charles duly took place at Tisbury on 24 August. What Benett thought of the reputation and family of his new son-in-law cannot be imagined, although the marriage of one of his children to a member of the aristocracy was perhaps a matter of satisfaction to him. Having in one year lost his wife by her death and one of his daughters by her marriage, the conduct of his son, John, was a cause of further anxiety to him. It seems that Benett had insisted that if his son was to go up to Oxford then he should study seriously and take a degree. This did not appeal to the 18-year-old John who wrote to his father:

> My dear father
> I have now made up my mind and write to inform you that I would prefer the army to Oxford, if I could not go to the latter without taking my degree. Mr Wright thinks it would be better for me to go to Oxford even without taking a degree however, I know your mind with regard to that. I should not like to go into a heavy regt – or the 15th, nay, I would rather go to Oxford on your conditions and I should prefer the 9th 3rd 8th 10th or 7th. However, I must take any regiment in which you can get me a commission but I suppose you will be able to get me one in one of the last mentioned .
>
> What has become of Ld and Lady Charles. I wrote to Ethel in Albermarle St where I suppose they are some time since but received no answer. . . I do not wish to say any more about money but of course the

sooner you can send me any the better as I positively do not know which way to turn and am literally afraid or rather ashamed to show myself in our village. Has Mr Wright written to you? I am glad to hear that you are at last settled comfortably. With love to Lucy[222]

John added a postscript 'My letters must begin to be as troublesome as Mr Chitty or rather more so'. Philip Mathews Chitty was a prominent Shaftesbury solicitor who had acted for Benett for some time. He was mayor of Shaftesbury in 1821 and 1826 and practiced in partnership with Charles Bowles, who was Recorder of Shaftesbury and the youngest brother of Benett's friend, the poet William Lisle Bowles.

During 1827, Benett spoke only twice in the House of Commons, on 18 June showing his pleasure that the corn bill had been rejected by the Lords.[223] Lucy's death was perhaps the cause of his unaccustomed silence, as well quite possibly as the work that was involved in preparing his *The National Interest Considered or the Relative Importance of Agriculture and Foreign Trade*, that was published in London at this time. In this work he set out all his arguments in defence of agricultural protection. At the end of a long review in the *Devizes and Wiltshire Gazette* (during the course of which reference is made to Benett having followed up his arguments with great ability and skill), it was stated that:

> It would afford us much pleasure, if it were in our power to devote a larger portion of our columns to the review of this interesting pamphlet: but we are obliged to be concise, and must therefore content ourselves by yielding a hearty assent to its concluding remarks. Indeed, we think every lover of his country, whether an advocate of Agriculture or Free Trade, must join in the eloquent language of Mr Benett and say:
>
> 'When we contemplate the diminutive spot occupied by Great Britain in the Map of Europe, and we compare her resources with those of other nations possessing similar or greater advantages – when we look back for a century only, and taking a view of her resources at that period, we compare them with what she now possesses – when we recollect that we have long supported the burden of a debt of eight hundred millions, without having been pressed to the earth by its weight – when we feel that we have, even with this pressure of debt, the power to defend our national honour and security by arms should it be required of us, we should pause, in these days of speculative philosophy, before we adopt an entire new theory on a subject which affects us so deeply, one of the great and leading interests of the country; to the protection, hitherto, of which interest we probably are indebted for the long continued advancement of our national prosperity, for our present greatness, our future wealth and power'.[224]

In May and June, he was in attendance in the House and presented on no less than five separate occasions petitions against the Test Acts. While Parliament was sitting he was, of course, living as usual in his house in Albermarle Street, and on 17 June Moore recorded in his diary:

> Was to have dined with Benett today, but my old friend Lady Bective invited us also, preferred it; See the Benetts almost every day, as he receives my letters under his cover from Bessy and I call there for them – the girls very pretty and lively and want me to take up my abode there, but distracted as I am even in my secluded back room at Bury Street, what should I be among them?[225]

On 1 October 1827, the readers of the *Salisbury and Winchester Journal* would have learned that 'Miss Benett last week made a present to the Salisbury and Wiltshire Library and Reading Society of a considerable number of curious and valuable fossils'.[226] The Miss Benett referred to was, of course, Benett's spinster sister who lived with her sister Anna Maria at Norton Bavant, the home of their ancestors since the 14th century. Etheldred, named after her grandmother, Etheldred, daughter of William Wake, Archbishop of Canterbury, was a truly remarkable woman who enjoys the distinction of being regarded as the first woman geologist.[227] For at least the previous twelve years, and probably longer, she had been actively pursuing her interest in geology and fossils. Justin B. Delair writes that in about 1813 she:

> . . . independently investigated the geology of Upper Chicksgrove Quarry, Tisbury. Assisted by quarryman John Montague, she carefully measured the strata there bed by bed, the result being one of the very first scientifically compiled sections ever made. The scale drawing of it was presented to the Geological Society of London in March 1815, with a note stating that, at that date, she had still to determine which beds hosted the fossils found in the quarry.[228]

In 1818, she wrote to the noted geologist Gideon Mantell[229] to tell him that Sir Richard Colt Hoare, having already produced his *History of Ancient Wiltshire*, was now 'very anxious to get a modern history also'. He was trying to 'stimulate everyone that can assist in it' and had proposed that Etheldred should undertake the Geology of the area surrounding Norton Bavant. She told Mantell that she had 'undertaken to attempt the Geology of Wiltshire decidedly for publication both as a separate thing and for the County history'. She said that her brother 'who had long before wished me to attempt the whole County now again strongly advised it'.[230]

She thought that her brother would 'write the article on Agriculture'. This was not to be but eventually, in 1831, she published *A Catalogue of Organic Remains of the County of Wilts*. Her catalogue, together with a letter addressed to Sir Richard Colt Hoare, was published in *The Modern History of South Wiltshire*[231] and a revised version, entitled *A Catalogue of the Organic Remains of the County of Wilts* appeared soon after. This contained a number of lithographic plates of various fossils based on her own sketches and drawings.[232] Canon J.E.Jackson[233] writing in 1882 relates:

> I used, when a student at Oxford, to attend the lectures of the well-known Dr. Buckland,[234] who brought that science [i.e. geology] so prominently into notice, and I recollect very well his speaking most highly of this geological lady and how her merits met with a rather curious reward. She had sent a set of Wiltshire fossils as a present to the Museum at St.Petersburg. The Emperor of Russia, wishing to acknowledge the gift by an Imperial compliment, supposing from the Anglo-Saxon name of Ethelred that the donor must be a gentleman, caused to be sent to her a very grand diploma, conferring on Miss Ethelred [sic] the Honorary Degree of Doctor of Civil Law in the University of St.Petersburg.[235]

She was in touch with the most eminent geologists of her day, and one of the first provisions of her will [236] was a gift to her 'highly valued and esteemed friend' George Bellas Greenough[237] of ten guineas for a ring and 'out of my library *The Histoire naturelle de la Montagne de St.Pierre de Maestricht* a work which I believe is not in his library'. Greenough was the first president of both the Geological and the Geographical Societies. She also made a small gift to 'my geological friend Gideon Algernon Mantell'.

Although geology was doubtless her major interest the comparatively new pursuit of archaeology also claimed her attention. Her name appears amongst the list of people who visited William Cunnington's[238] collection of antiquities at his house at Heytesbury,[239] and it seems that it was at her request[240] that barrows were opened at nearby Scratchbury Camp. Colt Hoare in his *History of Ancient Wiltshire* mentions a number of objects including a large amber ring and almost 50 amber beads being 'at present in the museum of Miss Benet at Norton House'.[241] When the newly formed Wiltshire Archaeological and Natural History Society held at meeting at Warminster in 1856, Etheldred lent to the temporary museum set up in the Town Hall 'a round Shield, apparently of Norman date discovered at Berwick St Leonard and a Roman Urn found at Norton'.[242]

The history of her ancestors did not escape the attention of her enquiring mind. Her kinsman the Rev. Henry Wake possessed the manuscript of her great-grand-father Archbishop Wake's attempt at compiling a history of the Wake family, and in 1833 she published it under the title of *A Brief Enquiry into the Antiquity, Honour and Estate of the name and family of Wake with a summary deduction of the lineal succession of the chief branches, down to this present time.*[243] Although the history of the Benetts appears not to have excited her interest, she did arrange for a seal to be made bearing the merchant's mark of her clothier ancestor. According to a copy of an obituary affixed to one of her portraits 'In private life this excellent lady was highly respected and beloved by a large circle of friends, for her sincerity of manners and her never-tiring charity and benevolence'. Etheldred's achievements as an amateur geologist have brought her name to the attention of her fellow scientists working at the end of the 20th century, with one of her unique specimens (known for a while as *Drepanites benett*) becoming the subject of two research papers at the Academy of Natural Sciences in Philadelphia.[244]

At the beginning of October, Benett found himself with 30 others as a guest of George Watson Taylor[245] and his wife at an extraordinary dinner held at Erlestoke Park near Devizes. The extravagance of the Watson Taylors' entertainments was legendary, and so Benett would not have been surprised when he entered the dining room to find 'a plateau of massy silver gilt, (about 30 feet long, it is said) blazing with lights, and surrounded by classical and admirably executed Tripods or candelabra, and groups of figures, nearly filled the entire centre of the long table. . . the figures on the Plateau bespoke at once the taste and opulence of the proprietor; whether as related to the designs, the intrinsic value (we do not vouch for the exact amount, but we have heard £18,000) – or the skill of the artists employed in its execution'.[246] It was not to be many years before the income of the 'opulent proprietor', that was founded on estates in Jamaica worked by slaves, was reduced to such an extent that all the contents of the mansion, described in the sale catalogue as being 'of superior elegance and taste as that which adorned The Abbey of Fonthill', were sold in 1832 by public auction.

In November, Tom Moore was writing to Benett again:

My dear Benett
I hear you have got some Regal residence somewhere (all owing to that cursed loyal taste of yours) but, not knowing the exact direction, I will send this to Pythouse.

I hope you are laying in a good stock of health for the next campaign, as you will have Turks as well as Tories to fight.

My love to the girls, & hearty regards to yourself
Ever yrs
T.Moore

I hope you have heard of Bowles's war against the Bench – (not of Bishops, no-no-catch him at that!) but of Magistrates. Codrington's nothing to him[247]

Moore's light-hearted reference to some regal residence would seem to suggest that Benett had recently been visiting or meeting some member of the royal family.

Following Lucy's death, Benett doubtless felt free to throw himself into the activities of the county with even greater vigour than before. In January 1828, a preliminary meeting was held at the *Bear Inn* in Devizes for the purpose of establishing a friendly society upon the principles of mutual insurance, by which 'a provision for old age, sickness, or infirmity may be secured by means of a small monthly contribution'. Benett was the moving spirit behind the enterprise and it is most likely that it was he who arranged for a large number of well known and influential people to sign a notice, inviting others to attend the meeting, that was published at the beginning of the month.[248] Not only did he and Astley together with the High Sheriff appear on the notice but from Salisbury, for example they were joined by the Bishop, the lawyer John Pern Tinney, the cutler Henry Shorto and Benett's kinsman, the silversmith James Bennett.

Most of the 'gentlemen of rank and fortune' of the county, therefore, were present at the meeting that was chaired by the Marquis of Lansdowne. Benett had been in touch with a number of those present and it was decided that he should address the meeting to explain the evils that attended the system of parochial friendly societies. He told the meeting that the funds of many of these societies had been materially injured, 'by feasting and extravagances and placing money in insecure investments, so that the poor man, when sickness or old age fell on him he was disappointed in the expectation he had formed and was deprived of that pittance to obtain which he had laid aside the savings of his younger days'. He said that most of the old societies had from 60 to 100 members, whereas it had been proved that the lowest number needed to ensure security should be 200. These evils could be remedied by the formation of a County Society, and he made a forcible appeal to those present and anticipated, 'a benefaction and an annual subscription to be applied in aid of the objects of the institution worthy of the opulent county of Wilts'.

He observed that such institutions tended to improve the moral condition of the poor and that 'there could be no greater inducement to the meeting to support the Society than the conviction that it would make a poor labourer a better husband, a better father and a better man'. He said that he had been an active magistrate of a large district for more than 30 years, and in almost every parish in which there was a friendly society he had scarcely known an instance of a single member being convicted of any serious offence. The meeting was adjourned to reconvene in April, having passed a number of resolutions (probably drafted by Benett) approving the taking of steps to form the new society.[249]

Many years later, Benett recalled the events that led to the formation and ultimate success of the Society. He said:

> Seeing the failure which attended all the parochial clubs, this was what gave Mr Lear and myself the idea of establishing a county institution. Well, we commenced, but we got no members. We subscribed largely ourselves and had stock in hand to the extent of two or three thousand pounds – and, I believe, I was that obstinate man who would not agree to divide the money, when it was found that we could gain no ground. The consequence was, we rested upon our oars: we could get nothing, because the landlords of the public houses set their faces against us. The Society gave no dinners, no jollifications: and the cause seemed hopeless, till it was later taken up by new hands. Mr Sotheron[250] came among us: he at once saw the advantages the Society would afford to the labouring classes: he gave his personal attention to it, laboured hard in carrying out the object for which it was established, and to him alone I attribute the success with which it has been crowned.

Sotheron replied by saying:

> Mr Benett has given some account of the manner in which the Society was formed, and in so doing has been good enough to put forward my pretensions. Allow me to put the matter on a right footing. I was only the apprentice: he was the head gardener. I turned up the sod, he put in the acorn.[251]

In the same month Benett played a part in a controversy that reflected well on him. In the previous year a woman named Catherine Cook was convicted of stealing some cups and saucers valued at 4s. 6d. (22p.) from her employer and was sentenced to six months in prison and fined £40. On her being unable to pay the fine, the magistrates proceeded to commute it to six months' solitary confinement over and above the term of imprisonment. Benett's friend William Bowles, well known as an active but lenient magistrate, was outraged, and successfully petitioned the King to have the sentence mitigated.[252] As a consequence, at the general quarter sessions of the peace held in Devizes, a resolution censuring Bowles for his conduct was debated. Paul Methuen supported the motion which was carried by 21 votes to 11 despite being vigorously opposed by Benett , George Crabbe and Lord Folkestone.[253]

Parliament sat again as usual in February 1828, and almost immediately Benett presented three petitions against the Test Acts and, consistent with his tolerant views in matters of religion, voted for their repeal. In the following month he was on his feet addressing the House in a debate about whether parishes should be empowered to raise funds to assist emigration by the poor. He strongly disapproved of parish officers having anything to do with emigration because they had an interest in sending emigrants away and out of their parishes. He observed that some men who were sentenced to transportation were in fact left in the hulks for three or four years, only to return to their native places when their moral principles were no better than when they were when they were put on board. It is they who should be sent to a new country, for by meeting with their old companions they 'again fell into evil habits and vicious courses'.[254]

In 1828, the first Bill to attempt to achieve commutation of tithes on a national basis was introduced into Parliament. Benett must have been pleased that at last there was a possibility that legislation would reach the statute book, and that his long held wish to see a commutation of tithes would come to pass. After Sir Robert Peel had addressed the House on a motion that the committee on the Tithe Commutation Bill be instructed to limit the duration of agreements under the bill to 21 years, Benett was soon on his feet to give the House the benefit of his experience and advice. He said that the object of the bill was to allow tithe to vary according to the price of corn and so if the time was limited to 21 years, no man would cultivate land without being obliged to give a third of the capital expenditure on the outlay to the tithe owner. When Peel observed that Benett had said that difficulty would be experienced in executing the provisions of the bill, he duly gave a further long explanation of his position.[255] In the event the Bill did not proceed and five years were to pass before another attempt was made to bring the matter to a conclusion.

In the following months the perennial question of the Corn Laws was again before the House, and Benett presented a petition from occupiers of land to the value of a million pounds a year in the neighbourhood of Salisbury, Warminster, Devizes and Marlborough, that the House would not legislate on the laws. At the same sitting he said that he had prepared certain resolutions as an amendment to the bill that had been proposed in 1827, but that he would not move them at the present time, although he was convinced that the new resolutions were generally unpopular and deserved to be so. When, a few days later, he proposed a duty of 24s. 4d. when the price of corn was at 66s., followed by a graduated scale, after considerable discussion his amendment was defeated with only 30 members in favour and 232 against.[256]

So well known was Benett's reputation as an opponent of any alteration to the corn laws that later in the year a letter appeared in the *Devizes and Wiltshire Gazette* addressed to him and headed '*On the dangerous consequences of the native consumers of lessening the cultivation of British grain*' and commencing:

> Sir, I beg permission to address this letter to you as a skilful agriculturalist, and an enlightened legislator. I know of no one to whom I can better point out this danger than yourself, nor any other way of conclusively showing it, than by the events of this extraordinary year. . . [and concluding] I most implicitly rely that you will be pleased to point out in a much clearer manner that I have, the destructive consequences of the corn bill whenever the resumption of your parliamentary duties will enable you to do so.
>
>               Sam S Quilter, Walton 14 Oct 1828[257]

As an acknowledged expert on all matters relating to agriculture and the countryside, in April he gave evidence before a committee of the House considering the Game Laws. In response to a question as to whether the mode of poaching was much altered during the time he had been a magistrate, he replied, 'Certainly: men go in much larger gangs, and sometimes in disguise. I cannot say that that relates to my own estate, for this reason, that some years ago I had a great deal of fighting upon my estate with respect to game: and I have since given up the preservation of game almost entirely'.[258]

The treatment of criminals and the causes of crime were matters that were always of interest to Benett partly, no doubt because as a magistrate and chairman of the Grand Jury in Wiltshire, he was regularly faced with those who had fallen foul of the law. So when the House was considering the question of criminal trials in Scotland – not, one would have thought, a matter of great concern or interest to the member for Wiltshire – his opinion was that the increase in crime was not produced by an actual growth in vice and immorality, but by the hardness of the times which reduced the lower orders to the commission of practices of which they would not otherwise be guilty. The House was considering the provision of an additional circuit court in Scotland, and Benett expressed the exceedingly sensible and modern view that members of the House would do better to seek out the cause of crime and check it, rather than to direct their attention merely to the punishment of offenders.[259]

In April, the adjourned meeting of the proposed Wiltshire Friendly Society was held in Devizes. Benett addressed it and having been called to the chair was then elected president of the Society,[260] a post he was to hold for the rest of his life. It was reported that Benett 'in a clear and able speech, at once showing the deep attention he had paid to the subject, and the great anxiety he felt for the welfare of the working classes of Society, explained to the meeting the particulars of the system which the Committee proposed to recommend'.[261] The formation of the Society – which still flourishes at the present day – was looked upon with suspicion by some. At the meeting of the Wiltshire Society in London in 1830, Benett said that 'the lower orders, for whose good it was established, could not conceive why gentlemen should come forward and contribute large sums of money, solely for relieving the poor. They imagined that there must be some sinister motive and that it was done to relieve parishes and not them. This (he said) arose from ignorance, and he was happy to observe that the erroneous feeling was fast wearing away'.[262]

As one of the county members, Benett was expected to be assiduous in his support of the Wiltshire Society, and was present at its annual meeting held in the *Albion Tavern* in London in May. The Earl of Suffolk[263] as chairman proposed the health of both Astley and Benett and said that he believed that no county was better represented than the county of Wilts. For while his honourable friend on his left watched over the manufacturing interest his honourable friend on his right (i.e. Benett) kept a close eye on the agriculture. This remark was met with cheers and laughter and further applause, and laughter greeted his hope that when the poor Wiltshire lad would be coming to London, Benett would not let him starve on the road. Benett responded and took the opportunity of commending the newly formed Wiltshire Friendly Society to the assembled company.[264]

Apart from the Corn Laws and reform of the system of parliamentary representation, the other burning topic of the day was the Catholic question. In May, on a motion that 'it be expedient to take into consideration the laws affecting his Majesty's Roman Catholic subjects with a view to a final and conciliatory adjustment for the peace and strength of the United Kingdom, the stability of the Established Church and the concord and satisfaction of his Majesty's subjects', Benett was one of the majority who voted in favour. Benett's old parliamentary opponent and fellow county member, Astley, was one of the minority who voted against.[265] When, in the following February, Astley presented a petition signed by more than 5000 Wiltshire people praying the House to maintain the Protestant Constitution 'entire and inviolate', Benett was on his feet expressing his cordial approbation of the proposed Catholic Relief Bill, which he was convinced was 'the best calculated not only to uphold the protestant establishment but also to give peace and tranquillity'.[266] He spoke against the anti-catholic petition from Wiltshire, congratulating the Duke of Wellington and his colleagues for their courage in bringing forward and persevering in the measure of relief for Roman Catholics.[267] He signed the county's pro-catholic address to the King and in the following month voted for emancipation. Following the passing of the Catholic Relief Bill, a small number of Roman Catholic peers, including Benett's neighbour Lord Arundell, were able to take their seats in the House of Lords.

By 1830, Benett is thought to have built a new farmhouse and buildings at Pythouse Farm and installed a threshing machine there driven by horses; and similarly a new house and buildings at Linley Farm to the north-west of Pythouse, with a threshing machine driven by water.[268] He continued, so far as he was able consistent with his parliamentary duties that occupied almost six months of each year, to manage his farms and to engage in agriculture. This he described, at the time, as having been 'the greatest amusement of his life'.[269] It is certain that he kept large flocks of sheep, and in a broadsheet published at the time of the 1818 election it is stated that he 'on one occasion made his own wool into cloth as his adversaries express it, at a time when wool was *unsaleable,* and employs a number of mechanics and labourers, paying them by *measure, task work,* as an encouragement to ingenuity and industry'.[270] There is an enduring tradition that he was the first to introduce Merino sheep into the county, although there is no contemporary documentary evidence to support this. However, he certainly had such sheep amongst his flocks and was convinced that they could be successfully and profitably reared in Wiltshire. When George, the son of his old friend William Wyndham, emigrated to Australia in 1827, he engaged in sheep farming and, in August 1828, William wrote to his son:

I was much gratified to find the South Down rams so much approved at Van Dieman's land. I hope they rank equally high in New South Wales. If you would like to have more of them, you know where to send; but I suppose the Merino are the most profitable on account of the wool, and I am glad you took Benett's rams with you. I am sure he will be very much pleased to hear how highly they are valued. He (Benett) often enquires after you.[271]

William's letter to his son written in July mentions that some further letters would be carried to Australia by a young man named Felton Mathews who, through Benett's influence, had obtained the post of deputy Surveyor of New South Wales. Some years later, in 1844, George Wyndham received a letter from his brother John who was rector of Sutton Mandeville in which he wrote:

Matt Marsh, having taken himself a wife ( a Miss Merewether, daughter of the Serjeant of that name), is just about to return to Australia, his being to Pythouse, and got some rams of Mr. B. I should have thought he might have got better ones elsewhere. I was there myself yesterday, and it amuses me very much to hear the old Squire. He attributes your lack of success entirely to not having taken more of his rams, and to your taking the 2 or 3 Southdowns you did. Neither will he believe it possible that India can be supplied with horses by you, though I assured him that they could mount themselves both cheaper and better thence than the Desert; by the way, I see they are making a rail road across the sea of sand to Suez; we shall be running across to have a look at you soon.[272]

Here we have a picture of Benett, who always had a high opinion of his own abilities (which were undoubtedly great in many fields) becoming even more opinionated as he grew old!

The last year of the decade opened with the usual round of balls with Benett and his family in the company of 100 'fashionables' attending the first Town and County Ball in Shaftesbury.[273] Benett on his own appeared at a ball held in the Assembly Rooms in Salisbury in aid of Spanish and Italian refugees,[274] and his family joined him at the last Shaftesbury Ball at the end of the month. It was at this time that, having been a member of the Bear Club of Devizes since 1804, he was at last elected president.

The year was, however, to be a sad one for Benett, as it saw the death in October of his younger son Thomas. A copy was made of some tantalisingly brief extracts from diaries kept by his sisters Anna and Lucy and they both mention that on 6 September 'Tom had his leg off'. At the beginning of October the *Devizes and Wiltshire Gazette* reported:

> We regret to state that Mr T.E. Benett, youngest son of our county representative, has been obliged (in consequence of a chill caught whilst shooting) to undergo the operation of amputation of the thigh. The operation was successfully performed by Mr.H.Coates of Salisbury. The patient bore it with fortitude and is now in a fair way of recovery.[275]

However, his recovery was short lived, as the 16-year-old Thomas died shortly afterwards at Mudeford (near Christchurch) where he had doubtless been convalescing. It was less than three years since his mother had died and was buried at Boyton with her ancestors rather than in the Benett family vault at Norton Bavant, and so Benett decided that his son should also be laid to rest in the church at Boyton. It is a curious coincidence that Benett's elder brother, also named Thomas, died at much the same age in 1789. Soon afterwards, Laetitia Wyndham, writing to her son George, tells him that 'Mr Benett and his daughters do not go out at present, on account of the death of poor Tom'. However, in the same letter and on a brighter note, she reports that young John, Thomas's elder brother, has become 'a smart dancing young man'.[276]

At the beginning of June, when two petitions for the repeal of the Corn Laws were presented to the House of Commons, Benett contended that the distress felt in the country did not arise from the effect of these laws, since the duty on corn was then, and had been for a long time, at a comparatively low level. When his son-in-law's brother, the Marquis of Blandford, called the attention of the House to the existence of closed or rotten boroughs, where the number of electors was so small that they were liable to be influenced by bribery – something that the House can hardly have not been very well aware – Benett rose to thank him for bringing forward the motion, and hoped that the motion would be an annual one until rendered unnecessary by success. He said he was no wild visionary reformer but was anxious to give the people a full and fair representation, and would vote for any motion that was calculated to effect that object.[277] Shortly afterwards a member presented a petition from people in Kent relating to tithes, in response to which Benett declared what by now everyone must have known, that he was in favour of commutation of tithes and hoped that in the next session it would be brought up and set at rest for ever.[278]

In the early months of 1830, Benett found himself having to consider what his friend John Peniston so aptly described as a 'tiresome subject'. It appears that in recent years the practice of erecting small houses in Salisbury to be let to poor weekly tenants had greatly increased. The churchwardens and overseers whose task it was to collect the parish poor rates found that they were suffering a serious shortfall in the amount of rates received because the owners of such houses were exempt from making any payments at all. As a consequence, the city corporation was persuaded to promote a bill, to be called The New Sarum Poor Bill, the effect of which would be to impose a liability on the owners of such houses – who promptly formed a committee, of which Peniston was a leading member, to oppose the bill. In January Peniston wrote to Benett at great length setting out the arguments and the resolution of the committee.[279] Further correspondence took place and in May Peniston wrote to Benett asking for a corrected copy of the proposed bill, and enquiring whether a clause could be introduced for exemption from its provisions where the parties agreed. Benett immediately sent him a copy, but Peniston refused to accept it because had he done so, he would have been obliged to pay a postal charge of 18 shillings, as the copy of the bill had handwritten interlineations on it! Peniston duly wrote to Benett informing him that he had declined to receive it and asking for another copy to be sent by private conveyance. It was uncharacteristic of Benett, who was normally extremely businesslike in his dealings, not to have realised that the postal charge would fall on Peniston. Although perhaps he did and was becoming a little tired of the extremely tedious intricacies of the bill, and of the negotiations between the parties who would be affected by it!

To be constantly owing money and to be pressed by one's creditors was a way of life common to numerous people in Benett's position in society. Although there is no evidence that Benett lived particularly extravagantly, the expense of keeping an establishment in London and in maintaining the life style expected of a county member of Parliament was considerable. It was not only tradesmen who were embarrassed by his inability to settle their accounts but even close members of his own family. His younger brother William,[280] who had been called to the bar after coming down from Oxford, was living in London with his wife Ellen and their three daughters. He looked to his elder brother for payment of an annuity due to him as sole executor of their father's will. In June 1830, William wrote to his brother: 'We are going on a long and expensive expedition for the recovery of Ellen's health, and as I had no opportunity of seeing you I hope you will pay the £100 into Messrs Drummonds. . . I have much need of it and it is now increased to £150'.[281] On his return from abroad in August he wrote again:

> I was disappointed on looking at my account at Messrs Drummonds to find that you had not paid the annuity which I had hoped you would have done during my absence from town. I am very much in want of it having been put to great expense in our excursion to France and cannot pay my debts without selling out of the Funds if I do not get what you owe me which will increase to £200 at Christmas. I thought that in settling our affairs you would have provided for the regular payment of this which I hope you will not suffer in future to be so much in arrears.[282]

Benett appears to have been meticulous in dealing with his business affairs and one must conclude therefore that he had not overlooked the payments that were due to his brother, but simply did not have the money available to pay what was owing to him.

Notwithstanding the appalling conditions endured by most of the agricultural labourers of the county at this time, and particularly those in the south-western corner of Wiltshire (where some of them must have been Benett's employees), the countryside itself, and indeed Benett's own land, had its attractions for such a critical observer as William Cobbett. On 1 September 1826 he had set out on one of his *Rural Rides*, travelling from Heytesbury to Warminster and passing through Benett's estate at Norton Bavant. He recorded:

> It is impossible for the eyes of man to be fixed on a finer country than that between the village of CODFORD and the town of WARMINSTER; and it is not very easy for the eyes of man to discover labouring people more miserable. There are two villages, one called NORTON BAVONT, and the other BISHOPSTROW, which I think form, together, one of the prettiest spots that my eyes ever beheld. The former village belongs to BENNET, the member for the county, who has a mansion there, in which his two sisters live, I am told.

In 1830 he wrote that if he were able to chose where to live his choice would fall on:

> some vale in Wiltshire. . . in short if Mr Bennet would give me a farm. . . in the parish of Norton Bavant just before you enter the village; if he would be so good as to do that, I would freely give up all the rest of the world the possession of whoever may get hold of it. I have hinted this to him once or twice before, but I am sorry to say he turns a deaf ear to my hinting![283]

# 6

## *The Battle of Pythouse 1830*

When speaking in the House of Commons for the very first time in 1819, Benett had urged that something be done to relieve the distress of the poor – and the rural poor in particular. It was the custom at this time for Parliament to resume its sittings at the beginning of February, and the wretched conditions in which many agricultural labourers and their families were compelled to exist was soon brought to the attention of the House. On 16 February 1830, Benett presented two petitions complaining of the general distress of the county of Wilts, and at the same time said that he could bear witness to it. He hoped that when the question of this distress came to the House, it would meet with the attention that its importance deserved.[1] In the following month the House debated the state of the poor, and Benett observed that he was certain that much of the distress that prevailed arose from the alteration which had been effected in the currency, because it took considerably from the means of those who were in the habit of employing the poor.[2] The three petitions complaining of agricultural distress that he presented to the House at the end of March were ordered to be printed.[3]

Parliamentary reform was also being debated again at this time and on 18 February Benett spoke almost immediately after an exceedingly long speech from his son-in-law's brother, the Marquis of Blandford.[4] He professed his admiration for the speech generally, although he could not promise him unconditional support, and he was disappointed that reform seemed to be taking precedence over measures to relieve distress.[5] At the end of March in a debate on whether there should be an enquiry into the state of the nation, he said:

> I am without party feeling on this question; and without agreeing with those gentlemen who profess to oppose the government on party grounds – although I think the government has done well in the reductions they have made, and I only wish they had made more – yet I feel myself obliged to vote for this enquiry, because it is demanded by a large class of people.

In June, he was on his feet again, this time speaking in a debate on proposals for the New Police. He said that one of the objections to the new system was that land in the neighbourhood of the metropolis gave aid to the rates, although its owners never required the attention of the police. If the system were extended, he said that we should, by and by, have a military police, the whole expense of which would fall on land.[6] Amongst the myriad of matters upon which Benett voted during May were the labourers' wages bill, the abolition of capital punishment for forgery that he favoured, and a proposal to reduce judges' salaries. On this vote he acted as a teller for the minority who favoured a reduction.

On 26 June, George IV died, and Benett was no doubt one of those who packed the chamber of the House at the end of the month to hear Sir Robert Peel complimenting the new monarch on ascending the throne, and condoling him on the loss which he and the country had sustained by, ' the demise of their late much lamented Sovereign'.[7] A few days later, on a third reading of the Beer Bill, Benett, rather surprisingly, said that he did not see how it necessarily followed that an increase in the consumption of beer would produce an increase in intoxication! It seemed to him that it would only place a wholesome and nutritious beverage within the reach of the labouring poor who most needed it. He thought that the number of beer shops would tend to keep the 'lower orders' from public houses and therefore promote both morality and comfort![8]

The death of the King resulted, of course, in the dissolution of Parliament and so, once again, Benett decided to present himself to the freeholders of the county for re-election, notwithstanding rumours that recent poor health would force him to retire. On 8 July, the *Devizes and Wiltshire Gazette* declared that the report that he might retire was altogether unfounded and:

> As proof of the vigour of the hon. Gent's health, we need only mention that within the last five months, (during which period, it will be recollected, the House of Commons has sat for more hours, on average, than on any former occasion) Mr Benett has been at his post, for a greater length of time than any other Member of the House, with the exception of the Speaker.[9]

His resolution to stand again was confirmed when, at a meeting of the Wiltshire Agricultural Society, both he and Astley expressed their intention to offer themselves for the county and, ' if returned, of honestly and zealously performing the duties attached to their high station'.[10]

In his letter to the freeholders, Benett said he would continue to pursue the same course of strict independence which he had hitherto maintained. He would not relax his exertions to reduce the peoples' burdens, and to secure for them all liberty, both civil and religious, which they could and ought to enjoy.[11] The election took place as usual at the ancient cross at Wilton and, as Benett and Astley were the only candidates, they were both duly returned. In addressing the electors, Benett told them that he had voted for a reduction in public expenditure, and it was his wish that all useless places (i.e. sinecures) should be abolished. This would reduce the taxes that pressed upon productive industry, it being his opinion that taxes should be borne by the rich and not by the poor. In particular, he lamented that he had hitherto repeatedly found himself voting with the minorities in the House.[12] Following the election at Wilton, both Benett and Astley proceeded to Salisbury and it was reported that the crowds who lined their route were amply supplied with alcoholic refreshment, presumably at the expense of their new representatives. In accordance with a tradition that has survived to the 21st century, the new members addressed the crowds who had assembled outside the *White Hart* and 'at the conclusion, Mr Benett proposed three good cheers for the ladies of Wiltshire, to whom he and Sir John were indebted for their election for (said the hon. gent.) if your wives had been opposed to us (being under their influence) you would not have dared to vote for us'![13] As supporters of reform, both the candidates found favour with the *Devizes and Wiltshire Gazette* that 'trusted that Wiltshire would long have to boast of her two loyal and patriotic representatives.'[14]

In August, a county meeting was held at Devizes for the purpose of congratulating the new King on his accession to the throne. Benett seconded the Marquis of Lansdowne's proposal by declaring that he was a sincere friend of a limited monarchy, conceiving it best calculated to promote the true interests of the people and seeing that it had raised the country to the highest pitch of glory.[15]

Parliament sat again in August and Benett spoke in favour of civil and religious liberties. In November he presented a number of petitions from the people of Wiltshire against slavery and distress, and in presenting a petition against malt duty he was rash enough to boast that there had been no disturbances in Wiltshire. Although in his election speech he declared that he entered this Parliament with the intention of supporting the Wellington ministry, he was listed by the ministers as one of their 'foes' and, dismayed by Wellingon's declaration against parliamentary reform, he voted against the government on the civil list on 15 November, which led to their replacement by a ministry led by Grey.

Although no longer mentioned in Tom Moore's journal after June 1827, it is clear that the poet remained in touch with Benett and corresponded with him from time to time. On 1 September, 1830 Moore recorded in his journal that on returning to London he met Richard Sheil,[16] the dramatist and noted advocate of Catholic emancipation. They walked together for a while and Sheil mentioned that Moore would have 'no difficulty in getting into Parliament for some Irish seat if he would but look for it'. Earlier in the year, Sheil had ignominiously failed to secure election as member for Louth, and their conversation must have reminded Moore that he had promised to do something to help Sheil find another seat. On the same day, therefore, he wrote to Benett:

> My dear Benett
>
> I ought to have written to you on the subject of this letter long before and shall therefore take it as the greatest favour if you will, as far as in you lies, repair my transgression by furnishing me with the answer as soon as possible. The matter briefly is this – Sheil you may have seen, has been by ill management thrown out of Louth and there is great anxiety among his friends here to get him into Parliament. In talking on the subject the other day it was mentioned by some one that our friend Lord Charles Churchill was anxious to transfer his seat at Woodstock and saying that I knew him a request was made that I would endeavour to find out whether such was his wish and to intimate that Sheil would be forthcoming with whatever sum would be requisite for the arrangement. This (though at the same time professing my misbelief in the report) I undertook to do but from the perpetual bustle and (what the old Irish used to call coshering) in which I am kept here have not had a minute to perform till now – and can run, having hardly written, I fear, intelligibly, as the clock is upon the very point of striking the last post hour – answer me I conjure you, forthwith
>
> > Bessy sends best regards
> >
> > Ever yours T .Moore[17]

In the event, Lord Charles remained as one of the members for Woodstock until the passing of the Reform Bill and later sat for a while as the only representative of the family in the one seat that survived. In the following year, through the influence of the Marquis of Anglesey,[18] Sheil was returned as member for Milborne Port in Dorset.

In October, the Wiltshire yeomanry cavalry met for two days' permanent duty, following which a grand ball and supper were given to the officers by the subscribers to the Devizes Assemblies. While Benett, as an officer of the cavalry, joined the 'fashionables' in the Town Hall in Devizes, the non-commissioned officers and several of the principal tradesmen of Devizes held a ball and supper in the Long Room at the *Bear Inn*. This, according to the newspaper report of the proceedings, 'was little, if any, inferior to the one just noticed' and continued until 5 in the morning, when 'God Save the King' was performed and 'the respective parties went home as merry as grigs'![19]

A few days later, Benett had an encounter, probably for the first time, with the girl who would, before very long, be Queen. The Duchess of Kent[20] had decided that her eleven-year-old daughter, the young Victoria, should see a little of the country over which she would almost certainly one day reign. So towards the end of October the royal mother and daughter were at Erlestoke Park, near Devizes, as guests of George Watson Taylor. Benett, who had on at least one previous occasion enjoyed the Watson Taylors' lavish and extravagant hospitality, was one of those present at a dinner given in their honour. Tom Moore records in his journal that he was also present, and it was doubtless expected that he would entertain the company. However, as the day was a Sunday, the Duchess protested against there being any music.[21] On the following day the royal party left Erlestoke Park and proceeded to Salisbury, visiting Stonehenge on the way. Having spent the night at the *White Hart* inn, the royal couple visited the cathedral and then 'partook of an elegant *dejeune a la fourchette*' at the College in Salisbury, the seat of Wadham Wyndham. Here, according to the newspaper report, the 'Earl of Radnor, Mr Benett and a number of other distinguished personages attended to pay their respects to their Royal Highnesses'.[22]

Whilst Benett enjoyed the Watson Taylors' hospitality and the officers and non-commissioned officers of the Yeomanry Cavalry disported themselves in Devizes, the poor labourer continued with the struggle to maintain himself and his often numerous offspring. Of course the poor had always been present in the countryside but, by the autumn of 1830, events had conspired to bring their grievances to a head. The want of employment amongst agricultural workers, exacerbated by the introduction of machinery, a cold summer followed by a poor harvest and the high price of bread, all resulted in the sufferings of agricultural labourers in the south of Wiltshire becoming acute. Indeed, Benett's friend and neighbour, Lord Arundell, described Benett's home parish of Tisbury as 'a Parish in which the Poor have been more oppressed and are in greater misery as a whole than any Parish in the Kingdom'.[23] Arundell may have been exaggerating, but in the unlikely event that Benett remunerated his workers more generously than his fellow landowners and employers, Benett must surely share in responsibility for this shameful state of affairs.

As a consequence, in the autumn riots and the destruction of machinery began to spread westwards across the southern counties, and the Wiltshire magistrates met to warn the yeomanry to be ready to act. Lord Arundell was commander of the Salisbury troop and William,[24] son of Benett's old friend William Wyndham, of the Hindon troop.

In the absence of a police force it was necessary to recruit large numbers of special constables, and on 14 November a meeting was held at Warminster chaired by the Marquis of Bath. At its conclusion a number of resolutions were passed and a large number of 'gentlemen and persons who volunteered' were sworn in as special constables.[25]

At the beginning of November, serious disturbances occurred in Salisbury and Charlotte Wyndham writing on the 14th reported:

> The whole county of Wilts is at present in a state of agitation, particularly near Salisbury, to which William[26] was yesterday ordered with the Hindon Yeomanry. We heard this morning that the mob was quietly dispersed in different directions, so we hope there will be no rioting of any consequence. We feel ourselves perfectly safe, as the parishioners of Dinton are all contented, and I believe neither Papa nor any of us ever oppressed or wronged a poor person. The mob's vengeance is chiefly directed against the machinery, which they burned, and not infrequently set fire to the ricks of corn and hay at the same time.[27]

Four days later, much machinery was destroyed in the neighbourhood of Alderbury to the east of Salisbury and not far from Longford Castle, seat of the Earl of Radnor. Having dealt with the disorder there and taken twelve of the rioters prisoner, the Hindon troop returned to Salisbury, and on the following morning received the news from a farmer who arrived from Hindon that very serious disturbances were expected in that part of the county. How right he was!

Benett was in London as usual attending to his parliamentary duties, and on 22 November, when the Marquis of Chandos[28] moved for leave to bring in a bill to amend the Game Laws and to legalise the sale of game, Benett said that he thought the motion should have been passed in the last session.[29] However, having heard that nightly meetings were being held in the neighbourhood of Pythouse, on the following day, on the motion of the Whig whip, he was granted three weeks' leave from the House on account of the 'disturbed state of his county' and hurried home. It seems that Benett's daughters, Lucy and

Etheldred, had been at Philip Chitty's house in Shaftesbury, as on the 25th he wrote to Benett:

> I am this moment returned from Motcombe and I am fearful that Miss Benett and Lady Charles have acted imprudently in leaving my House.[30]
> I hope I shall be disappointed in my expectation and fears. Again I advise you to leave Pythouse. I hope the meeting of Magistrates tomorrow will do good – nothing but positive orders from Persons in authority will make the Farmers take upon themselves the office of Special Constables. I cannot possibly go to Pythouse today. I am pressed on all sides more than you can imagine. I am happy the Motcombe labourers have separated. For God's sake take care of yourself . . . keep up the force at Pythouse – the Secretary of State has written to the Magistrates of this Division stating that Troops are at Hindon ready to come down on their sending for them.[31]

That Benett would take Chitty's advice and desert Pythouse was the last thing he would have done.

Having arrived home in the early hours of the morning and having been in bed for only two hours, he was woken by his bailiff who told him that people had assembled with the object of destroying firstly 'a manufactory' at nearby Fonthill, and then his own machines. Benett owned at least two large machines – one at the farm at Pythouse worked by six horses and the other worked by water at Linley Farm nearby. Such machines might be worth £100 or more.[32] Having written to a fellow magistrate to come to his assistance, he mounted his horse and called on a number of neighbouring farmers asking them to accompany him. None was willing to do so, saying that both they and he would be murdered if they did.

Benett set out to confront the mob and at about ten o'clock he came upon some 400 armed with sticks and led by two men, one of whom told Benett that they intended to break all his threshing machines and have 2s. a day for wages. He remonstrated with them, telling them where their conduct would lead, and that he had the King's proclamation (i.e. a copy of the Riot Act) in his pocket, which they would not allow him to read. Some of the mob said to him 'We are Hunt's men, not yours'; they would not hurt a hair of his head but would break his machines.

The mob, by then consisting of about 500 men, moved towards Pythouse and went into the farmyard to break the machines there. Benett told them that he had no means of stopping them by force, but entreated them not to proceed to extremes as he could afterwards punish them. He sat quietly on his horse for about ten minutes while they broke open the door of the barn and began smashing the machine, and was then suddenly hit by a stone and knocked unconscious. When he recovered consciousness, he discovered that his horse had carried him into a lane where he became entangled amongst a team of his own carts. The mob continued to pelt him with stones and so he drew a pistol saying to them: 'If you throw another stone, I will fire', following which he managed to escape to the house that was barricaded as effectively as possible with five armed men inside. An incident then occurred that was widely reported and believed at the time. If true, it makes it clear how close Pythouse came to being seriously damaged. It appears that a half-penny was tossed to decide whether the mob should attack the house, or break one of Benett's water machines about half a mile away. By the tossing of a coin, the house was saved.

Having retired to the house and to his bed, he was shortly afterwards roused by William Wyndham, who had come to see whether he was still alive and to tell him that the mob were engaged in breaking his machines. He accordingly set off with Wyndham and the Hindon troop of yeomanry cavalry, who had now arrived with Wyndham's kinsman and fellow magistrate Wadham Wyndham. They found the mob armed with hatchets, pickaxes, sticks and stones. Later, Benett told the House of Commons that Wyndham endeavoured, without success, to read the Riot Act. He then dispersed some of the mob, telling them that if they continued to throw stones, the troop would be ordered to fire. The stone-throwing continued and so Wyndham asked Benett whether they should fire. He replied: 'For God's sake do not, if you can help it; but we must, at all events, beat them'.

Wyndham must have then decided that his men had endured the assault of the mob for long enough, for he then ordered them to charge. The troop divided into two squadrons near a plantation of fir trees, one going to the right and the other to the left. The road being narrow for more than 100 yards, the mob pelted the yeomanry with stones from amongst the trees. At the end of the plantation, the two squadrons met again whereupon the mob armed with bludgeons, pickaxes, hatchets and other similar weapons commenced a furious attack. The confrontation, thereafter known as the Battle of Pythouse, lasted for about half an hour and at the end of that time the yeomanry force of 44 men, having fired several pistol shots and inflicted many sabre wounds, eventually dispersed the mob. Many of the rioters were injured and one, John Harding, was killed by one of the yeomanry, who fired on three or four of the rioters who were attacking him. However, local tradition had it that the fatality was caused by a farmer from Chilmark who snatched a gun from a gamekeeper's hand and shot one of the rioters.[33] Several of the cavalry were wounded but none seriously.

Benett then retired to Pythouse and immediately sat down to write a long letter to the Marquis of Lansdowne, the Lord Lieutenant, at Lansdowne House in London. This he appears to have done with some difficulty – as a result, no doubt, of the injuries he had sustained and of his exceedingly agitated state of mind. Indeed, some parts of the letter are illegible, commencing on quite small sheets of paper and continuing on larger. Having given a long and detailed account of what had occurred he continued:

> The magistrates here have all given way and I stand alone without any assistance. Even the Hindon Troop of Yeomanry are at Salisbury. We know many of the ringleaders but have no force to apprehend them with and I am now preparing to defend my House which they threaten to attack but I have only ten men and 3 fowling pieces. The party is now at work on a water threshing machine of mine and on a corn mill. 20 dragoons and 40 cavalry...would have beaten the whole body. If there are any troops at Dorchester not wanted could not a troop be sent to Hindon . . . after a severe engagement we have taken 25 prisoners. I regret to say one man has been killed on the side of the rioters. I still wish we had a troop of Horse at Hindon as the men [are] so drunk will now use firearms and hatchets. [34]

In the event, Benett had no alternative but to rely on a small detachment of men of the Hindon troop, who mounted guard throughout the night.

On the following day, Lord Arundell called at Pythouse with the intention, no doubt, of seeing how Benett had fared, and of obtaining a first-hand account of what had occurred. He immediately wrote to John Peniston, and his letter throws some light on how Benett was regarded by the people of the district at this time, as well as on Arundell's opinion on the conduct of the yeomanry cavalry:

> Dear Sir, You are probably aware by this time that Colonel Mair,[35] thinking my presence at home might tend to calm the ferment existing in Tisbury, requested me on Saturday to go home and return hither this morning. I obeyed his wishes. I yesterday saw Mr Benett; he has recovered his bruises, but surrounded by eighteen men of the Hindon troop, seemed to me in a considerable state of excitement and alarm. He complained that none of the people, farmers or gentry, would come to his assistance: a small party of twenty, farmers and others of Fonthill and Tisbury, went to him afterwards, and were sworn in as special constables. I announced in our chapel[36] my wish that people should be sworn in, and

at three o'clock p.m., Mr Thomas Grove[37] and myself administered the oaths to two hundred men at Ansty, Hatch and Tisbury, formed them into squads, and gave them leaders. Nothing can exceed the good feeling of the people towards me. I am sorry to say no goodwill to my poor neighbour. The mob who attacked him were composed of men from Swallowcliff, Tisbury, and the Fonthills, and would have desisted on Mr.Benett's persuasions had he not been persuaded to the contrary by the Hindon men after he had addressed the former. Mr.B. is now actively engaged in taking up prisoners, and sending them in under detachment every hour. All this may be necessary, but I fear may lead to bad consequences. Col.Mair is of my opinion and has gone off to Pythouse . . .

I know not what to say upon the conduct of the Hindon troop. It is a delicate question, and till I see the ground on which they fought I cannot help fancying they might have taken more prisoners by drawing the mob out, and not charging them when they did; mixed as they were with the people they could not do otherwise than wound those they did. I found at home two men not taken, one with a slice off his head, and another with his hand cut off. I have heard of many others . . .

Yours very truly, Arundell

Postscript. Young Lambert is making himself very obnoxious. Benett comes in with his witnesses on Wednesday. The men of the two Donheads and Semley assembled, and on the same day (Thursday the 25th) were addressed by Mr.Grove, who allowed them to burn his machines, and returned home peaceably; so much for conciliation.[38]

It is clear from Arundell's postscript that Thomas Grove's efforts at conciliation did him no good, and the conclusion may be drawn that the firm handling of the rioters at Pythouse was decisive in preventing any further disturbances in the district.

In his letter to Peniston, Arundell describes Benett as being 'in a considerable state of excitement and alarm'. Benett should be forgiven for being so. At about this time, and probably on the 27th, he wrote to 'My dear Wyndham', a letter, most unusually undated, in which, once again, his almost illegible handwriting is a clear indication of his state of mind:

We have had a quiet night but Messrs Thring and Ravenwood (?) were with me by seven o'clock to tell me that a large number of clothiers were appointed to meet early on Hindon Down . . . I think it highly necessary that you should bring your Troop to Hindon as soon as possible. This moment while I am writing a report is brought to me that a very large body is now at Chilmark intent on coming to this House. . .

The presence of a riotous mob threatening to destroy his house must have appeared reminiscent of the scenes that occurred in France at the beginning of the revolution there not so many years before. On the 26th he wrote from Pythouse:

I really do not know whether I will be able to go to Salisbury or not on Monday or if I may be able to spare the evidence agst the man so soon. I will however let you know on Sunday and I must request the Magistrates to detain the prisoners for which should there be any difficulty I will be answerable. To discharge them at this moment of excitement would be highly dangerous

In gt haste

I am yours

John Benett

We have been quiet all day though many alarming and unfounded reports have been spread and I am told that my House is to be attacked by a large mob.

While I am writing I have rec'd a letter from Lord Radnor which puts all in spirits as he tells me that we are to have 20 Lancers together with the Hindon Troop at Hindon tonight. I'm much disfigured but not seriously hurt. Pray tell Lord Radnor I am much obliged by his letter which I have not time to reply to at present as I cannot get a single farmer or brother magistrate ever to come to my assistance nor can I rely on any of my own men to fight as you know.

Show this to Wadham Wyndham and I write with difficulty not being able to see very well

I hope you are not quite disabled.

I am yours

most truly

John Benett[39]

On 27 November, Benett wrote once again to the Lord Lieutenant:

The night passed over in quiet but the exasperation of my resistance is great and the Farmers terrified so much . . . that I have not been able to get any of them to serve as special constables or to come here to assist me, although they all expect this House to be attacked and destroyed every hour. Some of the farmers are . . . to me and others acting on encouraging the rioters. I believe under the influence of Cobbett's writing on Hunt's advice as he has been in every part of the neighbourhood and riots have followed him. The storm I am told and believe is for me in every quarter because no one in this part of the county except myself has shown any resistance and I am therefore singled out by the rioters as the only enemy. I have only 16 of the Hindon Troop of yeomanry in the House and 5 or 6 tenants on whom I can rely but we shall defend the House I trust with every success. We sent over 29 prisoners to the prison at Salisbury in the night safely under the care of the Hindon troop which is detained yet in Salisbury . . . I wish it may be possible to have a troop of cavalry at Hindon as the yeomanry are much exhausted. I expect the rioters may use firearms. I wish also that I could get 25 good muskets to defend my House with . . . I have only 3 fowling pieces and a few pistols . . .[40]

Benett's fears were ill-founded as, in the event, no attack was made on Pythouse and peace returned to the countryside. News and false rumours, however, travelled very quickly. On 27 November, Lady Elisabeth Fielding[41] wrote to her son William Fox Talbot[42] at Lacock Abbey, 'Last night at Mrs Hope's it was reported that Mr Bennett the Member for Wiltshire, was dead of his wounds, but it turns out not to be true'.[43]

On the same day, an inquest was held on the body of John Harding and a verdict of justifiable homicide returned by the jury.[44] Benett very sensibly decided not to be present. As Harding had apparently been killed by a pistol shot, the coroner called on Benett before the hearing and asked to see the cartouche-boxes of the yeomanry to see the size of the balls. However, as many of the yeomanry made their own cartridges, they appeared of various sizes. The coroner asked Benett whether he should go and see the place where the affray took place, to which he replied, 'Go where you like, I shall not say a word to you on the subject'. After the inquest, the coroner told Benett that three people offered to perjure themselves, and to swear that the man was killed in a different way from that in which he really was killed, and that he never knew of any case in which so much perjured testimony was offered.[45]

Laetitia Wyndham, writing on the following day to her son George, who had emigrated to Australia, gives her version of the events:

. . . The riots, which you will see by the papers, began in Kent, extended through Sussex and Hampshire, and had just reached Wilts; the Yeomanry in consequence was ordered out. They dispersed the mob at Salisbury, and prevented the destruction of an iron foundry. At Wilton and Barford the machines were all broken. By the active exertions of your father in swearing in constables, etc., aided by Mr Lear and Mr King, the villages of Dinton, Teffont and Chilmark were kept perfectly quiet but at Tisbury etc., the rioting was dreadful. The mob marched to Pythouse, demolishing all the machines on the way, and when there tossed up, after destroying all of Mr Benett's threshing machines, whether they pull down Pythouse, or go on to the next. They went on to the next, and while there the Hindon troop of Yeomanry arrived, and after a desperate affray routed the mob, consisting of six or seven hundred, and took twenty-eight prisoners. Your brother received a severe contusion in the face from a stone, but was not otherwise injured, and is now nearly well. This defeat of the riots has, I trust, done much good, and has prevented it extending farther in the country.[46]

In reporting the 'battle of Pythouse', the name that soon became associated with the events of the previous month, the *Devizes and Wiltshire Gazette* concluded by declaring that, 'the manly and high spirited behaviour of Mr Benett on this occasion cannot be mentioned in too high terms of commendation',[47] a judgement by no means shared by all his compatriots.

On 1 December, an examination of the prisoners took place in Salisbury before a number of magistrates, led by the Earl of Radnor and Lord Arundell. Benett was, of course, present, 'directing the prosecution' according to the *Devizes and Wiltshire Gazette*. The use of this phrase no doubt contributed to the widely held belief that Benett acted as prosecutor, judge and jury in the trial of the rioters. In reporting the examination of the prisoners, the *Gazette* observed that Benett's face 'exhibits the signs of a black eye and a lacerated nose', and that 'the number of bandaged and plastered heads, shades over the cheeks and eyes, and other symptoms, amongst the persons present in court, attested to the severity of the affray'. The newspaper reported that ' many of the prisoners received excellent characters from their masters and others. One of them (a mason named Abery), upon being asked if any person could speak in his favour, appealed to Lord Arundell. His Lordship said he knew the man, who had worked for him for the last year; that he was an industrious fellow, and he was very sorry to see him here. He added that he was the very person, who, when Salisbury Cathedral was repaired, was hauled up to the top in a basket'. Benett also testified to the character of several of the prisoners and applied for their release. Almost all the men were married, but when the first of them to be asked whether he had a family, declared that he had nine children, the question was not put to any of the others!

No questions were asked as to why they had taken part in the affray, nor were they given an opportunity to air their grievances. But when later a newspaper reporter asked several of the discharged prisoners their motive for joining the mob, they replied that the farmers were at the bottom of it; that they gave the men beer and urged them to excess. He writes that he would not have thought this statement worthy of record had not 'Mr Benett, in the course of the examination, distinctly referred to one farmer, *by name,* as having encouraged the men to these acts of disorder'.[48]

In the view of Ella Wyndham, writing to her brother in New South Wales in the April of the following year, 'the law was administered with the utmost leniency, for the magistrates rarely committed the common labourers unless there was proof positive of their having been guilty of some great offence, and it is said that they were chiefly shoemakers and little tradesmen who made so much disturbance and destroyed so much property'.[49]

The Government made very speedy plans for a special assize to be held in Salisbury to try the prisoners committed by the magistrates following the riots both at Pythouse and elsewhere. Witnesses to be called swore depositions setting out details of the evidence they would be able to give and, on 20 December, one James Snow came to Pythouse to sign with his mark and then swear before Benett his deposition showing that he had witnessed the destruction of the threshing machines at Lawn Farm and Linley Farm.[50]

Benson and Hatcher, writing thirteen years after the event, painted a succinct picture of the commencement of the proceedings:

> Friday, December 31, the preliminary arrangements were completed for the holding of a special assize to try the captured rioters. That day the judges arrived, and were escorted into the city by the High Sheriff, and a hundred of the yeomany and gentry on horseback, while the carriages of others closed the procession. At the entrance of the city they were met by the mayor and corporation in several carriages. The streets on both sides, from the entrance of the city to the cathedral, were lined with special constables. At the cathedral they were received in the usual form by the dean and residentiaries. The number of persons committed for trial amounted to 330.[51]
>
> On the following day, the court sat and commenced by hearing the case against seventeen of the rioters, including James Blandford, a Tisbury labourer who was considered to be one of their leaders, and a blacksmith named Edmund White. The Grand Jury presented that:
> at Pythouse farm . . . [they] unlawfully maliciously and feloniously did cut break and destroy a certain threshing machine then and there being of and belonging to one John Benett Esquire and of great value to wit the value of one hundred pounds to the great damage of the said John Benett . . .[52]

Benett was named in the presentment as the prosecutor and gave evidence himself, describing what had occurred and identifying some of the prisoners. John Brigell, Benett's carter, James Jay his bailiff and Thomas Ball his coachman also gave evidence. Other witnesses were called to prove that all the prisoners were active in, and present at, the breaking of the threshing machine, with the exception of Edmund White. No witnesses were cross-examined, nor were the men legally represented, although they were permitted to address the court themselves. Most of the prisoners said that they had been pressed by the mob and expressed their sorrow at having joined them.

Lord Arundell and Benett and several others gave six of them excellent characters, with Benett speaking for Andrew Moxam, who was found not guilty, and declaring that 'Moxam is an excellent and industrious labourer'.[53] In no time at all, fifteen of the rioters were found guilty with Edmund White and another found not guilty and so discharged.[54] By modern standards of justice, none of them would have been considered to have had a fair trial.

On the following day, James Blandford, Edmund White and four others were charged with another offence of machine breaking. Benett's bailiff gave evidence once again, following which Blandford exclaimed that he had 'sworn very falsely as a great many others had'. This time, they were all found guilty with White and three others (but not Blandford) being recommended to mercy.

On the next day, Blandford (who in 1827 had been convicted for stealing from the person of Henry Lambert a purse containing £14 in gold and silver and a one pound promissory note[55]) was sentenced to be transported for 14 years, 13 others for 7 years with the remaining two being sentenced to be imprisioned for a year with hard labour.[56]

The Grand Jury had also presented that James Blandford and five other Tisbury labourers:

> with force of arms . . . together with divers to wit four hundred other persons to the Jurors aforesaid unknown of an evil seditious and turbulent disposition unlawfully riotously routously and tumultuously assembled together armed with sticks staves stones bludgeons and other offensive weapons to disturb the peace of our said Lord the King . . . and riotously routously tumultuously in a threatening offensive and alarming manner went armed as aforesaid to a certain farm of one John Benett Esquire . . . and there at the said farm . . . did riotously and violently assault beat bruise and wound the said John Benett he the said John Benett being one of his Majesty's Justices of the Peace in and for the said County to the great injury alarm and disturbance not only to the said John Benett and

other of his Majesty's liege subjects who were then and there quietly inhabiting and residing on the said farm but also of all other his said Majesty's subjects inhabiting and residing in the neighbourhood...[57]

This charge appears not to have come before the court. As will be seen, Benett later said in Parliament that he had refused to prosecute some men, who, if convicted (and they surely would have been) would almost certainly have been sentenced to death. This is no doubt the reason why the charge relating to the assault on Benett was not brought before the court.

After the special assize had sat for a week, Benett came on the Bench and addressed the Court:

> Mr Justice James Parkes, as Foreman of the Grand jury, I have a most pleasing duty to perform, which is to read a paper they have written and which I will now do. The grand Jury beg leave to present their thanks to Mr Justice J Parkes for his able charge on Saturday. Thinking that such a clear exposition of the law would at this time be highly useful to all orders of the community they request his Lordship will allow them to have it printed. In which request and thanks I beg, my Lord, most cordially to join.[58]

Several of the rioters had written to Benett hoping for mercy. Edmund White, who was probably known to him, wrote:

> Your Honour
> i have sent to you to beg your pardon and am sorry that I should have went with the mob but i hope your honour will forgive me as i most humbly beg your pardon and was forced to go as my life was threatened by some of the ringleaders before it was light but i Own myself in fault and do most humbly beg your pardon for to forgive me i shall remain
> your obedient and humble servant
> Edmund White

Benett endorsed this letter 'I tried to save this man from transportation but without effect. He was a young Blacksmith with a good previous character but did much mischief'.[59]

Edmund White had earlier written a letter to Benett from Fisherton gaol:

> Mr John Bennett esqr pythouse
> Sir i am Sorry that i should have offended you on this occasion but i hope Your honour will be favourable to me as it is the first offence and being forced possible to leave my work being pulled out of shop by two persons

by the name of Samuel Ares and Thomas hayter early on Thursday morning as the rioting began by which i said i was bisy and would not go went to my work as usual for the space of an hour or more till the mob returned as i was going to breakfast Ric Chivrel entered the door with a . . . sledge in his hand and said come thee must go with us which i answered i was busy and would not go and he pushed me to the door where there stood william snook of ansty with a large ash blugeon in his hand and said go on or else i will make thee. I went into shop and said i wouldnt go for I was going to shoe the doctors horse by which several went out of shop and Charles Garred their Captain as he called himself said is not he coming by which the mob answered he is going to shew the doctors horse which Answer Charles Garred said damnation cease the doctors horse make him come or else beat the bugers damnation brain out by which several and said that if I offered to go back be darned if they would not kill me i am sir your Obedient and humble servant Edmund White[60]

Benett was not the only one who had an interest in the welfare of young Edmund. Laetitia Wyndham writing again to her son George in New South Wales in January 1831:

Papa has done much to get one of the men's sentences mitigated. He is a native of Chicksgrove or Tisbury, and a blacksmith. He was always reckoned the most quiet, industrious young man in the parish. He was absolutely collared and taken away out of his father's house by violence; but, of course, when his spirit was up he was active enough, and being a blacksmith he well knew how to break the plows and rollers. Now don't laugh at me very much for what follows, because I know there is hardly a chance of your ever seeing poor Edmund White, but if you do, don't forget that Papa has interested himself in his behalf. He has seven years to spend at Botany Bay.[61]

Laetitia may have forgotten that she had already mentioned Edmund White to her son, as in April when writing to him again she tells him that in her view it would be a pity that he should be left with common convicts and thinks him very likely to make a good and useful servant.

If Benett is to be believed (and there is no reason to suppose that Benett ever deliberately told an untruth, despite Paul Methuen's assertion that he was a man devoid of common truth and common honesty) he had in the past been remarkably charitable towards one of the prisoners named Sanger. In his later statement to Parliament, he told the House that he had been convicted several years before when in his service of an act of dishonesty against him. When he discharged him, he procured him a situation as a gardener. While in that situation, the man committed another act of felony and Benett subsequently got him another place as a gardener with his son-in-law! Sanger was clearly an incorrigible rogue as he then committed another offence and was yet again dismissed. Benett said in his speech that he had no revengeful feelings towards the rioters and had, indeed, taken several of them into his service when they had come to him seeking steady employment.

Benett had for very many years sat as a magistrate and also as Foreman of the Grand Jury.[62] As a consequence he has been widely criticised, because it was thought that he acted not only as prosecutor, but also as witness and judge in the trial of the rioters, and that he was the magistrate who committed the prisoners to trial and foreman of the Grand Jury that found bills of indictment against them. These were amongst the charges raised by Henry Hunt when, in the following February, the Commons debated Hunt's motion: 'That an humble Address be presented to His Majesty from this House praying His Majesty would be graciously pleased to grant a general pardon and amnesty to those unfortunate agricultural and other labourers who had been tried and convicted at the late Special Commissions'.

In his speech made during the debate, Benett was able to make the true position clear after he had given a brief account of the course of events during the affray at Pythouse. He said that as soon as his wounds permitted, he went to Salisbury where the magistrates proceeded to investigate the cases. He there pleaded on behalf of many of the men whose characters he had in the meantime ascertained, and had pleaded that those who were of good character but could not get others to provide bail should be let out on their own bail. As a consequence twenty-one of them were indeed let out on bail.

Benett obviously realised that his position as foreman of the Grand Jury was a delicate one, and so he applied to the court to decline being on the panel, as he would have to appear as prosecutor in some of the cases that were to come before him. The reply of the Court was, 'You must act as Foreman of the Grand Jury, Mr Benett; but you will know what course to take when your own cases come before the Grand Jury'. As a consequence, he did not sit where cases in which he was to be a witness were heard.

Another charge made by Hunt was that he had given evidence to hang some of the men. Benett said that he objected as much as Hunt to hanging men at all, except in extraordinary cases and for extraordinary crimes, and indeed he had refused to prosecute two men and give evidence in those cases where, had he done so, they would almost certainly have been sentenced to death. Instead these were prosecuted by other persons merely as machine breakers rather than as rioters who actively attacked the yeomanry. In the course of an extremely lengthy speech in response to Hunt's motion, speaking of the affray at Pythouse, he said that though many had been wounded, only one had been killed; and that was owing to the good sense and humanity of the brave officer who commanded the troops and directed that his men were to strike principally side-blows, so as to wound the mob in the arms, but not to aim at the head where the blows might be mortal. He concluded by saying that he had no revengeful feelings, and that he would have got every man off if he could have done so consistently with the peace of the county. Several of those who had been implicated in the disturbances he had since taken into his service, because they had come to him seeking steady employment, and expressing their determination to defend him and his property.

In his response, Hunt said that Benett had accused him of exciting the mob by his speeches. Rather, Hunt declared, Benett had excited them by the low wages that he gave that were enough to drive men to desperation. Although there was rarely any truth in many of Hunt's allegations, there would seem to have been some truth in this one, as Benett replied that he had indeed raised the wages of his employees since the riots had occurred. On 9 February, Lord Ellenborough[63] recorded in his diary, 'There were two debates in the Commons last night – one a motion of Hunt's respecting the men convicted for machine breaking etc., recommending them to the mercy of the Crown, which gave rise to some lengthened talk of no great moment'.[64] It is unlikely that Benett thought that his lengthy speech was 'of no great moment'! At the end of the debate, the House divided, and it cannot have been any surprise that there were only two votes in favour of Hunt's motion and 269 against.

So many rumours had circulated and false reports published about the riot at Pythouse and the subsequent trials, that Benett must have welcomed the opportunity of speaking at length in the House of Commons in an effort to correct what he would undoubtedly have seen as slanderous and damaging attacks on his character and reputation. He was probably pleased that on 10 February 1831, the *Devizes and Wiltshire Gazette* placed before its readers some of Benett's arguments:

> Our readers have no doubt heard the manner in which Mr Benett's conduct as relates to the recent Special Commission, has been represented by Mr Hunt, and some of the Editors of the London Papers. Our worthy County Member thus answers the particular charges against him:-

First, in reply to the assertion that I gave evidence against 'men on whose criminality' I 'had, half an hour before, sat as judge'. I deny the fact altogether. I was, against my own expressed wish, appointed Foreman of the Grand jury: but I did not officiate as foreman, or remain in the room during the time when the causes in which I was concerned were under consideration, or for the first two days of the business of the assize.

In reply to your second charge, I have merely to observe I did not 'follow the mob from place to place, for the purpose of watching their criminal conduct, with a view to their future punishment' but with a view to save the deluded men from the consequence of such conduct by repeated remonstrance and entreaty: and which I have the satisfaction of knowing had its desired effect on many who, but for my persevering and admonishing them would now be suffering the penalties of the law. It is well known that I did not identify more than two persons whom I had seen with the mob on that day, and that I did not give evidence against those two as to the crimes of which they have been convicted. It is also well known that I saved, probably, the lives of two men (Thomas Topp and Samuel Banstone) who had committed a most cowardly assault on myself, by refusing to prosecute them for that assault, when I was well assured that the punishment of death would be the result of their conviction, of which there could not be the slightest doubt. I refused to prosecute another person for the same reason: but as he is now at home with his family, having given ample security for future good behaviour, I will not mention his name.

It is very irksome to be thus obliged to defend that part of my conduct which I consider as deserving of praise instead of censure. By no means unaware of the personal danger I was incurring, I nevertheless alone persevered in performing my duty as a magistrate, and as a friend to the deluded men who were incurring very heavy penalties by their conduct.[65]

A week later, the *Devizes and Wiltshire Gazette*, clearly a firm supporter of Benett, devoted more of its space to his replies to the charges brought by Hunt in the House of Commons and declared that:

The hon. Member for Preston appears (to use a professional term) to have been completely floored. Scarcely a statement he made as regards Mr B. but what was proved to be incorrect, or explained to the satisfaction of the House.

The reader would have learned at the conclusion of the lengthy report that Benett had said that he had not prosecuted any man with any malignant feeling; on the contrary, he felt as much attachment to that class of persons as ever. Many of the rioters he had since taken into his service, because he felt that they had been misled. He now felt that he lived again in a peaceable neighbourhood, and was confident that it would require the utmost art on the part of the evil disposed to excite the multitude or give rise to burnings again.[66]

It was not only Benett whose conduct was attacked by Hunt in the House of Commons but also the yeomanry cavalry who, according to Hunt 'attacked a peaceable and unoffending multitude on 25 November last near Pythouse'. One of the Hindon troop felt compelled to write to the *Salisbury and Winchester Journal*:

> ... never were poor fellows more bullied or insulted than we were before we attempted to hurt any man; and our noble Captain, though grievously wounded, would have made us forebear longer, if he could. We did bear with ill treatment as long as flesh and blood could bear it, and did not rise our swords and pistols till we were obliged to do it in defence of our lives. I hope Mr Hunt will in future be more particular as to the persons from whom he picks up his information. I think if he had been one of us, he would not have liked to have been pelted with stones, and beaten about with sticks as we were, without trying to defend himself.[67]

As can be gathered from Lord Arundell's letter to John Peniston, there appears to have been little goodwill felt towards Benett by those living in the neighbourhood of Pythouse. As a practical and progressive farmer, he was at the forefront of the movement for the modernisation of agricultural machinery, and was therefore seen as one who added to the current chronic unemployment. Further, his long held and well known views in support of the retention of the Corn Laws were perceived as contributing to the high price of bread, thus causing further misery to men already finding it difficult, if not impossible, to support their families. It was even suggested that some of the farmers had secretly encouraged the rioters, and that at Tisbury labourers said 'that the farmers were at the bottom of it: that they gave them beer and urged them to excesses'.[68] To Benett, the mob's enmity must have been difficult to comprehend after the rapturous reception that he had received from the people after his election triumph so few years before. The many speeches that he had delivered in which he expressed his concern for the distress of the people appear to have been either forgotten or ignored.

In 1883 a witness to the events of November 1830 dictated his account of them. Although fifty years had elapsed, there is no reason to believe that it is anything other than a reasonably accurate description of what occurred.

I'll tell ee about the fight up at Pythouse, yes sur, of course I can – Lets zee, t'were just fifty three years ago come November next, I were a strong lusty chap with the Squire's six horses hauling stone up from Lawn Quarry, to make the new road to West Lodge, by t'abbey when they did come along – oh, a lot on 'em – I should think 900 men. They wanted I to join 'em and they said they should take my horses – I zaid – where them horses goes, I goes – so I went up in the midst on 'em with two of the horses and some of 'em rode to their homes zum of 'em were awful drunk. When they got up to Home Farm – they set to and did smash up the 'drashing machines' and got up on roof, and broke all the zlates and tiles and made awful work – there – they were for all the world like mad folk – The t'old Squire he did ride up along wi' Mr Legge – the steward (terrible nice old man he were) he were a broken down gentleman he were – one of the mob did throw a brick at he – and knocked 'm off his horse they did – and stunned 'm. – 'nother stone hit the Squire and his face were all covered with blood, but there he did try and persuade not to carry on there, he did talk beautiful; but t'were no good, they were all mad drunk more or less. They talked of going down to Mansion and setting house on fire but Mr Benett he had his men there with loaded fire arms about 20 on 'em and the mob they were afeare – so they did march along across the park and went down to Linley and I followed 'em.- They smashed up everything there – and made dreadful havoc and took the Beer Barrel out of Bailiff's house – and knocked the bung out and got more drunk and they couldn't smash the big bar of the machine – till one of 'em said – here – let I try – and he smashed 'm in one blow. He was a blacksmith you see he were – and he did know just where to hit – he did – There – his name were Turner and he got transported for life. Then just as they were acoming up Park to Pythouse the cavalry did come – there – they did gallop splendid and the mob they made for the plantation, but zome of 'em did 'Voight' wonderful – armed were they? – oh! Yes they had all manner of Iron bars and great sticks – and all sorts. But the cavalry they did lay about 'em wonderful – there – they slashed 'em about awful and one man he were just agetting up into wood when one of the cavalry did let off his horse pistol and shot 'em – the bullet did go in at back of his head and out t'other side – His name were Harding – he were brother to Butcher's father down at Hatch – What became of his body? Why his people lived at Knoyle and they come and carried 'm home and he do lay in Knoyle churchyard now he do. – Mr Benett he did beg of the cavalry not to fire, he said he didn't want no man killed – but there they did fire – lots on 'em – Mr Wyndham he did command 'em – and then they surrounded 'em and took 'em all, and we had to get our farm horses and waggons and take them to Salisbury – and the blood did trickle out of the waggons the whole way to Salisbury – I was carter and drove the first wagon – when we got to Blackhorse at Chilmark they did cry out for summat to drink poor fellows, but the Cavalry wouldn't let 'em have nothing – They wouldn't. It were awful cold that night and they were shramm'd with the frost and some on 'em couldn't wag a bit – When we got to Salisbury we took one load to 'infirmary and t'others to Jail. There were special zizes were – and they lasted a fortnight – lots on 'em got transported. There – It was a bad job – Who were the ring leaders? – Well he were one '———' of Anstey he were – but they never took 'm. I heard as how they searched all Lunnon through to find 'm. But there – they didn't catch 'm and how be young John zur? And I do wish you'd have summat done to my front door. Goodnight zur and thank 'ee for calling.[69]

Rewards were granted to many of those who informed against and identified the rioters. The members of the yeomanry cavalry did not seek any reward, but seventeen men received amounts of money ranging from the astonishingly large sum of £102 (equivalent to more than four years wages for a labouring man with which to support himself and his family), down to £17 granted to James Snow, who had sworn his deposition in front of Benett before Christmas.[70]

Throughout 1830, the Government had come under increasing pressure to do something to alleviate the plight of the poor, and in almost every issue of his *Political Register* William Cobbett was asking what had turned the honest labourer into a criminal and who was to blame. To add to Benett's misery after the traumatic events of the previous month, on 4 December Cobbett wrote:

There is now before me a Report of a Committee of the House of Commons, on the subject of the Corn Laws. This Committee report the evidence of certain persons examined by them; and, amongst the rest, of a great landholder, in Wiltshire, named BENETT, who, upon being asked how much a labourer and his family ought to have to live upon, answered, 'We calculate, that every person in a labourer's family should have, per week, the price of a gallon loaf, and three-pence over for feeding and clothing, exclusive of house-rent, sickness and casual expenses'

Mark! Pray mark! A gallon loaf, that is to say, not quite a pound and a quarter of dry bread and a half-penny a day for FOOD AND CLOTHING! And a SPECIAL COMMISSION is gone into Wiltshire! There is a God of Justice, to be sure! That God will do justice, in the end, to be sure! Talk of blasphemy, indeed! Talk of Atheism! Who is not to be an Atheist, if he believe that there is no God to show displeasure at human creatures! (and those, too, who make all the food and all the raiment to come) being doomed to exist on a pound and a quarter of bread a day, and a half-penny for clothing, and nothing for drink, and nothing for fuel, and nothing for bedding, washing or light! And, what are we to think of the Parliament that received this evidence, and that never bestowed so much as one moment on the subject? What are we to think of that Parliament! Why, just what the people did think of it, to be sure.[71]

As a consequence of this and other articles, Cobbett was charged with seditious libel and the Attorney General chose the article naming Benett and the gallon loaf in support of his case. Cobbett subpoenaed the Prime Minister, the Lord Chancellor and other members of the Cabinet as witnesses to the fact that the Government had in 1817 sought Cobbett's permission to re-publish his *Letter to the Luddites* in order to persuade the rioters of the folly of their actions! The trial generated an enormous amount of interest throughout the nation and Cobbett said that every county in England was represented in the company that broke, from time to time, into storms of cheering. Benett was amongst those present and, in the opinion of the Hammonds when describing the trial in *The Village Labourer*, was 'a spectre of vengeance'![72] In the event, Cobbett was acquitted and left the court in triumph, while the name of John Benett was for many years thereafter associated not only in Wiltshire but throughout the country as a man who considered that a labourer should be expected to subsist on what was, in effect, a starvation diet.

It was Benett's misfortune that it was he, and not some other Wiltshire landowner and magistrate, who had given evidence to the Parliamentary committee on the Corn Laws and on what should be allowed for the subsistence of a labourer and his family. The opinion he gave was not his personal opinion (although he may well have agreed with it) but the opinion of his fellow magistrates. The fact remains that his statements to the committee were, at the time by his contemporaries and later by historians, taken as evidence of his 'uncompromising attitude to the poor', and resulted in him being labelled 'one of the most hated men in the county by 1830'.[73]

# 7

## *His Parliamentary Activities, a Public Attack on his Character and Family Affairs 1831-39*

To see the pattern of his life return to something like normality must have been a great relief to Benett, although he could not have been certain, of course, that there would not be a repeat of the events of the previous winter. In the event, the ruthless and speedy punishment of the rioters, not only from Wiltshire but also from other parts of the country, doubtless caused many potential troublemakers to think carefully before attempting to give vent to their grievances by force. So it was that Benett could once again turn his mind to the affairs of agriculture. In April, the first exhibition of the newly formed and wonderfully verbosely named Wilts and General Arboricultural, Horticultural, and Botanical Society[1] was held in the Guildhall in Salisbury. Benett's brother-in-law, Aylmer Bourke Lambert, who was certainly the most eminent of Wiltshire botanists, became president of the society, and it is no surprise to find Benett joining 23 others as one of the first vice-presidents.[2]

More importantly to Benett, however, was the prospect of the year 1831 being dominated by the question of Parliamentary reform. On 7 April, Ella Wyndham began writing a long letter to her brother in New South Wales in which she wrote:

> I cannot think what would become of you were you in England at present. Reform, Reform, you hear everywhere nothing else but Reform; but no annual Parliament, no Universal Suffrage. But I must tell you, Lord John Russell brought in a Bill and a plan of Reform on the first of March, with the concurrence of the Ministers and the approbation of the King. After a protracted debate of eight nights leave was given to read the Bill for the first time without division of the House . . . Of course there is a strong, a very strong party against it, but chiefly the Aristocracy, the country gentlemen being nine out of ten in favour of it . . . Berkeley Portman[3] and Mr Benett are enchanted with this measure, and Mr Coke of Norfolk, the Father of the House of Commons, is delighted to have lived to see the day it was brought in by the Ministers.

Mr Benett is just announced.

April 8th. – Mr Benett entertained us for a long time yesterday with Country Politics, arising out of the Reform Question. The à Courts, as Heytesbury has to go, are most violent, so much that they show the absolute necessity of the measure most fully. Report says that Colonel à Court is canvassing everyone in the county to stand and raise an opposition to our sitting members. Most disgraceful conduct! I should like to duck him well for it. Though without any great deal of difficulty they might find a cleverer man than the worthy Sir John.[4]

It is likely that the reference to the 'worthy Sir John' is a reference to Astley, who received a baronetcy soon after entering Parliament. However it is possible that the writer of this letter is mockingly referring to Benett as 'Sir' John. As one of the county members of Parliament he was a Knight of the Shire but was never knighted nor did he ever receive any honour. Had he shown less independence in the Commons and ingratiated himself to Ministers by his support of the Government of the day, he might also have expected to receive a baronetcy, although his somewhat precarious financial position following the enormous expense of the 1818 and 1819 elections would almost certainly have precluded this. There were undoubtedly more erudite men than Benett who might have stood for Parliament in his place, but surely none who would have more conscientiously discharged the duties expected of a man in his position both in Parliament and in the county.

As Parliament re-assembled in February 1831, Benett was in his place as usual, and soon presented a petition signed by nearly 14,000 people living in Wiltshire in favour of general reform,[5] and again at the end of the month two petitions from different parts of the county also praying for reform.[6] Denis Le Marchant,[7] the Lord Chancellor's principal secretary, records that in the debate on Lord Althorp's budget[8] on 11 February, when Benett tried to speak on behalf of the agricultural interest, 'the Speaker would never notice him when he rose'.[9] Despite this he did eventually manage to speak that day in favour of the budget.

On the 25th of the month, a County Meeting to consider the necessity of the reform of the House of Commons was held in Devizes. So great was the crowd of people attempting to enter the Town Hall that the meeting was adjourned to the Market Place. Here a wagon was placed in a strategic position, upon which the speakers could stand to address the crowd of over a thousand people, all of whom seemed to be in favour of reform. After the Earl of Radnor and Lord Andover[10] had spoken, it seems that the crowd (who had, of course, come to hear some rousing speeches) was about to be disappointed until Benett, who had not intended to speak, stepped forward. He congratulated the county on being able to assure them that they must have Parliamentary Reform, which was always a favourite subject of his, but he had feared that it would not come in his time . . . He said that nothing would satisfy him but the complete destruction of the horrible borough system:– it had given influence to men, backed with money, who, for their own interests had made a complete trade of it . . . the franchise must be widely extended, as there was nothing more absurd than that a freehold property of 40s should give a vote; that a farmer who rented a farm and employed capital of £5000 in stocking it should not have one was ridiculous, and it was equally so that a tradesman should not have one. He had not made up his mind about a ballot. Two years ago he would have given the boroughmongers some compensation for their ill-gotten gains, but now he would not give one halfpenny to any of them.

What started as a meeting that was unlikely to be anything but harmonious now became the scene of considerable confusion, when Benett was followed by John Mayne,[11] the squire of Teffont Evias, a village not far from Pythouse. He said that whilst he did not believe there was a sincerer well-wisher to the people than Mr Benett, he wished he could say the same tribute to the other member [i.e.Astley]. He had refused to support their petition signed by 14,000 people because he could not support a modernised property tax. Uproar followed as Mayne, a barrister who appears to have been an inveterate and rambling public speaker, proposed an alternative petition that Benett persuaded him to withdraw. Eventually Lord Radnor put to the meeting the original petition that was then duly adopted.[12]

Benett spoke in the House on many occasions in the Spring of 1831. In one of the debates, on a reform of the Game Laws, it had been suggested that magistrates hearing cases involving these laws did not always act impartially. Benett denied that magistrates in Quarter Sessions were actuated by personal feelings, or acted with severity in administering the Game Laws. For his own part, he said that he never sat on any trial of a poaching case – a rather surprising assertion for a magistrate who sat in a rural area to make.

In March, Benett found himself becoming deeply involved with the extraordinary events that had occurred in Liverpool in the previous autumn. In 1830 a parliamentary election had taken place at which William Huskinson[13] and General Isaac Gascoyne,[14] an ultra Tory, were returned. However, Huskinson was killed when, at the opening of the Liverpool and Manchester Railway on 15 September, a railway engine ran over his leg and so a by-election ensued. Two candidates,

William Ewart and John Denison, sought to replace him and D. Ben Rees wrote:

> The result was: – William Ewart, 2215: John Denison, 2186. the market price of the vote increased as the voting went on, reaching the sum of £40 per man. Out of 4401 freemen, not 1000 voted without being bribed. The resident voters received sums varying from £5 to £40 each. Some of the non-resident freemen having to come a distance received larger sums. The highest on the list was a person from Belfast, styled as a merchant, who voted for Denison and received £80 . . . Thomas Sephton was offered £12 10s. by his employers to vote for Ewart and threatened with the loss of his position if he did not. He was, eventually, persuaded by a canvasser with the offer of £50 to vote for Denison.[15]

As a consequence of this blatant bribery, a petition against Ewart's election was presented and, on 18 March, Benett was appointed to a committee to enquire into the election. He chaired all the meetings and no time was wasted, as only ten days later he reported to the House that, as a result of gross bribery, Ewart had not been properly elected. On the following day, he moved to suspend the writ until the House could consider the matter. When on 21 April the reactionary Gascoyne opposed Benett's motion that the system of bribery and cheating demanded the serious attention of the House, he declared that, 'he could truly say that if there was a spot in all the world free of corruption' – laughter prevented the House from hearing the conclusion of this sentence that would have undoubtedly continued with the words, 'it was the borough of Liverpool'. He continued by declaring that, 'he had never witnessed any of those practices which were resorted to by others, whose estates were already deeply mortgaged', the implication being that Benett's conduct at his own original election to the House had not been entirely blameless. Later in the debate, Benett referred to, 'some very invidious remarks that had been made in the course of the present discussion' and declared that, 'not one shilling of the large sum I spent at my election for Wiltshire was spent for any dishonest or illegal purpose'.[16] The problems of Liverpool were to occupy a good deal of Benett's time and energy over the next three years.

The question of reform was debated in the House on a number of occasions during the month of March. The bill aimed at removing the right of representation from no less than 56 rotten boroughs, and the 143 members thus gained would go to the counties and large towns that had not previously sent any members to Parliament, extending a £10 householder qualification for borough voters and extending the county franchise to leaseholders and copy holders. Various compromises and half measures had been proposed and on the 28th Benett said in the House that the country would not be satisfied if the disenfranchising part of the Bill was not retained. In his view, if this plan were rejected, and reform delayed, it would not be long before the measure would be forced on the House in a revolutionary shape – a vote by ballot and annual Parliaments. Benett was one of the majority who voted for the Bill on its second reading when, according to Francis Thornhill Baring,[17] the narrow majority was 'received with extraordinary cheers and demonstration of pleasure, the more grotesque as they came from the gravest country gentlemen, such as Benett of Wiltshire and others of his stamp'.[18] Following this the matter was adjourned until 18 April.[19] On rejection by the House of Lords the ministry, lead by Earl Grey,[20] decided to appeal to the country and so Parliament was dissolved and Benett had to face another election.

Before the election Paul Methuen, who had, of course, represented the county some years before, was under some pressure to stand. He wrote to Lord Radnor:

> I am very well content – as far as my views on the county stand – to be where I am. I believe I should have a good chance of coming in, but I had much rather not be concerned in opposition to the present members which I should have great difficulty in avoiding were I now at liberty. They have both of them more enemies than is convenient for County Members to have and these malcontents are of course with the third man, which I believe I owe as much to these as I do to myself, probably more. Benett has the most friends of the two.[21]

The election of two members to represent the county took place, as usual, at Wilton, and in his letter to the freeholders Benett said he went there with a mixed feeling of confidence and anxiety. He arrived in the town at 10 o'clock in the morning attended by a number of electors on horseback, preceded by a band and banners. Astley appeared in the same way and, as no other was nominated, he and Benett were duly returned. After the election, Benett addressed the voters and said that he had gone to Parliament with a decided feeling in favour of the Wellington administration, from which he had anticipated a measure of reform sufficient to satisfy the country. However, when, in the event, the Duke of Wellington turned his back on complete reform, he had opposed his ministry. At a dinner held in the Assembly Rooms in Salisbury in the evening, when the Marquis of Bath[22] proposed the health of the officers and members of the Wiltshire yeomanry cavalry,

Benett responded as a major of the regiment and 'alluded to the exemplary conduct of the regiment during the unfortunate disturbances in November last. He was proud to belong to such a company'.[23]

There is seldom a hint of any humour or levity in the many reports of Benett's innumerable speeches, save that in a report of the meeting of the Wiltshire Society held in London a week after Parliament re-assembled on 21 June it was said that, 'Mr Benett was unremitting in his endeavours to promote the objects of the Charity, and add to the hilarity of the evening, which was kept up until a late hour'.[24] Although he appears to have been an extremely fluent and eloquent public speaker, it is more than likely that most of his speeches were well prepared in advance. In July in the previous year at a meeting of the Wiltshire Agricultural Society at which he would surely have been very much at his ease, he was caught unawares when called upon to respond to Astley's speech proposing his health. It is reported that he said that, 'being a nervous man, he was not yet prepared to return thanks in the manner he could wish; however, they must take the will for the deed'. Now, of all the adjectives one might employ to describe him, 'nervous' is perhaps the last that would come to mind. One can only assume that the lack of preparation was the cause of his nervousness and the company was probably not surprised that he nevertheless then, 'dilated at some length on the prospects of the farmer'.[25]

In the new Parliament, Benett spoke on several occasions during June, and in July had something to say in a debate on the laws of settlement and hiring. In his view, the unhappy situation of the labouring classes was mainly caused by the impediment thrown in the way of free circulation of labour under the existing laws. For once he was in agreement with his old adversary Henry Hunt (who spoke before him), and said that it would be a great hardship to deny settlement to a man who had worked in a particular parish for several years.[26] As a countryman, he also made sure that his views on the game laws were known not only to the House but also to the electors, who would have read the reports of his speeches that appeared in the county newspapers. Earlier in the year in a debate on these laws, he said that the legalising of the sale of game would render it too cheap to make poaching profitable[27] – not one of his more accurate predictions! One of his much repeated assertions, and one widely held at the present time, was that a reduction in taxes would benefit the economy at large and that it should be the rich rather than the poor who should bear the largest burden. Therefore it is no surprise to find him approving the statement made by the Chancellor of the Exchequer proposing a tax of a half per cent on the transfer of funded property (i.e. Government securities), to enable the government to reduce taxation on 'those articles that operated against industry and to transfer it to the higher orders'.[28]

In the summer, Benett was on his feet in the House participating in debates on all manner of subjects, but the most important and controversial matter in which be became involved was that relating to the Liverpool election of 1830. On 29 June, he rose to perform a painful duty, as he put it, as chairman of an election committee that had been under the necessity of depriving the member for Liverpool of his seat. He now sought leave to bring in a bill for putting an end to bribery and corruption in the borough where, as he reminded the House, the freemen possessed the franchise for their lives, with it then passing to their children. He spoke at such length on the matter that eventually the house rose due to the lack of members remaining.[29] One suspects that it was realised that a general reform of parliamentary representation would soon become a reality and what had occurred in Liverpool would not be repeated. On 11 July, Benett tried again. He rose to bring forward his motion and when he said that he hoped that the House would hear him, he was greeted with cries calling for him to be stopped One member said he really must put it to the House whether, at that time of night, such a question ought to be discussed. Benett agreed to postpone the matter until the following Monday.[30] On that day he was thwarted yet again. Lord John Russell asked Benett to postpone his motion to allow the Reform Bill to go early into committee. As the committee was destined to occupy no less than forty parliamentary days[31] one can understand Russell's insistence that reform should take precedence over the problems of Liverpool. However, Benett was not one to be silenced. He said that he had been accused not only by a portion of the press but also by the honourable member for Preston [his old adversary Henry Hunt] of not being in earnest in the intention he had expressed of bringing the question forward. He did, however, assure the House that he most earnestly desired to make the motion of which he had given notice and nothing would prevent him from doing so but the want of physical strength. He therefore did entreat the noble Lord to allow him precedence on that day. However, he was now prepared to postpone his motion on the understanding that no writ would be issued for the borough of Liverpool until his motion had been heard.[32]

Benett's name is generally conspicuously absent from lists of subscribers to appeals of a religious or ecclesiastical nature, although he was always willing to give assistance to the parish churches of his home parishes of Norton Bavant and Tisbury. So it no surprise to find that he was one of the minority of 27 who voted in July on Hunt's motion for a reduction of the grant to the Society for the Propagation of the Gospel in Foreign Parts from £16,000 to £8,000, with a view to its entire discontinuance in the following year. He was particularly active in the House during the summer of 1831, being appointed to select committees on such diverse matters as molasses and steam carriages. But his most noteworthy performance was to be found when, having voted for the second reading of the re-introduced Reform Bill on 6 July, and again against the proceedings being adjourned, on 12 July, he demonstrated his stubborn determination to see the cause of reform being advanced. On that day, the House was debating a motion that it should go into committee on the Reform Bill, and sat until 7.30 am the following morning. According to Lord Ellenborough there was 'much disorder and violence'[33] and Thomas Babbington Macaulay[34] writing on the 15th relates:

> The scene on Tuesday night beggars description . . . towards eight in the morning the Speaker was almost fainting. Old Sir Thomas Baring[35] sent for his razor and Benett, the Member for Wiltshire, for his night-cap and they both resolved to spend the whole day in the House rather than give way.[36]

An enormous amount of time was spent in debating the *minutiae* of the Reform Bill, and in particular as to how many members (if any) should be returned by each individual borough. On 21 July, a very full House went into committee and began by debating whether the borough of Downton in Wiltshire should be disenfranchised. Henry Hunt spoke and was firmly of the opinion that Downton should no longer be represented in Parliament. As one of the county members, Benett felt that he should be heard but, according to one report, 'with much difficulty obtained a hearing for a few moments'.[37] Benett was well known as an exceedingly verbose debater, and so it is likely that many members feared that once he was on his feet – and especially in opposition to Hunt – an inordinate amount of time would be spent in listening to his arguments. In the event, he did speak quite briefly in favour of the borough retaining its representation and, although 243 other members agreed with him, 274 were of the opinion that, although Downton had been first represented in Parliament as long ago as 1275, it should no longer continue to do so.

In the summer Benett was on his feet in the House on several occasions. He always took great pride in the fact that he represented the whole of Wiltshire in Parliament, and on 11 August voiced his strong opposition to one of the provisions in the Reform Bill that Wiltshire should be divided into two divisions for electoral purposes. Despite this, he was strongly in favour of the principle of reform and on 25 August it was reported that 'Mr Benett and Sir J.D.Astley do not intend to leave town, for a single day, until the Reform Bill shall have passed and so the venison feast (should there be one this year) will be deprived of their company'.[38] It was at this time that Edward Littleton,[39] one of the members for Staffordshire, recorded in his journal that on:

> Seeing that Mr Bennet, the Member for Wiltshire was about to 'trouble the House' today, I bet him five Shillings that he would speak more than five minutes – I thought it would be to buy him cheap – He sat down within a moment of the time. I paid the Money with pleasure, for he is generally desperately long-winded.[40]

However, on the morning of Saturday 22 September, the Reform Bill eventually completed its passage through the Commons with Benett voting, of course, with the majority in its favour. The question then was how would it fare in the Lords. Predictably, the upper house voted that the bill should be laid aside for six months, so effectively rejecting it.

By September, Benett appeared at last to be making some progress in his attempts to bring the problems of the Liverpool representation to a conclusion. On the 5th, his amendment to the motion for a writ that there had been gross bribery was passed by a majority of 76 to 35, and later in the month he presented a bill to alter the franchise of Liverpool. In October he agreed to the committee stage being deferred for three months and, when a member proposed that a new writ be moved for an election in Liverpool, Benett said that he was sorry to hear the reformers attempting to defend a case of such corruption as that of Liverpool. Out of 4,300 voters only 300 were not found guilty of corruption. How could the House, therefore, when they had a bill still upon their Table to punish the corrupt electors, send them a writ to elect another member? Notwithstanding Benett's objections, a writ was successfully moved.

To see the end of slavery throughout the British dominions had, for some time, been the wish of most people, although strongly opposed by the planters in the West Indies in particular. In 1823 the Anti-Slavery Society had been formed, following which Thomas Fowell Buxton[41] had assumed William Wilberforce's mantle in attempting to force a measure through Parliament to achieve a total abolition. Public meetings were held throughout the country and, somewhat belatedly, in Wiltshire the first annual meeting of the Wilts Anti-Slavery Society was held in September, with the Bishop of Salisbury as patron and Benett as president, although his parliamentary duties prevented him from being present.[42] In the following year, the second annual meeting took place, when it was reported that the Society, 'desires to record the lively feelings of satisfaction it experienced on hearing that its President, John Benett Esq and its Vice President, Sir John Dugdale Astley were in the minority of 90 who voted in favour of Mr Buxton's motion on the 24 May last for the appointment of a select committee to consider the measures to abolish slavery'. In the event, the life of the Wiltshire society was short lived as, on 28 August 1833, the bill for the total abolition of slavery received the royal assent.

In September Benett had another encounter with his old enemy Henry Hunt, this time in the Commons. Hunt had moved that the House should resolve itself into a committee to consider the effect of several Corn Importation Acts. During his exceedingly long speech he made reference to an estate that the Honourable Member for Wiltshire knew well, and that 40 years ago had been let at £600 per annum when the weekly wage of a labourer was 6 shillings. Now it was let at £1,800 per annum when a labourer's weekly wage was 7 shillings.[43] The estate being referred to was, of course, Benett's own property, and the implication being that he had harshly and unjustly racked up the rent to nobody's advantage but his own. Benett could not let such a slur pass unchallenged, and so proceeded to answer Hunt's allegations. This included pointing out that he had paid £10,000 for the tithes of the estate, which would not, of course, then have to be paid by the tenant. Both Hunt and Benett were somewhat reprimanded when Joseph Hume, the radical politician, regretted that, 'on a subject of such great importance the Honourable Member for Wiltshire has thought it necessary to mix up any personal dispute or squabble he may have had with the Honourable Member for Preston about the value of this or that'.[44] In the event 194 members voted against Hunt's motion with only 6 voting for it.

In the same month, some of the aristocracy and gentry of the county who were in favour of reform of the House of Commons – and most of them were – decided that yet another County Meeting should be held. It is not unlikely that one of the motives for calling another meeting was to demonstrate to the people their particular enthusiasm for reform. In accordance with the usual practice, it was necessary for as many of them as possible to sign a requisition addressed to the High Sheriff. There would clearly be logistical difficulties in arranging for one document to be signed by all who would wish to be signatories to it, and so one or more copies were circulated. The difficulties that were experienced are demonstrated in a letter written on 23 September by G. Poulett Scrope[45] to William Fox Talbot:

> Having been disappointed in my finding you at Lacock yesterday, and not being quite confident whether I was fully authorised by you to sign your name to the Requisition for a County meeting, I send you a Copy with some (but not all) the names already attached, begging you to return it to me with your's, or what would be better to call at Benett's 19 Albermarle Street, and leave word with him to add your name to the Copy he has, and which he is . . .[46] forward to Methuen (at Brighton I believe) by tomorrow's post. I hope you will be able to attend, but if not, as I think you told me, Your signature will be yet more desirable to the Requisition that it may influence others to attend in your place.[47]

In the event, not one but two county meetings on the question of reform were held soon after in Devizes. At the first, Benett said that he was happy to see that there was no feeling of disaffection, no revolutionary spirit, amongst the people and that, though the Reform Bill should, this time, be strangled in the Lords, the Ministers would not desert the people and if they did he would desert them.[48] At the other, having been received with loud cheers, he addressed the crowd at great length and somewhat adventurously said that the reform of Parliament would also lead to the reform of other abuses, for instance in the law and perhaps in the Church.[49] At the meeting held on 30 September, it was unanimously agreed that, 'the cordial thanks of the Meeting be presented by the Chairman to John Benett Esq and Sir John Dugdale Astley Bart, members of Parliament for the county of Wilts, also to Hon. D.P.Bouverie,[50] member for New Sarum, for their unwearied support of the Reform Bill, during its progress through the House of Commons'. A copy of the resolution was duly sent to Benett who responded to Robert Waylen,[51] the chairman of the meeting, in the following courteous terms:

> My dear Sir
> It is exceedingly gratifying to me to learn by the vote of thanks which you forwarded to me a short time since that my public conduct has been in unison with the views and wishes of so large and respectable number of friends at Devizes. I request you to communicate to them my grateful acknowledgement for this much valued mark of their kindness and I assure you, my dear Sir, that not only the vote of my friends, but the manner in which it has been conveyed to me by yourself will never be effaced from my mind. I hope to meet you on Friday next at Devizes.[52]

The people of Wiltshire appear to have been particularly adept in organising petitions for submission by their members of Parliament, and it is to Benett that they mainly looked to present them to the House. Everyone was anxiously awaiting the passing of the Reform Bill and in the meantime made sure that their views and desires were known to the legislators. When, at the end of August, Benett had presented a petition from the people of Chippenham praying for annual Parliaments, universal suffrage and vote by ballot, he said if the people were dissatisfied with the Reform Bill they would have expressed their disapprobation through the medium of petitions. In fact, they were convinced the bill must be passed and were waiting with anxiety the result.[53]

The existence of slavery in the empire was another topic that concerned all thinking people, and earlier in the year Benett had presented a petition in favour of total repeal of the Acts permitting the continuance of slavery in the West Indies.[54] It was not only petitions signed by large numbers of people that were given to Benett for presentation to the House. In September he presented a petition signed by sixty clergymen in Wiltshire against the Beer Bill, and in so doing said that he could not see why a poor man should be barred from going to a beer shop for refreshment, while the tavern was open to the more wealthy.[55]

In November a dinner was given at the *Bear Inn* in Devizes by the Reformers of Wiltshire, in honour of the Marquis of Lansdowne, ' as a testimony of the public gratitude for the course the noble Marquis had pursued with respect to the great measure of Reform'. In proposing the healths of the county members, the lofty Benett and, presumably, the short Astley, the High Sheriff, Paul Methuen, amused himself and his audience by comparing them to a pair of horses drawing a carriage:

> They worked together in the Reform Coach or Diligence like a pair of good ones: and if the coach was a slow one, it was no fault of theirs; they did not want any whip. To be sure with regard to size, they were not a perfect pair, but they were like a couple of pills taken out of a box: – as I acted the part of ostler in putting them together at Wilton, I feel somewhat proud of the turnout.

One of the honoured guests and speakers was Tom Moore, the poet, who, it may be recalled, had described Benett as a 'haranguing gentleman' when writing about him in his journal some years before. He cannot therefore have been surprised to hear Benett deliver what must have been one of his more vehement and outspoken speeches, during the course of which he said:

> They (the Ministers) had been well advised to look to the maintenance of the peace of the country and to repress popular impatience, which was the only thing they had to fear. Mob tyranny was the worst of tyrannies: and if the Reformers should split among themselves, and the Tories again be returned to power, what Reform could they hope for? He knew that persons were striving to excite the people by representing the measure of Reform as inefficient, – stating that from a Tory administration they would receive universal suffrage. He was satisfied, however, that if the Tories gained ascendancy they would coerce the country by the sword. After drilling the mob into soldiers they would silence the just demands of the community by the force of the bayonet.[56]

In 1831 Benett's son and heir was still without any occupation and in financial difficulties, and presumably surviving on whatever allowance his father made him – and, of course, on credit and loans from his friends. In June he wrote from Rookwood to his father:

> I am particularly sorry to hear of yr indisposition especially as it immediately precedes a time which will occasion you so much interest and mental exertion.
>
> I am still here living on Ld Charles's bounty and am likely to remain so till I hear more effectively from you. I have only brought a small stock of clothes with me and have left the greater part of my things at Cambridge as a sort of honourable pledge that I will return to discharge some particular 4 bills which I have promised to pay so I cannot return for them without redeeming my pledge honourably. I am aware that Mr Higan's bill must remain til the sale of Enford, though I told him the other day on his mentioning its longstanding that it would be discharged very shortly. I received a letter yesterday from Ld St John[57] which I send you. The time he wishes to set off is exactly that which I should wish. I could reach home if I liked as Ld Charles has very kindly offered the money to carry me there but as I must return to Cambridge shortly, I would only be increasing the expense so I shall remain here awaiting a letter from you. I saw my aunt Ethel and likewise my uncle William from the space of five minutes as I was passing through town on my way to this place. I was surprised to find her in Albermarle St as no one had appraised me of it . . .
>
> Believe me my dear Father
> Your affectionate son
> John[58]

The young twenty-two year old John spent most of the summer on a tour of Scotland and the Lake District with his friend St John (who as a young child had succeeded his father as 14th Baron St John) and as usual was living beyond his means. On 21 September he wrote to his father:

> My dear Father
> We arrived at this place yesterday in the morning from Perth. I found your three letters waiting me and rescued the twenty pounds safe for which I feel very much obliged to you. It is about the amount that St John had expended in advances so I have repaid him but there is still thirty owing to Fane which I am sorry to be obliged to leave the country without paying, but I must send it to him. I am fully aware of the great trouble you have been put to on my account which I regret extremely but situated as I was I was obliged to bother you for money. We think of quitting Edinboro' tomorrow and intend to go at once to Bedfordshire where I shall remain some time with St John at Lisbourne where Lady St John will be. The 4th have just received orders to leave their quarters here for Glasgow, which they attribute to the damn reform bill as they call it saying that it is about to be thrown out and they are consequently ordered there to keep the mob down which is expected to rise on the occasion. I have seen a good deal of Fane lately, we left him shooting at Ruthven Castle near Perth . . . Has anything been done with regard to raising the money to purchase the Hatch House estate? . . . I imagine you are heartily sick of reform and London – how you bear it I can't conceive. I am glad you acted so perseveringly in the Liverpool business.
> Evr yr affectionate son
> John[59]

It is clear from this letter that Benett had told his son that he had an opportunity to purchase part, if not all, of West Hatch manor. Hatch House and its estate of about 400 acres immediately adjoined the Pythouse park and estate, and since 1769 had been owned in two separate moieties. By 1816, a moiety had passed to one John Dillon who, by his will proved in 1837, devised it to his sister Henrietta. She immediately decided to sell to Benett, who then had the satisfaction of knowing that a share in the estate so close to his own had passed into his ownership. By this time, the other moiety belonged to Sir Hyde Parker.[60] Benett must have been extremely anxious to acquire the other half of the estate, and so was doubtless delighted when in 1841 he was able to buy Parker's share from him.[61]

By the beginning of December, John was back in Cambridge and writing to his father:

My dear Father

Don't be alarmed at this paper. I have no other. [it was edged in black] The letter you have from St John is to ask him to Pythouse for the yeomanry dinner if it will be convenient . . . How do you propose to extricate yr deeds from Chitty's hands without entering into the mazes (?) of the Court of Chancery? I hope to get away from this place about the beginning of next week as I am anxious to get home to arrange the dinner. What shall I do about the stewardship of the Salisbury balls? It may await, I suppose, my return.[62]

Benett must have fallen out with Philip Chitty, his Shaftesbury solicitor, who was, perhaps, retaining some deeds or documents as security for unpaid fees. John wrote another letter to his father in December, 'I received both your letters this morning – alarming news with regard to Chitty. What is to be done? Can't he be compelled to give them up?'[63] Chitty appears to have been a domineering and difficult person who until the early 1830s had, with his partner Charles Bowles, acted as local agents to Earl Grosvenor[64] but then ceased to act for him. Benett too, in due course, ceased to instruct him.

As the year 1831 drew to a close, Benett took the opportunity of showing his appreciation to the Hindon troop of yeomanry cavalry for their conduct some twelve months before, when their presence at Pythouse undoubtedly saved his property from further destruction. The *Devizes and Wiltshire Gazette* carried this report from a correspondent:

On 25 ult. the Hindon Troop of Wilts Yeomanry Cavalry, under the command of Captain Wyndham, assembled in great numbers on the lawn before Pythouse, where they were sumptuously entertained by Cornet John Benett, the eldest son of their highly respected Major – our county member. At the conclusion of the elegant repast, the Major – after a very feeling and appropriate speech to the Captain and the Troop presented an extremely large Silver tankard, beautifully chased, to Captain Wyndham, as proof of the high approbation he entertained on a very trying occasion – The whole party were afterwards regaled in the Major's hospitable mansion, and they did not separate till the dawn of the day gave the signal for retreat.[65]

The silver tankard was inscribed, 'To Captain Wyndham and the Hindon troop of R W Y C from John Benett Esq Major of the regiment as a mark of his sincere regard and gratitude for their prompt and gallant services in protection of his property and family on 25 Nov.1830'.[66]

Benett was in the House again at the beginning of 1832 when he continued to attempt to make progress with his Liverpool franchise bill. At the end of January he duly presented it but then agreed to defer its second reading. On 23 May the second reading passed through the House with 44 members voting for it and 10 against. In June he insisted that he would press its passage, and in July complained at its committee stage being put off for six months. Later in the month, doubtless to his dismay, he finally withdrew it.

In March, Tom Moore wrote to Benett acknowledging some favour that he had conferred on him – letting him and his family stay in his London lodgings perhaps, or even supplying him with some superscribed or 'franked' paper to enable him to send letters through the post free of any charge:

> My dear Benett
> You have your own plague with me and mine – but I shall write a Hymn to you some day or other & immortalize you for your pains. My invocation shall be borrowed from
>> Come, thou Goddess, frank and free
>> I did intend to have dined with the Paddies tomorrow, not having drowned the shamrock with them for ages – but cares constantly oblige me to defer coming up for another week
>> Yrs ever T. Moore [67]

Moore appears to have made a habit of taking advantage of the privilege enjoyed by his friends who were Members of Parliament in being able to frank items of mail. It was not long after this that he was writing to William Fox Talbot, then Member for Chippenham, 'Benett being at Salisbury I take my chance of your being at your post, as a trusty franker, and trouble you with the enclosed . . .'[68]

Throughout the whole country, pressure for reform was intense. In May, Benett received a petition from people meeting in Melksham, and his response, written from the House of Commons, shows how promptly and seriously he dealt with such matters. He wrote:

> The Melksham petition reached me in due course of post this day, and I brought it to this House with the full intent of presenting it, but in consequence of the events of the day, it has been thought desirable by the friends of Lord Grey's Government to withhold all petitions for the present. You may have knowledge of the events I allude to by the papers, but I will briefly state, that the Duke of Wellington has found himself unable to form an Administration, and the King has desired Lord Grey and his colleagues to remain in office, giving him, of course, power to pass the Reform Bill.

These facts are announced in the Houses by Lords Grey and Althorp, but the details must of course wait. We who are sincere friends of the Reform Bill are greatly rejoicing at this event, of course; and I most heartily congratulate yourself and our friends in Melksham at the certain success of that measure, which is so absolutely necessary to the contentment and prosperity of the country. I will do with your petition whatever the gentlemen from whom it comes may direct, but if they should think proper to leave it to me, I will present it or not, and so manage as to give the best effect to the great and good measure which we have so much at heart.

To yourself and the gentlemen of Melksham, who have so highly honoured me by their thanks for my conduct in Parliament, I beg to offer my most sincere acknowledgement, and assurance I shall ever consider the approbation of my public conduct by my friends and constituents, as the highest reward which any public man can receive.[69]

In June, the Reform Bill was at last accepted by the House of Lords and passed into law. Benett had always been an enthusiastic supporter of reform although, in the opinion of a later historian, 'his quite genuine efforts on behalf of reform had been mistrusted because of his uncompromising attitude towards the working classes'; and also that, although a Whig, he 'had become the embodiment of the most reactionary elements in an acutely class-conscious world'.[70] When one considers the contents and tone of the numerous speeches delivered by him both in the House and on other occasions, one might be forgiven for considering this judgement a little harsh.

Benett must have been delighted that the worst of the rotten boroughs were now no more, and must have been particularly glad that Heytesbury, where his father had suffered his spectacular defeat in 1754, would no longer be sending members of the Ashe and à Court family to Parliament. However, one of the rearrangements incorporated in the Act certainly did not meet with Benett's approval, and that was that Wiltshire as a whole would no longer send two Members to Parliament. In future the county would be divided into two divisions with each being represented by two Members. As a result, there was considerable speculation as to who would be the new Wiltshire representatives in Parliament. At the beginning of June, it was reported that 'Some of the London papers have given the representation of Wilts, in the ensuing Parliament, to Mr Benett, Sir J.D. Astley, Mr Methuen and Mr W. Long – of the return of the two former gentlemen there cannot be the slightest doubt'.[71]

On the 14th, the *Devizes and Wiltshire Gazette* published the following piece received from 'a highly respected correspondent':

Some of the supposed friends of Mr Benett and Sir John Astley are at the moment secretly endeavouring to undermine the interest of those gentlemen in the county. A gallant Colonel, not much accustomed to the smell of gunpowder, is understood to be the principal snake in the grass.

[Let the real friends of Mr Benett and Sir John be on the alert, and they will have nothing to fear, even if they be opposed by the united efforts of all the 'Gallant Colonels' in the Kingdom. – ED]

The public are at a loss to imagine who will be the 4th candidate for Wilts. The fear of a contest prevents, we have been informed, several gentlemen (who might otherwise feel inclined) from offering themselves . . .

[Since writing the above paragraph, we have been informed, from authority upon which we can rely, that the Hon Sidney Herbert, brother of the Earl of Pembroke, intends offering himself for the southern division of the county in opposition to Mr Benett and Sir John Dugdale Astley and that he and his friends are at this moment busied in retaining agents etc. This gentleman is an anti-reformer; it will, therefore, be base ingratitude, if the Reformers of the county suffer either Mr Benett or Sir John Dugdale Astley to be put to one shilling expense in a contest with a gentleman of such principles].[72]

The 'gallant Colonel' was undoubtedly Colonel Charles à Court, who had incurred the wrath of George Wyndham's sister by stirring up opposition to the sitting members.

Later in the month, Benett addressed the 2,540 electors of the new southern division of the county through the medium of the press. In his letter, written from 10 Grosvenor Street in London and published in the *Salisbury and Winchester Journal*, having heard that Sidney Herbert was canvassing the electors, he wrote that he regretted the division of the county:

which separates me from a large portion of my constituents who in the year 1819 were united with yourselves of the South, in the gallant support which you then gave me through a contest, more than usually protracted and severe . . . those who are the old Freeholders of the County, and my constituents, never asked me for pledges, and I never made any, except that I would discharge my duty honestly and diligently: I now offer this promise to you, my long-tried and steady friends, as well as to the electors, who have now for the first time, to exercise their important trust.[73]

Benett was in no position to bear the expense of a contested election in opposition to Herbert who, on attaining his majority in the previous year, had become the possessor of an immense fortune. Benett had the support of the *Devizes and Wiltshire Gazette*, that reported at the end of the month that it had, 'heard that Hon Sidney Herbert[74] will be opposed in the south. Should this be the case, a subscription will be set on foot in every town in the county, to pay Mr Benett's expenses'.[75]

Sidney Herbert was the 21-year-old second son of the 11th Earl of Pembroke. His half brother, the 12th earl, lived in Paris, having taken from Wilton many of the choicest pieces of French furniture.[76] He had arranged with Sidney, the heir presumptive to the earldom, that he should live in and maintain the great house at Wilton. Herbert was by all accounts an attractive young man possessing, as well as an immense fortune, engaging manners. His influential position would certainly lead him to expect to be returned to Parliament without any difficulty. One cannot imagine that Benett had not discussed with Astley, his colleague in the unreformed Parliament, how they should act faced with Herbert's intention to stand for the southern division. As Benett was the senior member, Astley conceded that Benett should have a prior claim to seek election in the southern division where the majority of his support lay and proposed that he should stand for the northern division where most of his supporters were to be found.

However, this arrangement did not meet with the approval of Lord Radnor, whose letter published in the *Salisbury and Winchester Journal* on 2 July suggested that the electors should question the decision of Astley to leave the southern division to make way for Herbert, who, with all his connections, had vehemently opposed the Reform Bill.[77] Astley responded by declaring, 'I frankly avow, that I have had too much experience to engage hastily in a contested election especially under a certainty of being brought into collision with my present colleague',[78] and a week later wrote:

> Your senior Member, Mr Benett, has made his election and offered himself for the Southern Division . . . Mr Benett, in his Address published this morning, offers himself 'wholly unconnected with any other candidate or with any party' and the Honourable Sidney Herbert is announced as canvassing the Electors of the Southern Division of the County. If under these circumstances, I offer myself for the same Division, I must calculate on being brought into collision with my respected Colleague, which, in justice both to him and to myself, I am most anxious to avoid.[79]

In the event, Astley offered himself as a candidate in the northern division of the county and in due course was duly elected unopposed. No doubt much to Benett's relief, no other person had the temerity or financial means to consider embarking on a contested election, and so the public was spared the immense amount of controversial letters, broadsheets and handbills that marked the contested elections of 1818 and 1819. Nothing more was heard of the impending election until the end of the year. Both the now quite elderly Benett and the young Herbert were present at a ball held at the Assembly Rooms in Salisbury at the end of July[80] when they must surely have met and probably congratulated each other on the prospect of being returned to Parliament unopposed.

Although Benett appears generally to have enjoyed good health, at this time he was suffering from some sort of ailment. On 3 July he wrote in an uncharacteristically shaky and illegible hand to S. Bartlett:

> I am really not well enough to go to Lord Goderich[81] or attend the public officers even if I thought I could render you any service by so doing which I doubt or believe is in my power.
>
> You have presented Memorials which have been read and acknowledged – I would advise you following them up by letter, if you cannot do so personally. I assure you that had I any interests and if my health would allow me I would exert them in your favour.[82]

It was in July 1832 that Benett first opened an account with the London bankers, Coutts & Co. He always maintained an account with bankers in the country and may well have also dealt with a bank in London before commencing business with Coutts – a relationship that was to last for the rest of his life. The account was opened with a payment in of the sum of £45,000 provided by Coutts on the security of a mortgage over his estate in Enford. This mortgage was doubtless entered into to enable Benett to discharge some very substantial debts, as almost immediately a total of over £25,000 was paid to six different creditors. Early in the following year, Benett and his son John entered into a mortgage in favour of the Bank to secure a loan of another £20,000, and in June of 1833 his account was credited with a further £14,000 advanced by Coutts. Having borrowed, therefore, the sum of £79,000 (perhaps between £2 and £3 million in 21st-century terms) much of it was used to pay a number of substantial creditors – as well as to discharge his normal living expenses. By the first anniversary of the opening of the account, almost £10,000 of the loan remained standing to his credit,[83] but soon, no doubt, this too would be spent.

As he had done in the summer of the previous year, Benett's son and heir was again travelling in the north with his friend St John and troubling his father for money. On 17 July, he wrote from Windermere:

St John and I have just returned from a walk amongst the hills of about 12 miles. We walked 20 yesterday . . . we caught a perch weighing 2 lbs the other day. When you write again direct me at the post office in Edinboro' as we expect to be there in a few days. Pray let me know as far as you can how long it will be before you can procure my money & how much you can spare me. It will take I find about £50 more to finish my [?] and unless I can get £200 besides in a few days, I will be in for a great scrape. I don't suppose they can seize my person as they won't know where to find me but they will I have no doubt lay hands on my goods and chattels at Cambridge. I speak this plainly as it will account for my being anxious that you should procure me money before I left town – I am dead tired so believe me my dear Father

     Yr affectionate son
      John[84]

Benett continued to take very seriously his duties as president of the Wiltshire Agricultural Society. At the annual dinner of the Society in Devizes in August, in response to the suggestion that one of the first acts of the reformed Parliament would be the repeal of the Corn Laws, he 'affirmed that there was no ground for this fear, it being impossible that a free trade in corn could ever exist in this country. With a debt of 800 millions and taxes in proportion, the idea was preposterous!'[85] In common with many other landowners at this time, Benett attempted to alleviate the plight of the poor. It was reported that he 'very liberally let upwards of 50 lots of land, for field gardens, to poor persons of the parish of Tisbury and Semley at 3d per lug'.[86]

In the same month, Benett's eldest daughter Lucy was married at Tisbury to Arthur, one of the four illegitimate children of Lt. Gen. Sir Henry Fane[87] and Mrs Isabella Cook, with whom he lived for many years. She refused to marry him when her husband died on the grounds, it is said, that should she and Sir Henry then have children, this would not be fair to the children that they already had and in particular to their first son. It may be that their children did not know that their parents were not married. If so, the truth certainly came to light when in 1857 the arms of Fane with the mark of illegitimacy were issued by patent to Arthur and Lucy's son, Vere, when he assued by Royal Licence the name of Benett in lieu of that of Fane, upon inheriting the Pythouse estate. He was granted the arms of Benett quarterly with those of Fane being blazoned with a bordure wavy, the mark of illegitimacy. After Sir Henry died, Mrs Cook lived for many years near Warminster and was always known as Lady Fane.

A transcription of a few lines from Lucy's diary have survived, and in this she records that she was given away by her brother John, and not by her father. He, perhaps, did not initially approve of the marriage. However, he was of course a party to the Marriage Settlement that was entered into shortly before the wedding took place.[88] Lucy's new husband was ordained deacon in 1837 and in the following year was licensed to the curacy of Knook with a stipend of £52 p.a. Later in the year he became the curate at Boyton with a stipend of £80 p.a. and in 1841 vicar of Warminster and domestic chaplain[89] to the Earl of Westmoreland[90] – an acknowledgement perhaps of the family connection, notwithstanding Arthur's father's irregular conjugal arrangements.

Benett and Tom Moore appear to have continued with their friendship, although it seems from the following letter written in November that Benett was somewhat neglectful in nurturing it. Moore wrote:

> My dear Benett
>
> I have written definitely to decline Limerick. They had, on my first refusal (which I gave on the ground of my not being able to afford the attendance upon Parliament) set on foot a national subscription for the purpose of providing me with a qualification, and were actually negotiating for the purchase of a small estate in Limerick! But this generous offer of the warm-hearted [?] boys I have also declined.
>
> I have had another invitation from a high and more flattering quarter (in the common acceptance of the word) which I would let you have particulars of, if we were together, but there are some things connected with it too confidential to write. This I have also refused.
>
> How are you? We long to hear how you go on
>
> Ever yrs T. Moore[91]

In October, Moore had earlier confided in his journal that ' the invitation from a high and more flattering quarter' had come from Lord Anglesey, who had said that with ministerial support there would be no difficulty in Moore being returned for Trinity College, Dublin. Had they met, Moore would undoubtedly have told Benett all about it, and that 'the limited state of my means was an insurmountable bar to my coming into Parliament' as he put it in his journal.

The election of the new members of Parliament for the southern division of the county took place just before Christmas. On 10 December, Benett addressed the electors and told them that he was:

> anxious to devote my humble service to my country; I am desirous of having a seat in the first Reformed Parliament that I may assist in a

continued system of honest Reformation such as seems to me absolutely requisite for the permanent security of our various and invaluable institutions.[92]

The election took place in the Market Place in Salisbury instead of in Wilton, the traditional place of election of the old Knights of the Shire who had formerly represented the whole of the county. According to one report, Benett and his friends breakfasted with the Wyndhams at Dinton and at one o'clock, 'the grand cavalcade appeared Mr H.King in the centre; on his right Mr Benett and on his left Hon.Sidney Herbert, followed by nearly 1000 gentlemen and the most influential farmers of the Southern division'.[93] Benett was proposed by William Wyndham (who described Benett as his 'old and dear friend') and seconded by Walter Long,[94] who said that Benett was ' a friend to civil and religious liberty, the enemy of slavery, whatever form it may assume, the advocate of economy and retrenchment and the supporter of that great measure that great charter of our liberties'.[95]

Benett then addressed the crowd at great length, and when he said that all men were reformers he was greeted with cries of 'the ballot!' In response he said that he was averse to the ballot on the grounds that 'it would destroy all popular influence'. He continued by advocating a general commutation of tithes and would 'contend for more equal distribution of church property, the restriction of pluralities, the residence of the clergy and the non-translation of Bishops'. He remarked that he was happy to see a bishop of the Church of England an advocate of commutation of tithes, and reminded his audience that twenty years ago he had been called a robber by a church dignitary for merely suggesting such a measure.

The proceedings were enlivened by the appearance of John Mayne, the squire of Teffont Evias and also, it seems, something of a radical agitator, who was greeted by such an uproar that for as long as an hour he made an effort to obtain a hearing but without success. Eventually Benett and Herbert were duly returned unopposed, and it was reported that they 'returned to the Council House where the usual formalities were gone through, then the two Knights of the Shire gird with their ancient insignia went to their respective inns'.[96]

Immediately after the election, Herbert wrote to his mother, the 'Russian' Countess of Pembroke[97]:

I am member for Wilts. We had a capital procession from Wilton of four or five hundred horsemen, and a very fine day; Mr. Casey on foot as drum-major. Grove and Poulet proposed me; Wyndham and Long Benett.

When I had done speaking, Mallett asked me a question on the Irish Poor Laws, which I answered. Mr Mayne then got up, and was received with roars and hisses. He spoke for an hour, not one word heard; dead rabbits thrown at him. I am just come from the hustings, and am going to the freeholders' dinner.[98]

It was the normal practice at this time, and in the depth of the winter in particular, for the wealthy to give some assistance to the poor. Benett would certainly be expected to do something for his less fortunate neighbours, and so in January 1833 it was reported that 'Mr Benett has as usual at this season distributed large quantities of fat beef and clothing among the poor in the neighbourhood of Tisbury'.[99]

Early in 1833, the reformed Parliament sat and in the National Portrait Gallery can be seen Sir George Hayter's[100] magnificent painting entitled, 'The Moving of the Address to the Crown on the Meeting of the first Reformed Parliament in the old House of Commons on the 5th of February, 1833'.[101] This picture, that took ten years to complete, includes no less that 240 portraits of Members of both Houses of Parliament, including Benett, who sits in the second row on the Speaker's right.

On 21 February Benett presented a petition from 3,000 people in Liverpool complaining of bribery and corruption, and praying for the disenfranchisement of the freemen.[102] Five days later the House continued to debate the second reading of Benett's bill to disenfranchise the freemen of Liverpool. In his opening speech he refuted the suggestion in the *Liverpool Standard* that his bill was brought forward and promoted by the secret instigation of Ministers, and that he was acting throughout as their tool. He disclaimed all such connection with Government and had introduced the bill strictly from a sense of duty, without any connection with Liverpool and depending on the support of those who honestly agreed with him on the general merits of the question. During the course of the debate, minute details of the alleged bribery were revealed, following which Lord Sandon,[103] one of the new members for Liverpool, said that he would shortly address himself to the observations of the honourable member for Wiltshire, of whom he had nothing to complain. That honourable gentleman had not indulged in exasperating language or sweeping accusations, but had made the statement which he felt himself called upon to address to the House in a way worthy of his high character. Unfortunately the honourable gentleman was the chairman of the Election Committee of 1830, and was directed by that Committee to bring the case to the attention of the House. When, however, the honourable gentleman got once engaged in a subject, it became a favourite matter with him, and he had persisted in urging it to a conclusion. He however thought that his honourable friend had before that time felt reason to regret the course he had taken and had so long persevered in. Lord Sandon had probably expressed a view shared by many members – that once Benett had decided that some course of action was correct, nothing would deter him from doing whatever might be necessary to achieve what he considered to be right. It appears that Benett's bill proceeded no further, but his perseverance certainly brought the bribery and corruption in Liverpool to the notice of Parliament and to the wider public.

On 6 March, Lord Sandon presented a petition signed by every member of his election committee complaining of the gross misstatements in the petition presented by Benett, to the effect that bribery and corruption had been practised in the last election in Liverpool. He said that he could present another petition signed by more than 7,400 people in opposition to it. Furthermore, he was instructed to say that some individuals who had signed Benett's petition had signed five or six names, and that passengers landing out of steam boats were invited to sign, and did sign, that petition upon an assurance that their not being housekeepers was of no consequence.[104] The sparring continued when Benett retorted that he had received a letter from Liverpool stating that some people had signed Lord Sandon's petition upwards of twenty times, and that several boys belonging to charity schools had signed it, placing the occupations of their fathers against them. The debate was brought to an end when a member said that Lord Sandon had known Liverpool for 28 months, whereas he had known it for 30 years. He could assure the House that for the last 30 years there had been a greater system of bribery and corruption carried on in Liverpool than had ever disgraced any rotten borough.[105] Early in March Benett spoke at great length about the Liverpool question and, after a long debate, it was agreed that an election committee should look into the proceedings of the last election there. Later in the month, he spoke again on the same subject and on the 14th a note of exasperation appears when he declared that he had already devoted himself for three years to the investigation of the Liverpool question and must oppose every proceeding which would lead to unnecessary delay.[106]

On 9th March, Benett was re-elected to Brooks's club. Having first been elected in 1824, it may be that he had allowed his membership to lapse, as now he was elected on the same day as Montague Gore,[107] the Whig Member for Devizes, their nominations both being seconded by the Marquis of Lansdowne. Benett's proposer was Lord Ebrington[108] and a few days earlier, the other Member for Devizes, Wadham Locke,[109] also became a member. It was Locke who, at a dinner held in Devizes in the autumn of the previous year, had described Benett as: 'as honest and faithful a representative as ever entered the House of Commons'.[110]

From time to time, London was at the mercy of the mob, and in April it was reported that, 'two of our county members, viz. Mr Benett and Mr Methuen have been among the sufferers by the prevailing disorder in town and have consequently been unable to attend to their duties in the House of Commons'.[111] Notwithstanding this, he was not prevented from voting against a motion for the abolition of flogging in the army;[112] nor (with Sidney Herbert) from voting with the majority against a proposal for the introduction of voting by ballot.[113] Thus it was that, although forward looking in many of his opinions, in others he remained conservative. However, he was always in favour of any proposal that would result in the reduction in taxation, so he voted with the minority for the repeal of house and window duties.[114] In June when the House was debating the Corn Laws, Benett was on his feet to offer his long-held and oft-repeated view that there was a fallacy in regard to the benefits said to derive from the free importation of corn. In his view importation would have the effect of making corn cheap only for a time, and would have a direct tendency to create fluctuations in the price of corn when it was expedient to keep it as steady as possible. If they could get rid of the national debt, he said, then certainly they might establish a perfectly free trade in corn as well as in every other commodity.[115]

Benett continued to attempt to persuade Tom Moore that he should feel at liberty to stay in his house when in London. In June, Moore wrote:

> My dear Benett
> I trust this will find you at Pythouse and already the better for the change. Your kind offer of your lodgings <u>almost</u> tempted me to come up to town for a short spell & Mrs Moore was generous enough to press me to do so – but money, money (that devilish 'sine qua non' which with me always 'non est inventus') was not forthcoming for such indulgences and I must content myself at home – not the less obliged to you, however, for your kind thoughtfulness.
>
> You have a good escape from the wretched scrapes which the half-faced policy of our friend the Whip is plunging their party
> Yrs ever T.Moore[116]

It was at this time that, having lived when in London at 19 Albermarle Street since 1824, Benett moved to 10 Lower Grosvenor Street, and this remained his London address for the next five years.

Benett continued to give his support to the Hindon troop of Royal Wiltshire Yeomanry Cavalry ( the prefix 'Royal' had been awarded in recognition of its conduct during the recent unrest) and was present at Dinton Park, the seat of his friends the Wydhams, when a field day was held there in November. The company sat down at 4 o'clock to, ' a sumptuous dinner . . . consisting of every delicacy of the season'. In response to the toast to his health and the other officers of the troop, Benett 'eloquently explained the original objects of the yeomanry corps, and feelingly alluded to the protection himself and his family had received from the Hindon troop during the melancholy riots of 1830'. On the table was the silver tankard that he had presented to the troop as a token of his gratitude. It was reported that 'the pleasures of the evening were much heightened by many excellent songs, and the party did not retreat from the festive board until morning's dawn'.[117]

After 1832, the Whigs had failed to address and remedy the grievances of the dissenters and, soon after Parliament met in February 1834, Benett presented to Parliament a petition from the Independent Chapel in Warminster complaining about paying poor rates, and also of the want of proper registration of birth and deaths in their congregation. They could not bury their dead according to the rules and ceremonies of the church, and in the case of marriages they were obliged to conform to certain ceremonies at variance with their conscientious opinions. Further, they complained that their children could not be educated in the National Schools without subscribing to certain articles which would make them members of the Established Church. In presenting the petition, Benett said that with most of the grievances he fully concurred and bore testimony to the respectability of the people who had signed the petition.[118] Before long the Marriage Act passed in 1836 was to satisfy many of the dissenters' demands.

In January, the readers of the *Salisbury and Winchester Journal* would have been able to learn that during 1833 Benett spoke in the House on 23 occasions and occupied 9 columns of *The Mirror of Parliament*.[119] During February and March Benett was on his feet in the House on very many occasions beginning with the debate on the Budget. He deprecated the attack on the agricultural portion of the community. They had been charged, he said, with combining. Never at any time had they combined for their own or mutual advantage. While congratulating Lord Althorp (soon to become 3rd Earl Spencer on the death of his father) on the surplus already declared, he could not help repeating the regret he felt that some portion of it had not been applied in relieving the distress of the landed interest.[120]

Whenever the vexed question of tithes was debated in the House, Benett was sure to make his opinions known. In a debate on tithes in Ireland, he said that it was not fair for Catholic landholders to complain of the burden of tithe, as they had taken their land with knowledge of this liability. As soon as the plan relating to Ireland was introduced into England the better it would be for all classes in the agricultural community of both countries.[121] In the following month, in another debate on the subject, he said that something had to be said respecting dissenters, of which body he had considerable knowledge – he had never met a dissenter who entertained any idea of doing away with tithes without giving fair compensation to the clergy. That they were hostile to the payment of tithe there could be no doubt and he was equally hostile to them. He said they should be honestly and fairly compensated.[122]

The Corn Laws continued to be a bone of contention between those who favoured free trade in corn and those, like Benett, who were convinced that the protection afforded by them was essential to the prosperity of agriculture. When a petition from Liverpool was presented to the House in March seeking a free trade in corn, Benett said that the real question was whether the farmer was or was not entitled to protection. In his view, if land could not be cultivated so as to give a profit to the farmer, the consequence would be that the landlord would become the farmer, and the farmer would become a labourer. There was another class, however, in whose welfare he felt a more deep interest than that of the farmer himself; that class was the agricultural labourer. It had been said that England was essentially a manufacturing country; he denied that proposition; he thought it essentially agricultural.[123]

Having successfully introduced a bill to disfranchise the freemen of Liverpool who had been guilty of bribery and corruption, in the spring of 1834 Benett's bill was read for a second time with a majority of 152. On 19 March the bill had its third reading and was duly passed with 109 members voting in favour and 52 against. Benett must have been heartily relieved that at last his crusade against the wrongdoing in Liverpool had born some fruit.

The removal of the disabilities suffered by those who refused to conform to the Established Church was also much debated at this time. Benett had a great deal of sympathy with the demands of dissenters and it was, of course, as long ago as 1819 that he was first publicly declared to be a champion of their interests. It was natural, therefore, for dissenting bodies to look to Benett to make their views felt in the House of Commons. So in March 1834, when presenting a petition from Tisbury and other parishes in the county praying for their disabilities to be addressed, he said that in particular something should be done in the way of removing the church rate altogether, the Church possessing sufficient wealth to pay it itself.[124] Whilst Benett was the advocate of the dissenters, Astley was well known as a churchman and so the natural choice of member to present several petitions from Wiltshire in support of the Established Church. It is perhaps significant that Benett was absent from a meeting held in Warminster in July in support of the Church.

In 1834, the Poor Law Act was passed and one of the effects was to replace the parish, with its narrow boundaries, by the wider area of the union, and the functions of the local magistrates by uniform central control. The result would be the setting up of Union Workhouses – extremely unpleasant places where the sexes would be segregated and the able-bodied compelled to undertake work far more arduous than they would have found outside the workhouse. Benett strongly opposed the measure, and in so doing found himself, somewhat surprisingly, in agreement with William Cobbett. Cobbett stated in Parliament that the bill, 'will totally abrogate all the local government of the kingdom: the gentlemen and the magistrates will be totally divested of all power tending to uphold their character and their personal safety in the country',[125] sentiments with which Benett must have wholeheartedly concurred. Col. Charles à Court, the assistant Poor Law Commissioner, needed the co-operation of the local magistrates to implement the changes, and in Benett he found a vehement opponent. Benett knew that there was nothing he could do to prevent the new unions being created, and so he raised all sorts of objections to the implementation of the commissioner's proposals. On 30 September he wrote to à Court:

> My dear à Court
> I regret to find by your letters that you are not disposed to reconsider your decision in regard to retaining Hindon in the Tisbury Union, and that already within a week of your meeting the Overseers at Hindon, the Union has been declared by the Chief Commissioners to be fixed on, not as you first proposed to all of us, which proposition included Sedgehill and East Knoyle, but with a subsequent alteration – leaving those parishes out & uniting Hindon, the worst part of and of them.
>
> On Tuesday the 15th Septr you proposed a Union of 21 Parishes with Tisbury which included Sedgehill and East Knoyle – on Thursday the 17th Septr you having determined to enter Sedgehill and Et Knoyle to the <u>Mere</u> Union, proposed a new Union (leaving these parishes out) to the Overseers who met at Hindon and on the 26th Septr an Order of the Commissioners is dated fixing the latter Union.

Now here there was no time given for land-owners & occupiers to take the matter into consideration, you had the silent sanction of the Overseers who were present, because as they tell me they did not consider themselves to have any voice or power in the matter, & they were not allowed to consult Parishioners.

Surely this is not a satisfactory mode of commencing operations under a new law so unpopular and severe in its enactments. – You call this a 'sadly pauperized district'. – I know not from what you take your information on this point, but I do know from 40 years observation that the poor were never so well fed – housed, or cloathed – or more contented than they are now, and the Paymasters are equally well satisfied, and have only dreaded your operations. – Be this as it may – the law is to be enforced, Physic we must take whether we want it or not. – All I wish then is that we may make the Government Union such as it ought in Justice to be – and in so doing alone can you secure the assistance of the best men in the several Parishes to act as Guardians &c &c.

I am sorry to occupy so much of your time, but the subject is of importance – I know the power rests with yourself and the Commissioners, and greater powers are you invested with than were ever before entrusted in the Country to a Select body of individuals. –

I trust therefore you will give more time for deliberation and remonstrance, should it be required than we have yet been allowed in this case.

I am dear à Court
Ever yours very truly
John Benett[126]

It is unlikely that anyone else would have had the temerity to address Colonel à Court in such terms and his response was immediate. As he mentioned in a letter written a few days earlier to Charles Shaw-Lefevre[127] in response to a suggestion that one of his reports needed revision: 'As a military man I always write offhand usually without a rough draft, my practice is to answer every letter as soon as I receive it even tho' I sit at my desk the whole night'.[128] It comes as no surprise, therefore, to find à Court writing to Benett on 2 October:

My dear Benett
I cannot tell you how much your letter vexes me, nor how sincerely I regret that my arrangements are contrary to your wishes.

When I first wrote to you on the subject of the proposed Union, my desire certainly was to have included East Knoyle and Sedgehill in it, but I told you when I called at Pyt House that I could make no definite arrangements until after I had met my colleague & the Dorset Magistrates at Shaftesbury. . .

He then explained why there had to be a change to his original suggestions and continued:

> My meeting at Hindon was publically known for many days before it took place; but no Magistrate & none of the neighbouring gentry did me the favour to attend it. I could of course address myself only to the Parish Officers from none of whom did I hear the slightest [ ? ] of dissatisfaction at my proceedings . . .
>
> As to the haste with which the Union was declared, I am quite ready to take all the blame of that proceeding. I always stated to you that it was desirable to introduce the new system of parochial management simultaneously thro' the whole of the district from Amesbury to Mere and you appeared to agree with me that it would be well to do so. It was for this reason that I slaved full 16 hours a day in order to attain my object . . .
>
> Let me entreat you to be persuaded that I can have no object in view but to ameliorate the condition of the labouring classes both morally and physically, whilst at the same time I hope to render essential service to the suffering rate-payers.
>
> Let me further beg you to assist me in my honest endeavours to effect this great good; & above all pray do not withhold your valuable services in conducting the proceedings of the Union as at present constituted.
>
> In great haste believe me
> Sincerely yours
> C A à Court
>
> P.S. With respect to the expression 'pauperised district' am I not justified in using it, when I tell you that on a surface of only about 40,000 acres, I find that in Winter there are generally some 350 labouring men, most of them heads of families, out of work – paid by the parishes for doing next-to-nothing on the parish roads and under no superintendence whatsoever? . . . [129]

In the opinion of the author of that part of the *Victoria County History of Wiltshire* dealing with county government since 1835, it was as a result of Benett's powerful influence that none of the magistrates or neighbouring gentry attended the meeting at Hindon called by à Court.[130] In October, Benett was still causing serious problems to à Court when he arranged for a petition that Hindon should be removed from the Tisbury Union to be prepared and signed and submitted to Lefevre. On 11 October, à Court wrote to Lefevre that:

It is strange that most of the signatures said to be affixed to the petition
are of those to whom I submitted my arrangements & who not only made
no objection to them, but decidedly gave me to understand that they met
with their approval. What influence can have been [ ? ] to have induced
them now to change their opinion?[131]

On the 13th, à Court reported once again to Lefevre:

I am told that Mr Benett's great objection to having Hindon in the
Tisbury Union is the dread of an equal rating settlement in all Unions
hereafter . . . Could I always be present in the neighbourhood, I should
have less dread of Mr Benett's influence: − I know that he will have the
power to thwart our proceedings in every way, should he feel inclined to
do so; & on this account will conciliate him if I can.[132]

By the 15th, he appears to have found a solution to his problems with
Benett when he wrote from Hindon to C.S.Lefevre that:

he is evidently fighting for his interests & his own interests only − he is
nevertheless a formidable opponent & in an endeavour to conciliate him
− the appointment of his accountant to be Clerk to the Union has been
very acceptable to him. He needs his occasional services; is so
embarassed in his circumstances, as to make it an object not to have him
enter upon his lands − his present appointment will therefore relieve him
from an expense which I fancy is inconvenient to him.

    I trust it will induce him to give us his assistance or at all events his
continuance hereafter . . .

As a postscript he added , 'I think Benett may be persuaded that my
arrangements are not likely to be attended with the great inconveniences
which he anticipates . . .'[133]

A final meeting was arranged to take place on the following day. At
this à Court expected no opposition and would then (no doubt very
thankfully) be able to take his leave of Hindon and the troublesome
Mr.Benett! As will be seen , however, this was not the last time that
Benett was to interfere in the operation of the Poor Law in his
neighbourhood. The new clerk to the Union was duly appointed at the
first meeting of the Guardians at a salary of £50 a year.[134]

In April Benett, together with Methuen and Astley, had received
letters urging them to support a petition to the House to reject a local bill
for the management of the poor of Lacock. However, in the light of his
opposition to the new centralised arrangements, it is unlikely that he
would have been willing to do this.[135]

In the following year, the *Devizes and Wiltshire Gazette* reported that 'in consequence of the demoralized state of the paupers in some of the southern parishes of the County, Colonel à Court had been compelled to defer his visit to Devizes'. Benett always seemed to be reluctant to accept that the state of the poor in the south of the county was any worse than anywhere else. He wrote a letter to *The Times*, as a consequence of which the Devizes newspaper rebuked him in no uncertain terms:

> In a letter to the Editor of the Times, Mr Benett, one of the Members for the Southern Division of this County, has not only taken upon himself to contradict a statement which appeared in our paper a few weeks since . . . but has cast an imputation upon our character as Journalists. Mr Benett has been acquainted with us long enough to know, that we should not have inserted such a statement as the above, without authority; and were we disposed to act as uncourteously towards Mr B. as he has acted towards us, we should probably place him in an awkward position.[136]

Notwithstanding his stance over the Corn Laws and the Poor Laws, Benett was generally in favour of reform, not only of Parliament but of those areas where privilege seemed to him to be abused. Although in the minority, he therefore voted for a select committee to be appointed to enquire into pensions charged on the Civil List, in order to ascertain the nature and extent of any abuses which may have occurred in the granting of pensions.[137]

In May, some of Benett's friends decided that subscriptions should be invited from those in the north of the county, and members of the agricultural community in particular, who would wish to contribute to the cost of a piece of plate to be presented to him as a mark of their respect. On the 29th the *Devizes and Wiltshire Gazette* carried a report to this effect[138] and on 19 June the names of the 37 members of the committee that had been formed to receive the subscriptions was published.[139] They were probably dismayed, and Benett perhaps embarrassed, when on 19 June a letter from 'A Manufacturer' appeared in the *Devizes and Wiltshire Gazette*. It declared that, whilst the writer was pleased to see that a subscription had been opened, he questioned why it was confined to North Wilts, and to agriculturalists. He hoped that some means could be devised so that every inhabitant of Wilts, whether 'a gentleman, an agriculturalist, a manufacturer, a tradesman, a mechanic or a peasant, may have the opportunity of contributing to it as a token of regard to this favourite member for the County'.[140] This letter produced a response from 'An Agriculturalist' who expressed surprise at its contents. In his view it was clear that the plate was to show public esteem for him as, 'an *agriculturalist without the slightest regard to politics*, not for his Parliamentary labours; but, a far higher compliment, for his successful application of his talents to measures of public utility, which are not matters of party, but in which the whole of society is deeply interested'.[141] The 'Manufacturer' would not let the matter rest, and in the next edition of the newspaper another letter from him appeared in which he enthused that Benett's, 'exertions for the public have been liberal, unlimited and unbounded: his mind is expanded and generous. I have seen and know much of his exertion in the House of Commons and in the county. In the House I have known his opinion sought on many subjects with great earnestness, and delivered with very great correctness; and in the county his employments have always been of the most useful kind; but in no places and on no occasion, have I ever seen him support a narrow or illiberal measure.'[142] The writers of the letters appeared at first to disagree with each other, but later seemed to view the character and talents of Benett as everything that was commendable and worthy.

However worse was to come. In August this notice appeared in the *Salisbury and Winchester Journal*:

> We have lately perused with great pain a gross attack on the private character of our most respected County Member, Mr Benett. The political conduct of this gentleman, as well as that of all others, who fill public situations, may be fairly the subject of discussion, but black must be the heart of that man who, like the cowardly assassin, would stab his generous enemy in the dark. We can tell the person who signs himself 'A Plain Wiltshire Yeoman', that we believe he is no yeoman, for the yeoman's characteristic is generosity. We can further tell him that the blow he has given has failed in its effect. Mr Benett, whatever his political sentiments may be (and we are not disposed to quarrel with them), is beloved, and deservedly beloved, by every respectable freeholder in the Southern Division of the County, which he represents; and the individual who has attacked him may rest assured, that, were he to dare to own his name, he would be held up to that public scorn and contempt, to which his base conduct so justly entitles him.[143]

This most unusual notice brought forth a response from Benett who, in a letter to the newspaper, said he considered it his duty to discover the real name of the, 'author of that composition, in which nothing seems so conspicuous as private malice towards myself'. He said that the editor of the *Salisbury Herald* had sent him the original letter by, 'a gentleman who avowed himself as taking an interest in that paper and this gentleman expressed regret that such a letter should have been allowed to appear in its columns'. Benett wrote that he had put the letter in the hands of his solicitor, Mr Cobb of Salisbury, who would be at liberty to show it to those he may consider likely to assist him in the discovery of the real name of, 'the personage, whose cloven foot may, I think, be detected, however dark the veil which he may attempt to conceal it'. He concluded by saying that his *private* as well as his *public* conduct and character should be a matter of discussion and animadversion. Fearless as he was, he would not condescend to notice any *anonymous* observations, and, were they not anonymous, in a case like this, he would not enter into a *wordy* contention with one who, 'had exhibited so much malignant personal feeling on the onset'.[144]

Many of the readers of the *Salisbury and Winchester Journal* must have been agog to know what slur on Benett's private character had been revealed to the public by the *Salisbury and Wiltshire Herald*, which had first appeared in the previous year as a rival to the old established *Salisbury and Winchester Journal*.[145] Had they been able to obtain a copy of the offending newspaper they would have read the following astonishing and libellous attack:

It having been lately announced in the Devizes Gazette and Salisbury Herald to be the intention of agriculturalists of North Wilts to subscribe towards purchasing a piece of Plate to be presented to Mr Benett, I cannot but say that such an intention surprises me much, as they can know little of Mr Benett, and of his real principles. I ask what has Mr Benett done in favour of the agricultural interest? Has he been able to fulfil his promise held out to many agriculturalists at the time he solicited their votes previous to the late contested election for the county of Wilts – 'that he would keep up the price of corn &c. &c.' presumptuously thinking he had the power of leading the House of Commons by the nose? No. But say the northern agriculturalists, 'he has used his best exertions for upholding the agricultural interest of his county, and therefore is entitled to some reward.' To be sure; for what will a man not lie and say when self interested? I ask the northern agriculturalists, have not your own members for that district been equally as strenuous in the cause of agriculture as Mr Benett? Why then pass them over to confer a favour on a man who is not resident among you, and who has not, nor can have, the least claim upon you, for what? A piece of plate! And when I consider the enormous sum subscribed for defraying Mr Benett's electioneering expenses throughout the county of Wilts, to which I contributed, I should have thought this liberal act would have sufficed, without again soliciting the public to contribute their aid for purchasing him a piece of plate.

Had this letter ended here it is likely that Benett and his friends, while doubtless disagreeing with the sentiments expressed, would probably not have taken undue exception to the views of the writer. However what followed constituted a most violent assault on Benett's character. The writer continued:

I am no admirer of Mr Benett's political principles; as to his religious principles, they are bad, and I abominate them. To declare publicly in my hearing, and in the hearing of many others, at the agricultural meeting at the Bear Inn, Devizes, 'that he was a friend to the Church' was saying what he knew in his heart was false; for how is it possible that a man can be a real and sincere friend to the Church who never puts a foot within its sacred walls? It is true, he built a chapel, but more for ornament that divine worship, it never having been consecrated. I have to observe that the only criterion to judge of a man's civil and religious principles, is by his doings and actions, not what he says; for the tongue does not always express the real sentiments of the heart. A man who violates the sacred ordinances of the Church would in all probability be glad were there no Church, no Christian Sabbath, or Lord's Day; and who would also be glad to see all the poor remainder of Church lands and revenues, all tythes and glebes, alienated and confiscated; as those men were who obtained good estates by the former ruin of monasteries, or the later spoilings of Bishops and Cathedrals. Certain it is that there are but too many of this description at this time, in as well as out of the House of Commons; many who would deem it precious liberty, could they but partake of the spoilation of Church property with a view of patching up their own broken fortunes. I allude to no one in particular, but if the cap fits, so let it be worn. No one, I presume, can be so weak and deficient in understanding as not to know that Church property is as sacred as any other property in the kingdom, and indeed much more ancient. Mr Benett entertains a very different opinion by asserting in the House of Commons, that Church property is State property, meaning that the State has a right to do as it pleases with it. Supposing, erroneous as the supposition is, that Church property is State property; then I scruple not to say, that every other property in the kingdom, be it what it may, is also State property. Not a mite, Mr Editor, will I subscribe for purchasing Mr Benett's plate. If I have a pound to spare, my landlord is ready to receive it, and I am inclined to believe that every other agriculturalist, as times are now, is of the same opinion. There was a time when I was a reformer, with the hope of seeing all abuses (if any did actually exist in Church and State) amended; but little did I expect to see the world turned upside down, under the specious name of reform. I am now become a conservative, and whenever an opportunity offers, will give my vote and interest to one who bears that honourable name.[146]

History does not record whether the piece of plate was ever purchased and presented to him and so it is likely that the effect of this correspondence was to abort the whole enterprise. It had been his very public correspondence with Archdeacon Coxe twenty years before that first persuaded many people that Benett was willing to attack the property of the established church. During the 1819 election campaign the writer of one of the many letters published in the press declared that, 'his religious principles have long been questionable', and that he was indifferent to the cause of the established church. This was not the first time, therefore, that his religious principles, or lack of them, had been attacked, but the thinly veiled suggestion that he might benefit financially from the spoils of the church was an attack that could not be ignored.

Benett continued to take an active interest in the affairs of the Bath and West of England Agricultural Society, and at its annual meeting held in December he, with Sir Richard Colt Hoare of Stourhead and others, was appointed to a committee to superintend a ploughing match to be held in the vicinity of Stourton in the following year .[147]

In January 1835, Benett was faced with another general election, and in his address to the freeholders he said that, 'should I be returned I shall, as I have ever done, exercise my free judgement on all subjects which may require my attention, consulting the public good in the performance of my public duty'.[148] The election took place before the Guildhall in Salisbury and Benett and Sidney Herbert arrived in the usual way, with the yeomanry on horseback accompanied by banners and music. Benett was proposed by his friend William Wyndham, who said that Benett was an old and trusted Member, a man who had been constantly at his post, and had ever proved himself the advocate of liberal principles. He was attached to no party, but advocated those principles, which he deemed best calculated to promote the true interests of his county.

In contrast to the peaceful way in which Benett's nomination had been greeted by the crowd, when Herbert, who had been proposed by Benett's old friend and neighbour Thomas Grove, said that he had joined the Administration of Sir Robert Peel he was greeted by tremendous shouts of ' No Peel, No Peel', and a barrage of hisses that prevented anyone other than those standing nearby from hearing anything he said. Both Benett and Herbert, who, although only 24 years old, was now Secretary to the Board of Control, were eventually re-elected unopposed, but not before John Mayne, the notorious and unpopular orator, had his say – although when he rose to speak– he was greeted by such a storm of protest that he also could only be heard by a fraction of the crowd. In the course of an extremely lengthy speech he did, however, say that, 'Mr Benett was an old and excellent reformer and deserved well of his county. Mr Sidney Herbert was doubtless an excellent and amiable man and the Tories had played their best card when they brought forward that gentleman who was so straightforward and well meaning a man, that he could not but regret that he had been induced to join the present Administration'.[149]

In February, the new Parliament sat and, although Benett was not in the House when the Speaker was elected, he was present a week later when he voted in the division on the Address. However, the place in which he now found himself was not the ancient chamber in which he had addressed his fellow Members for the first time in 1819. On the evening of the previous 16 October, a disastrous fire had broken out, destroying most of the old Palace of Westminster. Following the fire, the ceremony of the prorogation of Parliament took place in the Lord's Library, that was hastily fitted out for the occasion. Over the winter months urgent work was undertaken to enable the two Houses to meet as usual in the following February. Arrangements were made for the Lords to meet in the Painted Chamber and for the space that they had vacated to be reconstructed as a temporary chamber for the Commons. Although, according to one report, 'this building, even as it now appears, is perhaps one of the most elegant specimens of taste that can well be conceived', with all the seats covered in green Spanish leather and lit by nine chandeliers,[150] another thought that 'the new House of Commons is ill calculated for persons to hear the debates, however attentive they may be to the speaker. This arises from the walls of the chamber being lined in canvass, which absorbs and affects the sound, and prevents its progress'.[151]

His speeches in the new chamber in 1835 were few and far between. However, in March he did speak at length in a debate on the repeal of the malt tax. In the course of this he said that he desired to make beer cheaper than spirits, and it was because the labourer was not able to brew at home that he went to the beer-shops, which had increased, and was induced to stay out at night, and waste the means which more properly belonged to his family.[152]

In March, Lord John Russell tabled a motion that the House should resolve itself into a committee to consider the temporalities of the Church of Ireland and on the 30th Benett wrote to James Cobb, the Salisbury attorney:

> It is the common belief that should Sir Robert Peel be beaten tonight in the Division on Lord Russell's motion he will resign. I do not believe that he will do so and I am sure he ought not to should the motion be similar to his (Lord John's) statement in the House on Friday night. The opposition however in the House is very powerful. I know but little of the feeling out of the House but I think Sir Robert Peel's proposed measure of reform must be generally approved of. I have been confined to my room by illness the whole of last week, and shall not be able to go out today or tomorrow though I am recovering fast. I have in fact been ill for three weeks or more though I have been in the Doctor's hands only a week. Mr Herbert has been very ill for some time, but went out in his carriage for an airing yesterday for the first time.[153]

In the event, on 8 April, having been outvoted on a resolution to appropriate the surplus revenues of the Irish church to non-ecclesiastical uses (Benett voting with the minority against Lord John Russell's motion for a reform of the Irish Church[154]), Peel did indeed resign. Benett held strong views on these issues and, on the day before, Moore had written to him from Sloperton Cottage:

> My dear Benett
> I am very sorry not to see more of you while I was in town – but business completely swallowed me up in the mornings – From the little I had time to say to you one morning, on politics, I am afraid you thought me far more strong in my objections to the line you have taken than I really am. The fact is there never were times when people ought to be more tolerant of the different views they respectively take, – as it is come to a mere matter of nerve, and he that can best face what is inevitable before us and to help to give it in the safest direction is the man most fit for the crisis. For myself, I am staunch to my own party always when they are out – it is their natural position. But I never feel myself bound to them when in Let me have a line to say how you are, and beleive [sic] me ever most truly yours
> Thomas Moore
> Peel does his work most gallantly, I will say for him.[155]

In June, in a debate on agricultural distress, Benett suggested that the poor rates be thrown on the general fund of the country,[156] and, in a debate on a bill for securing relief to the poor of Ireland, when Daniel O'Connell suggested that the Poor Laws were productive of mischief, Benett retorted that they were not the cause of distress, but they were too often confounded in this country with the cause because they were always in operation where distress prevailed.[157]

The year 1835 saw the opening of the new Assize Court in Devizes. It is likely that Benett did not approve of the prospect of the summer assize for the county moving away from Salisbury, as his name does not appear amongst the other Wiltshire members of Parliament who subscribed towards the cost of the new building.[158] Be that as it may, he had for many years been the foreman of the Grand Jury sitting in Salisbury and so, in August, he travelled to Devizes for the first sitting of the assize in the new court house. The procession that formed to meet the judges as they approached Devizes on the Bath road consisted of at least 200 horsemen and over 100 private carriages and occupied more than half a mile of road. Benett was once again foreman of the Grand Jury and amongst his fellow jurors were Sidney Herbert and his old opponent John Dugdale Astley. The *Times* reported that, 'though the exterior of the Courts was handsome, the interior arrangements were the worst that could be imagined; that there was poor accommodation for the bar, and none for the attorneys; and that all who had business would have reason to regret the removal of the assizes from Salisbury'. *The Devizes and Wiltshire Gazette* thought little of this report and observed that, 'if there be a few trifling defects, they can be easily remedied; and however deep-rooted the jealousies of our Salisbury neighbours may be; whatever obstacles they may throw in the way, we have no doubt, that the Spring assizes will in future be held in this town; and that it is not improbable that in the course of a very few years we shall have the both'.[159] The assize court building, with its still handsome facade, now stands empty and neglected with the assizes no longer being held in the town.

The management of his farms and the improvement of agricultural practice continued to be Benett's enduring interest. The activities of the Wiltshire Agricultural Society were always close to his heart and at the society's meetings he could always be sure of the warmest of welcomes. It is no surprise to read, therefore, that when he rose to speak to respond to the toast to his health at the meeting held in July, it was 'sometime before he could be heard; each renewed effort to speak, appeared to excite to renewed cheering. Nothing could exceed the enthusiastic manner in which the toast was received'.[160] An undated subscription list to the society has survived. It is likely that it dates from the 1830s. Heading the list are the Marquis of Ailesbury and Sidney Herbert, who each subscribed £100, followed by Benett whose contribution was £50, and then some 350 other people who provided varying amounts down to the very modest sum of one shilling.[161] It was now more than twenty years since the Bath and West of England Agricultural Society had awarded him its Bedfordian Gold medal for his essay on tithes, and during that time he had been an active member of the Society and had attended many of the annual meetings that were held every December in Bath. In 1835 he acted as chairman and, at the dinner held after the meeting, in response to the toast to his health, said 'that he had frequently been present on occasions similar to this, but never with so much gratification as he now felt. No-one could feel more zeal for agricultural pursuits than himself. Every shilling which he had in the world was dependent on agriculture, to which he owed the whole enjoyment of his life. The principal pleasure which he had, and he felt it also to be a duty, consisted in superintending the concern of his farm, which he walked over every day: and let it be a comfort to every farmer who heard him, that his pursuits, if properly followed, would afford him more and more pleasure as he got older.'[162]

In December, his daughter Etheldred died leaving behind her five young children. In writing to John Parkinson, his London solicitor, about the Fonthill estate, Benett added a rather sad postscript, 'My dear daughter Lady Charles Churchill has been buried this morning at the new Cemetery near London'.[163] Her husband was to survive her by only four months.

Readers of the *Salisbury and Winchester Journal* at the beginning of January 1836 would have learned that:

> Mr Benett, our respected County Member, gave at Christmas, a substantial dinner at Pyt-house to the numerous labourers, workmen etc in his employ, an ox having been killed for the purpose. Each person was, in addition, provided with a gallon of real Wiltshire stingo,[164] to drink the health of his benevolent employer.[165]

As a widower with two of his three daughters married and his youngest daughter Fanny not yet a young woman, Benett was not in a particularly satisfactory position to attend the numerous assemblies and balls that were held in Salisbury, Shaftesbury and Devizes throughout the winter season. He was therefore conspicuous by his absence from the second Lady Patroness's Ball held at the Assembly Rooms in Salisbury in January, and at which Sidney Herbert, the new Lord Arundell[166] and his family and the Wyndham and Grove families were among the many fashionable members of county society attending.

Parliament re-assembled as usual in February and, although Benett once again did not vote on the Address at the beginning of the session, he was soon to be heard. On the 8th the member for Bath was rash enough to suggest in a debate on agricultural distress that landlords belonged to the 'non-productives', and were entitled to but little consideration – the cause of their distress arising from habits of extravagance, when, unhappily for the country, they enjoy a monopoly of supply, England being then cooped up within four seas. One can imagine Benett leaping to his feet and declaring that he belonged to the class of English country gentlemen, and that he rose to defend them against the allegations made by the Honourable Member for Bath, who appeared not to know much about their character . . . the country gentlemen had uniformly done their duty; they were loyal to the King and Constitution, and in their capacity as magistrates have rendered important service to the country. He went on to say that the agricultural labourers would never prosper until their employers, the farmers, were also prospering . . . the three classes, the labourers, farmers and landowners were all bound up together. He felt obliged to the Government for having proposed the Committee to look into agricultural distress, which he had no doubt would be fairly constituted.[167]

Soon after this, when it was proposed that the second reading of the Tithe Commutation Bill be postponed, Benett said that the plan had been before the country for twelve months and should now proceed to a second reading. He said that as a landlord who had nothing to do with the collection of tithes, but much to do with payment of them, he was quite satisfied with the bill. However, he was of the opinion that the commutation should be permanent and compulsory and that much waste land had been left unclaimed solely owing to the injurious operation of the law of tithes. For no man would lay out £20 upon the improvement of land if he was obliged to pay £5 for leave to lay it out.[168]

In April Benett demonstrated his liberal attitude to the observance of religion by voting with the minority (that included his son-in-law Lord Charles Spencer Churchill), in opposing a motion for leave to bring in a bill for the Better Observance of the Sabbath.[169] Once again he was with the minority in the following month in favour of a motion for the application of the surplus revenues of the county to the relief of agricultural distress.[170] Soon after this, Benett spoke in a debate on the Factories Amendment Bill, when it was proposed that children from the age of twelve upwards could be permitted to work twelve hours a day. To this he was firmly opposed, and said that he had seen a great deal of the manufacturing children, and comparing them with the mass of the agricultural population it was impossible not to be struck by the physical debility and moral corruption of the one compared with the other. He was quite convinced that it was impossible for children to be employed for ten or twelve hours a day without impediment of their health.[71]

In June, Benett had some rather hard and perhaps rather uncharacteristic things to say about the 'lower orders', as he would have put it. In a debate on the Parish Vestries Bill he said that as a country gentleman he could from long experience assert that no practical evil resulted from the present system of parish vestry voting. The effect of the proposed bill would be to place in many instances the whole control of the funds of a parish at the disposal of ten or twelve labourers, when influence could be purchased for ten or twelve quarts of beer, and who would be therefore easily excited by artful and designing men (of whom there were always enough in every parish) to enter into every hostile combination against the great landowners of the parish. Let the Honourable member for Finsbury [who was proposing the Bill] legislate for his own borough if he pleased, but let him not interfere with country parishes.[72] These remarks brought forth a severe rebuke from one member, who considered them an insult to the humbler classes inhabiting rural areas. Another member said that he had passed a great part of his life in rural areas and had always found that the landed interest endeavoured to oppress those who were poorer than themselves – not something Benett would have liked to have heard.

In many ways Benett's principles were forward-looking and even radical, and it is therefore perhaps a little surprising to find him voting against a motion for the introduction of the vote by ballot[73] – adhering to the still commonly held view, no doubt, that no man should be ashamed to let it be known for whom he has voted. However, he was happy to second the motion introduced by Joseph Hume, the radical politician, that hop gardens and market gardens be removed from the scope of the English Tithe Commutation Bill. In this instance, as in so many others, Benett once again found himself in the minority. As a truly independent member who always spoke and voted as he thought best, in the third reading of the Poor Law Amendment Bill in November, he was perhaps surprised to find himself named with the radical William Cobbett as one of the principal speakers against the bill.[74]

On 18 July, the House of Commons was occupied with the investigation of the charge said to have been brought by the engineer and architect Nicholas Wilcocks Cundy[75] against Sir Charles Burrell, of having been influenced by corrupt motives in the support he gave to Stephenson's Brighton railway line.[176] Cundy was brought to the Bar of the House and was made to answer questions put to him by the Speaker and by Members. Benett was absent attending the assizes and upon other business when Cundy was questioned, and was extremely upset to hear from his friends and from reports in the newspapers that his name had been mentioned and a number of incorrect answers given. As a consequence on 25 July, Benett made a long statement to the House in order to correct a number of statements Cundy had made. For instance when Cundy was asked whether he had solicited the attendance of any Member on the third reading of the Brighton Railway Bill, he replied in the negative. Benett now told the House that Cundy had indeed canvassed him to be in the House. Benett went on to give the House the substance of certain conversations which he had had with Cundy relative to the proposed Brighton railroad, in which Cundy had informed him that Sir Charles Burrell was, by way of a bribe, to receive for his support of Stephenson's line the sum of £15,000 for about 6 acres of land. Benett wrote to Sir Charles Burrell and now 'considered it his duty to make his statement as early as possible, since it had gone out to the country that he had overstated the case against Mr Cundy; and where his character was not known, it might possibly suffer, even from the evidence of a man who had imprisonment before his eyes, if he did not contradict that with which he was charged'. It was reported that Benett satisfactorily explained the circumstances of the case and satisfied the House that he had been grossly misrepresented by Cundy in his statement at the bar of the House.[177]

Consistent with his long-held view that those who did not conform to the established church should not be treated differently from those who did, in a debate on the Jewish Civil Disabilities Bill, he said that the Jews were good and loyal subjects and were fully entitled to equal privileges with all other British subjects. He strongly objected to mixing civil rights with religious opinion.[178]

The 1830s saw the beginning of the movement that resulted in the whole country being served by a network of railways. As a public figure in the county, Benett, with Earl Grosvenor,[179] Lord Arundell and others, was appointed at a public meeting held in Shaftesbury in January 1836 to a committee to superintend and assist in the management of the plan for constructing a railway from London to Exeter.[180] At a meeting held in London in the following month, Benett, together with his fellow Member of Parliament Sydney Herbert and others, was appointed to a committee to superintend the subscription of shares in a company that subsequently became the Great Western Railway Company.[181] Soon afterwards his son-in-law, Lord Charles Spencer-Churchill, joined the committee, no doubt at Benett's suggestion, and to add credibility to the promoters. In April they issued a prospectus to raise £2 million in shares of £50 each – the issue being quickly oversubscribed.[182] Benett was also a member of the provisional committee for promoting the Hampshire and Wiltshire Junction Railway to connect Salisbury and Romsey with Southampton,[183] and of the committee formed in 1838, that also included amongst its number Lord Arundell and Benett's old friend Henry King of Chilmark, to promote the construction of a railway from Winchester to Salisbury.[184] This enthusiasm for railways was by no means universal. Benett must have been displeased to find his son-in-law, Arthur Fane, and his wife's half-brother, Aylmer Lambert, amongst those who signed a resolution opposing the construction of the proposed line from Salisbury to Warminster, on the grounds that it was entirely uncalled for and would prove seriously detrimental to the agricultural interests of the neighbourhood![185]

Most of those prominent people who allowed themselves to be appointed to committees to promote the construction of the new railways were undoubtedly figureheads. They hoped to gain financially from their involvement, but it is unlikely that many of them were actively involved in organising and managing the great deal of work that had to be done before the trains themselves could begin to carry passengers from town to town, and to transform the way in which the products of the manufacturing towns were transported throughout the country. Not so Benett, a meticulous man of business who would certainly have wished to have been kept informed of what was being transacted in his name. Indeed in the following decade, between 1846 and 1848, he appears to have instructed John Peniston to carry out a number of surveys in connection with proposed railways in Somerset and Devon, and to arrange for his accounts to be paid. For instance, in December 1847 Peniston wrote to Benett at 18 Duke Street in London:

> Dear Sir
> I enclose herewith the statement of my account for surveys as requested which I think will be found correct. I have also to thank you for your prompt reply to my application which I should not have made, but I am really much in want of the balance to meet my liabilities, which at this time come rather thick for me.[186]

And in the following January, he wrote to Benett clearly hoping for some more instructions:

Please to present my thanks to Mr Brunel[187] for his remittance received this morning, and accept the same for yourself. I enclose as you request separate receipts for the balance of each account, and have divided the sums previously received on the separate accounts in a way which I hope will be satisfactory and correct.

Hoping soon again to have the pleasure of receiving your order to take to the field again.[188]

On 5 July 1836 a violent storm devastated a large area around Salisbury with hailstones – some up to 5 inches in diameter – causing great damage. An appeal was launched to assist those who had suffered. Benett's name is generally conspicuous by its absence from subscription lists,[189] particularly those with a religious flavour, but on this occasion he no doubt felt compelled to join the numerous subscribers, many of whom were clearly people of modest means, by giving £20.[190]

Although there is no evidence that Benett's lifestyle was in any way extravagant, the enormous cost of the 1818 and 1819 elections resulted in his financial position being exceedingly precarious, although for a 19th-century country gentleman to be heavily in debt to his bank and to other mortgagees was in no way unusual. Benett knew that he would soon have to complete his purchase of the Fonthill estate, and would have to look to his bank for assistance in raising the necessary funds. In 1836, therefore, as predicted by Charles à Court when writing to his brother in 1825, he was forced to sell his estate at Enford and Fifield on the north-east of Salisbury Plain that had been purchased by his father in 1769. Benett, as Lord of the Manor, must have been sorry to have to dispose of this estate of almost 2,300 acres, consisting of two large farms and farmhouses and some 25 houses and gardens.[191] The purchaser was Sir Edmund Antrobus[192] who paid £75,000 for the property.[193] To raise a little more money, he had also sold in the previous year the advowson of Askerswell in Dorset – another property that had long been in the possession of his family, in this instance since 1699.[194]

As, following the death of his younger son, Benett had only one son, who he doubtless expected would one day succeed him, it would be surprising if by now he was not hoping that young Benett would find a suitable bride, to produce in due course further offspring to ensure that his estates would remain in the family. In 1836, young John fulfilled his father's expectations, although whether entirely to his satisfaction is unknown. His bride was Emily Blanche, the youngest daughter of Sir Henry Titchborne[195] of Titchborne in Hampshire. The Titchbornes were a noted Roman Catholic family, and Emily was the sister of Frances, the second wife of Henry, 11th Lord Arundell of Wardour.[196] He had succeeded to the title on the death of his brother in 1834, and it must be that young Benett met his wife through his and his father's friendship with the Arundells. We know that although Benett was a great advocate for the removal of all disabilities suffered by those who did not conform to the Established Church, whether Catholic or Protestant, he nevertheless on many occasions made it clear that he was a firm supporter of the church as established by law. Consequently, to see his son becoming and marrying a Roman Catholic with the result that any children would be brought up as Catholics may have caused him some disquiet.

In the autumn of 1836 Benett was in Devizes with the Hindon troop when the whole of the Wiltshire regiment of yeomanry cavalry, consisting of 415 men of all ranks, assembled there for eight days permanent duty, with Benett commanding in the field.[197] The final order to the regiment stated that:

> Major Benett cannot issue this final order on the present occasion without again expressing his personal thanks to the officers, non-commissioned officers, and privates of the R.W.Y.C. for their strict attention to his orders – for the zeal, ability, and good feeling with which they performed their duty – and their personal kind feelings and attention towards himself.
>
> Major Benett feels justly proud of having commanded the Regiment on such an occasion and the greatest satisfaction to know that the character which the Regiment acquired so many years since has not been tarnished while it has been under his command. He trusts that the Regiment never stood higher in public estimation than at the present moment.[198]

From the time of his election to Parliament in 1819 until the passing of the Reform Act, Benett regularly addressed the House of Commons, but as the years went by, only quite infrequently were any speeches made by him reported in the county newspapers. However, he continued to show his independence by sometimes voting with the Government and sometimes against. In March 1837, he voted with the majority against a motion for leave to bring in a bill for the introduction of voting by ballot at elections for members of Parliament[199] and, as one would expect, against any alteration to the Corn Laws.[200] He also voted for the abolition of church rates.[201] Whenever the question of tithes or church rates or other ecclesiastical matters was raised, Benett usually felt compelled to speak and so in a debate on the Government's proposal, with which he agreed, to abolish church rates he said that in

many parishes it was impossible to collect them. He pointed out that
before the spoliation of church property by Henry VIII there were no
such thing as church rates, the churches being kept in repair by the
voluntary contributions of the parishioners. He stressed that the whole
of the church's property was subject to the control of Parliament and
might be modified by Act of Parliament.[202] In view of his well known
opposition to church rates, the readers of the *Salisbury and Winchester
Journal* must have been surprised to learn that he did not vote in the
division in favour of the ministerial measure, particularly as he had done
so in March. However, all was made clear when they were later informed
that he was prevented by illness from voting in favour of the bill.[203]
Despite this, he had been well enough in May to attend the meeting of
the Wiltshire Society. This was held, as usual, at the *Albion Tavern*, when
the chairman congratulated the company on having present their 'old
tried, and valued friend, Mr Benett'.[204]

On 27 March, the Marquis of Bath, the Lieutenant Colonel
Commandant of the Royal Wiltshire Yeomanry Cavalry, died. The news
of his death would certainly have travelled to Benett, who had every
expectation and hope that he would succeed him in command of the
Wiltshire Yeomanry regiment. One can imagine his dismay and horror,
therefore, when on 14 July he opened his copy of the *Devizes and
Wiltshire Gazette* to read. '*Commission signed by the Lord Lieutenant of
Wilts – Royal Wiltshire Yeomanry Cavalry* – G.W.F. Earl Bruce[205] to be
Lieutenant Colonel Commandant, *vice* the Marquis of Bath
deceased'.[206] Benett lost no time in putting pen to paper and that very
afternoon wrote to Lord Lansdowne, the Lord Lieutenant:

> My dear Marquis
> I have this morning observed in the Gazette the appointment of Lord
> Bruce to the command of the R W Yeomanry Cavalry.
>
> I consider it due to myself and the officers whose promotion
> would depend on my own, to express to your Lordship my feeling of
> dissatisfaction at having been passed over, after forty years of service in
> that Regt in every grade from Private when the Regt was raised (and when
> noblemen as well as commoners enlisted as privates) to that of a Field
> Officer, and that an officer of inferior regimental rank to myself who has
> never been one day with the Regt on duty, should be placed over myself
> who has never, to the best of my belief, been absent from the Regt in any
> day of duty during the whole period of forty years,
>
> I might have been induced to believe, however extraordinary I
> should have thought it, that your Lordship considered a commoner not fit
> to hold the chief command of a yeomanry regiment had not Col Baker

told me that you had offered the Regt to him but he had refused to accept it. Thus then, as Col Baker who like myself is a commoner, was considered by your Lordship a fit person to hold a yeomanry regiment, I think no great presumption on my part, the considering myself as a fit person to hold such a position. Your Lordship will readily believe that it will be most painful to me to withdraw myself from the commission which I have been so long proud to hold with the RWYC... but I have no alternative between that of submitting to what I consider, to use the mildest term, a personal slight towards myself and which in a great degree affects the other officers of the Rgt who are near to me in rank, or to withdraw from the Regt by which some promotion must be had by others though not to the extent they had a right to expect.

I trust your Lordship will, under the circumstances in which I am placed, excuse the length of these details of facts and reasons, and that you will be pleased to accept my resignation from my commission of major of the Royal Wiltshire Yeomanry Cavalry.[207]

Whether Lord Lansdowne ever considered Benett as a possible candidate for the command of the regiment will probably never be known, but if he did, it is more than likely that Benett was thought of as much too controversial a figure to be appointed. Fewer than seven years had passed since the traumatic events of 1830, when he was considered by many to be the most hated and unpopular man in the county. Lansdowne must have thought it much safer to appoint another aristocrat to succeed the Marquis of Bath, to what was in reality a symbolic position as head of the regiment. However, Benett was a proud man, so probably never doubted for a moment that he should resign his commission rather than serve under a man with no experience in the field, and more than thirty years his junior. Despite this disappointment, he was probably pleased that his son John continued to serve in the yeomanry cavalry. In 1842 Cornet Benett was one of the officers who accompanied the regiment when between four and five hundred of them assembled for duty in Devizes.[208]

Whatever his disappointment in severing his connection with the yeomanry cavalry might have been, the usual pattern of his life went on, with his attendance at the assizes as foreman of the Grand Jury. On 20 July, it was reported:

The following written presentment was handed over to the Lord Chief Justice Tindal[209] by the Grand Jury after they had discharged their duty in finding the various bills against the prisoners committed:

The Grand Jury beg leave to present to your Lordship that we see

with great regret that the calendar contains a very unusual number of cases where death has ensued from affrays arising from the great intemperance and irregularities taking place in beer houses; and that as this is a very fertile and increasing source of crime of the greatest enormity, the subject demands some immediate and effectual interference on the part of the Legislature.
JOHN BENETT, Foreman of the Grand Jury[210]

The King having died, Parliament was dissolved as usual and so Benett was faced with another election. He must have been confident that he and Sidney Herbert would be returned unopposed. Herbert was the *de facto* master of Wilton House and of the immense estates of the Earls of Pembroke in the south of the county and elsewhere, and Benett having served most conscientiously as a county member of Parliament for the last eighteen years, their positions were unassailable. However, in accordance with the usual practice both the candidates addressed the electors. In his letter to them, Benett said that while he would uphold the connection of the national Church with the State, he would nevertheless support such reforms in regard to the affairs of the Church as he might consider calculated to give efficiency and security to that Establishment; at the same time assuring perfect liberty of conscience and community of right and equal justice to all – sentiments that would not be out of place in the 21st century.

The election took place in the Market Place in Salisbury, and in his speech to the electors he said that it was more than twenty years since he first solicited their votes. He had received no reward for his public services but that which he had derived from their good opinion. He felt proud to be a commoner, and did not consider that he was fit to be raised in rank. This remark brought forth laughter from the crowd, that perhaps thought that the very tall speaker certainly did not need to be raised! He continued by saying that when he should feel himself no longer fit to be a commoner, it would be time enough for him to seek a higher rank. More laughter greeted this observation. The emergence of parties in the commons was by now well advanced, but Benett continued to distance himself from them. He told the electors that although the people of this country were at present divided into two great parties, he belonged to neither of them. His party was the party of the people. However, when a list of the members of the new Parliament was published, he was described as a 'liberal' rather than as a 'conservative'.

Benett and Herbert having been declared the new Members, more lengthy speeches were expected from them at the dinner held in the Guildhall in the evening. According to the newspaper report, Benett delivered a 'long and able address'. In his younger days, Benett's speeches were invariably exceedingly serious, but now that he was in his sixties, in more and more of them a touch of humour appears. In this speech, he said that he was an old Whig, not an old Whig become Radical. His principles would lead him wholly to reform abuses wherever they might be found to exist. Whether proposed by Whigs or Tories, he would support good measures, not caring from whom they came, on the same principle that he would take good milk whether it came from a black cow or a white one. This was greeted with cheers and laughter. Speeches on these occasions were generally non-controversial and received with unanimous approval. However, Benett then touched on a subject that was greeted with perhaps unexpected disapproval. When he said that in his view the opinion of the people as expressed through the House must prevail over the will of the House of Lords, cries of ' No! No!' were heard. Benett said that he would preserve the heredity of the House of Peers, and considered the existence of the House a blessing to the people – it was like the escapement to the clock; take it away, the clock would run down and the machine would fall to pieces. The House of Commons, the People's House, however, would still be found all powerful. 'No! No!' was heard once again to which Benett replied, 'Yes! Yes!'.[211]

Benett duly took his seat but spoke on only a few occasions during the year. He had spoken, however, in March in a debate on Church rates. He could not agree with some members that it was desirable that there should be a separation of Church and State. On the contrary, he said that he would always exert himself to promote that union. It had been laid down that the property of the Church was altogether sacred from the control of Parliament. This was a doctrine he could never sanction. He held that Church property was entirely subject to the control of Parliament.[212] In the following month when, in a debate on the question of County Rates, a Member declared that the county magistracy were unfit for the administration of justice, Benett defended magistrates from the attacks which had been made against them. He was certain that the people were quite content with their present control over the magistracy.[213] In June, he spoke on just two occasions and, being always anxious to see any possible abuses being brought into the open, voted in December with the majority on the motion of the Chancellor of the Exchequer for a committee to examine the merits of the pension list.[214]

In the debate on the pension list, the Chancellor of the Exchequer, Thomas Spring Rice,[215] was asked whether the name of Thomas Moore was in the list of pensions charged on the Civil List and, if so, 'whether it was placed there for making luscious ballads for love-sick maidens, or for writing lampoons upon George IV, of blessed memory'. Spring Rice's spirited explanation of the reasons why Moore was in receipt of a pension was greeted with cheering from all quarters of the House, and in which Benett doubtless joined.

On 1 December, Moore wrote a particularly affectionate letter to Benett with whom he had by now been on very friendly terms for almost twenty years. One wonders whether he still recalled one of their first meetings, when he found Benett 'a very haranguing minded gentleman' and Lucy, 'odious – full of airs'! He now wrote:

> My dear Benett
> I should feel pretty sure of having the goodwill of such heads and hearts as yours, on the occasions you refer to, but to have my cause so warmly taken up as it appears to have been, by the great majority of the House, was really very gratifying – and I only wish that the gentleman who was the cause of such a triumph to me had a little of that sort of ovation for himself which rotten eggs are supposed to be the best means of bestowing – Though, poor fellow, it is only for the sake of the pun that I have wished him such a fate.
> Mrs Moore has been even worse in health than usual, lately – but a course of Blue Pill is making her daily better. I hope you keep well, my good fellow, for I know few (even among good fellows) that deserve it better.
> Ever most truly Yours
> Thomas Moore [216]

In 1838, Benett was at last compelled to complete his purchase of the Fonthill estate, a purchase that had commenced in haste so many years before and that he must surely have lived to regret. Following an action in the Chancery Court he agreed that a total of £114,380 18s 7d was due under the two contracts that had been entered into. Taking into account the sum of £10,000 that he had already paid, however, and also an agreed deduction of a further £10,000 and adding two other small amounts, the sum that was to be paid to settle the court proceedings amounted to £95,518 0s 11d, and upon payment of this Benett would accept a conveyance of the property.[217] He did not, of course, have such a large sum of money readily available, and it is likely that for some time he had attempted without success to effect a subsale of all or part of the property. He looked to his London bankers Coutts & Co to lend him the sum of £90,000 to enable him to complete the purchase, and then immediately placed the property, that included the remains of

Beckford's Abbey and the whole of the village of Fonthill Gifford, on the open market[218] but failed to find a buyer. By 1841 Coutts & Co were owed £124,000 (£34,000 having been secured by earlier mortgages entered into in 1832 and 1833) and in May of that year he wrote to them seeking to borrow a further £5,000. In order to attempt to satisfy them that there was adequate security for the additional loan, he set out in great detail the security already held by them, the additional security being offered, the acreage of the various properties and the rental income and his estimate of their value:

> Abstract of the settled property of John Benett Esq of Pythouse now in security to Coutts for a loan of £124,000 which with the addition of an estate called Lawn Farm is to be increased to £129,000.[219]

He firstly set out details of various estates including 'Norton Bavant Old Family Estate', 'Fonthill Gifford Purchased of Mr Farquhar' and 'West Tisbury Part Old Family Estate and part let by myself at various times including Pythouse mansion and garden' and then added:

| | | | |
|---|---|---|---|
| Recapitulation total 5596 1 31 acres annual rental | £8525 | 9 | 3 |
| After deduction of land tax | 197 | 16 | 1 |
| | 8327 | 13 | 2 |
| Deduct for repairs say | 327 | 13 | 2 |
| Clear rent | £8000 | 00 | 0 |
| Total asset £8000 at 30 years purchase | 240,000 | 00 | 00 |
| Value of timber on Fonthill Estate not less than | 20,000 | 00 | 00 |
| Value of timber on other estate not less than | 10,000 | 00 | 00 |
| Value of Advowson of Fonthill Gifford, tithes £320, Glebe £70 say 8 years purchase on £300 | 2,400 | 00 | 00 |
| Value of Norton Bavant mansion plus 6 acres | 2,500 | 00 | 00 |
| Value of Pythouse mansion and garden say | 5000 | 00 | 00 |
| Five insurance policies | 16,500 | 00 | 00 |
| Total | £296400 | 00 | 00 |

As Benett's sole income was derived from his farming activities and such of his land as was let, he sold as many of the building materials of the ruined Abbey as he was able, and in 1841 also offered for sale 1,300 maiden oak trees and 100 felled oak as well as 50 other trees, in order to generate additional income.[220]

Benett's long held conviction that tithes should be commuted by law came to fruition at last with the passing of the Tithe Commutation Act in 1836. The Wiltshire tithe apportionment awards, the first of which was published in 1838, enable us to obtain a picture of the extent of the land in the county owned and occupied by him in and around the year 1840. Not surprisingly, his largest holding was at Tisbury and in adjoining Semley and Fonthill Gifford, where he owned some 4,762 acres with almost 2,000 acres being held in hand and actually occupied – and presumably farmed – by him. He also owned a moiety of the nearby Hatch estate, the whole amounting to 358 acres, the other half belonging to Sir Hyde Parker.[221] His ancestral estate at Norton Bavant extended to 1,416 acres (including 83 acres of rectorial glebe) and at Boyton and Sherrington he held a further 640 acres. [222] On 13 October 1841 he borrowed a further £12,500 from Coutts & Co. secured by a mortgage over his share in the Hatch property, and in the following month consolidated all his borrowings by entering into a new mortgage in favour of the bank to secure the very substantial sum of £136,500 – at least five million pounds in 21st-century terms. The interest payable on these loans was, of course, enormous. For example, on 7 November 1842 he paid six months' interest to 25 December 1841 on the loan of £124,000 and three months' interest on the further loan of £12,500 amounting to £2,605.[223]

It is clear that having been deeply unpopular prior to the passing of the Reform Act, Benett was gradually became something of an institution in the county, and began to be seen as a man deserving of respect and even affection. So when, in 1838, the Wiltshire Agricultural Society at its annual meeting held at the *Bear Inn* in Devizes presented him with a magnificent silver candelabrum upon a triangular base supporting figures representing Spade Husbandry, Sowing and Reaping, with the base enriched with a chased rural subject in bas-relief with his coat of arms, it was said that, 'Rare indeed have been the instances in which all classes from every part of the county have united in a common mark of respect'.[224] The *Devizes and Wiltshire Gazette* reported in May that the piece of plate was available for inspection at the manufacturers, Payne and Son of Bath[225] and, in July, that ' a more magnificent piece of plate has rarely been witnessed. The workmanship is really exquisite; and the figures in particular have been pronounced by gentlemen who have made anatomy their study, as perfect'![226]

In 1838 he voted with all his fellow Wiltshire county members against the motion when what the *Devizes and Wiltshire Gazette* described as the 'annual Ballot humbug was enacted in the House of

Commons'.[227] However, during the year, he spoke only once, and this was when changes that would affect the yeomanry cavalry were debated – a matter very close to his heart. He said that he was probably the oldest member of yeomanry cavalry in the House. He had served forty years in that force but having now left it, he had no personal interest in the question. He had never in that force seen the slightest symptom of partisanship. He spoke as an old Whig when he said that the institution was the constitutional force of the country. Indeed, he was old enough to recollect the time when there was a great dread of a standing army. A new principle of a standing army had been introduced and he feared it would be followed by another, which he dreaded still more – a general police force . . . He had now, owing to private circumstances, left the corps to which he had belonged, and he might therefore say that the Wiltshire yeomanry had performed good service during the riots of 1830. The corps behaved with great perseverance, and with great leniency towards the parties, and they stopped all the great riots in Wiltshire. That corps was now to be disbanded, which he regretted.[228]

Although Benett continued to do his duty by attending the House of Commons, he spoke on only two occasions during 1839. When the Corn Laws were being considered Benett was certain to make his views know. In March he spoke at some length and, during the course of his speech, he declared that the Corn Laws were nothing more than a just protection to the landed interest;[229] and on 24 April he made another extremely long speech.

It may be recalled that, in 1835, Benett was a constant 'thorn in the side' of Colonel Charles à Court when setting up the new unions covering the south-western corner of Wiltshire under the Poor Law Amendment Act. In the autumn of 1838 à Court must have been dismayed to learn that Benett was now interfering in the work of the guardians of the Tisbury Union. On 20 December, à Court wrote an immensely long letter to Benett in the course of which he wrote:

> My dear Benett
> Before I proceed to reply to your letter of yesterday, which I am particularly glad to receive, let me express to you my real regret that I was unable to call at Pythouse immediately after my late visit to Tisbury. I almost passed your very door, but as the Shaftesbury Guardians were waiting for me, I was compelled to deny myself the pleasure and the advantage of a personal communication with you.
>     I reached Tisbury on the morning of the 16 instant before the Guardians had assembled & I had time to inspect the workhouse establishment before the Board met. From the Clerk of the Union I learnt

that you had attended the Board on the 26 Nov & had urged the absolute necessity of administering parochial relief to married men with large families, where miserably low wages were totally insufficient to enable them to maintain their families.

À Court then recited in some detail the course of action that the Guardians had decided to take and declared:

> Acting up to the intention of the legislature & the spirit of the Poor Law Amendment Act, I do not see what other course they could have taken.
>
> In consequence of their suggestions, it was added that you had prevailed upon the ratepayers of Semley and West Tisbury to consent to a private rate in aid, to be distributed by the overseers according to a given scale – without reference to charities or circumstances – to every child above three in number 1s. 6d. per head. That you objected to discriminate in the most important point, viz the earnings of the labourers, because you alone gave 9s. whilst the farmers generally paid only 8s. and some even as low as 7s. a week, your men would not receive their fair proportion of the monies collected. It was against such a system that I totally protested:- a system which tends to equate industry & indolence, honesty & dishonesty & to release the whole County to that state of [ ? ] and demoralisation which occasioned the passing of the Poor Law Amendment Act.

The letter continues by setting out in great detail, 'in what way and under what impressions I had reason to think that you were personally opposed to the Guardians, who have devoted so much of their valuable time & attention to carrying out the provisions of the Law as at present established'. He continued:

> Now, my dear Benett knowing that you to be the father of the original 'Hindon Scale system' hearing that you had privately introduced nearly a similar one in the two parishes in which you are interested, and hearing that you had directed a large number of labourers in private employment to demand out door relief in case of refusal to enter the workhouse, had I no reason to believe that you were opposed to the views of the Guardians and anxious again to establish parochial assistance in aid of wages? I do not hesitate to say that I did think so – nor does your letter incline me to alter my opinion . . . That we all seek the same end – viz the amelioration of the condition of the labouring classes I firmly believe but we differ widely as to the means. You would tamper with the labour market . . . I would have it free and unshackled – more especially in the Tisbury Union where, looking to the very few perquisites enjoyed by agricultural

labourers, they appear to me to do as badly, if not worse paid, than in any other union under my inspection.

I write in such haste & under great interruption but I would not allow a post to pass without replying to your letter. I hope to be able personally to communicate with you when my engagements will permit me again to visit your neighbourhood.

Believe me, my dear Benett,

However we may differ in opinion

Yours very truly

C A à Court[230]

Benett's reaction to this letter is not known, nor whether subsequently he was content to allow the Guardians to carry out their duties without further interference. It is likely that at their meetings the Guardians would have discussed Benett's activities, and that a record would have been made in the minute book kept by their clerk. It is perhaps significant that whilst the two minute books for the years 1835-1837 and 1840-1843 have survived, that for the years 1838-1839 is unaccountably missing.

Having lived in Lower Grosvenor Street when in London since 1833, he now moved to 73 Baker Street, but then, in 1840, to Limmer's Hotel at 1 George Street Hanover Square, where he was to remain until 1849. Limmer's was one of London's foremost hotels, where Benett was doubtless most comfortably accommodated during most of his last years in Parliament. According to Mogg's *New Picture of London and Visitor's Guide to its Sights* published in 1844, at Limmer's Hotel 'the first families will find themselves, comparatively speaking, at home'.

Since inheriting the Norton Bavant and Pythouse estates from his father, it appears that he farmed a substantial part of the land himself rather than letting it in the usual way. As he was in London attending to his parliamentary duties for many weeks in each year, he must have employed able men to manage the farms for him, at the same time taking an intense interest in what was being done. In some notes on the Norton Bavant estate, John Fane-Benett-Stanford, his great-grandson, wrote: 'up to his death in 1852, John Benett farmed the whole of Norton Bavant as well as the Pythouse property himself'.[231] This statement was not entirely accurate, however, as in 1847 he was in dispute with the tenant of one of the farms in Norton Bavant. In July 1839 when addressing the Wiltshire Agricultural Society, of which he had, of course, been president since its foundation, he spoke with approval of artificial manures and the application of the science of chemistry to agriculture. He also spoke of the subsoil plough. He had commenced farming in Berwick Farm 30 years ago and was told that the land was scarcely worth ploughing up. He had persevered and by ploughing half an inch every year it became one of the deepest and best hill soils in the county.[232]

Shortly after this, Sidney Herbert spoke of Benett's farming activities. One cannot imagine that he took kindly to Herbert's somewhat flippant comment, that he could only express his hope that his colleague (Benett) had made a better thing of his farming than he did of his; but if he (Benett) had made a good deal out of it, he was the first gentleman or amateur farmer that ever did. If the truth were told, perhaps it would be discovered, that for every shilling that Mr Benett had made, he had lost ten in some other part of his life![233]

An entry in the Court Book of the Manor of Semley in 1839 shows that Benett, although a Member of Parliament, a magistrate and major landowner, was not so important or influential as to escape the notice of the humble manor court! In that year it was recorded that: 'We present that John Benett esq opened a quarry in Semley Common and we hereby give notice to enclose the same within 2 months after notice of this presentation under penalty of 40s. and that he be fined 40s. for opening the same'.[234]

In October, he made a surprise appearance at a public meeting held on behalf of the Salisbury Diocesan Board of Education. Although on many occasions he expressed his firm support for the Church of England as established by law, he seldom demonstrated this by actively participating in the various appeals and initiatives emanating from the ecclesiastical authorities. He clearly knew that his appearance would be a cause of astonishment in many quarters and so, in his speech made after the Bishop of Salisbury had addressed the meeting, it was reported that:

> he hoped that he would be excused for mentioning matters personal to himself, as he felt some excuse was due from him for not having before attended the Board. No one was more anxious than himself to diffuse education through the whole mass of the labouring classes but he had looked to a different source for effecting it. He thought the wisdom of Parliament would have devised some system, supported by the national purse, but he feared this could not now be expected. An attempt had been made during the last session, which had signally and entirely failed – it was opposed by all classes and opinions. He himself felt that education without religion, would do more evil than good. He had come therefore to support the Board . . . those possessing large properties, whether of land or manufacture, had weighty duties incumbent on them; they held their property, not for themselves – one of their first duties was to provide for

the comfort and happiness of the poor . . . From the observation he had made, during a long life passed in the county, he found that those who could read and write and were truly religious were the most sober, orderly and useful workmen. . .[235]

By the 1830s, the church of All Saints at Norton Bavant, in which many of Benett's ancestors were buried, was in such a ruinous condition that, 'the floor was deeply sinking, the walls rent and dangerously out of perpendicular and the roof decayed and almost ready to fall.'[236] As a consequence the church was rebuilt, with the 14th-century tower and possibly earlier entrance arch to the Benett aisle being retained. As Benett was the lay rector he was responsible for bearing the cost of rebuilding the chancel and, as head of the family, he also paid for the reconstruction of the family aisle,[237] all the family memorials and grave slabs being carefully preserved. A brass plate prominently displayed on the chancel arch proclaims: 'This chancell rebuilt by John Benett Esr. M.P. for South Wilts 1839'. However, shortly before the church was rebuilt Benett and his sister Etheldred (who, with her sister, paid for most of the cost of rebuilding not borne by their brother) were unsuccessful in persuading the patron, the Lord Chancellor, to present to the living a neighbouring curate, who, in her opinion, was 'eminently qualified for the situation'. In her view, as she had lived at Norton House for 35 years, and as she and her sister were the only 'resident Gentleman's family', they had a good right to make a recommendation. However, the Lord Chancellor thought otherwise and appointed the Archdeacon of Barbados. Etheldred thought that it would be, 'hard to have such an utter Stranger poked close to our Noses for the rest of our lives; his way into the Village is by our door and our gardens . . .'[238]

Benett, as Lord of the Manor and the owner of more than half of the land in the parish of Norton Bavant, and Etheldred as the occupier of the manor house, both took an active interest in the welfare of their poor neighbours. Many years before, Catherine Mompesson gave the sum of £20 to trustees, the income to be distributed annually in or about the month of November in linen cloth for shirts and shifts. The trust money was in danger of being lost when Benett's grandmother, Etheldred Benett, recovered £16 of the legacy, provided the balance herself and then administered the charity until her death in 1766. Benett's aunt Catherine continued to make the annual distributions until her death, and his sister Etheldred was doing likewise when a report into the charity in 1839 recorded that the sum of £20 was in Benett's hands, the vicar and churchwardens being in possession of a written statement to that effect.[239]

# 8

## His Final Years in Parliament, the Death of Three of his Children, and his Withdrawal from Public Life 1840-1852

Benett was in his place as Parliament sat once again as the new decade opened, and the members would have found the temporary chamber, still in use after the fire of 1834, being lit in a new way – by gas. Benett was soon on his feet to say that he was a very old member of the House (as he was only in his late sixties we would not now consider him to be a particularly old man, although perhaps he intended to convey that he had been a member for a very long time!) and was agreeably surprised on seeing the new light. He found that, though a little gloomy at first, on taking a paper of small print from his pocket, that he had not been able to read for many years past so well as on that occasion. He was perfectly satisfied that this light was the best the House had yet tried and so he would vote for a longer trial of it.[1]

During his long life Benett received numerous letters, a number of which have survived. While it is clear why some were retained by him it is surprising that a note he received at the end of January was not immediately discarded. It read:

> Sir
> On your vote tomorrow night depends your seat as our member, if you are bought or duped by the Whigs, we have resolved to oppose you.
> Your obed. Servant R Bevan Smith
> A [ ? ] Liberal not a Whig Elector for South Wilts

Benett endorsed this letter, 'I have no knowledge of this Mr Smith nor do I wish to know anyone as little entitled to the name of Liberal which he would disgrace by his assumption of it. John Benett'.[2]

Early in April, the House was debating yet again the vexed and ever controversial Corn Laws. As an ardent protector of the agricultural interest and opponent of any repeal, Benett delivered a lengthy speech that was considered so important by the *Salisbury and Winchester Journal* that it was reported in full rather then in a truncated form in its usual Parliamentary columns.[3] Since time immemorial, magistrates had heard cases brought before them in private and even in public houses. One of the provisions of the Juvenile Offenders Bill debated in May was that hearings in these places, that we would now think quite unsuitable, should be discontinued, and should instead be heard in proper court houses. Benett strongly objected to this on the grounds that great expense would be incurred in erecting sessions houses and that this expense would fall on the counties.[4] In June, Benett had his say in a debate on the Seduction Bill and said that something should be done to suppress indiscriminate seduction, and that some protection should be given to the female which the present law did not give her.[5] Shortly afterwards the County Constabulary Bill caught his attention. Having dropped all constitutional objection which he had felt at other times to such a measure, he was now decidedly of the opinion that if they were to have a rural police, it ought to be under 'centrical' control and paid from the general public funds, for he said that it was the duty of the Government to maintain the peace of the country.[6] During the second reading of the bill, Benett asked why all the expense of the county constabulary should fall on the whole county, 'when nine-tenth of crime was in the four principal manufacturing towns'. In reporting this part of his speech, the *Devizes and Wilts Gazette* declared that he had, 'fallen into a very common and very great error' in suggesting this. Benett was quick to acknowledge that he was indeed mistaken, and on 8 April wrote to the newspaper from the House of Commons to say that, 'My friend Mr Ludlow Bruges[7] very promptly corrected me and I have great satisfaction in knowing from him that crime in the manufacturing towns has been much diminished by the activity of the old constabulary force, under the influence of vigilant and able magistrates'.[8]

Early in June, as Queen Victoria and her twenty-year-old husband Albert were driving up Constitution Hill in an open phaeton, a waiter named Edward Oxford fired a pistol at them from only about six paces away. He missed and fired again and so incompetent an assailant was he that the monarch and her consort escaped uninjured. As a result, patriotic and loyal fever spread amongst the populace of the capital and into the country. A County Meeting was hastily arranged to take place in Devizes[9] so that popular support could be obtained for the preparation of an Address, 'to express their horror and indignation at the atrocious attack and to offer congratulations to the Her Majesty on her happy preservation from so great a danger'. Benett seconded the Marquis of Lansdowne's proposal and, after being received with loud cheers, declared that he was, 'a man of few and plain words and these words he could deliver but in a plain way'. Some of those who heard him speak must surely have smiled at his description of himself as a man of few and plain words – 'plain' they might have been but certainly rarely 'few'! He continued by saying that, 'he was old enough to recollect the attempt that had been made on the life of George III – during the remainder of his short days, or of the days of the youngest among them – he fervently prayed that no such attempt would again be made'. After a number of other speeches had been made, he moved that the Address be presented to the Queen and Prince Albert by the High Sheriff.[10]

In June, he received a copy of a letter that was perhaps the last reminder of the extraordinary events that had taken place while he was a child, and which in due course resulted in him becoming master of both the Norton Bavant and Pythouse estates. The letter he received was addressed to his solicitor and read:

> You will oblige us by informing Mr Benett that unless the £137 19s. 5d. due from him to the estate of the late Mrs Jane Parry be paid to us for the use of the executors on or before Tuesday next the 7th July we must issue process for the recovery of the amount.
>
> It is now nearly two years since Mrs Parry's decease the annuity was ever then in arrears – this is the 4th letter we have been put to the trouble of writing and we do not recollect any instance in which our forbearance has been so abused.[11]

Mrs Jane Parry was the widow of Benett's first cousin William, the only son of his father's elder brother, who had inherited the Norton Bavant estate on the death of Benett's grandfather in 1754. It may be remembered that on William's death in 1781, it was discover that he had left the whole of his residuary estate to his widow Jane who promptly married William Parry. Following this, after unsuccessful attempts to have the will set aside, the Chancery Court ordered the estate to be sold. As we have seen, its purchase by Benett's aunt Catherine, who died in 1798 and who left the property to him, resulted in the two estates once again being united. It may be that the annuity was charged on the Norton Bavant estate, and whether Benett's reluctance to pay it promptly was due to his lack of funds, or to a wish to inconvenience his cousin's widow and her executors will never be known. As his brother had also experienced difficulties in extracting his annuity from him, it is likely that the shortage of ready money was the true cause of Benett's dilatory behaviour.

Although Benett had sold his estate at Berwick St Leonard as long ago as 1823, it appears that he prudently retained his lordship of the manor. In December 1840, an Inclosure Award was made and enrolled as a result of which, as lord of the manor, he was allotted no less that 724 acres of land in Berwick St. Leonard. Before the award was made, Benett and William Beckford, who was lord of the manor of Fonthill Bishop, agreed to exchange some of the land that was allotted to them in the two parishes, and this was confirmed by the Inclosure Commissioners before the award was made.[12]

During 1840, Benett's attendance in the House was not as constant as in his younger days. In February he was absent without pairing in a vote of confidence in the Administration, and in September, when a table of the attendance record of Members was published, it was reported that out of 256 divisions in the 1840 Session, Benett had voted in only 28 of them, compared with 45 in which Herbert had voted and an impressive 107 recorded by the Salisbury Member, William Brodie.[13]

The 1841 census provides an opportunity of a glimpse into the household at Pythouse at that time. In 1840 Benett's 34-year-old daughter Anna Maria had married Marmaduke Robert Jeffreys,[14] a barrister of Lincoln's Inn. He was also in his early thirties and the eldest son of the Rev. John Jeffreys, formerly the rector of Barnes and then living in Eaton Place in London. With Benett being away from home, his remaining unmarried daughter, Fanny, was the only member of the family shown on the return with Martha Ingram, her former governess. The indoor staff living in the house comprised three male and four female servants, who would probably have been the butler, footman and groom with the housekeeper, cook, kitchen maid and housemaid.[15]

Benett was, of course, frequently away on parliamentary or county business, and so it is gratifying to read that although a young teenager, Fanny accompanied her widowed father on what would be thought of as adult occasions. For instance, in 1839 she and her father attended a ball held in Salisbury after the races,[16] and in the following year they were seen at a brilliant fête given by Sidney Herbert at Wilton House, where she doubtless enjoyed the spectacular display of fireworks, and at its conclusion when 'countless number of Bengal light simultaneously sparkled from all parts of the park and river'. We cannot know whether she attended the ball held in the Double Cube room but we do know that 'the respectable inhabitants of the town and neighbourhood were politely admitted to all parts of the park'![17]

In the Spring of 1841, the Government was faced in the Commons with Sir Robert Peel's motion of no confidence, and how members would vote was of considerable interest to the public. A correspondent to the *Devizes and Wiltshire Gazette* wrote:

> It has been asked, how Mr Benett will vote upon Sir Robert Peel's motion? We answer, that he will vote like an honest man – against Ministers. Opposed, as Mr Benett has shown himself, to the ministerial proposition on the sugar duties, and decidedly opposed as we know to any attention to the corn laws, it is impossible that he can do otherwise than divide with Sir Robert; and say, 'that her Majesty's Government does not sufficiently possess the confidence of the House of Commons to enable them to carry measures which they deem of essential benefit to public welfare, and that their continuance in office under such circumstances is at variance with the spirit of the constitution'.[18]

Benett did indeed vote to bring down the government and so found himself facing another election to take place in Salisbury on 7 July. It was rumoured that he and Sidney Herbert might not be returned unopposed, and so Benett would have been relieved to read in the *Salisbury and Winchester Journal* published on the 5th that, 'We understand that there is no foundation for the report that Mr Ashley and Lord Huntingtower are about to offer themselves for the Southern Division of the county in opposition to Mr Bennett [*sic*] and the Hon.Sidney Herbert.[19] In his address to the electors he wrote that:

> I have faithfully redeemed the pledge which so long since I made to you on the Hustings, by not having servilely attached myself to any political party, and have not sought or accepted either emoluments or honours as rewards of public or party services . . . to have a watchful care, also, over the welfare of the labouring classes, whose position and daily engagements do not allow them deliberately to partake in matters of legislation, but whose importance and service to the great community give them special claims on the attention and protection of all who have the power to guard their interests.[20]

The candidates arrived in Salisbury with a large number of gentlemen and farmers on horseback and it was reported that:

> Most of the horsemen dismounted; but about fifty of them quietly ranged themselves to the right of the hustings. At this time there were at least 5,000 persons assembled: and the cry of, 'Off! Off! Pull them off!' became general. Finding this had no effect, some fellows seized the horses, whilst others endeavoured to pull the riders from their seats; but they merely got a rap over their knuckles for their pains. They then set up the most horrid yell and by their gestures, it might be presumed, that they

would speedily annihilate both rider and horse, if they dared. The horsemen, however, stood firm and undaunted, and their horses appeared equally so.

The High Sheriff made his appearance and claimed attention, but he might as well claim the attention of the winds. The general cry was, 'Turn them out, turn them out!' and some wretches exclaimed, 'Stone them! Stone them'!'[21]

When William Wyndham and Charles Phipps came forward to propose and second Benett's nomination, neither of them could make themselves heard, being completely overpowered by cries of 'Turn them out, turn them out'. Several large stones were then thrown at the horsemen, whereupon five or six of them dashed into the crowd defending themselves from the blows of the assailants. Eventually, some sort of order was restored and in the course of his speech, Phipps declared that, 'In Mr Benett they had found everything that could be expected of a Member of Parliament. He possessed a high private character, great capacity for business, and he entertained sound political principles'.

In his speech, Benett was to be found indulging in a little humour and also alluding to the financial price he had paid as a consequence of his long years in Parliament. He said that he had the honour of representing them for 23 years and had thus served three apprenticeships to the trade of politics. From long experience he could safely pronounce it to be a very bad trade indeed for an honest man (laughter and cheers). He came before them now a poorer man that when he commenced – poor in pecuniary point of view and poor in courtly honours – but the honour of representing them was to him the greatest of all honours.[22] He and Sidney Herbert were, of course, duly returned unopposed.

Not everyone was as satisfied with this comfortable state of affairs as the successful candidates. The *Western Times* carried a report of the county elections and apologised for so doing, declaring that, 'the County Elections have become so perfect a matter of arrangement between the aristocracy now, that it may almost be considered impertinent for the Press to intrude its Reporters upon the great constitutional farce...'[23] It is perhaps some indication of the respect that was generally accorded to Benett as he grew older that, for as long as twenty years, there was no contested election in the southern division of the county, until his retirement from public life shortly before his death in 1852.

In the evening of the election day, the usual dinner was held in Salisbury, during which a large number of congratulatory speeches were delivered. Benett told his audience that he would tell them a short story. He had, he said, some years ago, been congratulated on having gained his seat, and was asked if when he went into the House he intended to recover all the money he had spent in the contest. He had doubtless spent a great deal, and would doubtless get it back by his votes. In answer, he told the inquirer, that he could not honestly receive public money – that he was not a trading party man, that to represent the county of Wilts was an honour that would amply repay him. In his speech, Herbert said that he had now served three Parliaments with his honourable colleague Mr Benett whom they had just heard with so much pleasure; and although he had at times differed from his opinion, he had ever entertained for him a feeling of friendship. Wadham Wyndham, one of the Members of Parliament for Salisbury, said that they were well aware that the venerable gentleman on the right of the President had not always answered the helm in the House of Commons, but he thought he had redeemed himself, and that he was prepared to fight against Ministers. By his vote on the want of confidence question, he had caused the present Administration to dissolve Parliament. By that vote he had manifested himself an opponent of the weakest and most selfish Administration that ever existed.[24]

In 1841, Benett's son-in-law Arthur Fane was collated vicar of Warminster, and while he was probably pleased that his eldest daughter Lucy was living not far from Pythouse, Fane's uncompromising attitude to the large numbers of his parishioners who had deserted the Church of England in favour of the various dissenting bodies in the town cannot have met with his approval. Although on many occasions he publicly asserted his loyalty to the established church, Benett was also extremely tolerant of all those, whether Catholic or Protestant, who chose to worship in their own way. No sooner had Fane arrived in Warminster than he made it his business to attempt to persuade the poverty-stricken but numerous congregation who worshipped in a chapel under the leadership of William Daniell, commonly called the Bishop of Warminster Common, to cease doing so, on the grounds that Daniell had never been ordained and so should desist from preaching. Daniell recorded in his diary the long meeting that he had had on 18 November with Fane who remained, of course, intractable. Fane wrote to Daniell on the following day telling him, as he recorded, 'that he should certainly refuse to administer the sacrament to me, were I to desire it'[25]. Although Fane's intolerant behaviour would have been mirrored by that of many other Anglican clergymen of the time, it is certain that it would not have met with his father-in-law's approval.

Benett did not contribute to any of the debates in the House during 1841, although in December he and Fane found themselves addressing a very large number of people at a County Meeting held in Devizes in December. This was to approve the presentation of an address to the Queen and Prince Albert on the birth of an heir to the throne, coupled also with a proposal to consider the best means of dealing with the 'urgent distress' at Bradford on Avon. In seconding the Marquis of Lansdowne's speech, Benett wisely limited himself to the first and uncontroversial object of the meeting by observing that it was but a little while since he had the honour of seconding an address on the birth of her Majesty. He referred to the occasion when as a girl the Queen had visited Wiltshire with her mother and he had had the honour of meeting them in Salisbury. His remarks were greeted with approval. The Earl of Radnor then spoke on the question of distress, that inevitably provoked varying ideas as to what should be done to alleviate it, and when Fane attempted to speak on the same subject it was reported that, 'it was with difficulty that he obtained anything like a hearing'.[26] It may be that this was the first time that Fane had attempted to address an unruly public meeting. His father-in-law had, of course, on many occasions been confronted with a hostile audience, and so would have been able to give him the benefit of his experience.

After Parliament sat as usual at the beginning of February in the following year, the Commons were soon debating yet again the question of the repeal or modification of the Corn Laws. Benett voted in favour of Peel's proposals for a modification of the laws,[27] and at the end of the month he told the House that the 'operatives' (presumably meaning manufacturing workers) were now aware of what the effect of a repeal of the Corn Laws would be on their wages. He was anxious that corn should be cheap and that the people should have the means of purchasing it. In his opinion the measure being proposed by Peel would keep the price of wheat at 56s. His constituents were anxious that the Bill should pass, and he hoped that those who had intimated their intention to propose amendments should not throw obstructions in the way of the measure.[28] He also attempted to demonstrate that support for the Anti-Corn-Law League was waning, by pointing out that it had been able to attract only 400,000 signatures to its petitions compared with 1,300,000 in the previous year, and that the West of England labourers thought that their wages would be reduced if the Corn Laws were repealed.[29]

In the debates on the Corn Laws, Benett always spoke against a total repeal and on behalf of the wheat farmers, although in so doing he believed that he was also attempting to relieve the distress of the rural poor. On the other hand, Herbert argued that the competition from imported grain would not be great and that the poor would benefit by repeal. Whatever the merits of their respective cases, it has been said that: 'There was still much ignorance and prejudice abroad and, as the speeches of the Wiltshire members show, a lack of objectivity in the approach to agricultural problems. The economic arguments were in the main specious; the great diversity of the county's agriculture was ignored'.[30]

It was not only the agricultural labourers in the rural areas who continued to suffer considerable distress but also, and perhaps to an even greater extent, workers in the towns. From time to time, appeals were launched to raise money to alleviate the hardship, and in February Benett gave £10 towards the relief of distress in and about Bradford on Avon. Sidney Herbert's immense wealth enabled him to provide £100[31] – a sum approaching £5,000 in early 21st-century terms and a major contribution towards the total of £1,716 8s. 6d. raised by the committee chaired by Benett's old friend Thomas Sotheron.

Although always in favour of the reform of abuses, Benett continued to insist that certain practices that are now considered anachronistic and indefensible should be retained. In June, having returned to Parliament having, 'sufficiently recovered from his late severe accident'[32] he voted with the majority against a motion to substitute the vote by ballot for the prevailing system of voting.[33] At the time the idea of a secret ballot was thought of as 'unmanly'. No man should be ashamed of the way in which he voted.

In the following month, changes to the Poor Laws were being proposed. Benett had always taken the view that the administration of the laws should be conducted at a local level and so he told the House that he saw no necessity for a law that would take the poor out of the hands of the ratepayers. He could not consent to a system of forcing into a workhouse a man with a large family and selling up his furniture. Some discretion should repose with the poor law guardians.[34] On 5 July, once again showing his concern for the welfare of the vulnerable in society, he made it clear in a debate on the Mines and Collieries Bill that, while he acknowledged that he had nothing to do with collieries and mines, the House was justified in interfering in all cases where the poor were oppressed, and it was disgraceful that children employed underground in mines should be exposed to such treatment as had been described.[35]

In the summer of 1842, Benett continued to busy himself with his agricultural interests. When the Royal Agricultural Society held its annual provincial meeting in Bristol in July, Benett was, of course, present and acted as one of the stewards (with 'Mr Miles M.P.', probably William, the son of his old friend Philip Miles) in the trial of implements held at nearby Sneyd Park. Soon after, when responding to the toast to the County Members at the dinner held following the 3rd annual exhibition of the South Wilts and Warminster Farmers' Club it was reported that:

> Mr Benett returned thanks, and at the close of a powerful and animated address, urged the young Gentlemen of Lord Weymouth's school (who occupied the gallery) to prefer agricultural pursuits to those of any other walk of life – as being more honourable, more healthy, and more conducive to a happy old age than any other occupation.
>
> John Bleek Esq suggested that the very excellent advice offered by the esteemed Member for the county would be more likely to be impressed upon the minds of his youthful auditors, if enforced by a moderate supply of those accessories to social enjoyment with which the company below stairs were regaled – a proposition which was loudly cheered and speedily carried into effect.[36]

In the autumn, the *Devizes and Wiltshire Gazette* carried a particularly deferential report of festivities at Pythouse when it described how Benett:

> Gladdened the hearts of his labourers, upwards of 200 of whom partook of a plentiful supply of 'Harvest Home' cheer. The festivities were greatly heightened by the presence of Mr Benett and his amiable daughter, whose kind condescending, and encouraging address to the numerous assembly elicited ebullitions of gratitude and joy. The evening of Friday was spent in rustic amusements, 'the young contending as the old surveyed'. The children of the newly formed National School on this gentleman's estate (for whose well being Miss Benett has evinced an anxious solicitude that cannot be too highly praised or admired) were not forgotten. On the following Tuesday, about eighty of them assembled in their schoolroom and partook of refreshments suited to their tender age. It affords us much pleasure to add that the schoolroom, which is both elegant and commodious, was built at the sole expense of the worthy Member for South Wilts, and affords another proof of the desire of the more wealthy part of the community to afford their poor neighbours the opportunity of obtaining an education based upon the principles of our Scriptural and Apostolic Church.[37]

It was at this time that a contributor to the *Morning Chronicle* enabled a readership beyond the confines of Wiltshire to learn of Benett's agricultural prowess. He wrote:

Mr Benett is a spirited agriculturalist . . . In one of his plantations of oaks where trees stand at from ten to forty yards distant, and where a bottom of course brush wood has been growing, I saw as fine a crop of potatoes as any cultivator could reasonably desire. These potatoes were the property of the poor of Hindon, who, with Mr Benett's permission had grubbed up the brushwood and reclaimed the soil. I was told that the wood which they had taken off the ground had paid the expense of the labour so they had this crop of potatoes for nothing. Next year Mr Benett takes the land to himself, and gives the people another piece to break up . . . I had no opportunity of speaking to any person connected to Mr Benett's farm . . . One thing was visible at a glance, that his crops were better than other crops, the land cleaner that other land, and the style of working different, and also that by personally attending to his own estate the poor were to some extent provided for, while his profits were augmented. All I hear of Mr Benett, 'John Benett' as he is familiarly called had reference to his position as a Member of Parliament . . . Mr Benett may be a conservative in Parliament but he is an innovator at home, a radical reformer in agriculture, a true patriot and benefactor of his county. I will leave anti-corn law men and others to deal with him on his politics and only remark, that it would be a true and unspeakable blessing to England, if all land-owners attended to their land like John Benett.[38]

Benett would always attend as many of the meetings of the Wiltshire Agricultural Society as possible and, as the effective founder, permanent president and usual chairman, was always warmly received. In July it was reported that Mr Neeld[39] 'highly eulogised the chairman and proposed his health. Mr Neeld said he had only one word to say by was of reproof, and even that in kindness – he ought to have sent some animal from his stock to the Bristol exhibition'. Benett responded by saying that although he had a spark of ambition about him, he should be sorry to send his stock so many miles across the plain to compete with that against which he had no chance of success. Further, his stock were of that wild disposition, he feared they would run their heads against the stone erected to the memory of the highwaymen on the Plain; at any rate, there would be great difficulty in getting them there'.[40]

Although Benett continued to regularly take his seat in Parliament, in 1843 he spoke only once in the House. Having attained the age of 70 years, he was, perhaps, content to leave to younger men the cut and thrust of debate. However, when the Corn Laws were considered yet again in March, no one would have expected the veteran opponent of repeal to remain silent. On the fourth day, he rose to say that he considered the motion before the House to be in effect a total repeal of the Laws. People could not live more cheaply than in other countries because taxes were heavier here. He was in principle a free trader and all he wished was to see this country placed on such a footing that the manufacturers and merchants might be able to exchange freely their commodities for those of other countries. He entreated the Government to take up the whole question [meaning a reduction in taxation in order to relieve distress] in a manner more worthy to the dignity of this great country.[41]

If he did not speak as frequently in the House as he had done in the past, he was very content to continue to support and attend the meeting of the various societies with which he had been associated for many years. At the anniversary dinner of the Wiltshire Society held in London in June, the chairman, Ambrose Hussey,[42] proposed Benett's health. He said that he was highly esteemed by everyone who knew him in the county and to whom the Society was indebted for his valuable assistance for the last 20 years. He had attended each of their anniversaries during that long period, and was only absent last year from having met with an accident. He had known him in boyhood, and, whatever slight differences of opinion there might be between them, he felt assured that his honourable friend was guided in all his acts by the strictest principles of honour, integrity and noble independence.

For once Benett was at a loss for words! He said in reply that he felt quite at a loss to express himself. He was not naturally a shy man, but when he was so highly complimented as on this occasion, words in which to express his gratitude fell short; all he could say was, that he was exceedingly obliged to them. Needless to say, he did not sit down until he had delivered a speech that included a tribute to the merits of the Wiltshire farmer.[43] In view of his life long interest in the welfare of the farming community, it is perhaps a little surprising that he did not attend a meeting that was held in Devizes in July for the purpose of establishing an agricultural college for Wiltshire, Gloucestershire, Oxfordshire and Berkshire.[44] It is inconceivable that he would not have been invited to become involved, but it is probable that he thought that at his age such matters should be left to younger and more active men.

By 1843, the Anti-Corn-Law League's nationwide campaign to secure an unconditional repeal of the Corn Laws was reaching a crescendo. John Bright[45] and Richard Cobden[46] were the foremost leaders and advocates of the League and they toured the country speaking to enormous numbers of people. In August, some 4,000 people assembled in the Greencroft in Salisbury to hear these celebrated orators, who delivered immensely long speeches. During the course of his speech, Cobden reminded the crowd that Benett had said in evidence before the committee of the House of Lords in 1814 that land could not be cultivated unless the farmer got 80s. per quarter for his wheat, and if he obtained less that 75s. he could not pay his rent. He insisted that every protective duty must be abolished, and raised a great deal of laughter from the assembled company when he declared that they would not permit the continuance of the Corn Laws, 'even although it were to enable Mr Benett to pay off his mortgage'.[47] Cobden's lengthy oration was reproduced in full in the *Salisbury and Wiltshire Herald* , in the course of which he said:

> We shall, I say, never see any real improvement in agriculture till the Corn Laws are gone. The landlords I have said make use of the farmer at the day of Election – mind, not some of them who have leases – but they want them at the day of Election to keep up the system of monopoly, for the purpose of paying their own mortgages and dowries. John Benett himself has declared as much in Parliament; and I remember very well that Mr Hume who is a larger holder of landed property than many of the foremost supporters of the Corn Laws said 'he thought the Hon. Member (Mr Benett) might perhaps speak feelingly, but he did not, and should be most willing to assist in doing away with the Corn Laws altogether'.[48]

In the following month, Wadham Wyndham, one of the Members of Parliament for Salisbury, died whereupon the second son of the Earl of Radnor, Edward Pleydell-Bouverie,[49] (having failed to gain a seat at the election that took place in Salisbury only four months before), stood once again. Although he and his father were strongly in favour of a repeal of the Corn Laws, they attempted to distance themselves from the activities of the Anti-Corn Law League, that in turn was determined to give them every support. It would be a triumph for the League if a seat in the centre of an agricultural district could be captured by a supporter of repeal. However, despite intense activity in the city by League activists, Pleydell-Bouverie was defeated by the protectionist candidate by a margin of 317 to 270 votes. One can well imagine Benett's delight that the League's activities, of which he strongly disapproved, were to no avail.[50]

However secure he might have thought his position to have been as one of the members of Parliament for the southern division, Sidney Herbert clearly thought it necessary to join with Benett in attending what, one might be forgiven for thinking, were not particularly important events. By attending the dinner held after the Warminster Farmers' Club

Show in August, both the men would have been able to meet and talk with members of the farming community – many of whom would undoubtedly be potential electors whose favour had to be sought and maintained. The Marquis of Bath presented a fine buck, Lord Heytesbury was present and Benett was probably pleased that one of his bulls secured him a prize of 20s. at the show. Amongst the other prizes were three of £2 each for three men or women who had brought up the largest family without parochial relief, although only two were actually awarded.[51]

On 16 November, the following announcement appeared in *The Globe* as well as in *The Times*:

> Death of John Benett Esq M.P. – Devizes Nov.14. John Benett Esc., M.P. for South Wilts, died on Sunday last after a short illness. In him, the Pro-Corn-Law party have lost a staunch advocate of their interests. Thus there is another vacancy in the representation, and for an agricultural county; so that the Anti-Corn-Law League have plenty of work – but, supported as they are, no doubt will do their duty.[52]

It is likely that this mischievous notice was inserted by a supporter of the Anti-Corn-Law League. It was reproduced in the *Salisbury and Winchester Journal* in order to amuse their readers and also 'Mr Benett, who, we are happy to say, is in the enjoyment of good health at Pythouse'.[53] However, Benett may in fact have been near to death at this time, as at the end of the month, the readers of the *Devizes and Wiltshire Gazette* would have learned:

> We are sincerely happy to state, and we are persuaded our readers will be rejoiced to hear that Mr Benett, the much esteemed representative of South Wilts, is nearly recovered from the accident he met with a short time since by falling from his horse, and that he is enabled to take his usual daily exercise on horseback.[54]

On 5 January 1844, Benett's son John, with his wife and son, left Pythouse for Tichborne. Little did he know that he would not again see his son alive. Young John appears still to have had no regular occupation, although he was an active officer in the yeomanry cavalry and, in the previous May, the Lord Lieutenant signed a commission in which. 'John Benett the younger Esq' was advanced from cornet to lieutenant.[55] Benett later recorded in his diary that, prior to his son leaving Pythouse, he had 'a very slight cough occasionally, though he was daily working hard by shooting, or with the hatchet cutting and thinning trees and shrubs. He was then feeling slightly unwell but thought nothing of it, though he immediately took medical advice'.[56]

The repeal of the Corn Laws was by now one of the controversial topics of the day, with meetings being organised by those supporting both sides of the argument. In February both Benett and Sidney Herbert addressed a meeting held at the *Bear* in Devizes in opposition to the Anti-Corn-Law League, 'to show Sir Robert Peel how he could rely on the support of the agricultural interest to maintain the existing laws'. Benett said that he had frequently been called upon to address his friends in that room but never on so important an occasion as the present. Hitherto they had met together to consider the best mode of cultivating their land and improving the breed of stock. They were now called upon to unite their efforts for the purpose of maintaining a protection of the land itself. It was of little use to plough deeply or to manure liberally, with a view to increasing the crops, unless they could get a profit for those crops when produced. Many other speakers, including Herbert, addressed the meeting in similar vein with all those present being firmly opposed to a total repeal of the laws.[57]

Lord Radnor, one of the two great aristocratic landowners in the south of Wiltshire was, of course, a firm advocate for a repeal of the Corn Laws. In the following month, a meeting of the Anti-Corn-Law League was held at the Covent Garden Theatre in London. Benett took great exception to what was said at that meeting and his letter to Lord Radnor was published in the *Salisbury and Winchester Journal*. He wrote to:

> Complain of your want of candour and fairness in giving your audience your own version of some evidence of mine given before the Corn Law Committee of the House of Peers as long ago as the year 1814. You are reported to have said you have read 'my' evidence and then, without naming the period in which that evidence was given, you say 'he declared that corn could not be grown in this country under 96s. per quarter, and yet he passed an Act by which a pretty stout change was effected' . . . I must state to yourself and the public the question which was put to me before the Committee on the 22 June 1814 and my whole reply.

Benett then proceeded to set out in detail the evidence he had given, and that it had applied to the prevailing conditions of 1814 and not of 1844. He continued:

> I have been attacked by others both in the House of Commons and at anti corn law meetings. I have not before now noticed such attacks, mixed, as they have sometimes been, with extraneous and personal observations, because I have had little or no respect for the parties who have made them. But for your Lordship's character, talents, and honesty of purpose I

have much respect. I therefore address myself to you, and cannot for a moment allow myself to believe but that your Lordship will be glad to be set right in regard to the subject of this letter.[58]

This letter brought forth the expected reply from Lord Radnor who said that, in his speech as reported in the *Morning Chronicle,* he did indeed name the relevant year and so effectively rejected Benett's complaint.[59] Benett most wisely let the matter rest, and if he did make a further response it was not published.

It was not until 1844 that Benett at last found a purchaser for the Fonthill estate. Richard, Earl Grosvenor, agreed to buy 2,156 acres with the advowson of Fonthill Gifford for £89,500 . The sale was to be completed at Michaelmas 1845 and a postscript to the contract stated that: 'It is agreed that this purchase should be made as little public as possible till after Michaelmas 1845 and that the price should not be named'.[60] The whole neighbourhood must have been anxious in the extreme to know the identity of the new owner, and have been aware that secrecy was the order of the day. John Wyndham writing to his brother in Australia on 18 January 1845 passed on the news that Fonthill had been sold but, 'it is not known who the purchaser is, it being kept a profound secret'.[61] In the event it appears that further land was sold to Earl Grosvenor, as in March of the following year Coutts & Co wrote to Benett to tell him that they had received £95,000 from the buyer (by now the 2nd Marquis of Westminster), £9,762 7s. of which was applied in payment of outstanding interest and £70,500 towards the discharge of the enormous sum of £140,000 (some £7 million in early 21st century terms) then owing to them.[62] His indebtedness to the bank was now therefore reduced to £70,000.

Benett once wrote:

> In my time I have been enabled by circumstances which occurred to others to increase the Estate around Pythouse very considerably. Confidence in my own judgement as to the value of land has enabled me to do this by giving me boldness and decision in transacting the business of purchasing and selling land.[63]

Despite this assertion, it is difficult to determine what possible benefit he gained from his hasty and ill-judged purchase of Fonthill Abbey and its estate. Clearly the proceeds of the sale of the materials of the ruined abbey produced some income, but cannot have made sufficient to pay the interest on the money that he had been compelled to borrow. The final sale of the estate certainly failed to produce the profit that he had probably expected to make. Having made this declaration of confidence in his own judgement, he added the words, 'May those who succeed to me preserve the Estate entire as I trust I shall leave it'.

Although Benett was now largely silent in the House of Commons, his speeches made at various dinners in the county continued to be reported, and so his thoughts on the topics of the day were widely known. As president of the Wiltshire Agricultural Society, he was always expected to speak at the society's annual dinner, and so in July 1844 one of the topics of his speech was the question of agricultural wages. He said that he had heard that in some parts of the country it was not uncommon to employ a labourer for three days in a week, and then turn him adrift for the remaining three days. Such a custom did not prevail in Wiltshire. For himself, he could say, that he had never stopped a man's wages because he had nothing for him to do. The provision of allotments for the poor was another topic touched on in his speech. For forty years he had been anxious to promote the system. There was a bill now before Parliament but he did not like it. It empowered the overseers to grant each poor family as much as an acre of land. In his opinion this was more than he could manage. From 40 to 60 perches was as much as he could attend to with benefit to himself. He did not wish to make them farmers but gardeners.[64]

The year 1845 was an exceedingly sad one for Benett, now an elderly man of 71, for it began with news that his only son, John, had died just after Christmas in Madeira at the age of 35. John Wyndham, writing to his brother in Australia, tells him that John, 'was sent there last Autumn by his doctors, with scarce a hope of his recovery, being in deep decline'.[65] It is known that Benett kept a diary. Entries made by him in this year alone and headed, most prophetically, 'This I expect will be a *fatal* year', were copied by one of his grandchildren, after which the diary is thought to have been destroyed. Benett records that on 9 January he, 'went at night to Norton to attend my dying sister Etheldred'. She died early in the morning two days later, and on the 18th she was buried in the family vault in the church at Norton Bavant. Benett noted that the vault would hold 'two more'.

On the 13th he recorded that he had been informed by letters from his daughter Lucy, 'that the Duke of Marlborough had finally resolved that my three Churchill Granddaughters should no longer remain under his care at Blenheim and that she wished to send them for two months to Pythouse to which I consented'. Benett's second daughter Etheldred and her husband were survived by two sons and three daughters. It is clear that the duke was happy to continue to take a personal interest in the upbringing of his two nephews but not of his three nieces. In the normal course of events one might have expected the orphaned daughters, Susan, Lucy and Etheldreda,[66] to have been cared for by Lucy, as Etheldred's eldest sister. However, by this time she was seriously ill and, as she already had six children under the age of ten, the arrival of three more would have placed an intolerable burden on the household of her husband, Arthur Fane, the vicar of Warminster. At Pythouse, their aunt Fanny would have had plenty of time to devote to the supervision of their care.

On the 21st Benett received a letter from his daughter-in-law, Emily, to say that she had landed in Portsmouth with the body of her husband. 'Poor Jack!', Benett wrote, 'he is dead at the age of 35. I am here writing at nearly 72! Such is the uncertainty of life'. Emily travelled first to Tichborne, her family home, where her husband's body rested in the chapel. Benett recorded in his diary that on 28 January, 'Poor Jack's remains brought to Wardour Chapel from Tichborne Chapel, Emily and one of her sisters having arrived at Pythouse the day before'.

Three days before, Benett's three Churchill grand-daughters had arrived from Blenheim with their governess and maid – a most unfortunate time for them to be introduced to their new home, that surely would have seemed to them to be a most modest establishment after the splendours of Blenheim Palace.[67] Emily let it be known that her husband had told her that he wished to be buried either in the Arundell family vault beneath the chapel at Wardour Castle, or in the nearby burial ground that had been consecrated for the burial of Roman Catholics in 1836. Perhaps not surprisingly, Lord Arundell did not think it appropriate for his late wife's brother-in-law to be buried in the family vault beneath the floor of the chapel, and so John was buried in a deep brick grave on the east side of the cemetery, with full Roman Catholic ceremonies and with his brother-in-law Arthur Fane assisting – an unexpected display of ecumenical tolerance that Fane himself did not emulate in his own dealings with other denominations. The burial was preceded by a High Mass and Solemn Requiem in the chapel of Wardour Castle, conducted by Lord Arundell's two chaplains, assisted by Sir Henry Tichborne's chaplain. Benett walked to the cemetery[68] with a party including John's widow, her sister Catherine and her eldest sister's husband Lord Dormer[69] and Lady Arundell,[70] with the coffin being carried by sixteen of his labourers and all followed by a 'numerous and respectable tenantry and a very large assemblage of persons anxious to testify their respect towards one so deservedly regretted by all who knew him.'[71]

Over his grave was erected a massive tombstone bearing an inscription that was probably composed by his father, and reading, 'In memory of John Benett esquire who was the eldest and last surviving son of John Benett esquire of Pythouse M.P. for the Southern division of Wiltshire and Lucy his wife. Born the 13th day of August 1809, married the 25th day of July 1836 to Emily Blanche the daughter of Sir Henry Joseph Tichborne Baronet died the 16th day of December 1844 at Madeira leaving his widow and a son. His remains were deposited under this stone the 29th day of January 1845'.[72] In addition, a brass plaque in his memory was erected on the wall of the vestibule to the chapel in Wardour Castle, and another memorial in the Benett aisle of the church at Norton Bavant. His personal estate was exceedingly modest and consisted of £89 19s 2d in his bank, furniture, wine and personal effects valued at £158, his horses at £45 and his chariot and guns at £50.[73]

During the whole of February, Benett was laid low with an attack of influenza. For some two weeks his sister Anna, who had lived for many years at Norton Bavant with her sister Etheldred, had been at Pythouse, 'full of anxiety about myself' as Benett put it. Benett was clearly fond of Anna and noted:

> She is much worn by her late griefs – the Summer I trust will restore her health and spirits; she is the kindest of sisters and the best woman on earth – If conduct and works are to be allowed any merit, I would myself rather have her works to rely on than all the faith of all the weak headed pretty female enthusiasts of the present day, when under the doctrine and direction of young sprigs of parsons. Young women change their forms of religion, as they would, under the management of their dressmakers, change the shape of their dresses or bonnets. This is the age of Coxcombs of young England in politics Puseyism in the Church – love of novelty with each of the present generation – but time will shake the fools down to their proper level.

No sooner had Benett recovered from his illness than he heard that his daughter Lucy was extremely ill and not likely to recover. On 2 March, Ella Wyndham wrote to George Wyndham: 'Mr Benett has lost this winter his only surviving son John. He died at the Madieras of a deep decline; his eldest Sister too is gone, a clever, agreeable woman; and his eldest daughter (Mrs Fane) is at Torquay in a deep decline, not expected to live much longer'.[74] On 17 March, Benett recorded that that he had been out of doors for an hour after the snow and was, 'tolerably well except as to spirits'. He then proceeded to record some reflections on what had passed since the start of the year and his own religious philosophy:

I feel that I have lived too long for my own comfort, though I really believe I have lived for the advantage of my family. I have this year attended my eldest sister to the grave [and] My eldest and only son, too prematurely, he being only 35 years of age. My eldest daughter will not I believe live 2 months and her life will have been sacrificed to religious enthusiasm – she will leave 6 children. Religious enthusiasm is the bane of many families and of mine, in which I fear its increase when I am gone. I have a very strange mixture here of religious people in a few days. My very much beloved daughter Fanny who lives with me is far advanced in Puseyism under the auspices of my son-in-law Arthur Fane, though her good sense has as yet restrained her. I have three granddaughters here (Churchills) who are under the charge of a Miss Jenner who is low church and one of Arthur Fane's children who is too young to be anything (Vere) and on the 25th inst. my son's widow and child are coming here. She is a rigid R Catholic and I hold my own opinions which I keep to myself. I respect them all and believe them all to be right while they think themselves so, but I lament extremes which lead to mischief and in fact are little short of madness. Extremes in attention to religious forms proceed from selfishness and fear; those who adopt them endeavour to take Heaven by storm. But while they are so anxious about forms they are apt to forget or neglect their good works on earth which will, according to my simple judgement avail far more than all the forms and ceremonies which the ingenuity of priest craft ever devised or invented for their own influence by rendering our duty to our Maker mystical which is simple according to my view of it while they profess to render other matters simple which are, and ever will be, mystical'.[75]

Benett then recorded the death of one of his employees, by adding: 'James Grey an honest labourer on my farm for more than 30 years, died after a long illness with disease of heart and lungs and I felt much [his] parting'; and on 3 April he wrote: 'John Ford a very honest ploughman on my farm died of Influenza after a fortnight's illness in the 73rd year of his age. His father was my father's carter, and John had passed all his life in my service. I had much regard for him'. A few days earlier, he mentioned the death of his friend Philip Miles whose mansion, Leigh Court, had been built more than 30 years before, using Pythouse as its pattern. He wrote: 'He was one of my oldest and most valued friends – he was a sensible and prudent man; highly honest in all his mercantile dealings with the world – a kind husband, father and master to his servants, and in money matters I should say liberal. He was a steady and sincere friend and as such I lament the loss of him. He died surrounded by 13 children and his wife'. Benett must have known that his daughter Lucy's life was drawing to a close and that his friend should die surrounded by so large a family contrasted starkly with his own position – a widower soon to have but one child as a companion in his old age.

Lucy eventually died in Torquay on 6 April at the age of 42 and was buried at Boyton. In Benett's opinion: 'She was an enthusiast in matters of religion (*High* Church they now call it) though it used to be called Evangelistic or *low* Church. Her constitution was destroyed by her zeal to serve God and man beyond what her *strength* would endure, having given birth to so many children etc. etc. etc.'

Lucy had given birth to six children, one each year from 1835 to 1840 and so her husband Arthur was left with a large family of small children, the youngest only four years old. In March he had become embroiled in a very bitter and public dispute over his refusal to allow a member of the congregation of the Old Meeting in Warminster, called Presbyterian but in reality Unitarian, to be buried in the parish church yard. On 8 March, Arthur, who was in Torquay caring for his terminally ill wife wrote to the widower:

> Haynes
>
> I understand your wife has died, as awfully suddenly as others of your family. She died in an awful and damnable heresy, which renders it impossible for her to be buried in the Church Yard. I refuse her burial there. If you chuse to have her buried without any Service you may do so; or (least I should appear to deal harshly with you) I will pay the charge for her burial in the unconsecrated ground at Townsend; but in the Church Yard, with the burial service, she shall not be buried.
>
> I trust Almighty God may open your eyes to repentance, if such a thing may be, but I fear Haynes, you have sold your Saviour for thirty pieces of silver.
>
> Arthur Fane

This seemingly uncharitable note, together with correspondence between John Owen and the Bishop of Salisbury resulting from Fane's behaviour, was published by Owen in an appendix to a letter addressed by him to the inhabitants of Warminster. In this he declared: 'I can myself bear witness, how assiduously the Vicar labours to destroy that peace and harmony [earlier referred to by Owen as formerly existing between various sects of Christians], and to promote amongst you sectarian discord and strife'.[76] It is more than likely that this publication came to the notice of Benett, who must have deplored the ill feeling that his son-in-law appears to have been causing between various religious denominations. Fane's mother, writing in 1851, told her friend Herrietta Penruddocke, that her son the vicar, 'labours hard believe me in his Lord and Master's vineyard'[77] and his zeal contrasts starkly with Benett's decidedly tolerant attitude and impatience with divisions between religious denominations. However, amongst the many admirable qualities attributed to Fane on the brass plaque in the church of St Denys in Warminster (placed there 'by some of the sons and daughters of toil who knew the self-denying labours of his ministry'), is, 'a strong sympathy with the Poor in their sickness or their toil'; and so his character was not, perhaps, quite as black as a reading of Owen's letter would lead one to believe.

It must have taken Benett some time to recover from the events of the first few months of the year. Not only had he lost his only surviving son, his eldest daughter Lucy and his sister Etheldred, but also one of his oldest friends, Philip Miles. To add to the woes of the family, his sister-in-law Ellen, wife of his brother William, also died – less than three weeks after Lucy. In June, illness prevented him from attending the annual meeting in London of the Wiltshire Society,[78] and later he failed, 'through a series of domestic afflictions', to attend the dinner of The Wiltshire Agricultural Society held in Devizes as usual in the summer.[79] In a letter to the Society explaining his absence, he said that in addition to 'his numerous trials' another member of his family had been taken seriously ill.[80] However, in the following month, as president for the year, he felt able to be present, with Sidney Herbert, at the annual dinner of the South Wilts and Warminster Farmers' Club.[81]

In October a memorable event took place in Wilton when the magnificent new church, paid for by Herbert, was consecrated. The *Salisbury and Winchester Journal* reported that, 'the Rt. Hon. Sidney Herbert, in the new church which he has bestowed upon the town of Wilton, has evidently set no bounds to the cost of the building bringing together the treasures of the ancient world with all that the genius and talent of modern artists could apply to render it by far the most magnificent specimen which the annals of modern Ecclesiastical Architecture can furnish'.[82] *The Times* reported that, 'Mr Benett and Miss Benett' were amongst the principal guests who assembled at Wilton House before the service[83] and the Earl and Countess Bruce, the Earl and Countess Nelson[84] and of course, Sidney Herbert, were also amongst the Dowager Countess of Pembroke's party,[85] who moved to the church. Here they were joined by a large number of 'clergy, gentry, yeomen and others', who had assembled in the new school room opposite the church and all of whom were later lavishly entertained to lunch at Wilton House.

The vexed and long-standing issue of a repeal of the Corn Laws, so strenuously opposed by Benett, was now coming to a head. On 23 December 1845 Sir Robert Peel met Queen Victoria and confirmed his intention finally to abolish the Laws. Parliament opened again in the middle of the following January, and in addressing the House, Peel made it clear that he proposed to reduce the duty on corn to a nominal level. On the 27th Peel spoke for three and a half hours and, in proposing that duty on imported corn would be lowered gradually over the following three years, effectively signalled the end of the Corn Laws. Having been silent in the Commons for the whole of 1844 and 1845, Benett felt compelled to make his views heard. One recurring and rather endearing theme found in many of his utterances was his wish to see the price of beer reduced for the benefit of the poor labourer. In this debate he declared that Sir Robert Peel had forgotten the interest of those who consumed hops! He had expected to see the malt tax repealed. He had always contended, and would still contend, that the labouring classes might, consistently with the interests of every class, enjoy all the common luxuries of life. He felt that there should be no duty on hops, no duty on malt, no duty on anything which affected the welfare of the labourers.[86]

One of the speakers who followed Benett in the debate asked, 'does not the Hon. Gentleman, the member for Wilts, consider the scheme is not calculated to improve the condition of the people? Why, is it not for reducing the price of bread? Is it not for reducing the price of meat? Is it not proposed with the hope of improving the condition of every family?'.

In reply, Benett said that he had come to the House perfectly free; he had given no pledge, and expressed no opinion; he had purposely abstained from it, thinking he might possibly consider it his duty to vote with the right hon. Baronet [ i.e.Peel ] in what he did propose. He had pursued an honest course for forty years, in public as well as private, and nothing should have induced him to do what he could not have done honestly and conscientiously. He had expected more from the right hon. Baronet; but he was perfectly free now, if he had approved of the proposition, to vote for the repeal of the corn tax. The only pledge he had given was to do what he considered the best for the people of this country. He had not attended a single meeting in favour of agricultural protection, either in the country or in London; nor had he given a single intimation, by word or letter, to anyone, how he should vote on this occasion. His hon. Friend talked of agitation, and seemed to think that the friends of agriculture were about to agitate. Had the hon. Gentleman never heard of agitation before? Had no agitation been going on the other side? Had not the emissaries of the League been sent into every village? He had had them in his own village, at his own door, getting hold of his labourers and seducing them. But the agitation might now be turned another way, by the good sense of the labourers.[87]

On 5 January, an extraordinary meeting of labourers had taken place at Goatacre, a small village some six miles from Wootton Basset in the north of Wiltshire. Two days later *The Times* carried a full report of all the speeches made, commencing with a very emotive description of the rustic platform that had been erected. It was capable of supporting the chairman and one speaker at a time, below which were placed a small deal table, and some rush-bottom chairs, borrowed from a neighbouring cottage, for the accommodation of reporters:

> Four or five candles, some in lanterns, and others sheltered from the wind by the hands that held them, threw a dim and flickering light upon the groups on this spot, before and around which were gathered nearly 1,000 of the peasantry of Wiltshire, some of them accompanied by their wives and children, who, thus collected, presented a wild and painful appearance. In the shadows of the night the distinctive garb of their class was everywhere discernable, but when the flitting clouds permitted the moon to shine brightly on their faces, in them might be seen written, in strong and unmistakeable lines, anxiety, supplication, want, hunger, ever responsive to the sentiments and statements delivered by the speakers, who merely described in plain unvarnished language the miseries of their rural auditors.[88]

Free trade and the immediate repeal of the Corn Laws were the themes of the speeches delivered by the chairman and the speakers, who, with the exception of two, were labourers. Charles Vine, who seconded the resolution protesting against the Corn Laws, drew to the attention of his audience a statement he had made not long before to the editor of the *Wiltshire Independent*: 'As Mr Bennett [sic], M.P. for south Wiltshire lately stated at an agricultural meeting that the poor of Wiltshire were always employed regularly at the rate of 8s. and 9s. per week, and that they were well fed and well clothed, and as I know from experience that this statement is false, I will, if you will be so kind as to allow me to occupy a small space in your valuable paper, prove that it is so.' He then proceeded to demonstrate that during 39 weeks in 1844 to maintain a family of eight he received on average not quite 3s. 1d. per week and had he not been able to rent a little land, he and his family must have died from starvation. He continued:

> Now I will ask the hon. Gentleman if he thinks he is justified in stating such things at public meetings? I could say a great deal more on the subject, but I will leave these remarks for Mr Bennett's present perusal, and say a word or two at some future period, and I sincerely hope and trust that these remarks will open Mr Bennett's eyes a little, so that he may see that the poor are in distress; and I sincerely hope he will make speeches and try to adopt measures for the bettering the condition of us poor labourers, and I don't doubt but that it will redound to his praise, and I think he, in so doing, will glorify God, who alone knows the hearts of all, and the distress which we, as a nation, are labouring under; for there has been an increasing distress for years past; many in this parish are suffering greatly for want of work.

One cannot imagine that Benett took kindly at being preached at in this way. He sincerely believed that the distress of the poor would be increased rather than ameliorated by the repeal of the Corn Laws, and he did not need to be told by this speaker that many of the poor were in distress.

Early in February a great meeting, organised by the Wilts Agricultural Protection League, was held in Devizes to consider Peel's proposals to abolish the Corn Laws. Benett was prevented by ill health from attending, and his absence did not pass unnoticed by one of the speakers, who said that he would have been pleased to have seen Mr Benett and Mr Sidney Herbert, but that he very much doubted whether Mr Sidney Herbert would ever again make his appearance at a protectionist meeting.

On 19 February, the seventh night of the adjourned debate on the Corn Laws, Benett was fit enough to speak at great length. He began by saying that he was not influenced by ill-will or animosity either against the right hon. Baronet at the head of Her Majesty's Government, nor against those who now supported him. As for himself, he never gave any support as a party man to any Minister, nor to any party in that House. During the course of his speech, which was a formidable performance by a man in his 70s, he read out a most detailed account that he had prepared of the cost of farming Pythouse and Linley Farms during the current month. He was a very old man, and thanked God that he had once more the power of speaking honestly his sentiments. He should rejoice thereafter to reflect that he had taken that opportunity of requesting and urging upon the rich and great of the country to relieve the poorer classes of the people of those heavy taxes, and to take the burden upon themselves. He remembered on one occasion, some time ago, that at an agricultural meeting, when he had distributed some premiums amongst the small farmers and labourers, in his part of the country, for employing implements in farming, he had occasion to address them. In the course of his speech he had told them that he respected them as friends; for he looked upon them as such; and if he had to be born again, he would rather be born an honest labourer like one of them, than in any other class of society. He had made that statement in the excitement of the moment, it was true, but yet he felt it most sincerely; and he would wish to know if any of those Gentlemen opposite, who were connected with the manufacturing interest, would address the labourers as friends?

Benett said that a great many allusions had been made in the debate to the meeting that had been held at Goatacre, a place he knew well. In his view the persons who attended the meeting were not labourers of the place, but strangers who had been collected together in the night time. He had read the report of the speeches and would say without hesitation, that those delivered by the chairman (who, he said, had been taken out of the workhouse a short time previously and put in the chair), and by a Mr Edwards, were the manufacture of the League. There was one person who had admitted that he received a guinea a day for going about the country to get up these meetings. The people of Wiltshire were respectable men, and had nothing to do with that meeting; for, with the exception of some half-dozen lazy fellows, such as always were found in every locality, and were an annoyance to the place, they were as respectable a body of labourers as he had ever met with anywhere.

His concern was that the loss that landlords might sustain as a result of a repeal of the Corn Laws must eventually fall on the labourers, and he therefore protested against the measure for the sake of the poor labourers and the small but industrious farmers. In conclusion he declared that he had witnessed many important events in his time, but he confessed that he had not seen any more important than that would be – the passing of the measure under discussion.[89]

On 27 March, Peel obtained a decisive majority on the key principles of the bill on its second reading and, on 12 May, Benett spoke at length in an adjourned debate on the third reading of the bill. He knew that this would probably be one of the last, if not the last, time that he would address the House. He said that any man who had lived as long as he had lived would be well informed that seasons of prosperity did not last for ever. Great fortunes were rapidly made by manufacturers, but that could not always follow, and at last, the people would be left to starve, or else depend on the charity of landowners. He did not find himself equal to enter as fully as others into the intricacies of debate. He was a very old man. For fifty years at least he had practically advocated the happiness of the people. He spoke that night, perhaps for the last time in that House . . . Allow him to repeat, that the great duty of Government was the promotion of the greatest happiness of the people; and he was of the opinion that any system which curtailed the duration of human life should not have the support of those who legislate for the country at large.[90] These were his last words in the House on the Corn Law question, and he must have known that the argument was lost. On 15 May, at 4 a.m. on the Saturday morning the third reading was carried by 98 votes (with Benett voting in the minority against the Bill) and, on 25 June, the Bill completed its passage through Parliament. On the following day an Act to Amend the Laws Relating to the Importation of Corn reached the statute book.

In the event, the repeal of the Corn Laws did not have any immediate effect on the price of bread, and so Benett's long-held fears that a repeal would at once be catastrophic both for the farmers and the labouring poor proved to be ill-founded. However, the removal of barriers to foreign competition did eventually cause a slump in the price of wheat, and consequently great agricultural depression towards the end of the century – a scenario that Benett had always feared.[91]

Benett's speech delivered on 12 May was not in fact the last time he addressed the House. In June he spoke at great length on a topic that was to concern the legislature from that time to the present day, and it is perhaps fitting that he should have risen to his feet for the last time and addressed his still active mind to the problems of Ireland. What was being debated was the Protection of Life (Ireland) Bill, and had Benett been in the House when the bill was brought in, he said that he might have put confidence enough in the Government to have voted for the bill without enquiry. It was not, however, then in his power to be present. He had not then sufficient physical power to attend in his place or he might have fallen into the error of taking it for granted that the Government was quite right in bringing in this measure and have voted for it. What particularly concerned him was that under the bill a man would be liable to transportation for seven years on being out at night. He would not vote for it. What, then, had he a right to do as an independent Member of Parliament having no regard to parties? Either to absent himself from his duties, or to vote against a measure which he thought uncalled for?

In his view the Government was afraid to stop agitation in Ireland on account of its strength. He had asked a friend of his who was a supporter of the Government – 'Why did they not take the bull by the horns in Ireland?' And his friend's reply was 'Because the bull has got horns'. The Government was ready to attack the poor man and subject him to enormous punishment because he was found out of his house at night, but the bull with the horns was left alone. For this reason, though he was anxious that every possible measure should be taken to put down the dreadful system of assassination which prevailed in Ireland, he could not conscientiously vote for the second reading of the bill, and it would be cowardice, therefore, not to vote against it.[92]

During the course of this, his last speech in the House, Benett had said that until agitation was put down, it would be impossible to expect that peace and order could be restored. He recalled being present at the trial of 'the late Mr Cobbett', and suggested that part of Cobbett's defence, which Benett then proceeded to quote, should be adopted at the present time, as justification for taking strong measures against the prevailing agitation.

Although he had spoken for the last time in the House, Benett continued to take his place there and voted with the noes on 25 June on an amendment to the second reading of the Protection of Life (Ireland) Bill, and on two further occasions towards the end of July.

At a meeting of the Wiltshire Agricultural Society in July it was said of him:

> I believe there is no individual here in any way connected with the cultivation of land who has tried one half the experiments he has tried. Among the numberless improvements which are daily suggested . . . I have never found myself in a condition to ask Mr Benett about any one of them, without finding that he was able to tell me the results of the same experiment tried by himself some 20 years back. From which I derive much more information than all I could read upon the subject, and I think I may venture to say that no one who has been in the habit of attending our agricultural meetings has gone away without gaining some information from our worthy Chairman. But besides his great practical knowledge, his whole life both private and public has proved him to be the tried friend of that interest with which he is connected: for years past, he has gone in this county by the name honest John Benett and let me say, the longer I live, the more I think of that quality of honesty.[93]

In January 1846, certain friends of William Dyer, the perpetual curate of the remote village of Imber on Salisbury Plain, decided to petition Sir Robert Peel with a view to seeking some ecclesiastical preferment for the poor parson. His living was said to be worth little more than £100 a year, and his father, 'from the demands consequent upon a numerous family of 10 children', could not provide further for him. Benett, who would have been well aware that one of his agricultural labourers was expected to support himself and his family on less than £25 a year, was nevertheless prevailed upon, probably by his son-in-law, Arthur Fane, to support the memorial. He signed and added his reference to a number of others, declaring that: 'I have known Mr Dyer, the memorialist, the last eight years and from my own knowledge can say that he is fully entitled to all that is said of him by the Vicar of Warminster, and I strongly recommend him to the attention of the Government'.[94] William Dyer and his friends were doubtless disappointed when they heard that Sidney Herbert had received a letter from Peel saying that he was sorry that he, 'could give no assurances to Mr Dyer regarding Church preferment as it rarely happens that I have a living at my disposal'.[95] Poor Mr Dyer's living was, in fact worth £122 a year and he remained as perpetual curate of Imber until 1865.

Having at last disposed of the Fonthill estate, it may be that his slightly improved financial position encouraged him in 1846 to build a school and schoolhouse at nearby Newtown, endowed with land in Tisbury. It is said that the school was built to please his daughter Fanny,[96] who was particularly interested in the welfare of children.[97] In endowing the school Benett specified that, while teaching was to be on Church of England principles and services were to be permitted in the school room, he declared that the school should be under the exclusive management and control of the trustees, and that his daughter Fanny, one of the original trustees with the Marquis of Westminster, and the other trustees should exercise such control, free from all interference of the Church or any other establishment, whether ecclesiastical or lay.[98] In the same year, with his 'customary liberality' as reported in the *Salisbury and Winchester Journal,* he made a 'munificent gift' of £100 towards the cost of repairing Tisbury church.[99]

In 1846, a Warminster solicitor, Timothy Goodman, began acting for Benett and charged him 10 guineas for collecting his rents throughout the year.[100] In February he appeared on his behalf in the County Court sitting in Hindon when an action was brought against him by a man named Willes.[101] In the following year, he also acted in connection with a claim by Benett's tenant William Melsome for compensation for the loss he had sustained as a result of the passing through Norton North farm of the Wilts Somerset and Weymouth railway. As landlord, Benett had received compensation from the railway company, and so the tenant claimed the sum of £600 to compensate him for his own loss. Benett told Goodman that he would pay no more than £200 and, as this was not accepted, the dispute proceeded to a hearing in the Sheriff's court with a jury, as a result of which the tenant was awarded the sum of £450.[102]

In the following year, the Marquis of Westminster once again came to Benett's financial rescue by purchasing Westwood Farm in Semley, having already bought Hart Hill farm and Bowmarsh farm,[103] thus enabling Benett to reduce the sum owed to Coutts & Co to £54,000. In February 1848 he managed to repay a further £3,000 to the bank, the resulting balance owing, although still substantial , being considerably more manageable than the massive amount owed before the sale of the Fonthill estate.

Although now a very elderly man, Benett continued to take an active and acute interest in all matters relating to the improvement of agricultural practice. In 1847, there was laid before the council of the Royal Agricultural Society of England a report prepared by Benett and Mr W.R. Brown, in reference to the cutting of straw and using it as litter for livestock, as practised on Brown's farm at Winterbourne Stoke. Doubtless Benett travelled to the farm to inspect and monitor the experiment.

In this year in May, there was a meeting of the Wiltshire Friendly Society at Warminster, not far, of course, from Pythouse. On this occasion, he proposed the toast to the Bishop and Clergy of the diocese of Salisbury and made particular reference to his son-in-law, Arthur Fane, who as vicar of Warminster was present. Sidney Herbert proposed Benett's health by saying:

> I have received permission to propose a toast, and I will not detain you in proposing it by many observations, because the gentleman whose health I will drink, has by his own example through life and today by his precepts, so fully shown how benevolent is his character, and how entitled he is to our esteem . . . he has come here today at great sacrifice, for the state of his health and the infirmity under which he labours are such as to render the effort of speaking in public painful to him.

However, the effort referred to by Herbert did not prevent him from saying:

> I have through life endeavoured to perform the duties of a country gentleman. Indeed your reception of me today would almost convince me that I have in some measure at least succeeded. Belonging to

Wiltshire, I feel that here I am among my old friends; it was in this neighbourhood my father and my family for many generations resided: and if it should be in my power (though at my age, it is impossible to say what may occur) I trust again to see you, and again to receive the kind welcome I have ever had shown to me in the neighbourhood of Warminster.[104]

In 1847, Benett also faced what was to be his last election. In his address to the electors he declared:

After much deliberation, I have determined to request you to confer on me the honour of your representation in the House of Commons. The quietude of private life might have been more suitable to my age, and you might find an abler man to serve you; but you will never have a Representative more devoted to our Country's interests, or more anxious to maintain the prosperity and honour of the County of Wilts, than myself.

I am unwilling to sever the political connexion which has so long existed between us, and the more particularly at this period, when there is so much public promise in Parliament, and somewhat of public difficulty in prospect. I am anxious to assist in whatever ought to be done for good, and to resist whatever might be attempted for evil.

Professions, after so long in public service as mine, would be useless – and pledges I have not to make – except that one only which I did make thirty years since: viz that my conduct should be guided by measures and not by men – that I would not be the tool of any party – but that I would apply my best energies to the service of the State, irrespective of party or self interest. I have followed this independent course and have frequently been blamed for so doing by some who have considered party and faction of more importance than individual investigation, decision and action.

We have now since the abandonment of all confidence in party, and may fairly contemplate the general adoption of this my early-cherished principle of independence, and that the collective sense of the Representation of the people uninfluenced by the trammels of party, may have that just control over the Government, which it ought to have by the spirit of our Constitution in which our representative system so largely prevails.

I am not aware of any change of my opinions on any great public matters. I hope to meet you at the Hustings, and then to express my sentiments more at length than the limits of this address will allow.[105]

In a speech made on the day of the election, it was said: 'It was true that they could not regard Mr Benett as a strong a man, in the physical sense, as he had been in his heartiest time; but his mental facilities were never in a sounder state than at present'. Sidney Herbert, who was also returned unopposed with Benett as one of the members for the southern division, said, 'I wish I could fulfil the promise that my honourable colleague made for me, namely that I could make a better speech than his, because you will agree with me in saying that it came from a man of great experience, whom we all esteem'. Benett himself declared in addressing the electors that he had entered Parliament by the favour of their fathers, and in the case of some present their grandfathers, nearly thirty years ago . . . and he felt exceedingly grateful for their kindness, and was happy to find, after some thirty years, that he had not met a single enemy among them.[106]

During the whole of 1847, he does not appear to have voted in any of the divisions in the House, either before or after the election, although he probably continued to take his seat. In the following year he did vote in three divisions on matters in which he had a particular interest – the Parliamentary Electors Bill and the Sugar Duties Bill both in June, and the Corrupt Practices at Elections Bill in August.

By 1849, Benett's health was failing, and this was the last year during which he was listed in Robson's *London Directory* as living in Limmer's Hotel while in London. However, at the beginning of the year, he was fit enough to chair a meeting held in Warminster with reference to the unfinished state of the Wilts, Somerset and Weymouth Railway. The railway had reached Westbury but, much to the dismay of the inhabitants, work had stopped some five miles short of Warminster. Benett urged that the directors of the railway company be requested, 'in the most friendly manner', to continue the line to Warminster and then to Salisbury. At the end of the meeting, one of the speakers 'expressed his extreme pleasure in thanking so old and tried a friend as the Chairman for coming to the meeting, congratulating him on his improved health, and hoping that, for many years, his life would be spared to pursue his useful and valuable course'.[107]

In March, a great county meeting took place at Devizes for the purpose of 'considering the present distressed state of the agricultural and industrious classes'. The High Sheriff announced that he had received a communication, 'from Mr John Benett who had reached a green [sic] old age and would also have been present had his health permitted it'.[108] Although he continued to attend the House of Commons, he decided to resign as President of The Wiltshire Society for the Encouragement of Agriculture. On 19 June he wrote from 23 Berkeley Square to the Society:

I have come to the determination to resign my Post as President of the Wiltshire Agricultural Society. I have been so unwell lately that I feel any exertion quite uncomfortable. I have been really ill all this Summer, though I have gone much recently to the House of Commons but I must avoid fatigue as much as possible. Mr Sotheron will give you this and he will state to the Meeting the painful determination to which I have found it necessary to come.[109]

A general meeting of the Society was held and a resolution was passed and a copy sent to Benett:

... That we bear in mind that the Establishment of our society was mainly owing to the exertions of Mr Benett in 1813, and that since that period his time and untiring zeal and personal care have supported and maintained it year after year and contributing largely to its efficiency and success. That Mr Benett has throughout conducted himself in connection with this Society with a kindness of manner, a firmness and independence of character and a readiness to impart to all of us the Instruction with which his long experience in agricultural matters has stored his mind that has deserved our warm thanks and regard: and that he has uniformly shewed that the Poor Wiltshire Labourer as well as the Farmer has been the object of attention and interest to him. We feel deeply pained that a connection and intercourse of so many years should be brought to a close, and we offer to him our hearty acknowledgement for past services, and our best wishes for improved health, during the remainder of his life, which cannot fail to be sweetened by the recollection of Honest Public Conduct, and eminent usefulness in all matters of local concern to the County of Wilts.

On 6 July, Benett wrote from Pythouse:

... I was too ill to attend the Annual Meeting this year and to look forward to improved health at my age (76) would be presumptuous. . . The Resolutions a copy of which you have sent me I consider as the highest compliment which can be offered to anyone who has been for so long a time as myself so much devoted to the agricultural interest and which I must still consider the leading permanent Interest of this Country – and I Confess I foresee much danger in any very large habitual dependence on Foreign Countries for an Article become so necessary to human existence in this country as wheat.

The meeting of the Society held in June was the first at which Benett did not occupy the chair. His successor as chairman addressed the meeting and said:

I have already said that I regret much that circumstances should have placed me in the situation I occupy among you this day – circumstances which have caused to you and to the Society generally the loss of an old friend who has filled the chair since 1813. Yes, for 36 years has this chair been filled by a friend who is acknowledged to be one of the first agriculturalists in the kingdom, we may say, one of the first agriculturalists in the world. To lose such a man is indeed a grievous loss – a loss which it is far beyond my power to express. . .

He was followed by one of Benett's oldest tenants, who said that nothing but ill health would have prevented the worthy member for South Wilts from being present, and that his absence was to him a cause of deep regret. Later, Thomas Sotheron, one of the Members of Parliament for North Wilts, said:

I, for many years, have had the honour of intimate acquaintance with him; and I cannot on this, the first occasion of our meeting since his resignation of the chair, rise to say one word, without bearing testimony to the truth and genuineness of the character of that man. The longer I live in the world, the more I feel (and so will you) the value of truth . . . of all the public men with whom I have associated, he assumed that truly English character of being exactly the man he seemed to be . . .[110]

It was at this time that Benett sold to Richard Bentley,[111] the publisher, more than 1000 letters from leading royalists relating in particular to the life of Prince Rupert[112] (whose private secretary it will be recalled was Thomas Bennett[113] of the original Pythouse family of Bennetts). This led to the publication in three volumes of *Memoirs of Prince Rupert and the Cavaliers, including their Private Correspondence now published from the Original Manuscripts.* According to the very critical review of this work that appeared in the *Gentleman's Magazine,* 'this gentleman (i.e. Benett) it is remarked by the present editor placed a high value on such records, 'that is a high money value', and it was by a very speculation on Mr Bentley's part that he became their proprietor and publisher'.[114] The 'high value' was £600 in cash and, in the memorandum of sale signed by Benett on 2 April 1844, he declared that, 'if I can find any other papers, or render any assistance to Mr Bentley in the publication, I feel myself bound to do so'.[115] Some 75 letters escaped the sale to Bentley and eventually descended to Benett's grandson, Vere Fane-Benett-Stanford, and were published in 1879.[116]

It is likely that during the last two or three years of his life Benett did not travel far from Pythouse, but was well looked after there by his many servants supervised by his daughter Fanny. From the inventory of every single item of the contents in the house that was prepared following his death, a picture can be gained of the appearance of the house in which he spent his final years, and even of the clothes that were available for him to wear. It was probably some time since he had worn his court dress consisting of a coat with epaulettes, a feathered hat, a pair of trousers, a silk sash with tassels and a pair of boots and silk stockings. Had he wished to call for a glass of sherry or port there would have been no difficulty in this being provided for him from the wine cellar. At the time of his death this contained no fewer than 419 bottles of sherry, 52 of old sherry, 77 of claret, 325 of old port, 192 of white wine and 60 of sweet wine, as well as large quantities of beer. There were 1,550 books in his library and 145 in his study. Benett appears not to have been in the habit of subscribing to new books, although he is named in the list of subscribers to *Wilton and its Associations* published in 1851. It may be he was persuaded to subscribe as amongst those at the head of the list was his parliamentary colleague Sidney Herbert, whose seat at Wilton and its magnificent new church paid for by him features prominently in it.[117] Also in his library would be found backgammon and draughts boards. Surrounding him were many portraits of his ancestors, although his own portrait painted when he was a boy of six, and that of his brother Thomas painted when he was five-years-old, were relegated to the schoolroom. In the entrance hall would be found the marble bust of his grandfather Thomas Benett, who had purchased the Pythouse estate in 1725, together with that of his grandmother Etheldred, the daughter of Archbishop Wake, sculpted after her death by Joseph Wilton, as well as the bust of Benett's own mother. Nearby in the entrance hall were twenty glass cases of stuffed birds, and amongst the things to be found in the room called the surgery were three electrifying machines and a model of Fonthill Abbey – a reminder of when Benett had been its owner.[118]

For many years Benett's financial position had been in a precarious state. In 1844 he had mortgaged his estates to Coutts & Co to secure the enormous sum of £140,500, although by the time of his death the amount borrowed had been reduced to £56,000. His sole source of income was derived from his farming activities and from the rents received from his tenants. At the time of his death rent amounting to a little more than £5,800 was owing to him. He also owed a large number of small creditors the sum of £574 19s. 10d. – just £100 short of the sum standing to his credit at his bankers in the country.

In 1850 Benett made his last will. After giving legacies and annuities to his daughters, grandchildren and his sister, he then proceeded to make what must be regarded as unusually extensive and thoughtful provision for his numerous servants and employees. He must have had great regard for his butler, Thomas Ball, as he was left a legacy of £80 – considerably more than the sum of £50 left to his under bailiff or £40 to his woodman, or £25 left to each of his footman, John Gray, his housekeeper Mistress Titt, his gamekeeper George Turner, and his carpenter Joseph Trim. Smaller sums were given to his groom, his Spencer Churchill grand-daughters' ladies' maid, his mason, carter, gardener, shepherd and ploughmen – not forgetting Sarah or Sally Ploughman, the washerwoman. All other indoor and outdoor servants were also not forgotten. Martha Ingram who had been Fanny's governess and who had continued to live at Pythouse was left a legacy of £50.

Small annuities and legacies were given to retired workmen, and most notably to a man named Cockburn (whose forename Benett could not remember or more probably never knew), 'who was formerly my gardener and now residing in Norfolk as a small acknowledgement of his manly and sensible conduct at Pythouse in the year 1830'. The large sum of £100 was given to Salisbury Infirmary, 'in token of my opinion of its great utility and the benefit conferred upon the poorer classes from its excellent management'. One enigmatic gift is a legacy to a Cirencester silversmith named Hartwill and his wife Mary, 'as a token of my remembrance of them'.

The pieces of plate presented to him by his friends in Wiltshire and by the Reformers of Liverpool were to be treated as heirlooms together with all his other plate, pictures, furniture and china. A most curious gift was made to his widowed daughter-in-law. She was to receive, 'all my wines liquors and household stores and pleasure horses and dogs, and all harnesses and articles in and about the coach-house in order to avoid any sale at Pythouse after my decease'. All his freehold land, including Pythouse itself, was the subject of a settlement entered into in 1830 and so did not pass under the will.

William Wyndham, the son of his old friend William Wyndham of Dinton who had died in 1841, and his London solicitor were appointed executors, and were left 20 guineas each 'as a small mark of my sincere regard and sense of obligation to them having promised to undertake the trusts of my will which I have endeavoured to make as little complicated as possible'.[119] Read as a whole, this appears to be the will of a thoughtful and caring man whom it is difficult to believe is the same person who, just over 20 years before, was said to have been one of the most hated men in the county.[120]

Despite his age, Benett continued to take an active interest in the management of his affairs, and on 9 November he wrote to his Warminster solicitor, Timothy Goodman, asking him to ride over to Pythouse to see him. This he duly did on the 12th and discussed various matters with him.[121] The non-payment of rent by his tenants was a perennial problem. On 15 February 1851 his solicitor saw one of them named Melsome about his rent account. He said that he intended to ride over to Pythouse to see Benett himself. As one of Benett's oldest tenants who had spoken in moving terms about his landlord at the meeting of the Wilts Agricultural Society in 1849, he no doubt much preferred to speak to Benett himself rather than to Goodman. There must have been a successful meeting for in April £652 7s. 4d. was paid on account of the arrears.[122]

He was also concerned about the fate of the estate at Boyton that was being held in trust for Edward, the first son of his daughter Lucy and her husband Arthur Fane. In May, he wrote to Goodman telling him to take care to see that Fane (doubtless Benett's son-in-law Arthur who was interested in the property as trustee) respects the Boyton House and manor, and to learn his views and wishes respecting it. If Fane had no-one in view who might lease the property pending his grandson attaining his majority, then Goodman was to advertise it and come over to see him the week after next.[123] In October Goodman rode to Pythouse to obtain Benett's signature to a conveyance of a property in Frome that Benett was selling. They had so many other matters to discuss that he stayed the night and recorded in his day book that for two days he was engaged in dealing with his client's affairs.

A final glimpse of the household at Pythouse shortly before Benett's death can be gained from the 1851 census return. On the day appointed for the census, his daughter Fanny was away from home, but his Spencer Churchill grand-daughters, Susan and Lucy – now young women of 20 and 19 – and Etheldred, a girl of 14, were still living under his care. Etheldred's governess was in residence, and visiting on that day was Benett's elderly sister Anna Maria with her maid. The living-in servants consisted of his elderly butler, Thomas Ball, his rather surprisingly named young footman, James Arundell; and his groom Edmund Ford and the housekeeper, Jane Titt, would have supervised the housemaid and two kitchen maids. The cook, in common with the many outdoor servants, lived elsewhere.

It is inevitable that at this time there should be speculation as to when Benett would resign his seat in Parliament and who might succeed him. On 25 January 1851, an unknown correspondent wrote to

Richard Penruddocke Long,[124] the eldest son of Walter Long of Rood Ashton and a person widely thought of as a possible successor to him:

> Dear Mr Long
> A friend of mine wrote to me recently to ask me to make what enquiry I could as to Mr Benett's resignation of his seat and pointing out many reasons (in which I fully agree) as to the expediency for his resignation and the advantage that would result from you coming in if possible before a dissolution. I so fully agreed in this reasoning, that, I went over to Pythouse this week and ascertained Mr Benett's mind as fully as I could. I imagine you may be curious very naturally to know the result. Mr B. is so well in health and so fully alive in intellect that he has not an idea of resigning his seat save and except to one who will not stand. He will never stand again, I am quite sure & should he outlive the present Parliament which he probably will as I never saw such a haler man of 78. I much regret this determination which I am powerless to alter . . .[125]

The identity of Benett's preferred choice is unknown, although it is not unlikely that it was William Wyndham, the executor of his will and the son of his life-long friend. What we can be sure is that the last person he would wish to see as his successor would be a member of the Long family.

Throughout the first seven months of 1852, Benett continued to concern himself with his business affairs, although ill-health prevented him from attending the House of Commons. In 1847, he had entered into an agreement with the South Western Railway Company to sell land for the construction of the railway from Salisbury to Yeovil, but the agreement had never been completed. In January, therefore, Goodman travelled to London to meet Parkinson, his London lawyer, to discuss what should be done.[126] Following the meeting, Goodman wrote to the directors of the company calling on them to perform the agreement, and early in February called on Benett at Pythouse to report to him that the directors had refused to comply with his request.[127] On 22 March he was at Pythouse and again on the following day when he drew up a short codicil to his will for Benett to sign.[128] At the end of April he was with Benett at Pythouse discussing the tenancy of Upper Hatch Farm, went to Shaftesbury on the next day to see Chitty the Shaftesbury solicitor about it, and on the following day returned to Pythouse to report to Benett.[129] On 27 July Goodman called for the last time to discuss various matters with him.[130]

On 1 July, Parliament was dissolved. For some time it had been assumed that there could be no question of Benett seeking re-election.

He had not taken his seat in Parliament for two years, and so it was assumed by all that he would at last retire. In its editorial, published on the same day that Parliament was dissolved, the *Devizes and Wiltshire Gazette* declared:

> The only change in the county representation will be the return of Mr RICHARD LONG as one of the members for the southern Division in the room of Mr BENETT whose retirement, unhappily rendered necessary by age and its infirmities, will long be felt as a great public loss. Before the County was divided, Mr Benett, after two of the severest contests ever known in the West of England, was our representative, and has continued to be so for thirty years. During this long period, he has been a distinguished member of the House of Commons, and the name of 'Mr Benett of Wiltshire' has been a parliamentary 'household word' over all England. A practical farmer himself, he has been, in the real sense of the word 'A Farmer's Friend'. On all questions his course has been dictated by sound principles and intelligent views; his habits have been those of a practical man of business; and, till forced to yield to the pressure of advanced years and declining health, no member was more assiduous in the discharge of his duties . . . In making these remarks, of course, we take it for granted (as is generally done) that Mr Benett will not allow himself to be put in nomination again, but it would probably have been satisfactory to the electors if he had made a formal declaration to that effect, as a very large portion of them would continue to give their votes for him.[131]

Shortly after this, Benett did indeed announce that he did not intend to stand again and his address to the electors, the last of many made during his long political career was duly published:

> Having for so long a period had the honor [sic] of representing the WHOLE county in Parliament before the county was divided, in now taking my leave of you, I must request that you will allow me to offer you jointly my most sincere thanks for the gallant and independent support which your forefathers and yourselves have given me since my first successful contest, which terminated on the 4th August 1819, after a poll of fifteen days. In the year 1818, I had a contest with Mr Long Wellesley and was beaten; but from the time of my first election (1819), I have retained my seat without any opposition until the late dissolution of Parliament, by which my public duty ceases. I need not say that it is most painful to myself to part from my kind friends who have not complained, when in the last two years, my state of health has not allowed me to be much in the House of Commons, but I must be allowed in my own

defence to observe, that few men, during the last thirty-three years (except the Speaker) have sat more hours in the House than myself, or have attended more anxiously to business.

I observe in the Devizes Gazette of Thursday 1st inst. an address from Mr Mills recommending to the Southern Division of Wilts, Mr Richard P. Long, son of Mr Long, of Rood Ashton, as successor to myself. I have no knowledge of, or acquaintance with Mr Richard P Long; but as the county has been divided, and now sends four members to Parliament, I lament that two of them should not be found in the Southern Division.

And now, I take my final public leave of you, which I do with great reluctance, in the 80th year of my age – which later fact will, I trust, be ample reason for my retirement – I must claim your indulgence for any difference of opinion which may at any time (during so long a period of public service) have occurred between any individual and myself.

Wishing you, my kind friends, all the health, happiness, and prosperity which you so well deserve.[132]

Benett must have been delighted that, in the event, Sidney Herbert and William Wyndham,[133] who must have been his preferred choice, and both, of course, from the south of the county, were duly returned to Parliament after an election in which they were opposed by Richard Long.

Within three months, Benett was dead. On Wednesday 29 September, he was seized with a severe fit of apoplexy. William Wyndham, one of the executors of his will, immediately wrote to Goodman, informing him of Benett's illness.[134] Goodman wasted no time in riding over to Pythouse, but when he arrived he was told that Benett had died that very morning at half-past-eleven. According to the report in the *Devizes and Wilts Gazette*, 'Doctors Lees and Mackenzie were in attendance as well as Mr Zinzan of Hindon, but no medical skill could avert his death'.[135]

Wyndham instructed Goodman to attend to the funeral arrangements and, on 5 October, he met Bedford, the Warminster stonemason, and told him to open up the vault beneath the Benett aisle in the church at Norton Bavant,[136] where the coffin bearing Benett's body was to be placed after a private service. Due to the proximity of the river, the churchyard and the burial vaults were liable to flood, and in the 1930s Benett's great-grandson John Fane-Benett-Stanford[137] related that he could remember John Brickell, who died in 1897, telling him that when he went down into the vault he found all the coffins 'higgledy piggledy like', as if they had been floating about![138]

His executors acted with commendable speed in commencing to administer his estate. On 3 October Goodman spent all day at Pythouse and on the 5th Lady Fane (presumably Arthur Fane's mother, Mrs Cook) was sent a cheque for £73 15s. 8d. in payment of the interest that had been due to her on her mortgage over the Boyton estate on the 29 September. On the 20th Goodman made out a list of no less than 102 servants and labourers who were to receive legacies, and nine days later went to Pythouse to pay several of them.[139]

Following his death, a memorial tablet was erected to his memory in the Benett aisle in the church at Norton Bavant. The tablet is perhaps the most unpleasing of all the nearby Benett monuments – so long and narrow that one is tempted to believe that it may have been deliberately designed in this way as being particularly suitable as a memorial to Long John Benett. A more visible memorial to him is the great house that he designed and built, and in which he lived for almost half a century and which eventually passed to Vere, the second son of his daughter Lucy Fane.

In December, *The Gentleman's Magazine* published an obituary in which an account of the 1818 contested election was given, describing it as, 'a contest of unusual severity', and as, 'the last great contest for the county previously to its division by the Reform Act'. The writer of the obituary declared that: 'During the thirty-three years Mr Benett sat in the House of Commons, few men devoted more hours than himself to his senatorial duties, or attended more anxiously to the business of the county. He was originally returned to Parliament as a Whig of the old school, but his predilections were of a truly Conservative character. Throughout his long political career, he was uniformly the advocate of protection to native industry; and, so strongly impressed was he with the truth of his convictions, that he gave important testimony before committees of the Houses of Parliament in favour of the Corn Bill of 1815 and on all occasions resisted in the most determined manner any relaxation of the protective duties on corn'. [140]

His contemporaries saw him in very differing lights. Having originally found him, 'a very haranguing minded gentleman', on further acquaintance the poet Thomas Moore thought him, 'all kindness and hospitality', and another found him, 'a pleasant hospitable companion'. Paul Methuen thought him, 'a man devoid of common truth and common honesty'; an anonymous writer as, 'a man whose principles and conduct have made him obnoxious to every man attached to the religion of his country'; and Lord Malmesbury as, 'in every light a very unfit [person] for the situation (ie a seat in Parliament) – a democrat, a suppressor of tithes and a supporter of the catholic question'. In contrast, Ambrose Hussey declared him to be, 'highly esteemed by everyone who knew him in the county'. One anonymous writer said that he had, 'a competent fortune', while Lady Holland called him 'a pauper'; and Thomas Moore confided to his journal that he was, 'at his wit's end for money'. Henry Hunt memorably called him, 'Black Jack, alias the Devil's Knitting Needle'; while another anonymous writer declared him to be a man of, 'unblemished character . . . a good husband, an affectionate father, a kind master, a firm friend'. Another thought of him as a man, 'of a very moderate private education . . . without literary attainments', while another was sure that he was a man, 'of superior talents, of learning and science'. Another considered that, in the controversy on the subject of tithes, 'he acquitted himself in a manner highly creditable to his own literary talents and has displayed a fund of knowledge on subjects of political economy that is rarely acquired by one man'. To Lord Malmesbury he was, 'such a strange man that he will keep up the spirit of animosity as long as he can', and Littleton declared him to be 'desperately long-winded'. After the events of 1830 one newspaper assured its readers that his, 'manly and high spirited behaviour', could not be mentioned in, 'too high terms of commendation', and another paper praised him as, 'an innovator at home, a radical reformer in agriculture, a true patriot and benefactor of his county'. However, as his life drew to a close, his contemporaries tended to look on him in a very favourable light – an honest, conscientious and hard-working Member of Parliament, and a tireless advocate of the interests of the agricultural community and the people of Wiltshire in general.

History and historians have not looked kindly on him. His name is primarily associated with the 'Battle of Pythouse', and as the owner of the machinery that was smashed by the rioters. His presence with the yeomanry cavalry has led later commentators to assume that he was instrumental in ordering the attack that ended in the death of one of the rioters, and to look on him as a wealthy landowner intent on suppressing the downtrodden labouring man. To add insult to injury, his position as a magistrate and as foreman of the Grand Jury, as well as his giving evidence in the trial of the rioters, has persuaded many historians that he acted as witness, judge and jury and is thus to be condemned.

The editor of one edition of Cobbett's *Rural Rides* asserted that, 'John Benett, otherwise known as 'Wiltshire Benett', was one of the bitter enemies of the labouring class . . . He was attacked by the labourers in the riots of 1830, and took an enthusiastic part in sentencing them to transportation'.[141] It is to be hoped that this account of the riot and subsequent trial will dispel this myth, and that the reader will agree that, far from being 'a bitter enemy of the labouring class', he consistently attempted to improve their lot.

Cobbett labelled, and others remember, him as 'gallon-loaf Benett', the man who declared that the working man and his family should be perfectly capable of surviving on what we would now consider to be a starvation diet. The fact that in saying this he was merely relaying to the parliamentary committee what was the practice of the magistrates in his part of the country is conveniently overlooked.

His reputation has not been well served by the writings of his arch-enemy Henry Hunt. Many of the wild allegations contained in his *Memoirs* and his *Letters to the Radical Reformers* have little or no foundation, and his statement in Parliament that Benett had acted unjustly as a landlord was quickly refuted at the time. On just one occasion Benett was foolish enough to declare that in certain circumstances he would pull down his labourers' cottages. One cannot believe that he would actually have done such a thing, but the fact that he threatened to do so has been interpreted as evidence that he did indeed demolish cottages on the Pythouse estate in order to improve the outlook from his newly built house.

At the time of the contested elections of 1818 and 1819 many unkind things were said about him. During the course of fiercely fought political battles many allegations are made, some of which have a grain of truth and most of which are quite rightly soon forgotten. So it should be in Benett's case.

He was a man whose views and very presence caused his contemporaries to hold very strong opinions about him. So far as can be discovered, his private life was irreproachable when the private conduct of many in public life was less than perfect. As a Wiltshireman he felt passionately about his native county and strove to improve the lot of those less fortunate than himself. He is far from being thought of as a great man, but should surely be remembered as a man of many and varied talents who worked tirelessly for the good of his fellow countrymen.

# Epilogue

At his death, Benett was survived by his eleven-year-old grandson, John Edward . This child, the heir to the Pythouse and Norton Bavant estates, was destined not to live to enjoy his inheritance, and died at Nice in 1856 aged 15 years and 8 months. Lucy Fane, Benett's eldest daughter having predeceased him, the two estates eventually passed to her son Vere Fane who assumed the additional surname of Benett and, on his marriage to Ellen Stanford in 1867, the third surname of Stanford. Their son John, commonly known as Jack Benett, succeeded to the estates and died in 1947. On the death of his widow Evelyn in 1957, Pythouse, with a small area of land surrounding it, was sold to Mutual Houses Association (later Country Houses Association), who converted the mansion into apartments. Most of the Norton Bavant estate was sold in the 1930s with the remainder being disposed of following the death of Evelyn Fane-Benett-Stanford. Happily, some of the land in the vicinity of Pythouse that had belonged to Benett remained in the ownership of his descendants and continues to do so.

# Notes

## Notes on Abbreviations

B.L.  British Library, Additional Manuscript
D.W.G.  *Devizes and Wiltshire Gazette*
K.W.  An Observer, *Kaleidoscope Wiltoniensis: or, A Literary And Moral View of the County of Wilts during the Contested Election for its Representation, in June 1818 . . .* (London 1818)
S.A.R.S.  Somerset Archive and Record Service, Taunton.
S.W.J.  *Salisbury and Winchester Journal*
V.C.H.  *The Victoria County History of the Counties of England: A History of Wiltshire* (London 1955-2002)
WANHM  *The Wiltshire Archaeological and Natural History Society Magazine*
W.A.S. (Libr.)  The Wiltshire Archaeological and Natural History Society (Library in Wiltshire Heritage Museum Long St. Devizes)
W.S.R.O.  Wiltshire and Swindon Record Office, Trowbridge
WT  Wiltshire Tracts in W.A.S.(Libr.)

## Introduction

[1] *D.W.G.*,1903, 1 July 1852.

## Chapter 1

[2] *V.C.H.Wilts.*, viii, ed. Elizabeth Crittall (1965), p.48.
[3] Richard Colt Hoare, *The Modern History of South Wiltshire* (London 1822-1843), iv, The Hundred of Dunworth, p.132.
[4] William Wake (1657-1737), Archbishop of Canterbury from 1716 until his death.
[5] *The Gentleman's Magazine and Historical Chronicle* (London 1749), vol. xix, pp.234-235.
[6] Martin Folkes (1690-1754). He succeeded Sir Hans Sloane as President of the Royal Society.
[7] Sir William Blackstone (1723-1780), legal writer and judge.
[8] Lambeth Palace Library, ms. VV1/4/5/19 contains the bill of costs and all the other papers quoted or referred to in the account of Thomas's appeal.
[9] L.S.Sutherland and L.G.Mitchell, eds., *The History of the University of Oxford* (Oxford 1986), v, The Eighteenth Century, p.234.
[10] W.S.R.O. 635/119.
[11] W.S.R.O. 413/323.
[12] W.S.R.O. 635/118.
[13] *V.C.H.Wilts.*, xi, ed. D.A.Crowley (1980), p.119.
[14] Richard Colt Hoare, *op.cit.* iii, The Hundred of Warminster, p.78. This pedigree further suggests that John Benet of Enford may have been descended from a John Benet who was sheriff of Wiltshire in 1267. On one occasion at least when Benett was fighting an election to secure a seat in Parliament, he did not hesitate to claim that he was descended from his 13th century namesake.
[15] John Burke and John Bernard Burke, *Genealogical and Heraldic Dictionary of the Landed Gentry of Great Britain and Ireland* (London 1846), i, p.308.
[16] W.S.R.O. 413/387, account books for 1771 and 1776/7.
[17] These ladies were almost certainly descendants of the original Pythouse family one branch of which lived at Hartgrove in the 18th century.

[18] W.A.S.(Libr.), Box 174, ms.1586,Diana Ladas, *History of Donhead*, pp.64-5. The Mr Bunbury referred to was probably Henry William Bunbury (1750-1811), an artist and caricaturist who executed many drawings especially burlesques.

[19] B.L. Add. 62081, photocopy in W.S.R.O. 413/378.

[20] Ibid.

[21] *S.W.J.*, 4282, 26 July 1819.

[22] *V.C.H. Wilts.*, xiii, p.72.

[23] W.S.R.O. 413/361, codicil to the will of Thomas Benet *[sic]* 1797.

[24] *V.C.H.Wilts.*, xiii, p.109.

[25] W.S.R.O. 413/361, will of Thomas Benet *[sic]* 1797.

[26] Ibid.

[27] Thomas Grove of Ferne (1759-1846) and his wife.

[28] Probably John Hungerford Penruddocke of Compton Chamberlayne (b.1770) and his wife.

[29] Ferne in Donhead was the seat of the Grove family, close friends of the Benetts.

[30] B.L. Add. 62081, photocopy in W.S.R.O. 413/378. It is noticeable that Benett's uncle spelt his name 'Benet' – a spelling commonly used by earlier members of the family and his father, Thomas, similarly made his will and signed it as 'Thomas Benet'.

[31] B.L. Add. 62081, photocopy in W.S.R.O. 413/378. This letter is inexplicably addressed to Thomas Benett at Pythouse and dated 12 Nov. 1794 but would appear to be Benett's response to his uncle's invitation to become godfather to his cousin George.

[32] *S.W.J.*, 2974, 8 June 1795.

## Chapter 2

[1] Beryl Hurley, *The Hair Powder Tax Wiltshire 1796 &1797* (Devizes 1997), p.39.

[2] W.S.R.O. 413/361.

[3] *S.W.J.*, 5126, 1 Feb. 1802.

[4] *London Gazette*, 14 Nov.1797 quoted in *S.W.J.*, 4000, 20 Nov. 1797.

[5] G.Neville Packett, *The County Lieutenancy in the United Kingdom (1547-1975) a brief history and "A" to "Z"*, pp.110-11. A copy in W.A.S.(Libr.).

[6] George Augustus Herbert, 11th Earl of Pembroke and 8th Earl of Montgomery (1759-1827).

[7] Sir John Methuen Poore of Rushall, 1st Baronet (d.1820).

[8] Michael Hicks Beach (1760-1830), married Henrietta Maria, daughter of William Beach of Netheravon.

[9] *S.W.J.*, 4076, 25 March 1799.

[10] W.S.R.O. 413/220.

[11] *S.W.J.*, 4141, 5 Aug.1816.

[12] W.S.R.O. 1214/144, redemption mentioned in 1809 Abstract of Title.

[13] *D.W.G.*, 456, 30 Sept.1824.

[14] *S.W.J.*, 2927, 14 July 1794.

[15] A.G.Harfield, *Captain William Wyndham of the Hindon Troop, Royal Wiltshire Yeomanry* (Army Historical Research), p.27. A copy in W.A.S.(Libr.).

[16] Arthur Bryant, *The Years of Endurance 1793-1802* (London 1952), p.128.

[17] A.G.Harfield, *op.cit.p.28*.

[18] *S.W.J.*, 3517, 18 July 1803.

[19] *Ibid.* 3510, 8 Aug 1803.

[20] *Ibid.* 3509, 1 Aug. 1803.

[21] Thomas Grove of Ferne (1758-1847).

[22] *S.W.J.*, 3509, 1 Aug. 1803.

[23] *Ibid.* 3510, 8 Aug. 1803.

[24] Henry Graham, *The Annals of the Yeomanry Cavalry of Wiltshire being a Complete History of the Prince of Wales' Own Royal Regiment from the time of its formation in 1794 to October 1884* (Liverpool 1886), p.50.

[25] *S.W.J.*, 5018, 13 Jan. 1800.

[26] John Hutchins, *History and Antiquities of the County of Dorset*, (Westminster 1863) Vol. II, p. 177.

[27] *The Clerical Guide and Ecclesiastical Directory*, (London 1836), p.8.

[28] John Hutchins, *op. cit.*

[29] Aylmer Bourke Lambert (1761-1842).

[30] For Lucy's descent from Archbishop Wake see John Hutchins, *The History and Antiquities of the County of Dorset*,

(Westminster 1870), Vol. IV, pp.66-7.

[31] Her arms on a lozenge on the portrait indicate that it was painted before her marriage.

[32] Sir Thomas Lawrence (1769-1830), portrait painter.

[33] B.L. Add. 62081, copy in W.S.R.O. 413/378.

[34] Richard Colt Hoare, *The Modern History of South Wiltshire*, iv, p.132.

[35] J.Mordaunt Crook, *The Greek Revival:Neo-Classical Attitudes in British Architecture 1760-1870* (London 1995), p.97.

[36] Simon Jenkins, *England's Thousand Best Houses* (London 2004), p.834.

[37] W.S.R.O. 413/330, statement in brief in Warner-v-Benett in Chancery.

[38] Howard Colvin, *A Biographical Dictionary of British Architects 1600-1840* (Yale 1995), p.121.

[39] Jeffry Wyatt (1766-1840), architect.

[40] William Wyndham of Dinton (1769-1841).

[41] W.A.S.(Libr.), 1982-1852, pencil drawing.

[42] Although it is probable that Benett acquired these chimney pieces, it has been suggested that they were in fact inserted by his grandson, Vere Fane-Benett-Stanford, see *Country Life*, 6 Jan. 2005, p.40.

[43] Nikolas Pevsner, *The Buildings of England: Wiltshire* (Harmondsworth 1963), p.319.

[44] William Beckford (1759-1844).

[45] *S.W.J.*, 5108, 28 Sept.1801, advertisement of proposed sale.

[46] For an account of this gift see Robert Moody, *John Benett of Pythouse His life and Ancestors at Norton Bavant and Pythouse c.1450-1852* (East Harptree 2003), pp.136-8.

[47] Joseph Wilton (1722-1803), one of the foundation members of the Royal Academy and its keeper from 1790 until his death.

[48] W.S.R.O. 401/2,Thomas Miles, *Some Account of the Parish of Stockton Wilts*, (ms. 1847), p.79.

[49] Marcus Binney in *Country Life*, 9 Feb. 1984, p.337.

[50] Howard Colvin, *A Biographical Dictionary of British Architects*, p.121.

[51] W.S.R.O. 413/363, will of Edmund Lambert.

[52] The Department of the Environment in its Listing Schedule dated 22 Jan. 1990 considers the chapel to be ' circa 1827. Built by John Bennet...for his wife nee Lucy Lambert of Boyton' and Colt Hoare published in 1829 states ' in the shrubbery near the house Mr Benett has recently erected an elegant little Chapel, copied from the style of part of Canterbury Cathedral: and underneath is a sepulchral vault'. However in the light of the terms of Edmund Lambert's will it seems more likely that the chapel was built soon after 1802 for his wife while living rather than as a mortuary chapel for Lucy who died in 1827.

[53] W.S.R.O. 413/366.

[54] Philip John Miles of Leigh Court (1773-1845). For an account of his life and of Leigh Court see William Evans, *Abbots Leigh – A Village History: Manor, Estate, Community* (Abbots Leigh 2002).

[55] Thomas Hopper (1776-1856). He obtained many commissions after making alterations to Carlton House for the Prince Regent from whom he declined an offer of knighthood.

[56] For a detailed discussion see William Evans, 'Leigh Court, Thomas Hopper and Pythouse', *Somerset Archaeology and Natural History* , cxli, 1998, pp.115-123.

[57] Nikolaus Pevsner, *The Buildings of England: North Somerset and Bristol* (Harmondsworth 1958), p.77.

[58] Henry Addington (1757-1844) politician and holder of many offices including Speaker of the House of Commons and Home Secretary.

[59] For an account of the Bear Club see John Hurley, *The History of the Bear Club: A Social Club, Charity and School 1756-1875* (Devizes 1995).

[60] Henry, 8th Baron Arundell of Wardour (1740-1803).

[61] Barry Williamson, 'The ruin of a Great

Wiltshire Estate: Wardour and the eighth Lord Arundell', *WANHM*, 94 (2001), p.65.

62 W.S.R.O.413/43, sale contract.

63 W.S.R.O. 413/136 & 330.

64 Ibid. sale particulars.

65 W.A.S.(Libr.), Box 19D ms.267.

66 W.S.R.O. 413/330.

67 *V.C.H. Wilts.*,xiii, p.146.

68 W.S.R.O. 413/330.

69 *V.C.H.Wilts.*, xiii, p.70.

70 *Ibid.* p.216.

71 *Ibid.* p. 209.

72 W.S.R.O. 413/143.

73 *V.C.H.Wilts.*,xi, p.124.

74 R.E.Sandell, ed., *Abstracts of Wiltshire Inclosure Awards and Agreements* Wiltshire Record Society (Devizes 1971), xxv, pp. 70-71.

75 *Ibid.* p.106.

76 W.S.R.O. 1214/144.

77 W.A.S. (Libr.), Boyton Manor Archives: Calendar and Transcripts, Box 252, ms.2214.

78 Desmond Hawkins, *The Grove Diaries: The Rise and Fall of an English Family 1809-1925* (Wimborne 1995), p.55.

79 *S.W.J.*, 3784, 21 Aug. 1809.

80 Desmond Hawkins, *op. cit.* pp.99-10.

81 *S.W.J.*, 3605, 26 Aug. 1805.

82 Henry Hunt (1773-1835), radical politician popularly known as 'Orator Hunt'.

83 John Astley of Everleigh (d.1818), High Sheriff in 1775.

84 John Belchem, *'Orator'Hunt: Henry Hunt and English Working-class Radicalism* (Oxford 1985),p.31.

85 Henry Hunt, *Memoirs of Henry Hunt,Esq written by Himself in His Majesty's Jail at Ilchester in the County of Somerset* (3 vols 1820) ii, pp.336-8.

86 *Ibid.* p.403.

87 *Ibid.* p.405.

88 W.A.S. (Libr.),Wilts Cuttings, vol.16, p.153.

89 *S.W.J.*, 3313, 29 Aug. 1803.

90 Henry Penruddock Wyndham (1736-1819); Richard Godolphin Long (1761-1835).

91 *D.W.G.*, 470, 6 Jan 1825.

92 Paul Methuen (1779-1849), later 1st Baron Methuen of Corsham.

93 William Pierce à Court of Heytesbury (1747-1817), created a baronet in 1795.

94 *S.W.J.*, 3936, 5 Oct. 1812.

95 *Ibid.* 3938, 19 Oct. 1812.

96 Robert Gourlay (1778-1863), pamphleteer and proponent of reform.

97 Edward Adolphus Seymour, 11th Duke of Somerset (1775-1855).

98 *S.W.J.*, 3879, 17 June 1811.

99 *Ibid.* 5015, 23 Dec. 1799.

100 Thomas Davis, *General View of the Agriculture of Wiltshire drawn up for the consideration of the Board of Agriculture and Internal Improvement* (London 1813), p.246.

101 W.S.R.O. 574/318, WSEA Journal of Transactions ii , resolution to be put before the General Meeting, 1849.

102 *S.W.J.*, 3956, 22 Feb.1813.

103 Thomas Thynne, 2nd Marquis of Bath (1765-1837).

104 Charles Bruce, 2nd Earl of Ailesbury and 1st Marquis of Ailesbury (1773-1856).

105 Henry Petty-Fitzmaurice, 3rd Marquis of Lansdowne (1780-1863), later Chancellor of the Exchequer and President of the Council.

106 James Everard, 9th Baron Arundell of Wardour (1763-1817).

107 Richard Colt Hoare, 2nd Baronet (1758-1838), historian of Wiltshire.

108 *S.W.J.*, 3973, 28 June 1813.

109 *Ibid.* 3960, 22 Mar.1813.

110 Bath Record Office, The Royal Bath and West of England Society archive viii, p.112.

111 *S.W.J.*, 4025, 16 May 1814.

112 The Royal Bath and West of England Society archive, op.cit. p.128.

113 *S.W.J.*, 4056, 19 Dec.1814. It is noticeable that the newspaper incorrectly spelt Benett's surname – a mistake rarely if ever made by it in the future.

114 John Benett, *An Essay on the Commutation of Tithes to which was adjudged the Bedfordian Gold Medal by the Bath and*

West of England Society for the Encouragement of Agriculture, &c at their Annual Meeting, December 13, 1814 (Bath 1814).

[115] William Coxe (1747-1828).

[116] William Coxe, *Letter to John Benett, Esq. of Pyt-house Wilts, on his essay relative to the Commutation of tithes to which was adjudged the Bedfordian Gold Medal by the Bath and West of England Society for the Encouragement of Agriculture, &c. at their Annual Meeting, December 13, 1814* (Salisbury 1814), p.2. A second edition was published in 1815.

[117] Bath Record Office, The Royal Bath and West of England Society archive viii, p.136.

[118] John Benett, *Reply to the Letter of the Revd. William Coxe, Archdeacon of Wilts, on the subject of Commutation of Tithes; in which will be found an Enquiry into the origin and nature of tithes also The Prize Essay, which gave Rise to this Correspondence* (Salisbury 1815).

[119] William Coxe, *Three additional letters to J.Benett,Esq. on the Commutation of Tithe in answer to his Reply* (Salisbury 1815).

[120] John Benett, *Replies to the Three Additional Letters of the Rev.William Coxe...on the subject of commutation of tithe* (London 1816).

[121] There is a copy of volume 6 of *The Pamphleteer* in The London Library to whom the author is indebted for drawing his attention to it.

[122] *S.W.J.*, 4096, 25 Sept. 1815.

[123] *D.W.G.*, 312, 27 Dec.1821.

[124] Bath Record Office, The Royal Bath and West of England Society archive iv, p.35.

[125] William Coxe, *Three Additional Letters to John Benett Esq on the Commutation of Tithe, op.cit.* p.90.

[126] James Waylen (1810-1894).

[127] Charles Lucas (1769-1854), writer of novels and religious poems, curate at Avebury until 1816 and thereafter in Devizes until his death,

[128] [J.Waylen], *A History Military and Municipal of the Ancient Borough of The Devizes; and, subordinately, of the entire*

Hundred of Potterne and Cannings in which it is included (London 1859), p.516.

[129] Steven Hobbs, ed., *Wiltshire Glebe Terriers 1588-1827*, Wiltshire Record Society lvi (Trowbridge 2003), p. 432.

[130] *S.W.J.*, 4141, 5 Aug.1816.

[131] John Britton (1771-1857), antiquary and topographer.

[132] John Britton, *A Topographical and Historical Description of the county of Wilts...* (London 1814), p.251.

[133] William Lisle Bowles (1762-1850), divine, poet and antiquary.

[134] John Murray (1778-1843), publisher of the most important works of his day. He was latter to be Benett's neighbour in Albermarle Street.

[135] Garland Greever, *A Wiltshire Parson and his friends: the correspondence of William Lisle Bowles together with four hitherto unidentified reviews by Coleridge* (London 1926), pp.146-147.

[136] Dugaid Stewart (1753-1828), philosopher.

[137] Garland Greever, *op.cit.* p.148.

[138] W.S.R.O. 413/390.

[139] Anthony Wood, *Nineteenth Century Britain 1815-1914* (Harlow 1982), p.62.

[140] *Report from the Select Committee on Petitions relating to the Corn Laws of this Kingdom together with the Minutes of Evidence and an Appendix of Accounts* (London 1814), pp.59-71.

[141] *S.W.J.*, 4282, 26 July 1819.

[142] *V.C.H.Wilts.*, v, eds., R.B.Pugh and Elizabeth Crittall (1957), p.297.

[143] *S.W.J.*,4058, 2 Jan 1815.

[144] Henry Hunt, *Memoirs of Henry Hunt Esq.*, ii, p.229.

[145] *Ibid.* p.231.

[146] Unfortunately for Benett, Hunt also had an estate in Enford and so could speak with some personal knowledge.

[147] Henry Hunt, *Memoirs of Henry Hunt Esq.*,p.233.

[148] Desmond Hawkins, *The Grove Diaries*, p.126.

[149] *The Times*, 9416, 12 Jan.1815.

[150] Henry Hunt, *Corn Laws. The Evidence of J.Benett, of Pythouse, given before the*

Committee of the House of Lords, on the Corn Bill. An Impartial Report of the meeting of Landholders at Warminster. Mr.Benett's Letter in answer to that Report, Mr.Bleeck's Letter in reply, etc. (Salisbury 1815).

[151] *S.W.J.*, 4061, 23 Jan.1815.

[152] *S.W.J.*,4065, 20 Feb.1815.

[153] Henry Hunt, *The Memoirs of Henry Hunt Esq.*, p.353.

[154] *The Courier*, 6980, 21 Jan. 1815.

[155] *S.W.J.*, 4063, 6 Feb 1815.

[156] *Ibid.* 4059, 9 Jan. 1815.

[157] Philip Yorke, 3rd Earl of Hardwicke (1757-1843).

[158] B.L. Add. 35700, ff.332.

[159] *Ibid.* ff.342.

[160] W.A.S. (Libr.), Box 19D, ms.267.

[161] *Calendar of Prisoners in the County Gaol of Fisherton-Anger, and Devizes and Marlborough Bridewells* in W.A.S.(Libr.).

[162] *S.W.J.*, 4114, 29 Jan.1816.

[163] Material of course wool.

[164] *SW.J.*, 4117, 19 Feb. 1816.

[165] *Ibid.* 4121, 18 March 1816.

[166] Copy of the printed copy of the resolutions with Benett's hastily written note in W.A.S.(Libr.), WT 176.

[167] W.A.S.(Libr.), Box 19D ms 267.

[168] *S.W.J.*, 4153, 28 Oct.1816.

[169] *Ibid.* 4161, 23 Dec.1816.

[170] *Simpson's Salisbury Gazette*, 103, 18 Dec.1817.

[171] John Hungerford Penruddocke (1770-1841), later M.P.for Wilton.

[172] *S.W.J.*, 4172, 17 March 1817.

[173] *Ibid.* 4173, 24 March 1817.

[174] The man who was found guilty and hanged for the assassination attempt.

[175] *S.W.J.*, 4173, 24 March 1817.

[176] Henry Hunt, *The Memoirs of Henry Hunt Esq.*, iii, pp.464-70.

## Chapter 3

[1] William Pole-Tylney-Long-Wellesley (1788-1857), later 4th Earl of Mornington.

[2] *K.W.*, pp.311-312.

[3] W.A.S.(Libr.),Wilts Cuttings, vol.16, p.169.

[4] *S.W.J.*, 4232, 2 March 1818.

[5] *K.W.*, p.4.

[6] William Pleydell-Bouverie, Lord Folkestone (1779-1869), later 3rd Earl of Radnor.

[7] Berkshire Record Office. Radnor MSS, D/EPB/028/129a.

[8] John Pern Tinney (1777-1832), writer and lawyer.

[9] Berkshire Record Office, ibid. 133.

[10] Peter Henry Lovell of Cole Park (d.1841).

[11] W.S.R.O. 161/112.

[12] S.A.R.S., DD/WY Box 90.

[13] Ibid.

[14] W.A.S. (Libr.), Box 174, mss 1595.

[15] Susan (1767-1841), wife of the 5th Duke of Marlborough; George, Lord Blandford (1793-1857), later 6th Duke of Marlborough.

[16] *S.W.J.*, 4235, 23 March 1818.

[17] *Ibid.* 4236, 30 March 1818.

[18] *Ibid.* 4237, 6 Apr. 1818.

[19] Fulwar Craven (1782-1860).

[20] *S.W.J.*, 4237, 6 Apr. 1818.

[21] Thomas Calley of Burderop Park (1780-1836).

[22] William Bird Brodie, one of the Members of Parliament for Salisbury 1832-43 and for a time proprietor of the *Salisbury and Winchester Journal*.

[23] Wadham Wyndham of Salisbury (d.1843).

[24] Edward Duke of Lake (1779-1852).

[25] S.A.R.S., DD/WY Box 90.

[26] S.A.R.S., op.cit.

[27] Jacob, 2nd Earl of Radnor (1750-1828).

[28] James Everard, 10th Lord Arundell of Wardour (1785-1834)

[29] W.S.R.O.413/483.

[30] Ibid.

[31] S.A.R.S., op.cit.

[32] Francis Almeric Spencer, 1st Baron Churchill (1779-1845), 3rd son of the 4th Duke of Marlborough.

[33] S.A.R.S., DD/WY Box 90.

[34] Ibid.

[35] *S.W.J.*,4233, 9 Mar.1818.

[36] *Simpson's Salisbury Gazette*, 116, 19 Mar. 1818.

[37] *S.W.J.*, 4236, 30 Mar.1818.

38 S.A.R.S., DD/WY Box 90.

39 All these letters or contemporary copies of a few of them have survived and form part of the archive of the Wyndham family of Orchard Wyndham and Dinton. They are all bound together in one bundle and are catalogued under reference DD/WY Box 90.

40 S.A.R.S., op.cit.

41 Ibid.

42 Ibid.

43 Ibid.

44 K.W., p.26.

45 Ibid. p.34.

46 S.A.R.S., DD/WY 90.

47 S.W.J., 4237, 4 May 1818.

48 W.A.S.(Libr.), Box 138A.

49 S.W.J., 4237, 4 May 1818.

50 Ibid. 4238, 11 May 1818.

51 Ibid.

52 Ibid.4239, 18 May 1818.

53 K.W., p.131.

54 Ibid. p. 214.

55 S.W.J., 4241, 1 June 1818.

56 Ibid. 4242, 8 June 1818.

57 Alexander Powell of Hurdcott House (1782-1847).

58 K.W., p.26.

59 Ibid. p.234.

60 Ibid. p.235.

61 Ibid. p.320.

62 James Harris, 1st Earl of Malmesbury (1746-1820), diplomat.

63 Malmesbury mss, Malmesbury to Fitzharris, 26 Feb.1818.

64 K.W., p.126.

65 Ibid. p.157.

66 Ibid. p. 264.

67 S.W.J., 4242, 8 June 1818.

68 Ibid. 4243, 15 June 1818.

69 Ibid. 4244, 22 June 1818.

70 S.A.R.S., DD/WY Box 90.

71 Letter belonging to Eunice and Ron Shanahan see www.victorianweb.org/history/letters/crowdy2.html.

72 S.W.J., 4243, 15 June 1818.

73 K.W., p.286.

74 Berkshire Record Office, Radnor MSS, D/EPB/028/151.

75 W.S.R.O. 113/12.

76 Wiltshire Election Papers Devizes 1818-1868 in W.A.S.(Libr.).

77 There is no indication in the correspondence as to the nature of this list but it was probably a list of freeholders.

78 S.A.R.S., DA/WY Box 90.

79 W.S.R.O. 113/16

80 W.S.R.O. 113/15

81 V.C.H.Wilts., v, p.204.

82 S.W.J., 4244, 22 June 1818.

83 Wiltshire Election Papers Devizes 1818-1868, op.cit.

84 Ibid.

85 Ibid.

86 S.A.R.S., DA/WY Box 90.

87 Ibid.

88 Thomas Henry Hele Phipps of Leighton House (1770-1847).

89 S.A.R.S., DA/WY Box 90.

90 K.W.,pp.313-316.

91 Ibid. p.313.

92 Ibid. p.316.

93 John Peniston (c.1778-1848), surveyor and architect of Salisbury.

94 S.W.J., 4244, 22 June 1818.

95 No doubt an illusion to Lord Arundell of Wardour.

96 K.W., p.331.

97 George Purefoy Jervoise of Herriard Park, Hants (1770-1847), who was one of the Members of Parliament for Salisbury 1812-1818.

98 S.A.R.S., DA/WY Box 90.

99 Ibid.

100 S.W.J., 4244, 22 June 1818..

101 Ibid.

102 K.W., pp. 399-400.

103 Ibid. pp.401-2.

104 Ibid. pp. 402-3.

105 W.A.S.(Libr.), Wilts Cuttings, vol. 3, p.78.

106 Ibid.

107 John Gale Everett (c.1742-1825), cloth manufacturer and banker of Heytesbury. His brother, Thomas, had been M.P. for Ludgershall. For an account of John Everett's unusual will, see Kenneth Rogers, Wiltshire and Somerset Woollen

*Mills* (Edington 1976), pp.246-7.

[108] Benett was being a little economical with the truth in making this assertion. In 1718, his grandfather, Thomas Benett, was appointed one of the Registrars and Keepers of the Records and Muniments of the Prerogative Court of Canterbury as a result of the influence of his father-in-law William Wake, Archbishop of Canterbury who, at the same time, arranged for two other sons-in-law to be appointed joint registrars. These posts were certainly profitable sinecures.

[109] Receipts signed by all the special constables in W.A.S.(Libr.), WT. 17, p.121.

[110] *S.W.J.*, 4249, 27 July 1818.

[111] S.A.R.S., DA/WY Box 90.

[112] *D.W.G.*, 1361, 10 Sept.1842.

[113] *S.W.J.*,4245, 29 June 1818.

[114] *Ibid.*

[115] Desmond Hawkins, *The Grove Diaries*, p.137-8.

[116] *S.W.J.*, 4247, 13 July 1818.

[117] *Ibid.*

[118] John Scott, 1st Earl of Eldon (1751-1838).

[119] *D.W.G.*, 602, 26 July 1827.

[120] *S.W.J.*, 4250, 3 Aug.1818.

[121] Gideon Algernon Mantell (1790-1852), geologist and prolific writer.

[122] Alexander Turnbull Library, Wellington, New Zealand, MS Papers 0083, Mantell Papers.

[123] *S.W.J.*,4247,13 July 1818 and *Morning Chronicle*, 15360, 24 July 1818.

[124] *D.W.G.*, 648, 12 June 1828.

[125] *S.W.J.*, 4248, 20 July 1818.

[126] So great was the public interest in the election that this publication was advertised in *The Times*, 10464, 17 Sept 1818.

[127] (Devizes 1818). There is a copy of this pamphlet in W.A.S.(Libr.), WT 50. There are contemporary handwritten annotations on this copy declaring that several of the statements contained in it are 'a lie'.

[128] There is a copy of these letters in W.A.S.(Libr.), WT 30.

[129] Ambrose Goddard (d.1815), M.P. for Wilts 1772-1806.

[130] Andrew Bell (1753-1832) originator of the Madras system of education.

[131] *S.W.J.*, 4247, 13 July 1818.

[132] *S.W.J.*, 4249, 27 July 1818.

[133] Berkshire Record Office, Radnor MSS, D/EPB/028/169.

[134] *S.W.J.*, 4249, 27 July 1818.

[135] *Ibid.*

[136] *Ibid.* 4251 *[sic]*, 17 Aug.1818.

[137] *Ibid.* 4251 *[sic]*, 10 Aug 1818.

[138] *Ibid.* 4251, 17 Aug 1818.

[139] Henry King (c.1775-1844), occupied Manor Farm in Chilmark and by c.1825 was in possession of 4000 acres in various parishes and had flocks of 6500 Southdowns, see *V.C.H.Wilts.*, xiii, p.120.

[140] *S.W.J.*, 4252 *[sic]*, 31 Aug 1818.

[141] Robert Benson and Henry Hatcher, *Old and New Sarum or Salisbury* (London 1843), p.665-6.

[142] Thomas Moore (1779-1852), poet and author of *Believe me, If All Those Endearing Young Charms*.

[143] Wilfred S. Dowden ,ed., *The Journal of Thomas Moore* (Newark 1983), i, pp.83-4.

[144] Charles Lewis Phipps of Dilton Court (b.1782).

[145] Wilfred S.Dowden, *op.cit.* p.69.

[146] *The Dictionary of National Biography* (Oxford 1922), xiii, p.832.

[147] *Ibid.*p.831.

[148] *S.W.J.*, 4264, 15 March 1819.

[149] *Ibid.* 4253 *[sic]*, 21 Dec 1818.

[150] *Ibid.* 4253 *[sic]*, 14 Dec 1818.

[151] Thomas William Coke, Earl of Leicester (1752-1842).

[152] *S.W.J.*, 4280, 12 July 1819.

## Chapter 4

[1] *S.W.J.*, 4287, 30. Aug. 1819.

[2] John Dugdale Astley of Everleigh (1778-1842), later 1st Baronet.

[3] Desmond Hawkins, *The Grove Diaries*, p.141.

[4] Alexander Turnbull Library, Wellington New Zealand, MS Papers 0083, Mantell Papers.

5 Hampshire Record Office, 44M69/F10/ 53/1.

6 *V.C.H.Wilts.*, v, p.207.

7 *S.W.J.*, 4280, 12 July 1819.

8 *Ibid.*

9 John Fuller (1762-1839).

10 *S.W.J.*, 4281, 19 July 1819.

11 Perhaps John Bleek (c.1772-1846), a woolbroker of Warminster.

12 Berkshire Record Office, Radnor MSS, D/EPB/028/182. A copy of the printed declaration was sent with the letter and can be seen with it.

13 *S.W.J.*,4281, 19 July 1819.

14 W.S.Dowden, *The Journal of Thomas Moore*, Vol.1, p.214.

15 *The Morning Chronicle*, 15669, 20 July 1819.

16 One of these unusually small handbills is pasted in the front of the copy of volume 1 of *Memoirs of Henry Hunt, Esq.* in W.A.S.(Libr.).

17 W.C.Dowden, *The Journal of Thomas Moore*, Vol. 1, p, 200.

18 *S.W.J.*,4282, 26 July 1819.

19 *D.W.G.*, 192, 2 Sept.1819, speech by Mr Saunders of Bradford at the Venison Dinner.

20 *S.W.J.*, 4282, 26 July 1819.

21 *Ibid.*

22 W.A.S.(Libr.),Wilts. Cuttings vol. 1, p.334.

23 John Bleek (c.1772-1846), woolbroker of Warminster.

24 *S.W.J.*, 4288, 13 Sept.1819.

25 *Ibid.* 4289, 20 Sept.1819.

26 *K.W.*, p.211.

27 *S.W.J.*, 4289, 20 Sept. 1819.

28 *Ibid.* 4281, 19 July 1819. Further reports suggest that Bricker's statement under oath was entirely false.

29 *Ibid.* 4282, 26 July 1819.

30 W.C.Dowden, *The Journal of Thomas Moore.*, *op.cit.* p.201.

31 *V.C.H.Wilts.*, v, p.208.

32 A.M.Broadley and Walter Jerrold, *The Romance of an Elderly Poet: A hitherto unknown chapter in the life of George Crabbe revealed by his ten years' correspondence with Elizabeth Charter 1815-* 1825 (London 1913), pp.237-238.

33 *D.W.G.*, 186, 22 July 1819.

34 *S.W.J.*, 4283, 2 Aug 1819.

35 *Ibid.* 4284, 9 Aug 1819.

36 *Ibid.*

37 *The Morning Chronicle*, 25685, 7 Aug. 1819.

38 *D.W.G.*, 189, 12 Aug.1819.

39 *Ibid.* The British Library does not have a copy of this book, nor, so far as is known, any other institution and so it is likely that no copy has survived.

40 *S.W.J.*, 4287, 30 Aug 1819.

41 *D.W.G.*, 192, 2 Sept. 1819.

42 W.A.S.(Libr.), Wilts Cuttings, vol. 1, p.345.

43 *S.W.J.*, 4287 *[sic]*, 6 Sept.1819.

44 [J.Waylen], *op.cit.* p.434.

45 W.A.S.(Libr.), Cunnington Cuttings, vol. 2, p.382.

46 *Wiltshire Election Papers Devizes 1818-1868* in W.A.S.(Libr.).

47 *D.W.G.*, 192, 2 Sept.1819.

48 *Ibid.* 193, 9 Sept.1819.

49 *S.W.J.*,4290, 27 Sept.1819.

50 *Ibid.* 4290, *[sic]*, 4 Oct.1819.

51 W.A.S.(Libr.), Ms. Box 19D ms.267.

52 At this time, all Members of Parliament were entitled to send letters free of charge if franked (i.e. signed by the Member) and so it is evident that Etheldred wished to use her brother's new privilege to avoid the cost of her letter to Mantell falling on him.

53 Alexander Turnbull Library, MS Papers 0083, Mantell Papers.

54 *D.W.G.*, 200, 28 Oct. 1819.

55 A photograph of the sampler and an example of Gilmour's production are in W.A.S.(Libr.).

56 W.A.S.(Libr.), Wilts Cuttings, vol. 1, p.340.

57 Elizabeth Vassall Fox, Lady Holland (1770-1845), wife of Henry Fox, 3rd Baron Holland.

58 R.G.Thorne, *The History of Parliament – The House of Commons,*1790-1820, p.413.

59 *Ibid.*

60 *S.W.J.*, 4285, 16 Aug. 1819.

61 W.A.S.(Libr.), Wilts Cuttings, vol. 26, p.117.

[62] *S.W.J.*, 4436, 29 July 1822.
[63] W.S.R.O. 451/58.
[64] John Charles Spencer, Viscount Althorp, later 3rd Earl Spencer (1782-1845).
[65] *S.W.J.*, 4299, 6 Dec. 1819.
[66] Desmond Hawkins, *The Grove Diaries*, p.144.
[67] *S.W.J.*,4309, 14 Feb.1820.
[68] *Morning Chronicle*, 15849, 15 Feb. 1820.
[69] W.S.R.O., 413/485.
[70] Henry Wansey (1774-1855), clothier of Warminster and a nephew of Henry Wansey, the major contributor to that part of Colt Hoare's *The Modern History of South Wiltshire* dealing with the hundred of Warminster.
[71] W.S.R.O. 413/485.
[72] *S.W.J.*,4311, 28 Feb.1820.
[73] *Ibid.* 4312, 6 Mar. 1820.
[74] Henry Fox, 3rd Baron Holland (1773-1840) – prominent Whig politician.
[75] W.S.R.O. 413/485.
[76] Hampshire Record Office, 44M69/F10/54/2.
[77] R.G.Thorne, *The History of Parliament*, p.173.
[78] Letter belonging to Eunice and Ron Shanahan, see www.victorianweb.org/history/letters/crowdy.html
[79] *D.W.G.*, 218, 2 March 1820.
[80] W.A.S. (Libr.), Wilts Cuttings, vol. 13, p.222.
[81] A machine for dressing woollen cloth.
[82] W.A.S.(Libr.), Wilts Cuttings, vol. 1, p.346.
[83] *S.W.J.*, 4313, 13 March 1820.
[84] Tim Couzens, *Hand of Fate: The History of the Longs, Wellesleys and the Draycot Estate in Wiltshire* (Bradford on Avon 2001), p.95
[85] *D.W.G.*, 650, 26 June 1828.
[86] *The Dictionary of National Biography* (Oxford 1922), vol.xx, p.1136.
[87] Ambrose Goddard of Swindon (1779-1854).
[88] Rowland Hill (1744-1833), preacher. Attached to Surrey Chapel were 13 Sunday schools with over 3000 children on their rolls.
[89] W.A.S.(Libr.), Wilts Cuttings, vol. 13, p.121.
[90] *S.W.J.*, 4313, 13 March 1820.
[91] Abraham Ludlow of Heywood House (d.1822).
[92] Desmond Hawkins, *The Grove Diaries*, p.143.
[93] *S.W.J.*, 4314, 20 Mar.1820.
[94] Hampshire Record Office, Malmesbury mss, 9M73/G2459. Malmesbury to FitzHarris, 16 Mar.1820.
[95] *D.W.G.*, 222, 30 March 1820.
[96] *Ibid.* 226, 27 Apr.1820.
[97] William Pleydell-Bouverie, 3rd Earl of Radnor (1779-1869), Whig politician, a friend of William Cobbett and never a supporter of Benêtt.
[98] *D.W.G.*,860, 5 July 1832.

## Chapter 5

[1] *The Gentleman's Magazine* (London 1852), vol. xxxviii, p.637.
[2] *D.W.G.*, 374, 27 Feb.1823.
[3] *V.C.H.Wilts.*, xiii. p.243.
[4] W.S.R.O. 451/59.
[5] *K.W.*, p.251.
[6] *Ibid.* p.285.
[7] W.S.R.O. 413/329, note signed by Benett's sister Etheldred.
[8] *D.W.G.*, 239, 27 July 1820.
[9] *Ibid.* 242, 17 Aug.1820.
[10] *S.W.J.*, 4315, 27 March 1820.
[11] *Ibid.* 4357, 22 Jan.1821.
[12] *Ibid.* 4358, 29 Jan 1821.
[13] *D.W.G.*, 226, 27 Apr.1820.
[14] *Hansard*, New Series, vol. 1 (1820) col.105.
[15] *Ibid.* cols.235-6.
[16] Henry Hunt, *To the Radical Reformers, Male and Female, of England, Ireland, and Scotland*, 10 Dec.1820 bound up in Addresses of H.Hunt Esq. i, pp.10-11, in W.A.S.(Libr.).
[17] *D.W.G.*, 242, 17 Aug.1820.
[18] *Ibid.* 346, 15 Aug.1822.
[19] *S.W.J.*, 4062, 30 Jan. 1815.
[20] *Ibid.* 4360, 12 Feb. 1821.
[21] *D.W.G.*, 277, 19 Apr.1821.
[22] Perhaps the widow of Sir Stephen Richard Glynne, 8th Baronet.

[23] William, Lord Folkestone (1779-1869) later 3rd Earl of Radnor.

[24] William Thomas Nugent, Baron Nugent of Riverston (1773-1851).

[25] D.W.G., 273, 22 Mar.1821.

[26] S.W.J., 4365, 19 Mar 1821.

[27] Ibid. 4368, 9 Apr. 1821.

[28] James Brownlow William Cecil (1791-1868), later 2nd Marquis of Salisbury.

[29] Hansard., New Series, vol. V (1821) cols. 18 & 46.

[30] Ibid. cols. 445-6.

[31] S.W.J., 4371, 30 Apr.1821.

[32] S.W.J., 4376, 4 June 1821.

[33] D.W.G., 279, 3 May 1821.

[34] Augustus Frederick, Duke of Sussex (1773-1843)

[35] D.W.G., 289,12 July 1821.

[36] V.C.H.Wilts.,iv, ed. Elizabeth Crittall (1959), p.70.

[37] Joseph Hume (1777-1855), radical politician.

[38] D.W.G.,290, 10 July 1821.

[39] Ibid. 229, 18 May 1820.

[40] Bernard Edward Howard, 12th Duke of Norfolk (1765-1842).

[41] D.W.G., 281, 17 May 1821.

[42] S.W.J., 4005, 20 Dec.1813.

[43] Dowden, The Journal of Thomas Moore, ii, p.500.

[44] A Catalogue of the Valuable Contents of the Mansion (Salisbury 1957), p.43.

[45] Sir John Andrew Stevenson (1760?-1833), remembered for his symphonies and accompaniments to Moore's works.

[46] WANHM, 24 (1889), p.254.

[47] S.W.J., 4389, 3 Sept.1821.

[48] Ibid. 4302, 24 Sept.1821.

[49] For an account of this dinner see Robert Moody, 'James Bennett of Salisbury (1797-1859): Jeweller and Newspaper Proprietor', WANHM, 94 (2001), pp.183-4.

[50] William Bennett (1596-1661). For an account of the original Bennett family of Pythouse see Robert Moody, John Benett of Pythouse:His life and ancestors at Norton Bavant and Pythouse c.1450-1852 (East Harptree 2003), pp.68-124.

[51] Benett was James Bennett's 5th cousin once removed. John Fane-Benett-Stanford mentions this entry in his great-grandfather's diary (now presumed lost or destroyed) in a letter written in 1943 to C.A.S.Bennett of Los Angeles.

[52] S.W.J., 4412, 11 Feb.1822.

[53] Hansard, New Series, vol. VI (1822) cols. 472-477.

[54] Ibid. vol. VII (1822) col. 788.

[55] S.W.J., 4420, 8 Apr.1822.

[56] Charles William Stewart, 3rd Marquis of Londonderry (1778-1854).

[57] D.W.G., 327, 11 Apr.1822.

[58] John Russell, 1st Earl Russell (1792-1878), statesman.

[59] D.W.G., 330, 2 May 1822.

[60] S.W.J., 4425, 13 May 1822.

[61] D.W.G., 331, 9 May 1822.

[62] S.W.J., 4428, 3 June 1822.

[63] Ibid. 4429, 10 June 1822.

[64] George Canning (1770-1827), statesman.

[65] Henry Hunt, To the Radical Reformers, Male and Female,23 Jan.1821, p.9.

[66] Ibid.12 Jan.1822, p.12.

[67] D.W.G., 320, 21 Feb.1822.

[68] Henry Hunt, op.cit. 8 Apr.1822. ii, p.19.

[69] Probably Sir Thomas Baring 2nd Baronet (1772-1848), M.P. for Wycombe and Hampshire.

[70] Ibid. 14 July 1822, p.7.

[71] Henry Hoare (1784-1836).

[72] D.W.G.,342, 25 July 1822.

[73] Ibid. 349, 5 Sept. 1822.

[74] Frederick Hastings Goldney, A History of Freemasonry in Wiltshire etc...(1880), p. 4.

[75] S.W.J., 4440, 2 Sept.1822.

[76] Mary Ann, Lady Arundell (d.1845).

[77] For a detailed account of the parlous state of the finances of the family in the 18th and 19th century see Barry Williamson, 'The Ruin of a Great Wiltshire Estate: Wardour and the Eighth Lord Arundell', WANHM, 94 (2001), pp.57-67.

[78] Richard Temple Nugent Brydges Chandos, 1st Duke of Buckingham (1776-1839).

[79] James Paine (1725-1789), architect.

[80] S.W.J., 4443, 23 Sept 1822.

[81] John Farquhar (1751-1826), millionaire

who had made a fortune as a government contractor in Bengal.

82 John Constable (1776-1837), landscape painter.

83 *S.W.J.*,4493, 29 Sept. 1823.

84 *Ibid.* 4495, 20 Oct.1823.

85 Perhaps Richard Heber (1773-1833), M.P. for Oxford in 1821 and in 1824 one of the founders of the Athenaeum Club.

86 Sir Alexander Charles Mallet, 2nd Baronet (1800-1886).

87 Dowden, *The Journal of Thomas Moore*, ii, pp.684-6.

88 *S.W.J.*, 4410, 28 Jan 1822.

89 *Ibid.*

90 *Ibid.* 4457, 13 Jan.1823.

91 Dowden, *The Journal of Thomas Moore*, p.611.

92 *S.W.J.*, 4463, 3 March 1823.

93 *Hansard*, New Series, vol. VIII (1823) cols.233-4.

94 *S.W.J.*, 4476, 2 June 1823.

95 *D.W.G.*, 375, 6 Mar. 1823.

96 *Hansard*, New Series, vol. VIII(1823) col. 520.

97 *Ibid.* vol. IX (1823) col. 81.

98 W.S.R.O. 413/67, contract for sale.

99 *D.W.G.*, 399, 9 Oct.1823.

100 *The Clerical Guide and Ecclesiastical Directory* (London 1836), p.17. .

101 *V.C.H.Wilts*, xiii, pp.103-104. The purchaser was Robert Grosvenor, 1st Marquis of Westminster (1767-1845).

102 W.S.R.O. 413/221.

103 Charles, 6th Baron Clifford of Chudleigh (1759-1831), married to Eleanor, youngest daughter of Henry, 8th Lord Arundell of Wardour.

104 W.S.R.O.2667/20/55. Further correspondence between lawyers in 1821 and 1822 suggests that there was to be another conveyance of the advowson that was never completed, see W.S.R.O. 2667/20/53.

105 John Francis, 12th Lord Arundell of Wardour (1831-1906).

106 *V.C.H. Wilts.*, xiii, p.240.

107 *Ibid.* p.216.

108 Dowden, *The Journal of Thomas Moore*, iii, p.812. Miss Houlton was probably one of the daughters of John Houlton of Farley Castle and Grittleton House.

109 Robert Benson and Henry Hathcher, *Old and New Sarum or Salisbury* (London 1843), p.584.

110 *S.W.J.*, 4486, 11 Aug.1823.

111 W.A.S.(Libr.), Box 19D ms 265.

112 W.A.S.(Libr.), Britton ms. Benett to Britton, 12 Sept 1823.

113 *S.W.J.*, 4538, 23 Aug.1824.

114 *Ibid.* 5585, 25 Aug.1828.

115 W.S.R.O. 413/361.

116 *D.W.G.*, 452, 2 Sept.1824.

117 *Hansard* New Series, vol.. X (1824) cols.919-20.

118 *D.W.G.*, 430, 1 Apr.1824.

119 James de Carle Sowerby (1787-1871), artist and geologist.

120 University of Bristol, Special Collections, Eyles Collection- Sowerby Archive material.

121 *D.W.G.*, 446, 22 July 1824.

122 William Wellesley, (1762-1845), created Baron Maryborough in 1821 and later 3rd Earl of Mornington.

123 *D.W.G.*, 443, 1 July 1824.

124 This was built in 1776 to Henry Holland's design.

125 William Philip Molyneux, 2nd Earl of Sefton (1772-1838).

126 The author is indebted to the Secretary of Brooks's Club for this information.

127 James Lees-Milne, *A History of Brooks's*.

128 Sir Robert Peel (1788-1850), statesman.

129 The author is indebted to Sarah Dodgson of the Athenaeum Club for kindly supplying a list of the first members of the club.

130 Dowden, *The Journal of Thomas Moore*, ii, p.761.

131 For an account of Henry Shorto's life see *WANHM* 83 (1990), pp.170-189.

132 Thomas Spring Rice (1790-1866), M.P. for Limerick in the Whig interest later Chancellor of the Exchequer and 1st Baron Monteagle.

133 W.S.R.O. 451/58.

134 *Ibid.*

[135] *D.W.G.*,456, 30 Sept. 1824.

[136] *Ibid.* 467, 16 Dec.1824.

[137] *Ibid.* 519, 22 Dec.1825.

[138] *S.W.J.*, 5398, 10 Jan.1825.

[139] *D.W.G.*, 470, 6 Jan.1825.

[140] *S.W.J.*, 5411, 11 Apr.1825.

[141] *Ibid.* 5410, 4 Apr. 1825.

[142] Robert Gourlay (1778-1865), radical agriculturalist.

[143] *D.W.G.*, 480, 24 March 1825.

[144] Henry Peter Brougham (1778-1868), later Baron Brougham and Vaux and Lord Chancellor.

[145] *D.W.G.*,483, 14 Apr.1825.

[146] *S.W.J.*,5415, 9 May 1825.

[147] *Hansard* New Series, vol. XIII (1825) col. 572.

[148] Ernest Augustus, Duke of Cumberland (1771-1851).

[149] *Hansard, op.cit.* col. 1048.

[150] *D.W.G.*, 491, 9 June 1825.

[151] *Ibid.* 489, 26 May 1825.

[152] Daniel O'Connell (1775-1847), Irish politician.

[153] William Cobbett (1763-1835), politician and agriculturalist.

[154] *D.W.G.*, 498, 28 July 1825.

[155] *Ibid.*

[156] Sir Astley Paston Cooper (1768-1841), surgeon, who had been created a baronet in 1821.

[157] W.S.R.O., 540/264.

[158] *S.W.J.*, 5446, 12 Dec.1825.

[159] *Ibid.* 5952, 30 May 1836.

[160] Charles Ashe à Court (1785-1861), a lieutenant-general in the army.

[161] William Ashe à Court (1779-1860), later 1st Lord Heytesbury. A distinguished diplomat and Lord Lieutenant of Ireland 1844-46.

[162] www. A-court.fsnet.co.uk/Heytesbury Letters/letter 12.htm. Letter in the possession of James and Penny à Court.

[163] W.S.R.O. 413/34, contract for sale.

[164] Desmond Hawkins, *The Grove Diaries*, p.161.

[165] W.S.R.O. 451/105, contract dated 27 Dec 1825.

[166] J.B.Nicholls, *Historical Notes of Fonthill Wiltshire* (London 1836), p.33.

[167] W.A.S.(Libr.), Wilts Cuttings, vol. 26, p.103.

[168] W.S.R.O. 413/69, Order in Chancery, 21 June 1839.

[169] *D.W.G.*, 616, 1 Nov. 1827.

[170] *Ibid.* 451/59.

[171] *Ibid.* 451/105.

[172] *Ibid.* 451/58-69.

[173] *Ibid.*

[174] Edward Blore (1787-1879), architect and artist.

[175] W.S.R.O. 413/58-69.

[176] *S.W.J.*, 5799, 22 July 1833.

[177] John Buckler (1770-1851), topographical artist.

[178] J.B.Nicholls, *Historical Notes of Fonthill Wiltshire*, p.39.

[179] Probably James Jay, Benett's bailiff.

[180] *S.W.J.*, 5570, 28 Apr.1828.

[181] *D.W.G.*, 658, 21 Aug.1828.

[182] *V.C.H.Wilts.*,xiii, p.163.

[183] *S.W.J.*, 5443, 26 Dec.1825.

[184] *Ibid.* 5398, 10 Jan 1825.

[185] *D.W.G.*,571, 21 Dec.1826.

[186] Bath Record Office, The Royal Bath and West Society archive xvi, p.50.

[187] *S.W.J.*, 5456, 20 Feb.1826.

[188] *Ibid.*

[189] *Ibid.* 5458, 6 Mar.1826.

[190] *Ibid.* 5459, 13 Mar.1826.

[191] *Hansard* New Series, vol. XIV (1826) cols. 1109-10.

[192] *The Times*, 12911, 10 Mar.1826.

[193] *Hansard.*, vol. XV (1826) col. 531.

[194] *D.W.G.*,538, 4 May 1826.

[195] Dowden, *The Journal of Thomas Mcore*, iii, pp.921-2.

[196] Sir Francis Burdett (1770-18<4), politician.

[197] Dowden, *op.cit.* p.929.

[198] Probably John Houlton of Farleigh Castle, Somerset and Grittleton House (1773-1844) and his wife Mary Ann In the following year, Houlton sold Grittleton House to Joseph Neeld.

[199] Dowden, *The Journal of Thomas Moore.*, p.935.

[200] *Ibid.* p.925.

[201] *Ibid.* p. 951.

[202] *D.W.G.*, 553, 17 Aug. 1826.

[203] A.Aspinall, ed., *The Letters of King George IV 1812-1830* (Cambridge 1938), pp.185-6.

[204] *Hansard*, New Series, vol. XVI (1826) col. 136.

[205] *D.W.G.*, 568, 30 Nov.1826.

[206] *Gentleman's Magazine:and Historical Chronicle* (London 1827), vol. xcvii, pt.1, p.189.

[207] *D.W.G.*, 597, 21 June 1827.

[208] Boston Public Library, Dept. of Rare Books and Manuscripts, Ms.Eng.553(4).

[209] Almost certainly Henry Crabb Robinson (1775-1867), diarist and founder of the Athaneum Club and of University College London.

[210] John Wilson Croker (1780-1857), politician and essayist.

[211] Dowden, *Letters of Thomas Moore*, ii, p.610.

[212] George Gordon, 6th Baron Byron (1788-1824), poet.

[213] Dowden, *The Journal of Thomas Moore*, iii, p.1036.

[214] Mary Wollstone-Croft Shelley (1797-1851), authoress and second wife of Percy Bysshe Shelley.

[215] Wilfred S.Dowden ,ed., *The Letters of Thomas Moore* ii 1818-1847 (Oxford 1964), pp.571-2.

[216] Lord Charles Spencer Churchill (1794-1840).

[217] George Spencer Churchill, 5th Duke of Marlborough (1766—1840). See the letter quoted above, p.56.

[218] George Spencer Churchill, Marquis of Blandford, later 6th Duke of Marlborough (1793-1857).

[219] Mary Soames, *The Profligate Duke: George Spencer Churchill, fifth Duke of Marlborough, and his Duchess* (London 1987), p.154.

[220] *S.W.J.*, 5597, 17 Nov. 1828.

[221] Dowden, *The Journal of Thomas Moore*, iii, p.1048.

[222] B.L. Add. 62081, copy in W.S.R.O. 413/378.

[223] *Hansard* New Series, vol.XVII (1827) col.1316.

[224] *D.W.G.*, 510, 22 Feb.1827.

[225] Dowden, *The Journal of Thomas Moore*, iii, p.1029.

[226] *S.W.J.*, 5540, 1 Oct.1827.

[227] See Sarah E.Nash, 'The Collections and Life History of Etheldred Benett (1776-1845)', *WANHM*, 83 (1990), pp.163-169. Aylmer Bourke Lambert was not Etheldred's brother-in-law as mentioned in that paper but her sister-in-law's half brother. See also J.B.Delair, 'Pioneer Geologists of the Salisbury Area', *WANHM*,87 (1994), pp. 127-141. However, Etheldred's father was never a member of Parliament as mentioned in that paper. For further details of Etheldred's work see her entry in *Oxford D.N.B.*

[228] Justin B Delair, 'Wiltshire's Contribution to Early Geological Science', *Wiltshire Archaeological and Natural History Society: The First 150 Years* (Devizes 2003), p.156.

[229] He was in this year elected to the Geological Society.

[230] Alexander Turnbull Library, Wellington, New Zealand, MS Papers, 0083 Mantell Papers.

[231] Richard Colt Hoare, *op.cit.*, iii, pp.118-126.

[232] Justin B.Delair, op.cit. p.159.

[233] John Edward Jackson (1805-1891), one of the founders of the Wiltshire Archaeological and Natural History Society.

[234] William Buckland (1784-1856), professor of mineralogy and reader in geology at Oxford.

[235] J.E.Jackson, The Eminent Ladies of Wiltshire History, *WANHM*, 20 (1882), p.40.

[236] PRO 11/2015.

[237] George Bellas Greenough (1778-1855), geographer and geologist.

[238] William Cunnington (1786-1846), archaeologist.

[239] *The Heytesbury Collection of Antiquities*, list of visitors, in W.A.S.(Libr.).

[240] *WANHM*, 38 (1914), p.296.

[241] Richard Colt Hoare, *A History of Ancient Wiltshire* (London 1810), part I, p.70.

[242] *W.A.M.*, 3 (1857), p.267.

[243] There is a copy in W.A.S. (Libr.).

[244] Sarah E.Nash, 'The Collections and Life History of Etheldred Benett' *WANHM,*83 (1990), p.163.

[245] George Watson Taylor (d.1841), M.P. for Devizes.

[246] *D.W.G.*, 612, 4 Oct.1827.

[247] B.L. Add. 57940, f.67.

[248] *D.W.G.*, 625, 3 Jan.1828.

[249] *S.W.J.*, 5555,14 Jan.1828.

[250] Thomas Henry Sutton Sotheron (1801-1876). He later resumed his paternal surname of Estcourt and was M.P. for Devizes 1835-44 and for North Wilts 1844-65 and briefly Home Secretary in 1859.

[251] *D.W.G.*,1637, 27 May 1847.

[252] Rene Huchon,*George Crabbe and his Times 1754-1832: a Critical and Biographical Study* (London 1907), p.462.

[253] *S.W.J.*, 5556, 21 Jan.1828.

[254] *Ibid.* 5563, 10 Mar.1828.

[255] *S.W.J.*, 5565, 24 Mar.1828.

[256] *Ibid.* 5570, 28 Apr.1828.

[257] *D.W.G.*, 667, 23 Oct.1828.

[258] *Ibid.* 638, 3 Apr. 1828.

[259] *Hansard*, 2nd series, vol. XVIII (1828) col. 1118.

[260] *S.W.J.*,5568, 14 Apr.1828.

[261] *D.W.G.*, 640, 17 Apr. 1828.

[262] *Ibid.*750, 27 May 1830.

[263] Thomas Howard, 16th Earl of Suffolk and 9th Earl of Berkshire (1776-1851).

[264] *S,W.J.*, 5571, 12 May 1828.

[265] *Ibid.* 5571 *[sic]*, 19 May 1828.

[266] *Ibid.* 5613, 10 Mar.1829.

[267] *D.W.G.*, 682, 12 Mar.1829.

[268] *V.C.H.Wilts.*,xiii, p.230.

[269] *D.W.G.*, 655, 31 July 1828.

[270] W.A.S.(Libr.), Box 138A, ms.1410.

[271] *Extracts from Dinton-Dalwood letters from 1827-1853* (1964 Edition), p. 15, in W.A.S.(Libr.).

[272] *Ibid.* p.109.

[273] *S.W.J.*,5604, 5 Jan.1829.

[274] *Ibid.* 5605, 12 Jan.1829.

[275] *D.W.G.*, 717, 8 Oct. 1829.

[276] *Extracts from Dinton-Dalwood letters, op.cit.* p.19.

[277] *Hansard* 2nd Series, vol. XXI (1829) cols. 1682-3.

[278] *S.W.J.*, 5626, 8 June 1829.

[279] W.S.R.O. 451/58-69.

[280] William Benett (1779-1859).

[281] B.L. Add. 62081, copy in W.S.R.O. 413/378.

[282] Ibid.

[283] William Cobbett, *Rural Rides* (2 vols. London 1912), ii. p.228.

## Chapter 6

[1] *S.W.J.*, 5663, 22 Feb.1830.

[2] *Ibid.* 5666, 15 Mar. 1830.

[3] *Ibid.* 5668, 29 Mar. 1830.

[4] George Spencer-Churchill, Marquis of Blandford (1793-1857), later 6th Duke of Marlborough.

[5] *Hansard,* 2nd series, vol. XXII (1830) col.699.

[6] *Ibid.* vol. XXV (1830) col.356.

[7] *S.W.J.*,5681, 5 July 1830.

[8] *Ibid.*

[9] *D.W.G.*, 756, 8 July 1830.

[10] *Ibid.* 758, 22 July 1830.

[11] *S.W.J.*, 5648 *[sic]*, 26 July 1830.

[12] *Ibid.* 5650, 9 Aug.1830.

[13] *D.W.G.*,761, 12 Aug.1830.

[14] *Ibid.* 800, 12 May 1831.

[15]*S.W.J.*, 5652, 23 Aug.1830.

[16] Thomas Richard Lalor Sheil (1791-1851), dramatist and politician.

[17] B.L. Add. 62081, copy in W.S.R.O. 413/378.

[18] Henry William Paget, 1st Marquis of Anglesey (1768-1854).

[19] *S.W.J.*,5659, 11 Oct.1830.

[20] Marie Louise Victoire, Duchess of Kent (d.1861).

[21] Lord John Russell, ed., *Memoirs, Journal and Correspondence of Thomas Moore* (London 1860), p.520.

[22] *D.W.G.*,772 , 28 Oct. 1830.

[23] J.L.Hammond and Barbara Hammond, *The Village Labourer 1760-1832: a Study of*

the Government of England before the Reform Bill (Abingdon 1995), pp.261-2.

24 William Wyndham of Dinton (1796-1862).

25 S.W.J., 5666, 29 Nov 1830.

26 Charlotte Wyndham's brother.

27 W.A.S.(Libr.), Extracts from Dinton-Dalwood letters, op.cit. p.39.

28 Richard, Earl Temple of Stowe and Marquis of Chandos (1776-1839).

29 S.W.J.,5665, 22 Nov.1830.

30 Chitty's house was a fine late 18th century house in Bleke Street in Shaftesbury and in 1830 was rented by him from Charles Bowles. Ex info. Mr Frank Hopton of Shaftesbury.

31 W.S.R.O. 413/23.

32 E.J.Hobsbawm and George Rude, Captain Swing (London 1969), pp.126-7.

33 W.H.Hudson, A Shepherd's Life: impressions of the South Wiltshire Downs (London 1910), p.248.

34 Microfiche copy of letter at Bowood, Box Lans (3) 4, original in the British Library.

35 Probably, in the view of Henry Graham, the author of The Annals of the Yeomanry Cavalry of Wiltshire, a professional soldier appointed by the military authorities to superintend the movement of the troops in the county.

36 The magificent Roman Catholic chapel at Wardour Castle, Lord Arundell's seat.

37 Thomas Grove of Ferne, Benett's friend since childhood.

38 Henry Graham, The Annals of the Yeomanry Cavalry of Wiltshire (Liverpool 1886), p.80.

39 W.S.R.O. 413/23

40 Microfiche copy of letter at Bowood, Box Lans (3) 4, original in the British Library.

41 Elisabeth Theresa Fielding (d.1844 ), daughter of 2nd Earl of Ilchester.

42 William Henry Fox Talbot (1800-1877), pioneer of photography.

43 Letter transcribed in the Talbot Correspondence Project, www.foxtalbot. arts.gla.ac.uk, Doc. No. 02083. Original letter in Fox Talbot Museum Lacock.

44 S.W.J., 5667, 6 Dec 1830.

45 D.W.G., 788, 17 Feb. 1831.

46 Extracts from Dinton-Dalwood letters, op.cit. pp.41-2.

47 D.W.G.,777, 2 Dec.1830.

48 Ibid. 778, 9 Dec. 1830.

49 Extracts from Dinton-Dalwood letters, op.cit. p.47.

50 Jill Chambers, Wiltshire Machine Breakers, vol. 1 The Riots and Trials (Letchworth 1993), p.265

51 Robert Benson and Henry Hatcher, Old and New Sarum, p.569.

52 Ibid. pp. 534-5. and W.S.R.O. 212B/6572.

53 Jill Chambers, op.cit. p.110.

54 S.W.J., 5671, 3 Jan. 1831.

55 Jill Chambers, op.cit. vol. 2 The Rioters, p.44.

56 S.W.J., 5672, 10 Jan. 1831,

57 WANHM, 47 (1937), pp.533-4.

58 S.W.J., 5672, 10 Jan 1831.

59 W.S.R.O. 413/67.

60 W.S.R.O. 413/23.

61 Extracts from Dinton-Dalwood letters, op.cit. p. 43. For an account of the later fate of Edmund White see Mary Dalton, 'The Pyt House Riot and the Tisbury-Tasmania connection', Hatcher Review, vol. 3, no. 30.

62 The function of the Grand Jury that always consisted of members of the aristocracy and gentry was to receive and enquire into indictments before being submitted to the court.

63 Edward Law, 1st Earl of Ellenborough (1790-1871), later Governor-General of India.

64 A.Aspinall, ed.,Three Early Nineteenth Century Diaries (London 1952), p.48.

65 D.W.G.,787, 10 Feb.1831.

66 Ibid. 788, 17 Feb. 1831.

67 S.W.J., 5675, 14 Feb 1831.

68 E.J.Hobsbawm and George Rude, Captain Swing, p.233.

69 W.A.S.(Libr.), Box 143 ms.1444. The story teller is said to have been one Giles Chawbacon – perhaps a pseudonym for John Brickle who is named as the narrator in the copy in W.S.R.O. 413/23.

70 Jill Chambers, Wiltshire Machine Breakers, vol. 1 The Riots and Trials (Letchworth

1993), pp. 323-4.

71 *Political Register*, 4 Dec.1830.

72 J.L.Hammond and Barbara Hammond, *The Village Labourer 1760-1832*, p.317.

73 *V.C.H.Wilts.*,v, p.296.

## Chapter 7

1 For some account of the early years of the Society, see W.C. 12, p.44 in W.A.S.(Libr.).

2 *S.W.J.*, 5676, 21 Feb.1831.

3 Edward Berkeley Portman (1799-1888), M.P. for Dorset 1823-1832 and later 1st Baron Portman.

4 *Extracts from the Dinton-Dalwood letters*, op.cit. p.46.

5 *S.W.J.*, 5675, 14 Feb.1831.

6 *Ibid.* 5677, 27 Feb.1831.

7 Sir Denis Le Marchant (1795-1874), politician.

8 John Charles Spencer, Viscount Althorp, most memorable for attempting to introduce duties on transfers of real and funded properties.

9 A.Aspinall, ed., *Three early Nineteenth Century Diaries* (London 1952), p.9.

10 Charles John, Lord Andover (1804-1876), succeeded his father as 17th Earl of Suffolk and 10th Earl of Berkshire in 1851.

11 John Thomas Mayne (1792-1843).

12 *S.W.J.*, 5677, 27 Feb. 1831.

13 William Huskisson (1770-1830), statesman.

14 Isaac Gascoyne (1770-1841), M.P. for Liverpool 1796-1831.

15 D.Ben Rees, *Local and Parliamentary Politics in Liverpool from 1800 to 1911* (Lewiston 1999), p.38. The author is indebted to Dr.Ben Rees for the background material relating to the 1830 Liverpool election contained in this work.

16 *Hansard* 3rd Series, vol III (1831) cols. 1756-1764.

17 Francis Thornhill Baring, 1st Baron Northbrook (1796-1866), statesman.

18 Thomas George, Earl of Northbrook, ed., *Journals and Correspondence of Francis Thornhill Baring, Lord Northbrook* (London 1905), I, p.84.

19 *S.W.J.*, 5681, 28 Mar.1831.

20 Charles Grey, 2nd Earl Grey (1764-1845), statesman.

21 W.S.R.O. 490/1381.

22 Henry Frederick, 3rd Marquis of Bath (1797-1837).

23 *S.W.J.*, 5688, 16 May 1831.

24 *Ibid.* 5693, 27 June 1831.

25 *D.W.G.*, 758, 22 July 1830.

26 *S.W.J.*, 5694, 4 July 1831.

27 *Ibid.* 5676, 21 Feb.1831.

28 *Ibid.* 5675, 14 Feb.1831.

29 *Hansard* 3rd Series, vol. IV (1831) cols.480-83.

30 *Ibid.* col. 1003.

31 Edward Pearce, *Reform: The Fight for the 1832 Reform Act* (London 2003), p.161.

32 *Hansard* 3rd Series, vol.V (1831) col.34.

33 A.Aspinall, *Three Early Nineteenth Century Diaries*, p.104.

34 Thomas Babbington Macaulay, 1st Baron Macaulay (1800-1859), historian.

35 Sir Thomas Baring, 2nd Baronet (1772-1848), M.P. for Wycombe and Hampshire.

36 Thomas Pinney, *Letters of Thomas Babington Macaulay* (Cambridge 1974), p.71.

37 *D.W.G.*, 811, 28 July 1831.

38 *Ibid.* 815, 25 Aug.1831.

39 Edward John Littleton, 1st Baron Hatherton (1791-1863), politician.

40 Staffordshire Record Office, D260/M/F/5/26/7, Journal of 1st Lord Hatherton, 1828-1832, p.115.

41 Sir Thomas Fowell Buxton (1786-1854), philanthropist.

42 *D.W.G.*, 818, 22 Sept.1831.

43 *Mirror of Parliament*, (1831) II, p.2153.

44 *Ibid.* p.2157.

45 George Julius Poulett Scrope (1797-1876), geologist and political economist.

46 Text torn away under seal.

47 Letter transcribed in Talbot Correspondence Project, www.foxtalbot.arts.gla.ac.uk, Doc.No.01592. Original letter in Fox Talbot Museum Lacock.

48 *S.W.J.*,5706, 3 Oct.1831.

49 *Ibid.* 5710, 31 Oct.1831.

50 Hon.Duncombe Pleydell Bouverie (1780-

1850).

51 Robert Waylen (1770-1841), cloth manufacturer of Devizes and father of the historian, James Waylen.

52 W.A.S.(Libr.), Wilts Cuttings, vol. 3, p.74.

53 *S.W.J.*, 5701, 5 Sept.1831.

54 *Ibid.* 5674, 7 Feb.1831.

55 *Ibid.* 5701 *[sic]* 12 Sept.1831.

56 *D.W.G.*, 827, 17 Nov. 1831.

57 St. Andrew Beauchamp, 14th Baron St.John (b.1811).

58 B.L. Add. 62081, copy in W.S.R.O. 413/378.

59 Ibid.

60 Sir Hyde Parker, 8th Baronet (1785-1856), M.P. for West Suffolk.

61 *V.C.H.*, xiii, p. 211 and W.S.R.O. 413/196.

62 B.L. Add. 62081, copy in W.R.O 413/378.

63 Ibid.

64 Robert Grosvenor, 2nd Earl Grosvenor (1767-1845), created 1st Marquis of Westminster in 1831.

65 *D.W.G.*, 837, 26 Jan.1832.

66 *S.W.J.*, 8841, 21 Nov.1833.

67 B.L. Add. 62081, copy in W.S.R.O. 413/378.

68 Letter transcribed in Talbot Correspondence Project Doc. No. 02959, see www.foxtalbot.arts.gla.ac.uk; original in Fox Talbot Museum.

69 *D.W.G.*, 853, 17 May 1832.

70 *V.C.H.Wilts.,v*, p.309.

71 *D.W.G.*, 856, 7 June 1832.

72 *Ibid.* 857, 14 June 1832.

73 *S.W.J.*, 5734, 25 June 1832.

74 Sidney Herbert (1810-1861), politician and later 1st Lord Herbert of Lea.

75 *D.W.G.*, 859, 28 June 1832.

76 Tresham Lever, *The Herberts of Wilton* (London 1967), p.210.

77 *S.W.J.*, 5744, 2 July 1832.

78 *Ibid.* 5745, 9 July 1832.

79 *Ibid.* 5746, 16 July 1832.

80 *Ibid.* 5748, 30 July 1832.

81 Frederick John Robinson, Viscount Goderich (1782-1859), later 1st Earl of Ripon and briefly Prime Minister 1827/8.

82 B.L. Add. 40878, f.177.

83 Letter 7 July 2004, Coutts & Co's Archivist's Department to the author.

84 B.L. Add. 62081, copy in W.S.R.O. 413/378.

85 *S.W.J.*, 5749, 6 Aug.1832.

86 *Ibid.*

87 Sir Henry Fane (17778-1840), succeeded his father, the Hon.Henry Fane ( a son of the 8th Earl of Westmoreland) as M.P. for Lyme Regis in 1802 and later M.P. for Sandwich and Hastings. Appointed Commander-in-Chief in India by the Duke of Wellington in 1835.

88 W.S.R.O. 1938/1.

89 W.A.S.(Libr.), Box 19C, ms.250, letter William E.Bigg to J. Benett-Stanford, 17 Feb.1938.

90 John Fane, 11th Earl of Westmoreland (1784-1859)..

91 B.L. Add. 62081, copy in W.S.R.O. 413/378.

92 *S.W.J.*, 5767, 10 Dec.1832.

93 *D.W.G.*, 884, 20 Dec.1832.

94 Walter Long of Rood Ashton (b.1793).

95 *S.W.J.*, 5767, 10 Dec.1832.

96 *D.W.G.*, 884, 20 Dec.1832.

97 Catherine, (1783-1856), widow of 11th Earl of Pembroke.

98 Lord Stanmore, *Sidney Herbert Lord Herbert of Lea: a Memoir* (London 1906), p.16.

99 *S.W.J.*, 5774, 28 Jan.1833.

100 Sir George Hayter (1792-1871), portrait and historical painter.

101 National Portrait Gallery ref. NPG 54.

102 *Hansard* 3rd Series, vol.XV (1833) cols.1026-7.

103 Dudley Ryder, Lord Sandon (1798-1882), later 2nd Earl of Harrowby.

104 *Hansard* 3rd Series, vol.XVI (1833) col.294.

105 *Ibid.* cols.294-5.

106 *Ibid.* col. 645.

107 Sir Montague Gore (1800-1864), M.P. for Devizes 1832-4.

108 Hugh, Lord Ebrington (1783-1861), later 2nd Earl Fortescue.

109 Wadham Locke (c.1780-1835), M.P. for Devizes 1832-1835.

110 *D.W.G.*, 885, 27 Dec.1832.

111 *Ibid.* 901, 18 Apr.1833.
112 *S.W.J.*, 5784, 8 Apr.1833.
113 *Ibid.* 5788, 6 May 1833.
114 *Ibid.*
115 *Ibid.* 5795, 24 June 1833.
116 B.L. Add. 62081, copy in W.S.R.O. 413/378.
117 *S.W.J.*, 5814, 4 Nov.1833.
118 *Ibid.* 5829, 17 Feb.1834.
119 *Ibid.* 5823, 6 Jan.1834.
120 *Hansard* 3rd Series, vol. XXI (1834) cols. 391-2.
121 *S.W.J.*,5830, 24 Feb.1834.
122 *Ibid.* 5832, 10 Mar.1834
123 *Ibid.* 5834, 24 Mar.1834.
124 *Ibid.*
125 Quoted in Anthony Burton, *William Cobbett: Englishman A Biography*, (London 1997), p.245.
126 P.R.O. MH 32/2.
127 Charles Shaw-Lefevre (1794-1888), politician later Viscount Eversley who, in1830, had entered Parliament as member for Downton, Lord Radnor's pocket borough.
128 P.R.O. MH 32/2.
129 Ibid.
130 *V.C.H. Wilts,* v, p.254
131 P.R.O. MH 32/2.
132 Ibid.
133 Ibid.
134 W.S.R.O. H. 14/110/1.
135 Letter transcribed in the Talbot Correspondence Project, www.foxtalbot.arts.gla.uk, Doc.No.02870. Original letter in Fox Talbot Museum Lacock.
136 *D.W.G.*, 1032, 22 Oct.1835.
137 *S.W.J.*,5841, 12 May 1834.
138 *D.W.G.*, 959, 29 May 1834.
139 *Ibid.* 962,19 June 1834.
140 *Ibid.*
141 *Ibid.* 963, 26 June 1834.
142 *Ibid.* 964, 3 July 1834.
143 *S.W.J.*,5860, 11 Aug.1834.
144 *Ibid.* 5863, 1 Sept.1834.
145 Mrs Herbert Richardson, 'Wiltshire Newspapers – Past and Present', *WANHM*, 41 (1920), p.491.

146 *The Salisbury and Wiltshire Herald*, 57, 2 Aug.1834.
147 Bath Record Office, The Royal Bath and West of England Society archive xvi.
148 *S.W.J.*, 5880, 5 Jan.1835.
149 *Ibid.* 5882, 19 Jan.1835.
150 *Ibid.* 5885, 9 Feb.1835.
151 *D.W.G.*, 999, 5 Mar.1835.
152 *S.W.J.*, 5890, 16 Mar.1835.
153 W.S.R.O. 413/383.
154 *S.W.J.*, 5893, 6 Apr.1835.
155 Thomas Moore letters, 1804-1847, MS 15, Woodson Research Center, Fondren Library, Rice University.
156 *S.W.J.*, 5901, 1 June 1835.
157 *Ibid.* 5907, 14 July 1835.
158 W.A.S.(Libr.), Cunnington Cuttings, vol.4, p.1, list of subscribers.
159 *D.W.G.*, 1023 , 20 Aug 1835.
160 *Ibid.* 1018, 16 July 1835.
161 W.A.S.(Libr.), Wilts Cuttings, vol. 3, p.49.
162 *D.W.G.*, 1039, 10 Dec.1835.
163 W.S.R.O. 413/330.
164 Strong beer.
165 *S.W.J.*, 5933, 11 Jan.1836.
166 Henry Benedict, 11th Lord Arundell of Wardour (1804-1862).
167 *S.W.J.* 5938, 15 Feb.1836.
168 *Ibid.* 5940, 29 Feb.1836.
169 *Ibid.* 5947, 25 Apr.1836.
170 *Ibid.* 5948, 2 May 1836.
171 *Ibid.* 5950, 16 May 1836.
172 *Hansard* 3rd Series, vol. XXXIV (1836) col. 753.
173 *S.W.J.*,5956, 27 June 1836.
174 *Ibid.* 5975, 7 Nov.1836.
175 Nicholas Wilcocks Cundy (b.1778).
176 *S.W.J.*,5960, 25 July 1836.
177 *S.W.J.*,5961, 1 Aug.1836.
178 *Hansard* 3rd Series, vol. XXXV (1836) col. 872.
179 Richard, Earl Grosvenor (1795-1869), succeeded his father as 2nd Marquis of Westminster in 1845.
180 *S.W.J.*, 5935, 25 Jan.1836.
181 *Ibid.* 5940, 29 Feb.1836.
182 *Ibid.* 5944, 4Apr.1836.
183 *Ibid.* 5947, 25 Apr.1836.
184 *Ibid.* 6080, 3 Dec.1838.

185 *Ibid.* 5953, 6 June 1836.
186 W.S.R.O. 451/65A.
187 Isambard Kingdom Brunel (1806-1859), civil engineer.
188 W.S.R.O. 451/65A.
189 He did, however, subscribe £10 towards the relief of those who suffered as a result of the disastrous floods in Shrewton and Maddington in 1841 when 36 cottages were totally destroyed, *S.W.J.*, 6206, 1 Feb.1841 and the same amount to the fund established to assist those in distress in Bradford in 1842, *S.W.J.*, 6242, 28 Feb.1842.
190 *S.W.J.*, 5967, 12 Sept.1842.
191 For a large plan of Benett's estate see W.S.R.O. 1236/64.
192 Sir Edmund Antrobus, 2nd Baronet (1792-1870).
193 *V.C.H. Wilts.*, xi, p.119. and W.A.S. (Libr.), Box 19D ms.265, note by John Fane-Benett-Stanford.
194 John Hutchins, *The History and Antiquities of the County of Dorset,* (Westminster 1863), Vol. II, p.177.
195 Sir Henry Titchborne, 8th Baronet (1779-1845).
196 Henry Benedict, 11th Lord Arundell of Wardour (1804-1862).
197 Henry Graham, *The Annals of the Yeoman Cavalry of Wiltshire being a complete history of the Prince of Wales' Own Regiment from the time of its formation in 1794 to October 1884* (Liverpool 1886), p.106.
198 *D.W.G.*, 1983, 13 Oct 1836.
199 *S.W.J.*, 5993, 13 Mar.1837.
200 *Ibid.* 5994, 20 Mar. 1837.
201 *The Wiltshire Independent*, 18, 23 Mar. 1837.
202 *S.W.J.*, 5994, 20 Mar. 1837.
203 *Ibid.* 6004, 29 May 1837.
204 *D.W.G.*, 1113, 11 May 1837.
205 George William Frederick, Earl Bruce (1804-1878), later 2nd Marquis of Ailesbury.
206 *D.W.G.*, 1122, 13 July 1837.
207 Microfiche copy of letter at Bowood, Box Lans (3) 4; original letter in the British Library.
208 *S.W.J.*, 6253, 16 May 1842.
209 Nicholas Conyngham Tindal (1776-1846), Chief Justice of the Common Pleas.
210 *D.W.G.*,1123, 20 July 1837.
211 *S.W.J.*, 6013, 31 July 1837.
212 *Hansard* 3rd Series, vol. XXXVII (1837) col. 429-30.
213 *Ibid.* col. 1146.
214 *S.W.J.*, 6030, 18 Dec. 1837.
215 Thomas Spring Rice (1790-1866), later 1st Baron Monteagle.
216 Thomas Moore letters, 1804-1847, MS 15 Woodson Research Center, Fondren Library, Rice University.
217 W.S.R.O. 413/67.
218 W.S.R.O. 413/69, sale particulars. The property included the remains of Beckford's Abbey as well as the whole of the village of Fonthill Gifford.
219 W.S.R.O. 413/330.
220 W.S.R.O. 413/45, sale particulars.
221 Sir Hyde Parker, 8th Baronet. The Hatch property had been purchased by his ancestor Laurence Hyde in 1570.
222 R.E.Sandell, ed., *Wiltshire Tithe Apportionments* Wiltshire Record Society (Devizes 1975), xxx, pp. 21, 56, 90, 91, 98, 82.
223 Letter 7 July 2004, Coutts & Co's Archivist's Department to author.
224 *S.W.J.*, 6061, 23 July 1838.
225 *D.W.G.*,1166, 17 May 1838.
226 *Ibid.* 1175, 19 July 1838.
227 *Ibid.* 1154, 22 Feb. 1838.
228 *Hansard*, 3rd series, vol. XLII (1838) col.638.
229 *Ibid.* vol. XLVI (1839) col. 817-9.
230 B.L. Add. 62081, copy in W.S.R.O. 413/378.
231 W.A.S.(Libr.), Box 18, ms.215.
232 *S.W.J.*, 6115, 29 July 1839.
233 *Ibid.* 6185, 7 Sept.1840.
234 W.S.R.O. 2667/14/41, Semley Court Book, 20 Nov.1839.
235 *D.W.G.*, 1239, 10 Oct.1839.
236 *S.W.J.*, 6063, 6 Aug. 1838. Statement made at the laying of the foundation stone by Etheldred Benett.
237 Colt Hoare, v, Addenda p.58.
238 Etheldred Benett to Samuel Woodward,

22 Apr 1837: The Norwich Castle Museum & Art Gallery (NWHCM: 1919. 44) Samuel Woodward correspondence Vol.1837-38, p.42.

[239] *The Charities in the County of Wilts selected from the Voluminous Reports of the Commissioners for Inquiring concerning Charities in England and Wales...*(London 1839), p.392.

## Chapter 8

[1] *Hansard*, 3rd series, LIII (1840) col.1346.
[2] W.S.R.O. 413/487.
[3] *S.W.J.*, 6158, 13 Apr. 1840.
[4] *Hansard*, 3rd series, LIV (1840) col. 659.
[5] *Ibid.* col.966.
[6] *Ibid.* col. 1270.
[7] William Heald Ludlow Bruges of Seend (b.1796), Recorder of Devizes and Chairman of the Devizes Quarter Sessions.
[8] *D.W.G.*, 1265, 9 Apr.1840.
[9] For a copy of the Requisition sent to the High Sheriff and signed by Benett and others see a transcription in theTalbot Correspondence Project, www.foxtalbot. arts.gla.ac.uk, Doc.No.04088.
[10] *D.W.G.*, 1277, 2 July1840.
[11] B.L. Add. 62081, copy in W.S.R.O. 413/ 378.
[12] W.S.R.O. EA 158 and R.E.Sandell, ed., *Abstracts of Wiltshire Inclosure Awards and Agreements*, Wiltshire Record Society (Devizes 1971), xxv, p. 24.
[13] *S.W.J.*, 6188, 28 Sept.1840.
[14] The Marriage Settlement whereby the sum of £400 p.a. was settled on Anna Maria and Marmaduke by his father is with the deeds of Lushill Farm, Castle Eaton and Hannington, W.S.R.O. 1040/4.
[15] These are the servants identified in more detail in the 1851 census return.
[16] *S.W.J.*, 6118, 19 Aug. 1839.
[17] *Ibid.* 6182, 17 Aug.1840.
[18] *D.W.G.*, 1324, 27 May 1841.
[19] *S.W.J.*, 6212, 5 July 1841.
[20] *Ibid.* 6211, 28 June 1841.
[21] *D.W.G.*, 1330, 8 July 1841.

[22] *S.W.J.*, 6213, 12 July 1841.
[23] *Ibid.* 6214, 19 July 1841.
[24] *Ibid.* 6213, 12 July 1841.
[25] W. Daniell, *Warminster Common: shewing the steps by which it has advanced from its former state of notorious vice, ignorance and poverty, to its present state of moral and social improvement* (Warminster 1850), p.262.
[26] *S.W.J.*, 6231, 13 Dec.1841.
[27] *Ibid.* 6241, 21 Feb.1842.
[28] *Ibid.* 6242, 28 Feb.1842.
[29] *Hansard*, 3rd series, vol.. LX (1842), col.859.
[30] *V.C.H.Wilts.*, v. p.306.
[31] *S.W.J.*, 6242, 28 Feb.1842.
[32] *Salisbury and Wiltshire Herald*, 457, 18 June 1842. The nature of Benett's 'late severe accident' has alluded discovery.
[33] *S.W.J.*, 6259, 27 June 1842.
[34] *Ibid.* 6020, 4 July 1842.
[35] *Hansard,* 3rd series, vol. LXIV(1842), col. 1002-3.
[36] *S.W.J.*, 6265, 8 Aug.1842.
[37] *D.W.G.*, 1395, 6 Oct.1842.
[38] *S.W.J.*, 6282, 3 Dec.1842. Following his death, his farm stock was valued at £5632 – an indication of the very large scale of his farming activities, see W.S.R.O. 413/ 376.
[39] Joseph Neeld of Grittleton House and M.P. for Chippenham for over 25 years. Apart from his great wealth and ill-stared marriage, he had much in common with Benett, being a staunch supporter of agricultural protection.
[40] *Salisbury and Wiltshire Herald*, 462, 23 July 1842.
[41] *Hansard*, 3rd series, vol. LXIX (1843) p.268.
[42] Ambrose Hussey, M.P. for Salisbury very briefly in 1843.
[43] *S.W.J.*, 6306, 20 May 1843.
[44] *Ibid.* 6312, 1 July 1843.
[45] John Bright (1811-1889), orator and statesman.
[46] Richard Cobden (1804-1865), statesman.
[47] *S.W.J.*, 6318, 12 Aug.1843.
[48] *Salisbury and Wiltshire Herald*, 517, 12 Aug. 1843.

[49] Edward Pleydell-Bouverie (1818-1889).

[50] For an account of this election see Ronald K.Huch, The Anti-Corn Law League and the Salisbury Election of November 1843 in *Canadian Journal of History*, vol. 6, issue 3, Dec.1971, pp.247-256.

[51] *S.W.J.*, 6317, 5 Aug.1843. John Alexander Thynne, 4th Marquis of Bath (1831-96) was an infant, and so the buck must have been given by his mother who was administering the Longleat estate on behalf of his trustees.

[52] *The Times*, 18456, 16 Nov.1843.

[53] *S.W.J.*, 6332, 18 Nov.1843.

[54] *D.W.G.*, 1454, 23 Nov.1843.

[55] *Salisbury & Wiltshire Herald*, 502, 6 May 1843

[56] W.A.S.(Libr.) Devizes, Box 19c, ms.246.

[57] *D.W.G.*, 1463, 8 Feb.1844.

[58] *S.W.J.*, 6349, 30 Mar.1844.

[59] *Ibid.* 6350, 6 Apr.1844.

[60] W.S.R.O. 413/67, minutes of agreement between Benett and Earl Grosvenor, 30 Sept.1844.

[61] *Extracts from Dinton-Dalwood letters, op.cit.* p.133.

[62] W.S.R.O. 413/69.

[63] W.A.S.(Libr.), Box 19D, ms.265, transcript of an extract from *A Book of Accounts of Estates and many other useful Memorandums beginning 1829 by John Benett Esquire of Pythouse.*

[64] *S.W.J.*, 6365, 20 July 1844.

[65] *Extracts from Dinton-Dalwood letters, op.cit.* p.113.

[66] Two of the children eventually married clergymen, Susan, the Hon. & Rev. John Horatio Nelson (2nd son of the 2nd Earl Nelson) and Lucy, the Rev. John Fletcher Dixon Stewart. Etheldred died unmarried.

[67] The girls' two brothers remained in the care of their uncle, the 6th Duke.

[68] W.A.S. (Libr.) Devizes, Box 19C, ms.246, transcript from *Our Grandfather's Diary 1845.*

[69] Joseph Thaddeus, 11th Baron Dormer (1790-1871). When reporting that, following the passing of the Catholic Relief Bill in 1829, he was then entitled to take his seat in the Upper House, the *Devizes and Wiltshire Gazette* declared that 'he had been abroad almost from infancy and was wholly unable to speak the English language'.

[70] Theresa, 3rd wife of Henry Benedict, 11th Lord Arundell of Wardour.

[71] *S.W.J.*, 6394, 8 Feb.1845.

[72] There is a certified copy of the entry (in Latin) in the register of Wardour Castle chapel recording his death in Madeira and burial in the cemetery with the deeds of Lushill Farm, Castle Eaton and Hannington, W.S.R.O. 1040/4.

[73] W.S.R.O., 413/376.

[74] *Extracts from Dinton-Dalwood letters, op.cit.* p.114.

[75] W.A.S.(Libr.), Box 19C ms.246.

[76] John Owen, *A Letter to the Inhabitants of Warminster in reply to a Letter addressed to him by the Rev. Arthur Fane with an Appendix containing Letters to the Bishop of Salisbury and his Replies* (London 1845), p.17.

[77] W.A.S. (Libr.), Box 19C, ms.250.

[78] *S.W.J.*, 6411, 7 June 1845.

[79] *Ibid.* 6419, 2 Aug.1845.

[80] *D.W.G.*, 1541, 24 July 1845.

[81] *S.W.J.*, 6418 [sic], 16 Aug.1845.

[82] *Ibid.* 6426, 11 Oct.1845.

[83] *The Times*, 19052, 11 Oct. 1845.

[84] Horatio, 3rd Earl Nelson (1823-1913) and his wife, Mary Jane Diana Agar (d.1904).

[85] *D.W.G.*, 1553, 16 Oct.1845.

[86] *Hansard*, 3rd series, vol. LXXXIII (1846), col.317-8.

[87] *Ibid.* cols. 321-2.

[88] The report in the *Times* was reprinted by J.Gadsby of Manchester as a 12 page pamphlet and doubtless widely distributed. Copy in W.A.S.(Libr.) Devizes, WT. 14.

[89] *Hansard*, 3rd series, vol. LXXXIII (1846), cols. 1213-1221.

[90] *Ibid.* vol. LXXXVI, col.434-438.

[91] The author acknowledges the assistance he has received from the research of Norman Longmate in *The Breadstealers* (London 1984) in tracing the course of the

legislation through Parliament in 1846.

92 *Hansard,* 3rd series (1846) vol. LXXXVII, col. 639-642.

93 *D.W.G.,*1592, 16 July 1846.

94 B.L. Add. 40582, f.317b.

95 B.L. Add. 40582.

96 Benett's eldest daughter Frances was always referred to as Fanny even in his will and in the deeds entered into when the school was endowed and on her memorial in Norton Bavant church.

97 Mrs E Miles,*Tisbury (Past and Present)* (Salisbury 1920), p.44.

98 *Endowed Charities (County of Wilts),* (London 1907), p.15.

99 *S.W.J.,*6450, 31 Oct. 1846.

100 W.S.R.O. 628/48/34, ledger book 6, p.343.

101 Ibid.

102 Ibid. pp. 344-6, 578.

103 *V.C.H.Wilts.,* xiii, p.71.

104 *D.W.G.,* 1637, 27 May 1847. The Norton Bavant estate is situated very close to Warminster.

105 *S.W.J.,* 6484, 24 July 1847.

106 *Ibid.* 6486, 7 Aug.1847.

107 *D.W.G.,* 1725, 1 Feb. 1849.

108 *S.W.J.,* 6569, 31 Mar. 1849.

109 W.S.R.O. 574/318.

110 *D.W.G.,* 1750, 26 June 1849.

111 Richard Bentley (1794-1871) the publisher of *Bentley's Miscellany* of which Charles Dickens was for a time editor and in which *Oliver Twist* first appeared. The letters that were purchased by Bentley were sold at Sotheby's in 1852 and nearly all of them were bought by the British Museum and are now in the British Library, Add. 62081-62086.

112 Prince Rupert (1619-1682), Count Palatine of the Rhine.

113 Thomas Bennett (c.1645-1688), brother of Patience, Benett's great-grandmother.

114 *The Gentleman's Magazine,* (London 1849), pp.143-150.

115 B.L. Add. 46651, f.9.

116 W.A.Day, ed., *The Pythouse Papers: correspondence concerning the Civil War, the Popish Plot and a Contested Election in 1680* (London 1879).

117 James Smith, *Wilton and its Associations* (London 1851). This book was printed by Benett's distant kinsman James Bennett of Salisbury who, with his elder brother William Coles Bennett, vicar of Corsham, is also named as a subscriber.

118 W.S.R.O. 413/376, probate inventory and valuation.

119 W.S.R.O. 413/367, will and probate.

120 *V.C.H.Wilts.,* v. p.296.

121 The Dewey Museum, Warminster, solicitor's day book 24 July 1850-30 Oct.1852, pp.27,28.

122 Ibid. pp.58,74.

123 Ibid. p.91.

124 Richard Penruddocke Long (b.1825), later M.P. for Chippenham.

125 W.S.R.O. 947/1843.

126 The Dewey Museum, op.cit. p.149.

127 Ibid. p.162.

128 Ibid. p.178.

129 Ibid. p.191.

130 Ibid. p.227.

131 *D.W.G.,* 1903, 1 July 1852.

132 *D.W.G.,* 1905, 15 July 1852.

133 William Wyndham of Dinton (1796-1862).

134 The Dewey Museum loc.cit. p.250.

135 *D.W.G.,*1917, 7 Oct. 1852. Why 'Mr Zinzan of Hindon' should have been present remains a mystery. He may have been a medical man although in the *Post office Directory for Wiltshire 1855* the name of 'Robert Zinzan esq' appears under the heading of Hindon 'gentry'.

136 W.S.R.O. 628/48/36, Goodman's bill book 7, p.369.

137 John Fane-Benett-Stanford (1870-1947).

138 W.A.S.(Libr.), Box 18, ms. 215.

139 The Dewey Museum, loc.cit. pp. 251,252,257,258.

140 *The Gentleman's Magazine,* vol. xxxviii, p.637.

141 George Woodcock, ed., *William Cobbett; Rural Rides* (Harmondsworth 1967), p.527.

# Index

disappointed that Wiltshire was to be divided into two divisions for parliamentary elections 221- 2; opens an account with Coutts & Co and borrows large sums of money 224; is again returned to Parliament 226-7; his bill to disenfranchise the freemen of Liverpool is debated 228-9; prevented by disorder in London from attending the House 230; speaks on many occasions in Parliament and his Liverpool bill is finally passed 231-2; dispute with the assistant Poor Law Commissioner following the passing of the Poor Law Act 1834 233-6; the proposal that he be presented with a piece of plate followed by an attack on his character 237-41; is again returned to Parliament 241-2; attends the opening of the new Assize Court in Devizes 244 ;death of his daughter Etheldred and entertains his employees at Pythouse 245; speaks in Parliament 246-7; satisfies Parliament that he had been misrepresented by Nicholas Cundy at the Bar of the House 247-8; his activities relating to the construction of a network of railways 248-50; sells his estate at Enford 250; his disappointment at not being appointed to the command of the Royal Wiltshire Yeomanry Cavalry 252-3; again returned unopposed to Parliament and amuses the electors in his speech to them 254; completes his purchase of Fonthill Abbey and estate and seeks the financial assistance of

Coutts & Co 256-7; is presented with a silver candelabrum by the Wiltshire Agricultural Society 258; in dispute again with the Poor Law Commissioner following the passing of the Poor Law Amendment Act 259-61; is fined by the manor court of Semley 262; pays for the rebuilding of the chancel of Norton Bavant church and takes an interest in the welfare of the poor of the neighbourhood
1840-52: takes his seat in Parliament and speaks at length on the Corn Laws and other topics 264-5; is pressed to make the annuity payments due to the estate of his late cousin's widow 266; the 1842 census returns reveals the occupants of Pythouse 267; offers himself again for election to Parliament and is returned unopposed 268-9; speaks on several occasions on the Corn Laws and other subjects 271-2; gives a Harvest Home for more than 200 of his labourers at Pythouse 273; a false report of his death 277; a dispute with Lord Radnor over the evidence he gave in 1814 to the parliamentary committee 278-9; sells Fonthill Abbey and estate 279; the death of his sister Etheldred 280; the death and funeral of and memorials to his only son 280-2; the arrival of his Churchill grand- daughters to live at Pythouse 280-1; the death of his daughter Lucy 284; attends the consecration of the new church at Wilton 285-6; is criticised at a meeting of

labourers for his statements on the state of the poor 287-8; addresses the House at great length and in great details in a debate on the Corn Laws 288-9; speaks for the last time in the House 290-1; builds a new school and school house at Newtown 292; actively manages his estates 292, 300-1; faces his last parliamentary election and is returned unopposed 294-5; his failing health 295; resigns as president of the Wiltshire Agricultural Society 296-7; sells his Civil War papers and letters 297; makes his last will 298-9; the 1851 census return reveals the occupants of Pythouse 300; decides not to stand for re-election to Parliament 301-2; his death and funeral 303
agricultural activities, 32-3, 34, 133-4, 150-1, 176 245, 261-2, 274, 291
ancestry, 3-4
appearance, 19, 21, 228
charitable gifts, 20, 48, 263, 292
financial position, 117, 143-4, 155, 224, 257-8, 279, 282, 293, 298
health, 147, 182, 272, 277, 295
litigation, 18, 27, 39-40, 48, 117-8
monument at Norton Bavant, 304
obituary notice, 304
opinions of his contemporaries, 62, 65, 66, 67, 73-4, 90, 93, 101-2, 109, 126, 190
oratory, 50-1, 107, 135-6, 255, 269
publications, 35, 37, 38, 167
religious views and perceptions, 68, 102, 124-5, 128, 240, 283
sobriquets, 'Long John' 21,